Jennifer Saunders is a comedian, writer and actress. She has won three BAFTAs (including the Bafta Fellowship), an International Emmy, a British Comedy Award, a Rose d'Or, two Writers' Guild Awards and a People's Choice Award. She also has a certificate for coming third in the discus at the Northwich Area Sports Championships, and numerous rosettes for clear round jumping and gymkhana on her pony.

She first found widespread attention in the 1980s when she joined **The Comic Strip** after graduating with an actual degree from the Central School of Speech and Drama. With her comedy partner Dawn French she wrote and starred in *French and Saunders*, the long-running hit sketch show.

She won worldwide universal and stratospheric fame and acclaim in the 1990s for writing *Absolutely Fabulous*, playing Edina Monsoon. Such is her fame she can barely walk down the street or go shopping without giving people her autograph or asking them to have a picture with her.

She lives in Devon and London with her husband Adrian Edmondson. She has three daughters who are all grown up and have left home. They have been replaced with a whippet called Olive. She has recently been forced to become a grandmother despite being only 55.

Bonkers is her first book. It was shortlisted for **Autobiography of the Year** at the **Specsavers National Book Awards 2013** and for the **RTÉ Radio 1 Listeners' Choice Award** at the **Irish Book Awards 2013**.

PODGE

@ferrifrump

BONKERS

MY LIFE IN LAUGHS

JENNIFER SAUNDERS

PENGUIN BOOKS

PENGUIN BOOKS

Published by the Penguin Group
Penguin Books Ltd, 80 Strand, London WC2R ORL, England
Penguin Group (USA) Inc., 375 Hudson Street, New York, New York 10014, USA
Penguin Group (Canada), 90 Eglinton Avenue East, Suite 700, Toronto, Ontario, Canada M4P 2Y3
(a division of Pearson Penguin Canada Inc.)
Penguin Ireland, 25 St Stephen's Green, Dublin 2, Ireland (a division of Penguin Books Ltd)
Penguin Group (Australia), 707 Collins Street, Melbourne, Victoria 3008, Australia
(a division of Pearson Australia Group Pty Ltd)
Penguin Books India Pvt Ltd, 11 Community Centre, Panchsheel Park, New Delhi – 110 017, India
Penguin Group (NZ), 67 Apollo Drive, Rosedale, Auckland 0632, New Zealand
(a division of Pearson New Zealand Ltd)
Penguin Books (South Africa) (Pty) Ltd, Block D, Rosebank Office Park,
181 Jan Smuts Avenue, Parktown North, Gauteng 2193, South Africa

Penguin Books Ltd, Registered Offices: 80 Strand, London WC2R ORL, England

www.penguin.com

First published by Viking 2013
Published in Penguin Books 2014
005

Copyright © Jennifer Saunders, 2013
All rights reserved

The moral right of the author has been asserted

Illustrations by Tom Jennings. www.tomjennings.me

Quotation from 'A Case of You' from the album *Blue* by Joni Mitchell,
reproduced by kind permission of Joni Mitchell and Alfred Publishing Co.

Typeset by Jouve (UK), Milton Keynes
Printed in Great Britain by Clays Ltd, St Ives plc

ISBN: 978-0-241-96726-3

www.greenpenguin.co.uk

For my father, who taught me the
importance of laughter

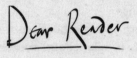

Dear Reader

I have been told that publishers these days like a particular type of memoir. They like a little bit of misery. They like a 'mis mem'.

Well, I'm afraid I have had very little 'mis' in my life, and nowadays I have even less 'mem'. So we can knock that one on the head.

In fact my brain is a bit soupy overall re the past. Sometimes it's hard to know what is an actual memory and what is simply a memory of a photograph.

Was I really called 'Podge' as a child? Answer: yes.

Was I really surly, apathetic and introverted at school? Apparently not. That is simply an image I invent for myself.

The truth is, I was fairly friendly, sometimes hard-working, and quite good at things.

My mother has kept all my school reports. I imagined these would be a rich source of hilarity and irony, but they turn out to be decidedly average. She has also stashed a good selection of my schoolbooks, clay models, posters from my teenage bedroom wall, a few *Fab 208* magazines and a selection of diaries: the Pony Club diary, the *Honey* diary, a diary with a small elf on the cover that was a present from my friend Karen.

All these diaries are written in remarkable detail for the first couple of weeks of January. Then nothing. So a lot of the incidents that I will write about in this book may all have occurred in January. I have scant info re summers and autumns.

One of the teenage diaries contained a code so I could write really important secrets. Each letter of the alphabet was represented by a shape taken from the capital letter A. Quite complicated, but luckily I had written the code down in the diary itself. I'm no fool! It is just about decipherable, so I could now read my deepest, darkest teenage desires.

This was thrilling in anticipation, but sadly not in practice. I knew it was going to be disappointing when the result of the first code-crack read: 'I really want a velvet hacking jacket.'

Memory is a liquid and strange thing. Researching my own life, I realize that there are major events I have totally forgotten, people I don't remember meeting, shows I don't remember being in and places I don't remember going. And that can leave you vulnerable.

Quite a few years ago, my agent Maureen rang me at home. Her normal voice said, 'Hello, love, a couple of things to go through vis-à-vis availabilities and dates and so on.'

We talked these things over and then she said, not in her normal voice, 'Love, just wanted to check.' Nervous laugh. 'Have you ever been in a porn film?'

Me. Not normal voice. 'Pardon?'

Maureen coughs. 'Have you ever been, do you think, in a porn film? I'll tell you why, love. The papers have been on to me to say they've seen your name on the credits of one such film and it looks like you in it.'

My heart is now beating fast. I think, *I know I have never been in a porn film*, but something is making me doubt myself.

'I don't know, love, I mean, I just thought I'd run it past you. I thought perhaps when you were in Italy?'

I spent seven months in Italy after I'd left school. Maureen knew this.

Now I'm seriously considering the possibility. Was I in a porn film? My memory soup is working overtime. Was I drugged by some boyfriend? How could this have happened? I eventually resolved that the best thing was to say, 'No.'

Maureen, relieved voice. 'No. I didn't think so, love. I suspect they're just fishing.'

This happens quite a lot, apparently. The press go fishing and cast out into the celebrity pool with outrageous bait, just hoping to touch a nerve and get a nibble.

I can honestly say to you, dear reader, that I have never been in such a film. However, there might well be a porn star out there with my name. Most people calculate their porn name by using the name of their first pet and their mother's maiden name. That would make mine Suki Duminy. Just so there's no confusion.

Another time my memory was severely questioned was when my husband, Ade, and I were living in Richmond and our three daughters were very little. One morning, Ade got up before me and went upstairs to get the older girls out of bed and down for breakfast, and then I got up a few moments later to get the baby.

I went into the tiny nursery and couldn't see her. The cot was empty. Empty cot. I stared at it a while. No baby. Heart skipped a beat. I went back to our bedroom and looked about. No baby.

It occurred to me that Ade had picked up the baby and taken her downstairs with the others.

I went downstairs. I was now having palpitations.

The other two were happily having breakfast with Ade. No baby.

I didn't say anything.

I went back upstairs. Still empty cot. I'm now not just looking for the baby, but looking for evidence that we've even had a baby. Perhaps there simply was no baby, and if I asked Ade where the baby was, he would look at me the way they looked at Ingrid Bergman in *Gaslight*.

I went back to our bedroom and sat on the bed. As I did so, I put my hand on the duvet at the very end of the bed and felt a small lump. I pulled the duvet away and there she was. Freya. Asleep. Perfectly alive and happy and asleep.

I had been breastfeeding her the night before, and must have fallen asleep with her still in the bed. She had gradually kicked her way down to where our feet were.

DO NOT TRY THIS AT HOME.
I KNOW!

Please, Mumsnet, I realize that this is not recommended practice, but all was well. It wasn't funny or clever, but Freya lives to this day. She has never given me any other reason to doubt her existence.

So, dear reader, I will tell you all I remember, and embellish all that I don't. For my publisher's sake I shall name-drop regularly and mention royalty as much as possible. Press on.

One

I am inside an egg.

Everyone on my course at the Central School of Speech and Drama is inside an egg. These are eggs that we have made from newspaper and Sellotape. All sixteen of us are inside our own eggs on the floor of one of the studios.

We are told to remain inside the egg until we feel ready to hatch. When we hatch, it will be into an unknown world where we can be anything we like. We may have to learn new methods of communication. We may be frightened. We may be aggressive. We must take our time and do it as it comes naturally.

The lights are dimmed.

There is silence.

Nobody wants to be the first to come out of the egg. It's quite nice in the egg. I think I may have a little sleep.

I am trying to study for a BEd in Drama and English, and, I think, Speech as well. We do have speech training and have to move around a room, breathing from our buttocks and rolling our voices along the floor and then saying, 'Arr ay ee ay arr, bar bay be bay bar, car cay cee cay car' (continued for whole alphabet), in order to get some mouth movement and find our embouchure. Mine is still missing.

I have an immobile top lip. I blame it on playing the flute, but it could just be my reluctance to move my mouth at all when speaking. (I took up the flute as it was the grown-up instrument to play after the recorder, and I had been excellent at the recorder. I mean, really excellent: I could even play the treble! But the flute is a very different kettle of fish, and I was found out when I had to join the school orchestra. It was a pretty scratchy old orchestra, but you were required to read music, which I could, and keep time, which has never been my strong point. So I would mime, vaguely follow the other flute, and move my fingers up and down randomly. Unfortunately one day 'lead flute' was ill and there was only me. Let's just say that during the flute solos there was silence, and a lot of tutting from the oboes.)

So, I'm on a teacher training course. Yes, I'm surprised too. This has never been part of my Plan – if indeed there has ever been a Plan. Plan or not, this was certainly not part of it. Everything in my life has been fairly random, happened by accident or just fallen into place.

That I am at college at all is something of a miracle. I left the Northwich Grammar School for Girls in Cheshire with three very average A levels in Geography, Biology and English, with no idea of anything that I particularly wanted to do, and no sense of having to do anything at all particularly urgently. The school careers officer (who was actually just the RE teacher earning a bit on the side) told me, in no uncertain terms, that I had chosen a strange mix of subjects and should apply immediately to become a dental nurse.

I, however, thought I should apply to some universities. Both of my parents had been to university, and my older brother, Tim, who was full of brains, was about to go to Cambridge to study Engineering.* Thankfully, this had taken the pressure off me a bit. My two younger brothers, Peter and Simon, were still at school.

I went to quite a few interviews at various universities – Leicester, Nottingham, Coventry – but wasn't accepted at any of them. Reluctance to open my mouth when talking, or even to talk at all, could have been a contributing factor. I couldn't really raise any enthusiasm about myself, so they didn't stand a chance.

'Why do you want to do Combined Studies here in Nottingham?'

'Er . . . because . . . (*Damn, I should have prepared this*) . . . erm . . . because I . . . like them?'

'Why do you want to come here to Leicester?'

The truth was, I didn't.

'What makes you particularly suited to Archaeology and Anthropology?'

Nothing. Nothing at all. I just liked the sound of it and imagined digging about in ancient tombs wearing khaki. And

---

* Since leaving university, Tim has spent his life in fascinating places, building underground systems and overflow tunnels for dams. He has worked on projects in Sri Lanka, Baghdad and Jakarta. Without fail, a revolution or a war has broken out within weeks of his leaving these countries. Tim is currently tearing his hair out redesigning the luggage system at Gatwick airport, so if I were you, I wouldn't be tempted to buy a home in the Gatwick area any time soon.

they knew it too. For them, it must have been like interviewing a bowl of porridge.

I have always thought I'd quite like to be an archaeologist. Actually, I'd still quite like to be an archaeologist. Or a psychiatrist. Or a casting agent. Did drama or performing feature in my life as a schoolgirl? Not really. Apparently, I once did quite a funny turn as a fortune teller in a school revue when I was in the sixth form, but I don't remember much about it.

The thing that Central had to recommend it over and above all of the others was that it was in London, and I wanted to go to London. I didn't particularly mind what I studied, I just wanted to study it in London. I had been to London only a handful of times in my life – mainly to attend the Horse of the Year Show, so only really to Wembley – but the thought of it excited me.

When I returned from my seven months in Italy *not* making a porn film, they asked me for an interview. I was instructed to bring a black leotard with me. A leotard!

On arrival, all us candidates were ushered into one of the studios and the girls were told to go off to put on our leotards. The horror! We didn't know each other and were having to strip down to bra and pants and put these things on. Mind you, I was glad of my tan. The boys had to wear T-shirts and tights and were confused about whether to wear the jockstrap outside or inside them. The results were not pretty.

We then had to show we could move and were put through some exercises by a movement teacher ('Swing your arms, touch the floor, skip about'). We were all lumpen and slightly confused, and luckily no one shone. I was still in with a chance, and after about fifteen minutes of sweaty hell and hitching up of jockstraps, it was over. After that, it was all pretty simple: a short interview, during which I actually spoke. They asked what theatre I had seen recently, and I told them I had seen Dostoyevsky's *The Rivals* at the Royal Exchange in Manchester. It was an obvious lie, but they didn't question it. The truth was that I had only ever seen *Charlie's Aunt* at a rep theatre in Worthing, but they must have been desperate to fill the course. We then had to sit near a piano and show we had an 'ear' by recognizing whether notes were higher or lower as they were played.

That was it.

A few days later, much to my surprise and my mother's joy, I got a letter of acceptance. I moved to London in the autumn of 1977.

Back in the egg.

I can hear someone inside their egg, crying with laughter, and I know this must be Joanna Bowen. JoBo.

JoBo and I had quite quickly become friends at college. She was tall and dark with extraordinary legs; legs that, she told us, featured in the Pretty Polly posters that were all over Tube stations. We never knew if she was telling the truth. About anything, really. JoBo even had us believing, at one point, that she had been raised by wolves in Africa. (It was entirely possible, although I have since discovered that she was raised by a very nice family in Hertfordshire, whom I have got to know quite well over the years.)

JoBo had a car. This was the greatest thing. JoBo drove me everywhere, at breakneck speed.

Up until then, my preferred mode of transport had been my shiny red bicycle. It was a solid, postbox red – I painted it myself – and shiny because I used thick gloss paint. There were a few drip marks here and there, and marks where my trousers had stuck to it before it had fully dried, but otherwise I was very pleased with the result. It had a basket on the front for my bag and was the picture of a good, old-fashioned bike. But it was a tough pedal: the gears often crunched into each other without any notice and, if I wasn't careful, my trousers would get stuck in the chain. Or the chain would fall off altogether.

Thanks to my bicycle, I arrived late every single day for my first term at college. Quite regularly I would arrive just as everyone was packing up their folders to go home. My problem has always been (and still is) that I believe I can get anywhere in London in twenty minutes. This has simply never been the case.

An awful lot of my life has been spent thinking up excuses for my lateness. My husband, Ade, has taken to giving me false timings, usually subtracting an hour, in the hope that I will be ready to leave the house on time.

JoBo made it her mission to shock me, or make me laugh, at every given opportunity. In those days, I generally appeared quite serious. Apparently it could be intimidating. I was the girl who never got wolf-whistled when passing building sites. Instead, they would stop and look puzzled and shout, 'Cheer up!' Even now, I get the odd 'It may never happen, love!', which fixes my face into an even grimmer state. People often think I'm frightening, when the truth is, I'm just really quite frightened myself.

A journalist once commented in an article, 'Why doesn't Jennifer Saunders smile more? She's got a lovely smile when she tries.' There is nothing more designed to make you not smile than someone telling you that you should. Just as there's nothing more likely to stop meaningful conversation than someone saying, 'I'm so glad we're talking.'

JoBo's favourite trick was to take her top off while driving. Next to her, I would be wracked with embarrassment and nervous laughter, panicking if we stopped too long at traffic lights and keeping an eye out for the police. She once pulled the car up next to a man and a woman who were walking along the pavement, got out and ran up to the man, kissed him, and then said, 'Darling, darling. Listen, I don't want you to worry about what happened last night. I asked the doctor and he said it's perfectly normal.'

We drove off, while the couple were left standing confused and slightly unsettled. It was JoBo's nerve that made me laugh.

Another time, she pulled the car up next to a pedestrian, pretended to be blind, and asked for directions. And could they be specific, please, because she was driving using only her Braille A–Z.

JoBo's fearlessness once almost killed us both. The novelty of the tits out was obviously wearing off and she needed more laughter from me. So she decided to steer the car with her legs. I laughed, so she went one near-fatal step further and pushed one of her legs through the steering wheel. This meant that she couldn't steer at all. She had to try madly to find the brake pedal with her accelerator foot while extracting her leg from the wheel, as we hurtled out of Hyde Park towards Queen's Gate, missing the Royal Geographical Society by inches before she finally regained control.

Back in the egg, nothing much is happening. I'm not aware of any hatchings. I can hear some whisperings and some chick noises, but no ripping paper.

Dawn French is in one of the eggs. Dawn French, later to be 'off the teleovision' and my comedy partner.

Much has been made (mainly by me, I suspect) of the fact that, when Dawn and I first met at college, we hated each other on sight. This isn't true. We were indifferent. She had come with a purpose, which was to learn to be a teacher. She actually wanted to teach. I had arrived not really realizing that it was a teaching course at all. A few terms in, when they sent us all into schools, I was genuinely shocked. I was hanging with the posh girls, as far as she was concerned, and she had her own gang.

To be fair, I was also actually living with posh girls. A friend of mine from Cheshire, Belinda Pritchard-Barrett (quite posh), was in London sharing an attic flat in Kensington with two other girls, Fiona Pelham-Burn (posh) and Charlotte Kennard (extremely posh).

I got on well with Belinda, who has a big laugh and a great sense of humour. She had done a cordon bleu cookery course and was now cooking directors' lunches for a firm in the City. The other two were secretaries.

I was a mystery to them. They never could quite understand what it was that I was doing, but they thought it terribly clever. They wore grown-up clothes, lipstick, court shoes and had drinks parties with young officers from the Welsh Guards. They had already become their mothers.

Occasionally I would be present at a drinks party wearing cord jeans, an army surplus shirt and a pair of bright red Kickers. I had to be explained.

'This is Fer. She's living with us. She's a student, doing something very high-powered. What is it again, Fer?'

(I should explain, dear reader, that close friends and family call me Fer. I never liked Jenny, so it's either my full name, or Jen, or Fer. Except for JoBo, who has always called me Foffy. Onwards.)

'Drama. I'm doing drama.'

At which point there would be general mutterings of 'Marvellous', 'Terribly high-powered' and 'Well done, you', before they returned to their general chatter and G&Ts.

Eventually I moved from that flat because, in my second year, a place closer to college came up. It was on the top two floors of a house in Steele's Road. There were six of us living in it, and Dawn was one of them. She shared a room with Angie, her friend from Plymouth, and I had a small room to myself. On the surface we had little in common, apart from the fact that both our fathers had been in the RAF. She listened to John Denver and Dean Friedman, and I listened to Elvis Costello and Patti Smith.

Dawn and I would walk to college together most days. I can't remember what we talked about,* but I remember enjoying it more and more. We laughed a lot. We laughed about everything, but mainly about people.

We became obsessed with an older actress who lived on the same street. We thought we'd seen her on television. We started inventing a life for her and hung out of the window to watch her comings and goings. I like to think of it as character study. I suppose it was our equivalent of animal study, which was done by the actors at college. This involved going to the zoo, choosing an animal, watching it for a bit and then going back to the studio and spending hours as that animal. We used to walk past and look in. Strange how many actors chose very slow animals that didn't do much at all – sloths, owls, etc. Occasionally you'd see an actress that regretted the decision to choose a flamingo and having to stand on one leg all day. Hilarious viewing for us.

Dawn and I can now both do vague approximations of an actress.

It is the best feeling when you find someone who isn't just a good audience, but who can actually add to the funny and keep it going longer. If you are doing an impersonation of someone or telling a story, there are people who will interrupt and stop your momentum and there are people who can make comments and observations that keep the plates spinning. We became great plate spinners.

*

* For extra detail on most aspects of my life and character, please refer to *Dear Fatty*, a wonderful, best-selling book written by Dawn French. You may be wondering why her book is called *Dear Fatty*, and that is because it is what she calls me. When we had a writing office in the BBC, on the door we wrote 'Fatty and Grumpy', which I believe we have been called on occasion. Anyone coming in would always nervously laugh and say, 'I think I can guess which is which.' Dawn would look at them aghast. Point at me. 'Well, she's Fatty, obviously.'

I had never considered myself funny before. Was I the class clown? No. One of my school reports, when I was seven, refers to my 'unusually developed sense of humour', but this surprises me. I feel like I was largely mute.

I had changed schools a lot, by virtue of the fact that my father was in the RAF. In my first thirteen years of life, we moved seven times. My first six years were spent abroad – initially in Nicosia in Cyprus and then in Ankara in Turkey. I remember the smell of pine trees and the heat. There are hundreds of photographs of this time, as my father and grandfather produced boxes and boxes of slides. We always look happy and are generally in a paddling pool.

I was rather accident-prone, and I like to think of this period as early training for physical comedy. My first memory, aged three, is of a swing to the head.

I am at my kindergarten in Nicosia and I am running, running, consumed by a sense of panic, a mixture of homesickness and abandonment. I am trying to get to my older brother, Tim, who is in the junior school. A small picket fence separates our two parts of the school, but I don't let that stop me. Oh no. I climb over that forbidden fence and run towards where I think he might be. The next thing I know is a bang on my head – *boom*. I've been floored by a swing.

From that moment, my early life was punctuated by a series of accidents. There was the brick that my brother threw in an alleyway that knocked me unconscious. The fall from a balcony wall down into a cactus bed, resulting in months of boils and cactus-spine removal. Then the plastic golf club that ended up rammed down my throat when I decided that leaping from chair to chair with it in my mouth might be fun. I was blue when my mother found me, and only choked back to full health once she'd pulled it out.

There was also the time I found myself sitting quite calmly at the bottom of the swimming pool. I remember looking up at the surface and being able to identify the rubber ring that I'd slipped through. I knew I shouldn't have been in the pool, so I just waited to be pulled out, which I was, eventually.

If you can avoid serious injury or death, then the odd accident can be a learning experience. Childhood seemed like quite a bloody affair. It's always nice to have a great big scab to pick at.

On returning from abroad we had a series of postings – Colerne, Camberley – and I also lived with my grandmother in Littlehampton when my father was posted abroad on his own. Our final Air Force posting was Melksham in Wiltshire. I was ten and we stayed there till I was thirteen, when we finally settled in Cheshire, where my father got a job near Manchester working for Hawker Siddeley (later British Aerospace), selling commercial aircraft.

By this point I had attended seven different schools – two of them twice. Changing schools that often had pushed me the other way from being the class clown; it had made me a great blender-inner. It becomes instinctive in you to position yourself so that you very quickly feel settled, and home life is always the most important thing. I don't ever remember moving house or there being a fuss when I left school or friends.

By the time I arrived, aged thirteen, at my final school, the aforementioned Northwich Grammar School for Girls, I had it down to a fine art. I was presented at the front of the class by the teacher; I was the only girl in the room wearing a shiny new school uniform and feeling sick with nerves.

'This is Jennifer . . .'

I hated my name at this point. Nobody was called Jennifer except 'Jennifer Eccles', and that song followed me round the playground. Later it would be 'Jennifer Juniper', sung to me by French boys on foreign exchange trips. They only ever knew the words 'Geniver Gunipair' and would sing it over and over again in their silly French accents, never knowing when to stop. I preferred Jennifer Eccles. And yes, I did have freckles.

Anyway, anyway . . .

'This is Jennifer Saunders. Now let's find you somewhere to sit.'

I looked round the class. Girls sitting next to each other shuffled their chairs closer together to show there wasn't room near them – the good girls at the front, the bad girls at the back. There was only one girl sitting on her own. This was the not-popular girl. I was sent to sit next to her at the front. I could hear mean sniggers from the back.

This girl was sweet, but I knew I couldn't stay her friend. I needed to be nearer the sniggerers to stand any chance of survival. Which, over the next year, I did. I blended myself into the the group at the back and became the bad girls' pet. Never doing anything to ruffle feathers.

I learned much later in life that laughter is a great method for breaking the ice and easing your way in socially. Which is strange, because the default setting in my family was laughter. That was where we all instinctively headed to; being in on a joke was absolutely the best place to be. And we had a cast of characters and a roster of in-jokes that could be enjoyed over and over, time and time again.

My father, Tom Saunders, was brilliantly deadpan and easily amused.

There was a Golden Rule in our family, decreed by my father: you can be serious, but you must never, ever take yourself seriously. Most things could be tolerated except pomposity.

He and my mother, Jane, always made each other laugh. They had first met on a date arranged by their respective mothers, Margaret (Maggie) Saunders and Jenny Duminy, who had been best friends at school. Despite the forced situation, they got on; they amused each other and they shared an adventurous spirit. When they first started courting, so the story goes, my father flew his plane upside down under telegraph wires, to impress her. At the time he was posted in Jordan, teaching pilots (including King Hussein of Jordan) how to fly. On one of his trips home on leave, they got engaged. Everyone suggested they wait until his posting was over before they got married, but my mother was adamant. She is very brave, my mother – still is – and the thought of going out there with him was too exciting a prospect to turn down.

My father had been born in Cambridge in 1926, the younger son of John Tennant Saunders and Margaret Saunders. Although my father's father had been christened John, he had come to be known as Fanny while at university in Cambridge, by virtue of the fact that he bore an uncanny resemblance to the college cleaner, Fanny.

Fanny (my grandfather, not the cleaner) was a brilliant academic who, by the time I was born, was a biology don at Cambridge and had written several books on practical vertebrate morphology (still available on Amazon!). My father himself went to Cambridge to study languages. During the Second World War, he joined the Air Force very young, and he didn't look back. He was a very good pilot and had a lifelong passion for flying. When the war ended he decided to remain in the Air Force for that reason, and was extremely good at his job. He helped to set up an Air Force base in Sharjah in the United Arab Emirates, and in 1969 was awarded a CBE.

The morning of the CBE ceremony we got up early and set off for London in our car. My mother was adamant that we shouldn't travel in our best clothes, just in case they got mucky or crumpled, so we got changed in a car park near Buckingham Palace. I was wearing a tartan cape and a Beatles cap. The most exciting thing of all was the palace toilets. When you pulled the chain, a flap opened at the bottom of the bowl – like the loo in a caravan, but very, very smart. When I'd finished, a person in some sort of livery escorted me back to where we were sitting. When he went up to get his CBE, my father looked like he had a good joke up his sleeve for the Queen.

He told us that she had said to him, 'So where are you now?'

And he had replied, 'I'm here in the palace shaking hands with you, Your Majesty.'

Always playing to the gallery.

My father left the Air Force as a Group Captain, but he never used his titles once he entered civilian life. He loathed men that retained their rank: Major so-and-so-up-the-road who hadn't been in the Army for twenty years. There was a man called Commander Cox who lived nearby and would occasionally come over for a drink with his wife. We knew my father – who had done impressions of him for us – didn't particularly like him, and when he arrived at the house my father would play up for us. He would go to the door to greet him with all the appearances of the perfect host.

'Ah, Commander Cox! Commander Cox is here, everybody! Do come in, Commander. Now, Commander, what can I get you to drink? Jane, Jane, Commander Cox is here!'

Commander, Commander, Commander Cox.

It was all for our benefit. My father loved nothing more than making people laugh. Deadpan face, silly hats, he was a great clown. During his early days in the RAF, he had done an act in the British Council Revue – the man who can't put up his deck-chair. I wish I'd seen it.

I think my love of physical comedy must have been inherited from him. He was never happier than when he was slouching in his favourite chair, gin and tonic in hand, watching Harry Worth or Morecambe and Wise on the television. Not Charlie Chaplin. We all thought Charlie Chaplin was an idiot. Too sentimental and not funny at all. Not funny like Dave Allen, Dick Emery, Victor Borge, Laurel and Hardy or Tommy Cooper. Or

Mr Pastry! Mr Pastry was my absolute favourite. I think it was while watching Mr Pastry that I properly first found the joy in real panto-ish physical comedy. I used to think I'd made up Mr Pastry, as nobody else seemed to remember him, until I met Miranda Hart, who said that he had inspired her too.

Nowadays, children are only allowed to look at young people being funny on the television. All the presenters are basically newborns. The crazy bowler-hatted Mr Pastry, otherwise known as Richard Hearne, was quite old, but then so was Doctor Who in those days. Mr Pastry would dance around a room, or fall through a wall, and usually ended up covered in flour, or twisted up in a tuba. Along with Lucille Ball, Mr Pastry was my greatest comedy influence.

So, in Dawn – who is truly a great physical comedian – I had found someone to play with, someone who was in on the joke. For me, comedy is about being allowed to be a child, to make things up and be silly. To play pretend and not be embarrassed in front of the person that you're playing pretend with.

Imagine you were eight and playing hospitals with dolls, teddies and trolls. As you were listening to Sindy doll's heart with a plastic stethoscope, the friend you were playing with said, 'What are you doing? That's just a doll. It doesn't have a heart. None of these toys is alive. You're just doing the talking for them. You're not actually a nurse. And look at the scale of these toys! Teddy is the same size as baby squeaky doll, but Sindy doll is tiny, and I don't understand where the trolls fit in. Are you mad? Look at yourself. What are you doing? Grow up!'

It just wouldn't work. Making up characters and scenarios is basically playing. I knew that I couldn't embarrass myself in front of Dawn and vice versa. We encouraged each other's silliness. On my own I would have struggled to find a voice, but when I was with her there was always somewhere to go with a joke – and that was wherever she took me.

The crucial element in our double act, then and now, has been our friendship. For us, the friendship has always mattered more than the career. And this, in a way, has fed into the career; people enjoy watching us, I think, because they enjoy how much we enjoy each other.

Our first act was called the Menopause Sisters. Actually, to call it an act is probably going a bit far. It was me and Dawn and a guitar. We had no idea what the menopause was, but thought it was probably something to do with periods. We dressed up as punks and had a song about a hamster that got trodden on, which we sang at parties (not always by request).

The Menopause Sisters then became the Menopazzi Sisters, who were an old Italian circus act. The sofas in the flat would be pushed back against the wall and whoever was there would be our audience (again, not always by request). They would have to sit through me and Dawn in black leotards and red swimming hats miming a series of circus tricks, like walking on big balls, or simply doing forward rolls followed by endless bowing. We would then exit into the hall applauding ourselves while the audience pushed the sofas back and continued to watch television.

We laughed and laughed. We didn't drink much in those days – wine was disgusting and gin rather expensive – so our thrills came from messing about. We were short on money, but long on free time, and whiled away many hours just being childish. Activities included:

- Dressing up as punks and seeing if we could scare people on the Tube.
- Hiding in the laundry basket and popping out to try and frighten our flatmates.
- Making severed heads out of cabbages and banging them on our friends' windows.

- Hanging out in Honest John's record shop in Camden, making ourselves laugh by seeing who could buy the naffest record. It was then that we discovered 'Kinky Boots' by Patrick Macnee and Honor Blackman, which was to become our favourite record of all time. Along with smatterings of Barbara Cartland, William Shatner and Gracie Fields, it was always played to the audience before live and studio shows.
- Debating whether or not to write to Rowan Atkinson, whom we didn't know, to ask him for tea.

DAWN: Do you think we should write Rowan Atkinson a letter and ask him for tea?
ME: Why?
DAWN: Because I bet no one ever does.
ME: Yes, and I bet he's just really normal, and since he's become famous I bet no one ever, like, just says, 'Come round and have a cup of tea.'
DAWN: We should do it.
ME: I bet he would come. I mean, I bet some people would find that weird, but it's actually just a nice, normal thing to do. We wouldn't ask him about being famous or anything, because I should think he's pretty bored of that now.
DAWN: And he seems like a really nice person.

Despite continuously convincing ourselves that, if we actually asked him, he would actually come, we never actually asked him. I told this story to Richard Curtis recently, who had worked with Rowan since the beginning of his career. He said, 'You know, I think if you had asked him, then he would have actually come.'

We were fools.

*

Back in the egg, I can hear some hatchings.

Paper is being ripped and I can hear the noises made by people taking it seriously. I think I'll stay put for a bit and let them get it out of their system. This whole thing was an exercise that we might be expected to take into schools and use in a lesson. Really? Well, I suppose those who actually wanted to be teachers might, but I couldn't imagine it at all.

I hated teaching practice. I have never really liked schools. It's bad enough being in a classroom, but being in a staffroom was even worse. All the teachers seemed depressed, chain-smoked, and if they spoke to you after lunch, there was always a whiff of cider on their breath.

The first school I was sent to teach in was an Ursuline convent in Wimbledon, which was an unremarkable experience. My last school was in Peckham Rye, which wasn't. It was quite a rough school in quite a rough area. As a student teacher, I was given some of the roughest classes, the remedial groups who were told to take drama as a way of not having them in another lesson that they would disrupt. There was very little I could actually teach, and my main job was just to keep them in the room by whatever means possible.

For one group, I had a lesson plan that somehow involved post offices (don't ask), in which they had to set up a post office for themselves. I knew this class and I knew it was going to be tough. They knew I was a student teacher and ruthlessly took advantage. As I walked into the classroom, I noticed that they had set up a record player.

'What's that for?' I asked.

'For dancing.'

'We're not doing dancing.'

'Yeah, but when we have this lesson, the teacher lets us bring our records in and do dancing.'

'Right.'

I decided to negotiate.

'OK. You do some work and then, at the end, you can do dancing.'

By now, we were halfway through the lesson anyway, and after a short spell of 'work' the records began to be played. There was nothing I could do. After about ten minutes, they got bored and turned to me.

'Why don't you dance, Miss?'

'No, no. I don't dance.'

'Yes you do. Come on, Miss, DANCE.'

So I danced and danced, to cries of 'Dance, Miss! Dance!'

It took me a moment to realize that the classroom door had opened and standing in the doorway was Miss Dawn French. She had witnessed the whole thing. Her school had closed that day and she had decided to pay me a visit. Everything she had thought about my commitment to teaching was confirmed, and to this day I haven't lived it down.

Dance, Miss! Dance!

Still in the egg, and I can now hear that, outside, the hatchers are starting to form some sort of primordial society. Squeaks and gibbon noises and grunts.

I open my egg, just enough so I can have a look. I was right. Quite a few are taking this very seriously indeed; some are gathering the newspaper shells of other people's eggs, and fights are breaking out. I can see JoBo's egg, and she is watching me. The look in her eye says, *Really, Foffy, do we have to?*

I shake my head. *Not yet . . .*

At the end of term every year at Central, there was an actors' cabaret where actors and actresses could show off their special skills – singin' and poncin' about. Dawn didn't like most of the actors because they really didn't want to be seen mixing with the teachers. We were considered slightly beneath them, and only the secure ones would ever break the pose. She still feels the hurt, and if you ask she will give you a twenty-minute rant on the subject. So she decided, out of sheer bloody-mindedness, that we should perform at the cabaret. The Menopazzi Sisters had their first gig. By now, we had embellished the leotards by sewing nipple tassels on to the back, as if we were wearing them back to front, and had put white make-up all over our faces. We put flour on our hands and feet, to represent resin. You have to use resin for grip if you're performing a dangerous circus act. And believe me, this was dangerous.

The actors' cabaret was invaded by student teachers on our course, who came to watch. After a couple of guitar strummers and singers and poetry readers, we were on. And, I have to say, I think we stormed it. We got our first real audience laughs, and that is the greatest feeling. Like the nicest tickle. I like that tickle. I've always liked that tickle. And once you know you can get a laugh, it's absolutely addictive. It's a very nice feeling, making someone laugh. It kind of makes everything OK. And even the actors laughed! We could afford a bit of a swagger next time we walked through the lobby.

When the next cabaret came along, we had really worked up an act: a reprise of the Menopazzis, followed by two American characters we wrote a sketch for. Double stormer. Dawn had had her revenge on every actor who had ever spurned her advances in the coffee bar. You know what? You may be actors, but you are just *not* funny!

So, there we were, at the end of the third year, poised for a comedy future – but it didn't happen immediately. We had never actually considered taking it further. Dawn went off to become a teacher, while I moved into a house in Chelsea with JoBo. Dawn and I kept in touch, but we believed that that part of our lives was over. And it was, for a while.

I have hatched and deserted my eggshell, and am watching from the sides.

There are the grunters, and the softly weepingers, and the completely-no-imagination-at-allers, just sitting still. It's silly, but not at all funny, and eventually it winds down. No one is quite sure where we are supposed to go with this.

We look around. The teacher who set the whole experiment has pissed off. He has gone to the pub.

Two

I am sitting on the steps outside the small house that I'm sharing with JoBo in Glebe Place, Chelsea.

JoBo has just gone up to the King's Road to buy a paper, so we can do the crossword. We have nothing else to do. We don't have jobs. The house was rented from the Church Commissioners by JoBo's boyfriend, and we have been allowed to stay in it while he is abroad. It is shabby, to say the least, and becomes shabbier the longer we live there. The whole house is slowly collapsing due to dry rot. There are holes in the stairs where feet have gone through. Throughout the house we have to tread quite carefully in order not to find ourselves a floor below.

Where the plaster has fallen off the walls and the original rotted wattling is exposed, we pick it off and burn it on the fire to keep warm. No, this isn't Dickens's time: it is 1980. By the time JoBo's boyfriend returns a year later, very little of the original house remains. We have even burned some of his old law books that we found in a cupboard, because we can't afford coal.

We sleep in a room together on two single mattresses on the floor. There are no curtains, but there is a cupboard that we don't use. We hang everything on something that's standing in the middle of the room. It's covered in so many clothes that we have no idea what it is. Turns out to be the Hoover. But we don't hoover. In fact, we can navigate our way to our mattresses by following a path that we have made through the thick dust on the carpet with our feet.

JoBo has rented out two other rooms in the house. Maggie, a teacher, and Sarah, then a secretary, are our housemates. They actually have jobs, but don't seem to mind the squalor. We also have a cat called Spider. As we have very little money, we often split a tin of pilchards with Spider.

This is going to sound awful. JoBo and I realize we should sign on, but cannot be bothered. The Social Security office is a long way down the Fulham Road, and that kind of energy is lacking. We are layabouts. We get up late, do nothing, talk a lot, scrounge drinks in the pub and then sit on the step.

Sometimes we'll go up the King's Road to see if anyone's about. I once saw Blondie in the grocer's.

When JoBo comes back from the shops, she will hopefully have got a copy of *The Stage* so that we can look for jobs. What we would really like to do is work on a cruise. Be entertainers on a cruise. Yes, you have to work, but you are on that cruise having a cruise.*

JoBo's friend Fi Cotter Craig (who would become a TV

---

* If you recognize those lines about a cruise, it's because Dawn and I used them in a sketch once and I have tried to work them into nearly everything I've ever done. I never tire of them.

producer, but at this moment is a secretary) often comes over in the evening. It's an easy house to get into. There is a wire coat hanger behind the empty window box and you just slide it through the letter box and pull the latch. We don't have keys. Fi sometimes gets us work in her office, stuffing leaflets into envelopes, for which we actually get paid. But, generally, money is tight and food scarce. Our favourite dish is frozen peas with margarine and pepper. Belinda PB pops in sometimes with leftover food packages from her directors' lunches, which keep us going for a while.

The other day, when we were really desperate, JoBo came up with a plan. She had to drop her cousin back at her old convent school in Hertfordshire and I was to come with her. While JoBo was taking the girl in and keeping the nuns occupied, I was to get out and go round the back of the school to the vegetable garden (JoBo drew me a map) and steal vegetables. I was terrified. When JoBo was out of sight, I followed the map round to the veg garden. If spotted by a nun, I had to appear nonchalant and admiring of the garden. I was wandering around with a huge basket and some plastic bags trying to look innocent. I find that so hard. It's a bit like when you have to use cue cards in a studio to help with lines that you keep forgetting. On 'Action', I make a point of not looking at the cue cards, in case it seems like I'm looking at the cue cards. Which completely defeats the point. Anyway, I got as far as the runner beans and filled a couple of bagfuls, but lost my nerve when it came to actually pulling things out of the ground. I know I don't believe in God, but what if he was watching?

I sensed JoBo's disappointment. We had runner beans to eat for the next two weeks.

I like sitting on the step and watching the world go by. I'm quite happy on my own and always have been.

We were given a lot of freedom growing up; the biggest

punishment was not being allowed out. The worst words I could ever hear were 'You can't go outside today.' Outside, I could do whatever I wanted: ride a bike, poke around with a stick, build a den, climb trees. I never had to tell my parents where I was going; I just had to be back for mealtimes. My parents never fussed. Nobody did then. You just sort of got on with it, really.

Growing up in RAF camps is comparatively safe. They are gated communities and there isn't a lot of traffic. We spent all day outside riding bikes, roller-skating and going to the perimeter fence to watch planes taking off. I would be quite happy to spend all day watching planes taking off and landing; quite happy to have a deckchair on a roof at Heathrow and see the aircraft coming in and out.

My mother never felt the need to check up on us constantly. The final RAF quarters we lived in were in Melksham, and they were nowhere near a runway. A whole camp had been demolished, leaving only the officers' quarters. Our address was 2OMQ (officers' married quarters), The Old Hospital Site, Melksham. To get to the houses, you had to drive through the overgrown remains of buildings; it looked like an atom bomb had been dropped. Tiny streets named after aeroplanes were lined with rubble – Vulcan Avenue, Hastings Way, Lancaster Drive. In the middle of the site was the old parade ground, a vast expanse of tarmac where people were taken to learn to drive. We went there sometimes in the car, and my father would let us steer. I have never lost that bug. Even now, if someone else is driving, I feel the urge to ask if I can steer.

The old site may have looked like a nightmare, but to us children it was heaven and we cycled around it whenever we could. We made dens in the shells of buildings and were thrilled by the amount of rude graffiti that we found on the walls. At night, the site became quite a different place, judging by the number of used condoms that had been tossed into the hedges.

When I asked my mother if she had ever worried about us, she said, 'Not really. I thought you were all probably quite sensible.'

Sadly, this is true. My fourteen-year-old self's diaries make a fairly humdrum read:

Friday, 28 January 1972
Barnaby rolled in mud. Received a letter from Fiona. Had needlework, did nothing. Mrs Dodd away. Thank god. Had a French lesson. Mrs Cross let us listen to tapes and look at pictures. Gave a letter to Stephen Okell who said he did not like Gill. Mucked out stables. Barnaby rolled in mud again. Have made up a code. Ate some AYDs. Radio sounds terrible.

Saturday, 29 January 1972
Put ponies out. Snowed slightly. Going into Chester to look at a flute. Bought it.
Groomed and rode. Took him out on the road. Watched telly. Ate enormous tea.
Watched Cliff Richard and The New Seekers on Songs of Praise. Man Utd lost 2–1 to WBA. Went to bed at midnight.

Thursday, 3 February 1972
Windy rainy night. Wore my new black boots. Forgot to do my Biology. Handed my German in on wrong pile. Oversewed my straps in needlework.
Started pouring with rain. Had my flute lesson. Did Telemann. Mum picked me up. After watching The Vera Lynn Show went to bed.
Am apparently in bad mood.

As I said, the much-anticipated teenage diary written in code was also disappointing. The first line I cracked was 'I really want a velvet hacking jacket.' Why was this a secret?

Home, from the age of thirteen, was Acton Bridge in Cheshire. The Grange was a large, red-brick Victorian house that sat squarely on a small hill, overlooking a millpond. It was idyllic. The area itself was quite industrial, but you wouldn't have known it when you were there. Occasionally, on a clear night, you could see the lights from Ellesmere Port and, if the wind was blowing in the wrong direction, you might get a faint whiff of burning oil. About three fields away was a big railway line, but it wasn't close enough to bother us really; the house was in its own little bubble. It had a huge garden, which my parents filled with vegetables, shrubs and specimen trees, with paddocks beyond. They were both great doers, and it was the first garden that they could see through to fruition. To reach town you had to walk down to the end of a long lane and then get on the bus, which provided the perfect excuse not to socialize.

I was a quiet child. I was a watcher. I liked to stare. My mother said I would often wander off and be found staring at people a little bit too closely, and have to be removed.

My mother dressed me and my brothers in similar outfits when we were little. It made sense as we did the same things. We rode bikes, climbed trees, made bonfires and dens. I wanted to be a cowboy and I always wanted a tommy gun for Christmas. I would still quite like a tommy gun for Christmas.

It was great growing up with brothers. I think it gave me a competitive edge. Not the kind of competitiveness that girls have with each other. I know about that, because I have witnessed it, first hand, with my daughters. If you have an argument with your brothers, you have a proper fight and try to hurt them and then forget about it. You don't sit and sulk and spend every mealtime giving each other 'the evils', and then perhaps bopping them hard on the head with a teaspoon.

We always had rusty old motorbikes lying around that my brothers had got going, and we raced them around the fields.

We did timed courses and small ramp jumps. Anything they could do, I wanted to do, and generally I wanted to do it faster.

Tim went away to school but would come back home in the holidays. His room was on the top floor at the back of the house and was always neat. There were Yes posters on the wall and a bit of Salvador Dali. He listened to Pink Floyd and David Bowie, while I was still into David Cassidy but moving towards a total T. Rex obsession. When Tim was back at school I would go up to his room and see if there was any chocolate. Tim was picky and always cut the fat off his ham, and never finished his Easter egg. He would hide it, and other chocolate, in his sock drawer. Sock drawer? I mean, that was the first place I would look! If you're looking for anything, the first place to look is in the sock or knicker drawer. Little by little, the egg would be eaten. With each nibble I thought, *Oh, he won't notice that*, until there was nothing left but the wrapping.

Peter, my middle brother, was three years younger than me. He was the most daring, and the naughtiest, a tall, handsome free spirit, and always wore a huge grin. He wasn't academic and went to the local Secondary Modern; but he was immensely practical and, when he wasn't off being naughty, he would be tinkering with machinery and chopping down trees. He was intensely infuriating and hugely lovable.

My youngest brother, Simon, set out his stall fairly early on in life. He was always a wonderful host. He had immaculate manners and an old-fashioned demeanour. At the age of twelve, he would wear a bow tie and a jacket and greet guests at the door. I know many of my friends mistook him for a butler. He would take their bags and ply them with drinks.

When people ask, 'Are you a close family?' I always think, *Yes, we are, but we just never talk about it*. Life at home was peaceful and uncomplicated. And full of animals.

For as long as I can remember, we always had animals. Whenever we moved to a new posting, it was accompanied by rabbit hutches, aquariums, hamster cages and a tortoise in a cardboard box. We had terrapins, newts, gerbils, hamsters, mice, guinea pigs, rabbits, stick insects, pupae ready to hatch, a cat and a golden retriever. I recently asked my mother if she minded the menagerie and she said she didn't; in retrospect, I think it was her who wanted them, really. She was a biologist, like my grandfather, and had studied at St Andrews University.

An only child, she had spent half of her young life in Scotland (her father was also in the RAF). Here, she had learned to skin rabbits, gut fish, and plough with heavy horses. She had grown up with a real passion for nature. She had, and still has, an encyclopedic knowledge, though she has always been modest about it. Flowers, leaves, insects: you name it, she can name them. We used to go on long walks, find leaves or insects that needed identifying, bring them home and get the books out. I have seen her pick up a rabbit with myxomatosis and put it out of its misery with a quick twist of her fingers.

It was she who instilled a passion for animals into all of us. When my father was posted to a staff college in Camberley, Surrey, we lived in a lovely big officers' quarters, and at the bottom of the garden were some old tree stumps, full of holes. Our favourite game was to put our hands in the holes and see if we could pull out a toad. In the spring they would be full of stag beetles. My mother would always make us examine them and work out the differences between a stag beetle and an ordinary beetle. By the time I had left home, she had become a biology teacher at a local school, and had never been happier.

At school, I used to love the biology labs – the tanks full of locusts and fruit flies, the bulls' hearts and eyeballs all ready for dissection, and the skulls and skeletons of various animals. I was very disappointed when I eventually discovered that the human skeletons they have in schools are actually fake! Not real dead bones at all, dear reader.

When I found myself in the first year at George Ward

Comprehensive School in Melksham, I quickly learned that if I made friends with the biology teacher, I could go down the 'Can I look after the mice?' route at break-time, thereby avoiding the huge playground full of huge children for whom first-years were an easy target. The added bonus of being the Mouse Looker-Afterer was being allowed to take the mice home for the holidays. Lovely big white mice. It was summer, so they could live in cages in the shed with the rabbits.

Looking back, I don't quite understand the attraction of small mammals. They are cute and you want them so badly to love you. You want to be able to cuddle them. You want them to behave like they do in films: live in your pocket and be your friend and do tricks. But really all they do is bite and scratch. Try to catch a gerbil by the tail and it will, like a ninja, turn itself in mid-air and land its tiny teeth into your flesh. A rabbit being cuddled will kick you in the chest with its hind claws and leave you looking like you've had a night out with Freddy Krueger.

So I had the mice. For the whole summer. In the shed. One of the mice turned out to be pregnant and gave birth to a lovely litter. I was in heaven. No one in the house was really even aware of the mice until, one day at breakfast, my father started to pour some cornflakes and a very small mouse jumped out into his bowl. 'What the bloody hell?'

How had a mouse got into the cornflakes?

But I knew. I knew where this miniature mouse had come from. Something apocalyptic had happened in the shed and I was no longer in control of it. The baby mice had been escaping through the bars of the hamster cage and, no matter how hard I tried to keep the sexes apart, they were breeding out of control. Every day, there was another litter of tiny, peanut-sized babies, and because they were breeding so young, they were gradually getting smaller and smaller and becoming a mutant strain. Then the inevitable happened, and wild mice started coming into the shed and breeding with them, so now there was a wild mutant strain. It was the stuff of nightmares.

Eventually, my mother had to be told, and she helped me sort them all out. School mice were separated and taken back to the lab, and the rest disposed of practically but humanely. The relief was enormous, and I have never wanted to see a mouse since.

When I was eleven, I got my first pony. It was nearing the time to go to 'big school' and the possibility was mooted that I might go to a nearby girls' boarding school called Stonar. A few of my friends were going there, but I didn't want to go. I wasn't even going to be a boarder, but I hated the idea and was no fan of *Malory Towers*, or *The Ten Marys*, or whatever it was called. And this was obviously going to cost my parents money! I told them that I didn't really want to go and perhaps they could buy me a pony with the money that they would be saving? Happily, they agreed, and I went to the local comprehensive.

I had been riding since I was little at various riding schools and on friends' ponies, but I was desperate to have my own. Having my own pony was a dream that became an obsession. All I did was read books about horses (*My Friend Flicka, The White Stallion*) and watch programmes about horses (*Champion the Wonder Horse, White Horses*). I had models of horses and pictures of horses. I had horses on the brain. Of course, we had nowhere to actually keep a pony, but my best friend Debbie Brown lived on a small farm not far from the school. Most nights I would go home with her and ride. So when Topaz arrived, he was kept there.

Topaz was 14.1 hands high, dapple grey and excellent at gymkhana. My poor mother must have spent her life in a car, taking me to or picking me up from Lagard Farm. Some nights I would stay over with Debbie. Everything became about ponies. Riding out after school to meet other girls with ponies and talk about their ponies, and other people's ponies, and ponies we'd read about or seen on the TV.

When not in school uniform, I spent my life in my other uniform, which was jodhpurs and jodhpur boots. I used to love jodhpurs, and at that time there were no such things as stretchy jodhpurs; they were tight down the lower leg and baggy above. When stretchy jods came in, the whole effect was much less pleasing, and girls used to wear them so tight that nothing was left to the imagination.

Dear reader, I have not forgotten that I'm still on a step in Chelsea. JoBo isn't back with the papers yet. I don't mind, because the step is the perfect place to start or continue a daydream. I am a serious daydreamer, never happier than when I'm alone in my own head.

Riding your pony out on your own is one of the greatest times to daydream. Back when I was first riding Topaz, my daydreams weren't exactly sophisticated. The main character who featured in them was my ideal man: tall, dark, good-looking and mysterious. He was a mix of James Bond and Mr Rochester, and he had an aristocratic title that he never liked to use. When I was a little older, and reading Victoria Holt novels and other bodice-rippers, I gave him a Cornish name. Lord James Petroc.

James Petroc was sometimes a spy, sometimes an Olympic rider, sometimes a racing driver, but always rich, unpretentious, carefree, funny and sensitive. No one quite understood him, but everyone fell in love with him. I think he was probably basically 'me', which was why he was never very successful at romance (there was no sex): he was actually just in love with himself.

By the time I was fourteen, all my daydreams starred me, and often Topaz. James was killed off. By then, I was in love with Marc Bolan anyway. Marc had replaced Donny Osmond, and Peter Tork of the Monkees. Marc was up there with George Best, whom I saw once, at Haydock Park Racecourse on Merseyside. Mrs Pritchard-Barrett, Belinda's mum, wouldn't let us speak to him. This was a source of great sadness because, as my fourteen-year-old self wrote in her diary, he did 'look super in the flesh'.

When I was growing up, I was genuinely more into ponies than boys. My greatest heroine was the showjumper Marion Coakes. She had taken her childhood pony, Stroller, into adult competition and won just about every big event going, including the silver medal in the Olympics in Mexico. Stroller was 14.2 hands high and the smallest horse jumping. Marion was actually living every pony girl's dream. Stroller was a hero and, in the minds of lots of pony girls, their pony could be that hero too . . .

Topaz and I have been jumping in local shows and he's been winning. All the other competitors really wish I wasn't there, because their ponies don't stand a chance. And then, one day, I arrive home and my mother tells me that I had a phone call. That's odd, because I rarely get phone calls. I ask who it was, and she tells me it was the Head of the British Showjumping Team.

I ring him back. He tells me that there has been a problem. They are due to fly out for the Olympics, and Stroller has gone lame. They need a replacement. Someone has seen me and Topaz jumping at the Cuddington Show and Gymkhana, and I am now the only one they are considering. Would I agree to become a member of the British team? They need an answer now! It would mean time off school, but I'm sure that would be OK, as it would be for Britain . . .

And so it was that I went to the Olympics and won gold. I don't want you to think that this daydream was a quick moment in the head. Sometimes, daydreams could take weeks. Each scene was rewritten and improved, and jeopardy added. Once they were fully formed, it was quite nice to run through them more than once.

When I was older, my daydreams became a little more sophisticated, with more complicated relationships. Once I had my first car, the best time to daydream was when I drove it, particularly as the cassette player meant that I could add my own soundtrack. In my head, I was generally a friend of the star, Emmylou Harris or Joni Mitchell, and had – for a bit of fun – sung on one of their albums. Now they found that they couldn't sing those tracks without me. My gap year was spent just hanging out with all these musicians, but it was never going to be a serious career . . .

> *Joni is onstage, playing to a huge crowd. I am standing at the side of the stage and she doesn't know I'm there. After a few numbers, she announces that she's going to sing 'The Boho Dance'. This is one of the tracks I half-wrote and sang on for the album. She starts the song and then, just as she's getting to the first chorus, I walk on and, at the microphone slightly to the back of the stage, I join in, singin' my familiar harmonies. The crowd go mad, and Joni turns and smiles. She asks me to stay onstage and sing the whole album with her.*

Which I do. In my car.

In all my daydreams, I am a version – an ideal version – of myself. I can do anything. I speak many languages, i.e. I have many tongues at my disposal, and I am often the perfect spy or secret agent, with a mysterious past. This person could be worked into any scenario. She was in an episode of *Prime Suspect* once. Not the one on the telly. The real one.

The other thing I am in my daydream is thin. Immaculately dressed in outfits that are given to me by all my designer friends, and Ralph Lauren.

If I could go back and say one thing to my younger self it would be: YOU ARE NOT FAT.

I started diets when I wasn't fat, but diets were becoming the in thing. Calorie counting was everywhere, and my mother had caught the bug. Everywhere you looked in our house, there were tea towels and chopping boards with calorie charts on them. In the back of my schoolbooks, there were lists of what I had eaten that day, followed by their cal numbers. Black coffee, one piece of toast no butter, salad. At school we were all at it, off and on. Dieting for a week and then forgetting about it and just eating Mars bars for the next four.

There were things called Ayds that were like little toffees full of sugar and appetite suppressant, which frankly never worked and we just ate them like toffees. They were quite moreish.

My mother drank PLJ, which is a vinegary lemony cordial that she was convinced burned fat.

Luckily, I exercised, so the Mars bar binges never took a terrible toll. I knew that, if I rode for a day, I could lose three pounds. It happened. And the pathetic thing is that I still think I can. I can't.

I still do a bit of exercise though, and that does seem to work, extraordinarily. Who'd have thought? I mean, really, who would have thought that eating a bit less and taking more exercise would be the solution?

Nowadays, I try to do a big walk every day. I don't wear tracksuits or exercise gear any more as I find it raises people's expectations. And mine. They seem to think I should be moving faster. I do wear trainers. I have to, because they have orthotics in them to stop my knees collapsing. I am in the early stages of crumble but pushing this body to its very limits.

In the house, we have a machine that you stand on and it vibrates until you think your teeth will fall out, and a big rubber ball that I sit on occasionally. Exercise fads and personal trainers have come and gone, and I have drawers full of weights and bits of elastic, and devices that electrocute your stomach trying to find a hidden six-pack. I am at the age when mostly what I do is stretch and take glucosamine and complain about the noise my joints make as I walk upstairs. It's so loud I sometimes have to stop, because I think someone is following me.

It's all a kind of hell, but it keeps the old bod in a shape that vaguely resembles a female human.

I never wore dresses as a teenager. I wasn't a girly girl and generally went around in wide baggy jeans and my brother Tim's old Sea Scouts jumper. It was tight-fitting because he had been in the Sea Scouts when he was about ten. It was wool, with a round neck.

I bloody loved this jumper. My going-out outfit, when I went to the local disco, was red cord jeans and the jumper. If I had worn it a lot, it started to smell BO-ey so I washed it by hand, but always at the last minute. With ten minutes to go before I had to leave to get the bus into town, I would wring it out and lay it on the boiler, willing it to dry. After ten minutes, I would pick it up, still steaming and heavily damp, and put it on. I steamed all the way on the bus and all the way through the disco. By the time I got home later, it was only moist. No one had many clothes then, and the new items were rare. Desired items were Ben Sherman shirts and a pair of platform shoes. I had one of each, and a maxi-length denim coat that I bought on a trip to London and never took off. I wore it with jewellery that was made out of horseshoe nails. Otherwise, it was basically back to jodhpurs.

My social life moved between girls I knew locally whom I would go riding with, and a Saturday disco in Northwich called Stan's. Girls I knew at school went to Stan's, which was conveniently near the bus station, and we would dance around to Slade and T. Rex for a few hours and then hang about near the buses, smoking. Boys from the town would come and talk to us, boys we knew were a bit dangerous.

There was one boy, nicknamed Joe 90, who was a real

skinhead. He wore the uniform, and the rumour was that he was very bad and had been in prison. Other boys were afraid of Joe 90. He hung around, but always in the distance. Then, one day at school, a girl came up to me and said that Joe 90 wanted to go out with me. Huge aghast-ness from all my friends and even the girl telling me. Surely this was a joke? Why would Joe 90 want to go out with Sea Scouts jumper?

It was always a mystery to me, but it was true, and we started to meet. We would meet outside Stan's – he was too cool to go in – and go for walks around the precinct in Northwich or into the pub. He was quiet, but terribly nice, a good kisser, and we dated for a while. He was nicer than a lot of other boys I went out with, who would just spend the whole evening trying to stick their tongues down my throat or touching my boobs. Boys who would take you to the cinema and then never want to watch the film. I had to push them off.

'Will you stop it! I am trying to watch *The Exorcist!*'

When school ended, I was at home, with nothing on the horizon and nothing much to offer the world. I did attempt to get some work locally, mucking out stables, but to no avail. A lot of my friends had landed temp jobs at the local Ski yoghurt factory, which was something of an eyesore and would occasionally discharge various yoghurt flavours into the nearby waterway. Our house – a big Victorian grange – was built just above a mill-pond that was filled by said waterway. Sometimes we would wake up in the morning to find the whole pond was blackcurrant flavour and – on occasion – banana. Despite this, I applied for a job, but even they wouldn't have me. I couldn't believe it! I mean, *everybody* got a job there.

It was my mother who pointed out that I couldn't just hang around at home, as lovely as that was. And it was. But something had to be done. I had to be moved on. I was obviously going to have to have a gap year, although such a thing didn't really exist then (it was just called 'wait-a-year-and-try-again year'). My mother discovered an agency that set up au pair jobs in Italy, and I was eventually found a job working for a family in Milan. I was fairly placid, so this didn't seem too terrifying, despite the fact that I had never been to Italy, spoke not a word of Italian, would be gone for six or seven months and only really knew how to look after animals.

So, thanks to my mother, I found myself in Milan.

I arrived at night, armed with only a piece of paper with the address written on it – Via Cappuccio 21 – and some traveller's cheques. A cab took me through the city and plopped me out in a narrow, deserted little street. This couldn't be right. The family I was going to work for were supposed to be rich. They were called Zucchi and had made a fortune in linen. He was a tablecloth magnate. (That's *magnate*, not *magnet*. He was not attractive to linen.)

The driver pointed through the gloom to a pair of double doors and I faintly made out the number 21. He drove off and I pressed the buzzer. A tiny door, set into the big doors, opened and I was admitted by a doorman, who led me into a beautiful courtyard surrounded by what appeared to be a palace. I was directed to the back door, where I was met by Signora Zucchi. As it turned out, they only owned half the palace. It was a semi! And it would be my home for the next three months.

I was given a tiny room off the kitchen, which by day was full of maids and a cook called Jana, who would talk at me incessantly. By the time I had learned enough Italian, I realized that they were just gossiping about the Zucchis' relationship, the fact that he had other women, and that one of the two sons took drugs and had girls staying over.

The Signora was a frightened-looking woman who was obviously making herself sick with nerves. Neither of the two sons, Luca and Paolo, wanted anything to do with me at all. I didn't push it. I did general tidying in the morning and took the Signora a breakfast tray that was prepared by the cook. I went to the baker and got the daily bread. I was expected to have lunch with the family. This was eaten in a vast room with nothing in it except the dining table – and generally eaten in silence, because the rule was that conversation at lunch had to be in English.

They struggled to find things for me to do, and the atmosphere in the house was never less than strained. I was eventually relieved of the silent lunch duty and given the job of opening and closing all the shutters in the house every day. This I loved because I was on my own and doing something practical. The rooms were the size of ballrooms and never used by the family.

Luckily, I had been signed up for Language School, and was later surprised when a diary I wrote at the time suggested an extremely complicated social life. My memory was of being fairly solitary but, as it turns out, I had a string of boyfriends and was going out with two or three at a time.

This extract sums up a typical day:

1 March 1977

Got up at 7 when the alarm rang. No school this morning, so no desperate rush. Took my nightshirt off the rack where it had been drying. Still a bit damp, but I had to wear something to wake Paolo.

Did the Signora's breakfast as usual. She wants coffee now, instead of tea. Got dressed at 8.30. The boys' rooms weren't in too bad a state so they didn't take long. Listened to Labelle, Nightbirds.

Finished the rooms about 10.30 and had a fag before tidying myself up to go to the library. My ticket arrived this morning. Caught No 1 tram to Via Manzoni, then walked to the library. Decided I must read some Ernest Hemingway, so I took down Old Man and the Sea and Farewell to Arms, which I didn't think I would enjoy. So I sat and watched the American lady in the black dress with the awful American accent watching a video tape of Jimmy Carter. I think I looked conspicuous, so I moved across to the poetry section, selected Robert Frost, and then went into a daydream for about quarter of an hour. Got up to leave, whereupon the man sitting opposite me asked me how to spell 'definitely'.

Decided to walk home. The sky was clear but it was slightly chilly. Arrived back at 1.00. Ate in usual silence. Didn't want to go out in the afternoon so stayed in and read Robert Frost.

I should have met Mimo at 3 but couldn't be bothered.

Ironed some sheets, laid the table, shut the shutters.

Signora arrived home and put herself to bed. She remained in bed the rest of the evening.

At 8 I started to get ready to go out having arranged to meet Oscar outside at 8.30. It was a beautiful night and Milan looked like a painting against the blue-black sky. The Gallerie was especially beautiful. We had a panini and cappuccino in a bar and then went upstairs to the American Bar. I had a Gin Fizz with an umbrella stuck in it.

I got quite tipsy on the Fizz and, coming back towards Via Cappuccio, started singing rather loudly, at first Led Zeppelin, then Amarillo. Got back. Signora opened the door. I did the kitchen. Went to bed.

The Signora was always suspicious of me. Where had I been? Who was I with? I was never allowed a key to the house and never allowed to bring anyone into it. It was a time when the Brigate Rosse, a Marxist paramilitary gang, were kidnapping and murdering the children of the rich, so maybe she had good cause to worry. One of my many boyfriends was actually a policeman, so I told her this and it seemed to calm her.

I did eventually escape.

A friend of mine from school, Helen Newman, had got a job working with a family in Orbetello, on the coast above Rome, and I took a few days off from shutter shutting to go and visit her.

She was working for a family called Von Rex. He was a Bavarian count in his sixties – tall and imposing. His wife, Adriana, was tall and imposing and in her forties. They were the most extraordinary couple, with two sons, and couldn't have been more different from the Zucchis. They were eccentric and funny.

He had built the house, a large sprawling bungalow surrounded by olive groves. The main rooms of the house were filled with the remains of the contents of a Bavarian castle that had once belonged to his family. They had dogs and horses and chickens, and I loved it.

Adriana was quite wild. She had been Adriana Ivancich, daughter of a Venetian aristocrat, who in her youth had been Ernest Hemingway's muse. He wrote *Across the River and into the Trees* about their relationship. 'Then she came into the room, shining in her youth and tall, striding beauty. She had pale, almost olive-colored skin, a profile that could break your or anyone else's heart, and her dark hair, of an alive texture, hung down over her shoulders.' In a letter, written to her from Nairobi in 1954, Hemingway said, 'I love you more than the moon and the sky and for as long as I live.'

Adriana never got over this. She carried the air of the Disappointed Muse about her. The rest of her life could never quite live up to that moment in her youth. I became fascinated by her; she filled her days drinking and smoking and heading up an '*antinucleare*' campaign, which allowed her to let off steam. Her husband filled his days with his olive groves and horses. The two would row fiercely with him ranting in German and her in Italian.

They treated Helen as part of the family, and I was welcomed warmly. When I got there, I knew I never wanted to leave. I went to Milan and handed in my notice. Signora Zucchi expressed no disappointment or surprise. No emotion at all.

For the next four months, I was in a kind of heaven. We rode horses, moved irrigation pipes for trees, learned to cook pasta, shopped in local markets and made olive oil. We were taken out in yachts and had trips to Rome. We went to the beach for picnics in a horse and trap. We sat in on wild dinner parties where Adriana had invited writers and artists from Milan and she would be in her element, holding court and getting drunker and wilder.

Once, on a shopping trip to the local town, we were all squashed into her 2CV when she realized she had just passed someone driving in the opposite direction that she needed to talk to immediately. She swung the car round without warning, mounting the pavement and crossing two flower beds, and drove after them at speed, only to be stopped by the police. They eventually let her go because they couldn't stop her talking. This was not unusual. She was erratic, and this made life interesting.

I see now that Edina in *Absolutely Fabulous* owes a lot to Adriana; certainly the sense that life has not lived up to her expectations, and authority is an irritant.

When I got home, my mother didn't recognize me. I had grown up. In truth I think I had just got a tan and lost weight, but perhaps she could detect a new-found confidence. She had the UCCA forms waiting, and what followed has led me to this step.

JoBo has arrived with the papers. Before doing the crossword, we flick through the jobs section at the back of *The Stage*. There are no jobs going on cruises, but there is an ad wanting comedy acts for a new club. Specifically, they want female comedy acts. I think there is a possibility that Dawn and I could be a comedy act.

She is doing her probationary year teaching, but if we took the job in the club, they would only want us in the evening, so there shouldn't be a problem. I call her that night. Please remember, young people, these are the days before mobile telephones, when you had to wait till the person was home in order to get them. Or you had to use pigeon post. I call her.

'Dawn?'

'Yes.'

'It's Jennifer. Do you remember me from college?'

'Yes.'

'Well, the thing is . . .'

'Oh, do get on, I've got books to mark.'

'Well, the thing is . . .'

'And lesson plans to do.'

'Well, the thing is . . .'

'Stop saying "the thing is" and get to the point.'

'Well . . . blah blah blah . . . the thing is . . . Oh no, now I've said "the thing is". I was trying to say "blah blah blah" instead of "the thing is".'

'What is it?'

'What?'

'The thing?'

'Oh, the thing is, could we be, do you think, a comedy act?'

'But I've got books to mark.'

'Could we, do you think?'

'But I've got lesson plans. I'm a teacher, Jen.'

'Just the odd evening. Shall we audition?'

'What, now?'

'Yes.'

'I don't know. Send me something by pigeon and I'll think about it.'

So onwards, dear reader. It's 1981.

My 23-year-old self is sitting in a small dressing room at the Comic Strip club with Dawn.

After Dawn had agreed that we might indeed be described as a female comedy act, I'd rung the club and was told to come along and audition. Dawn and I had decided to do the Americans sketch that we had performed at the college cabaret. We hadn't ever written it down, so we met after her school day to try to remember how it had gone. (I don't think Dawn and I ever wrote any sketches down until we had to, which was when we started doing television and directors insisted on knowing what we were going to say. Even then, we gave them only a scant impression. As long as we both knew the order we were doing things in, we were fine. I still find that scripting over-formalizes things and you start waiting for each other to say the written line, rather than just acting out the funny.)

The audition took place at the Boulevard Theatre in Raymond's Revue Bar in Soho, a popular nudey-show venue. Neither of us thought that being called to perform in a strip club was strange at all. We just went.

The Revue Bar was owned by the famous Paul Raymond, property magnate and porn king. It was one of the few legal venues in London that could show full-frontal nudity. Luckily, as it turned out, not Dawn's or mine.

Sometimes, we were taken to meet Paul Raymond in the bar and he bought us a drink. Dawn and I never quite knew what to say to him. I don't think he looked at us as if we were real women. We were a new breed. He was a strange-looking man, slightly built, and wore tinted glasses and often a long, waisted mink coat. But we have to thank him, because he was the one who eventually got us an Equity card.

The Boulevard was a 200-seater theatre. In 1980, Peter Richardson – with assistance from theatre impresario Michael White – hired it as a new comedy venue. The only other big comedy venue was the nearby Comedy Store, but Peter wanted his own place and brought with him the core group from the Store: Alexei Sayle (the compère), Adrian Edmondson and Rik Mayall (20th Century Coyote); himself and Nigel Planer (The Outer Limits); and a stand-up called Arnold Brown ('I'm Scottish and Jewish – two stereotypes for the price of one').

Ade and Rik had been at Manchester University together. Their characters the Dangerous Brothers had a crazed energy; I asked Ade recently how he would describe the act and he said, 'Bollocks done at 100 miles an hour. No jokes, just a huge amount of fear.' It was in fact a brilliant combination of non-jokes, great comic timing and extreme physical violence. Rik also had his own act as Kevin Turvey and Rik the Poet, and was being seen as the golden boy of comedy. He was a superb performer. Offstage Ade was the quieter of the two and would often come into the girls' dressing room. I remember liking him, but there was no bolt of lightning. He also wasn't available: he was married to his first wife, Anna.

All the boys were very civilized offstage. Alexei would storm on and off the stage in a blaze of screamed absurdities and 'Fuck's and 'Hello John, got a new motor?' and then be modest and shy. He and Pete and Nigel – and of course Arnold – were slightly older than the rest of us. Dawn and I got on best with the Coyotes initially.

They were all great acts, but Pete knew, or I suspect had been told, that he needed some females on the bill. Women. Hence the ad in *The Stage*.

We arrived, did our sketch and were hired. I have to admit, there didn't seem to be a great deal of competition. The other acts auditioning were fire eaters and jugglers. There just weren't many female acts around; most comedy clubs were bear pits. I think we got the gig by virtue of the fact that we were the first living, breathing people with bosoms to walk through the door. The 'Alternative Comedy' circuit was just taking off, and there weren't yet many proper venues. Just pubs and vegetarian restaurants.

Culturally there was a great sense of change. To be young was to be angry and resistant and to rail iconoclastically (not entirely sure what this means, but the dictionary suggests that it's what I mean) against what had gone before. Music was angry, and comedy was angry. But, generally, Dawn and I represented those who were just quite cross.

Dawn was more political than I was, because she was a teacher, I suspect, and had a real job. Whereas I was basically unemployed by choice. But neither of us could have been described as 'right on'. We were not Right-Onners, though we would shout 'Up Nicaragua!' or 'Down with Thatcher!' when required, and that was quite a lot. And we all hated Bernard Manning.

Now I had a job. Dawn had two jobs.

To begin with, Pete put Dawn and me on the quiet nights – Tuesdays and Wednesdays – which was a good idea as we really didn't know what we were doing. We were usually the first act on, presumably so that if we were very bad the audience would have forgotten about us by the end.

At first, we were so inexperienced that we thought we had to change our act every evening. Then someone pointed out to us that it was in fact the audience who changed and that we didn't have to. By this point, the pool of sketches that we could use had been getting shallow. In desperation one night, this happened onstage:

Dawn and Jennifer move around the stage attempting to look like Thunderbirds *puppets. Eventually . . .*

SAUNDERS: What's the time, Brains?

Dawn raises arm as if to look at watch, but wrist hits forehead.

FRENCH: Four o'clock, Mr Tracy.

Silence from audience.

SAUNDERS/FRENCH (*to audience*): Thank you.

They bow and leave the stage.

Every night, sick with nerves, we would stand side-stage waiting to go on and I would look out at the audience through a little window in the door and wish they weren't there, wish that they would all go home. We were only just getting away with it at that point.

Occasionally a man would make his way into the audience by accident. This wasn't the show he had come to see at all. They were easy to spot, men like these, sitting on their own in large macs looking confused when Alexei Sayle leaped on to the stage and opened the show with his loud Marxist-inspired sweary rant, before introducing me and Dawn. And then, to their total shock, we would come onstage fully dressed and remain so throughout the act.

The best thing about going on first was finishing first. We would make our way around to the back of the auditorium to watch the other acts. This is how we learned how to do it. They had been at it longer than we had, and were incredibly confident and funny.

One of our favourite guest acts was called Hermine. She was a French performance artist and beautifully weird and funny. She was accompanied in her act by a musician who was tall, softly spoken and smelt better than any other boy. This was her act:

Music starts.

Hermine enters slowly.

She is entirely covered by a cone of newspapers that have been glued together. It is the pink Financial Times. All you can see is her feet. She gingerly makes her way over to the microphone.

Inside the cone, she starts to sing the theme to Valley of the Dolls *in a low French drawl:*

> *'Got to get off, gonna get*
> *Have to get off from zis ride . . .'*

Then, very slowly, she starts to pick a hole in the paper (evoking our memories of the egg) and, while singing, gradually emerges from the cone.

It was mesmerizing. Her expression never changed. When she was totally out of the paper, she just leaned into the microphone.

'Sank you.'

And left the stage.

At this point we didn't have a name for our own act. We were just 'The first act this evening . . .' It was Alexei who eventually came up with French and Saunders, out of sheer frustration. We had knocked about a few names and our favourite was Kitsch 'n' Tiles. We thought anything with 'n' in it was cool. Luckily, Alexei disagreed and we have him to thank for that to this day.

So, backstage there are two small dressing rooms, as well as the fire escape where Peter and Nigel go out every night after coming offstage to have a shouty boys' row. I don't know what has happened between them, because the act had always appeared to go well and been fairly similar every night. The shoutings and fights, however, are regular. We think the problem is that Peter is a bit of a wild man and Nigel is a proper actor, and the mix is explosive.

Pete had spent a lot of his adult life travelling around Europe in a converted horsebox, and Nigel was currently understudying Che in *Evita*, which was the big new musical. My favourite musical, in fact. When I was in Italy, I had asked my mother to get hold of the cassettes and send them to me. It wasn't the stage version – Elaine Paige hadn't been invented then – and the part of Evita was sung by Julie Covington, whom I worshipped. She had given me hope when I learned that she hadn't actually become famous until she was twenty-seven, so I still had time . . .

My wanting to be famous started when I was at college and I wanted to be in a band. I wanted to be Patti Smith (not look like her, just have her life). I wanted to read Rilke and Rimbaud, and write crazy poems that didn't require punctuation or form, and sing to thousands of people. Popular, but cool and dangerous. It was a good daydream.

Truth is, I would have been scared to death of Patti Smith and all her friends. There is a line in Joni Mitchell's 'Case of You': 'I'm frightened by the devil, and I'm drawn to those ones that ain't afraid.' That's close to my truth. I love crazy people, eccentric people, people who are brave and 'out there', but I am always just quite safe myself.

Dawn and I have the smaller of the dressing rooms, which we generally have to ourselves, there being a lack of comedy females. All the boys are squashed into the other one, next door. We do go in and hang with them sometimes, but, to be honest, it stinks. They are always dripping with sweat when they come offstage, and the only facility to wash in is a sink which is always filled with bottles of beer. Their stage suits are hung up, wet with sweat, and left to dry out before being worn the next night. The funk of BO and fags is heavy in the air, spiced up with a whiff of old doner kebab, chips from the night before and the odd fart. It hums.

Occasionally, at various intervals, the boys come and see us in our nice, un-smelly dressing room. Including Ade. Quite often.

In our nice, un-smelly dressing room, we have a mirror with lights around it and a good shelf in front, where we can put a hairbrush and some make-up. We have only recently learned about make-up and its effects. Last week, we got into our dressing room to find another woman in it. Pauline Melville was slightly older than us and had a very funny act. She seemed to have lots of things laid out on the shelf, and we watched as she applied them to her face. She was putting on make-up! The effect was good, and it got us thinking that perhaps we should put on make-up too. We bought a light foundation and some brown mascara, and didn't look back.

*

Whenever Dawn and I have done a show together – in a studio or on tour – we always share a dressing room and, if possible, sit next to one another. It is comforting, and we chat and run lines and check each other's make-up before putting on our costumes.

Once, during a *French and Saunders* show, our make-up designer tried to have us separated. We were about to have a very long, tricky make-up session to become the Fat Men, involving prosthetics (moulded bits of latex that change your face shape) and bald caps. The designer had decided that it would be quicker if we were apart, because we wouldn't talk and interfere with the gluing process. It never happened. Within minutes, we were back sitting next to each other again, talking and laughing, sometimes to the point of tears, as we became the characters. This made the poor designer's job really difficult.

All dressing rooms in theatres have their differences, but they are invariably all shit-holes with poor facilities, bad plumbing and nowhere to be comfortable. But you make do. By the time we were doing big tours and large venues, we had a 'rider', a list of things we would like to see in the room when we arrived – not just a bowl of waxy, inedible fruit and some peanuts. We like Marks & Spencer sandwiches, lemons and honey (for Dawn's vocal-cord drinks), nice coffee, chocolate (preferably Crunchie bars), and a bottle of good Sauvignon Blanc for after (eat yer heart out, Mariah Carey!).

Dawn doesn't drink a great deal, but I do, given the opportunity. Never before a show though. If someone offers me a drink pre-curtain up, I hear her voice booming from a distance: 'NOOOOOO!!!!' You see I did it once, in the early days of the Comic Strip, and went a bit happy and woozy and lost any sense of timing. I have never been allowed to forget it.

Back to the Comic Strip, 1981.

Over the time we have been there, we have honed our act and written more substantial sketches. We have even found a way of getting into and out of them better. At first, we came onstage, went straight into character, and the audience only knew we had ended when we said 'Thank you' and took a bow. There was no real French and Saunders. But then we started going on in the second half of the show, and Dawn insisted we got equal pay with the boys, which took it up to about £15 a night, so that, instead of just being able to afford the bus fare home, I could have a doner kebab as well.

We were now part of the gang, and the reputation of the Comic Strip had grown. Through Michael White's connections, the audience had almost become more watchable than the show. It had become trendy, with famous (the word 'celebrities' hadn't been invented yet) Jack Nicholson and Bianca Jagger types watching. There was even a *Sun* headline: 'Bianca's 4-letter night out'. Lenny Henry came in one night and sat at the back. But most extraordinary was that Robin Williams came in, not only to watch, but to perform in the guest slot. We always had guests: Keith Allen, Tony Allen (the Guv'nor), Chris Langham, Ben Elton. But Robin Williams!

Dawn and I insisted that Robin share our dressing room because the thought of him entering the funk next door was more than we could bear. He was wired and never stopped talking, a different voice coming out of him every other second, like machine-gun fire. So we never stopped staring. He did a brilliant set. (Although the audience were slightly confused by the fact that Chris Langham, not realizing who the acts were that night, had gone on in the first half and done most of Robin Williams' material.)

But Robin Williams! Robin Williams on the stage where Dawn and I had performed our (very popular) rebirthing sketch – the one where Dawn is trying to rebirth me and I can't find my way out of a red duvet cover. Robin Williams! I had four comedy heroes at this time – Robin, Steve Martin, Richard Pryor and Joan Rivers – and throughout my life since have managed to meet them all. I've never been disappointed. All are, or were, geniuses and took risks. Mr Pastry took a back seat for a while.

When he came offstage, Robin was sweaty and didn't have a spare T-shirt, so I gave him mine. A blue striped T-shirt. I gave my T-shirt to Robin Williams. I told him he could keep it, hoping that one day, when our paths crossed again, I would strike up a conversation.

'Hey, Robin! Still got that blue stripey T-shirt with the red bit round the collar?'

'Why, I sure do. Let me buy you a drink . . .'

'Jennifer.'

But a week later it was returned, unfortunately washed and ironed. Heigh-ho.

Soho was a great place to work, and in 1981 it was very different from today. There was the sex industry and the film industry, but not yet the sprawl of bars and restaurants. And the Groucho Club hadn't been invented then. That didn't happen until 1985. It is now a much busier but, I think, less interesting area. There were some good cheap restaurants, a few bars, but mainly strip joints, clip joints, porn cinemas and sex shops. As you walked down the street, most of the door buzzers stated that there were prostitutes living there, should you feel inclined to visit them. Often they would be standing by the door, just advertising themselves. It was a beautifully scruffy place full of degenerates and generates, transvestites and vestites, comedians, artists and addicts. The streets smelt of rubbish from the market, smashed bottles of vodka and marijuana.

As I walked to get the bus late at night, I never got any hassle. I just wasn't the sort of girl that the men on the streets were after and – not supplyin' or requirin' drugs, or indeed carrying any more than £5 in my bag at any time – I probably wasn't a target. And there were enough heavies standing outside the venues to make you feel protected.

Back in the dressing room. We have all decided that, after the late show tonight, we are going to see some kind of sex show. We suspect that most of the boys have already seen one, but do not let on. Dawn and I are conflicted by our confused and largely non-existent feminist politics. We are just going to see what all the fuss was about.

SORRY, FEMINISTS, THIS IS A LONG TIME AGO AND I AM NOW MUCH CLEARER ABOUT IT ALL.

Back in the early days of the Comic Strip, Dawn and I played a couple of very scary gigs. One was at the Drill Hall, which we were told was largely a feminist venue. And it was. We were hissed throughout our set for showing women in a negative light.

The other scary one was the Comedy Store. The boys had played there a lot, but we had never had the nerve. Basically, you just had to play onstage and hope that the audience liked you. If they started booing, the compère would hoick you off. It was competitive. The level of booing depended on how drunk the audience were, how fast you could get through your act. I realize that this is why the boys' acts were fast and aggressive: you just couldn't allow the audience any thinking time.

We went onstage to the inevitable shouts of 'Show us yer tits!', which we ignored, and proceeded at speed with our sketch. But the shouts got worse and were coming mainly from a large group of men in the corner. 'Get yer tits out!' We tried to keep going, but just when I was happy to leave the stage, Dawn marched to the front and looked hard at these men.

'Will you just shut up! Do you realize how rude you are

being? There are people in this audience who actually like to listen. Stop it! Just shut up!'

The whole audience went quiet and so did the shouters. We finished our act and left the stage, to mild applause. Dawn had frightened them. Dawn was not only brave but she was also a teacher and she was having none of it.

Later, as we were about to leave, one of the group came up to us. He apologized profusely and explained that it was a stag do that had got a bit out of hand. Surprisingly, they were from the River Police.

Right, so now we are in the sex-show building. We have paid some money for a session. There appears to be a line of velvet-curtained booths. We are told that there is only one booth available and no more than two are allowed in at once. We say we will take it in turns. Which we don't. We all pile into a tiny booth and draw the curtain. It is totally dark.

Suddenly, a shutter goes up in front of us and we are looking at a near-naked woman on a bed (at least she has her pants on). She is playing up sexily to all the booth windows, stroking herself and pointing her bottom at them suggestively.

When she comes across to our booth, I see that she is not happy. All eight of us have our faces pressed to the glass, laughing. She isn't doing any of the stroking or bottom pointing for our benefit and, before we know it, the shutter is coming down and we are being asked to leave.

We can't even get our money back.

We think we'll go to Jimmy's in Frith Street for some chips.

four

It is May 1985 and I have just woken up in a huge bed in a huge hotel in the Lake District. Waking up next to me is a lovely man. I have married Adrian Edmondson.

We had a fantastic wedding at my home in Cheshire, which my mother managed to organize in six weeks. That was all the notice we gave her. In my 26-year-old mind, that seemed like ages. We told my parents that we were engaged just before we disappeared on a three-week holiday to St Lucia, the Iles des Saintes and Antigua, and left them to get on with it. Looking back on this – and having organized my own daughter's wedding – I can't believe we had the nerve. However, we did look gorgeous and tanned on the day.

Somehow, with help from our friends and some unseasonably good weather, they gave us a beautiful day.

My outfit was made by the costume designers we were working with on *The Supergrass*, a Comic Strip film we had just finished making. I absolutely didn't want a fluffy dress, so they made me an Edwardian-style outfit from cream silk. On my feet I wore very early Emma Hope shoes. Ade wore a dress coat that had been worn by Simon Ward in *Young Winston*, and looked very handsome. His best man was Rik Mayall.

I had two tiny bridesmaids. Tiny because they were children, not midgets. In fact, they were barely children. They were toddlers. One was JoBo's daughter, my god-daughter Cordelia, who was eighteen months old. The other was Peter and Marta Richardson's daughter, Alice, who was slightly older but had only just learned to walk. They were very beautiful and made a very good attempt at following me down the aisle and only fell over twice. I didn't fall over at all, which was a miracle. But then I had a sensible heel.

Can I just say (it's me now, dear reader, in 2013), what is it with the height of shoes nowadays? Shoe stilts that women are forced into? Six-inch heels? Really? I know, yes, they probably have a platform, which means they only have a five-inch heel – but very few women can actually walk in these things. Once a heel is that high, you are basically just walking on tippy toes. You would be better off just painting shoes on your feet and actually walking on tippy toes. It would be less painful.

A few years ago, Dawn and I were offered a BAFTA Fellowship. I managed to persuade Dawn (who loathes awards and prizes) to accept it, and to attend the ceremony. (I dealt a low blow by telling her not to think about it as an award for herself but as something that would make her mother very proud. So low.) And besides, there would be no pressure that evening because we had already won the award and so didn't have to be nervous or cross and could spend our time having a nice party and meeting people we admired. I really wanted to meet Harry Hill and hoped he would be there. Very few things have induced hysterical, pee-making, someone-may-have-to-slap-me-because-I-can't-stop laughter, but Victoria Wood's Acorn Antiques is one and Harry Hill's *TV Burp* the other.

Because we had a lot of notice and knew we were going to have to walk the dreaded red carpet (though Dawn always seems to manage to find a back door and avoid the whole she-bang), I decided, for the first time in my life, to prepare in advance what I was going to wear. Usually I leave it too late, convinced that I will shed a stone in a week, and then rush out and buy something I don't like, just because it fits and I'm desperate.

There are too many clothes in the world and a lot of them are fairly spiteful. If I take a wander down Bond Street, there are clothes in the windows that really don't want to be worn at all. They dare you to walk in the shop. They dare you to finger an item on the rail. They dare you to tell the spiky assistant that you're just browsing.

Shall I put it in the changing room for you?

No.

Why?

Because I haven't been able to look at the price ticket yet and I'm almost 100 per cent sure you won't have it in my size. And because you will try and make it fit and tell me it looks great and I will be forced to buy it out of embarrassment.

Then the evil clothes dare you not to leave the shop immediately, so you wander aimlessly towards the door, still fingering the rails, and then turn and say 'Thank you' before hitting the street and vowing never ever to go back.

I asked Betty Jackson to make me a dress.

Betty and I had been introduced by a brown tasselled leather jacket during the filming of a series of *French and Saunders*.

Alison Moyet, a friend of Dawn's, had worn the jacket on one of our shows and I had fallen in love with it. I wanted it. I wanted it bad. It fitted in with everything that I liked. It was just a bit cowboy, with shoulder pads.

Dawn somehow arranged this, with one catch: I had to go to Betty's shop and pick the jacket up myself. My idea of living hell. She was a famous designer; I was just a lumpy comedienne who didn't really have any nice clothes. But I really wanted the jacket and went to Betty's shop, looked at the floor a lot and mumbled. Betty was slightly braver and attempted to look me in the eye before I left, which resulted in us both getting quite embarrassed. However, the jacket was such a success that I went back for more clothes, and over the next few visits we even managed conversation and then laughter. It turned out that Betty and I had children much the same age and, gradually, we became friends, and our husbands became friends. As our kids grew up, we spent many happy and completely drunken Sundays together. The children would perform plays and fashion shows and sometimes weddings for us, while we disappeared into the bleary, happy world of eau de vie.

Anyway, back to the BAFTAs. I had lost a lot of weight on a detox diet, and didn't even have to ask Betty to make the dress quite tight, because on the day I actually *was* going to be a stone lighter than usual.

All I needed was to find some shoes.

I found a pair of black satin Louboutins. They were beautiful. A small platform and a cope-able heel. They fitted perfectly. Not too tight anywhere. Just snug and remarkably comfortable. I bought the matching clutch bag too.

For the first time in my life, I had got a whole proper outfit a week ahead of an event. I got a fake tan and a manicure and, by the time my make-up and hair were done on the night, I felt very swish. I felt comfortable and confident – a feeling I had never experienced before when dressed up. I was ready on time, not in a panic, and not running up- and downstairs in different dresses trying to drag an opinion out of Ade.

'Does this look mad?'

'No.'

'I think it does.'

'It doesn't. The car's here.'

'If you saw me, what would you think?'

'I'd think . . .'

'Look at me from behind. You don't think it looks mad? That I look mad?'

'No. The car's here.'

'I think it looks mad. I'm going to wear the other dress. FUCK, why can't I just wear jeans?! Do you think we have to go?'

'Car's here. I'll wait for you in the car.'

Ade was probably pleased to be busy on the evening of the Awards, so I took my friend, the set designer Lez Brotherston, and we set off for the Royal Festival Hall. Then the driver said he wasn't allowed to drive up the side of the Hall to the entrance and we would have to get out and walk. Walk? It was a long way. By the time we actually hit the red carpet, I was in agony; the shoes were rubbing at the back of my heel and the balls of my feet were burning. As I reached the end of the red carpet, I was beginning to hobble. So I rushed into the Hall and took the shoes off, stood barefoot on the marble floor, cooled my feet until they felt comfortable and then slid them back into the shoes. But a strange thing had happened. They didn't fit. My toes were squished into the toe space, as before, but now there was a centimetre gap between my heel and the back of the shoe. They had become Louboutin flip-flops.

Pain in toes now greater. Body trying to pipe itself through the peep toes. I found a toilet and attempted to pad the shoes with toilet paper. Nothing worked. I was in the grip of torture;

Louboutin high-heely flippy-floppy body-piping torture. Lez guided me from then on, supporting me by the arm as if I had been recently shot.

I sat through the ceremony, during which I could only think, *How am I going to walk up the steps without embarrassing myself?* Richard Curtis made a jolly and kind speech and then Helen Mirren came on and did the same. (What an honour. After all, she is, to all intents and purposes, the Queen.)

The time came for us to collect the award. Dawn annoyingly skipped on to the stage in flat pumps. I walked, stiff-legged, with a slight scooping action to bear pain and stop shoes falling off (gap at heel had doubled by now), made it without incident, got given heavy BAFTA – 'Thank you, Ma'am' – and curtsied. As the evening progressed, the pain lessened but I lost all sensation in my toes (I imagine it's a bit like frostbite). Got home and was frightened to take the shoes off in case my toes came off with them. Considered going to A&E to have them surgically removed. Never wore them again, but gave them to my daughter to wear to parties and trash.

And did I meet Harry Hill? Oh yes. Met comedy hero Harry Hill. During the walk into the auditorium I saw him. I let go of Lez's arm and attempted to move towards him nonchalantly.

'Harry Hill, how are you?'

'Jennifer Saunders. Why are you walking so strangely?'

I told my daughter to party in them, walk in mud in them, spill vodka on them. Kill the wicked evil shoes.

Anyhow, I've taken us well off track. Let's go back to 1985.

Screen goes wobbly.

Ade and I are getting married.

The ceremony took place in our local church in Crowton. It's a funny old church. On a Sunday morning, you would be amazed to hear the most beautiful bells ringing out across the fields. Amazed because the church itself didn't have a bell tower and so had, very obviously, no bells at all. Not even a small tinkler. It all came from speakers rigged up by the vicar who was going to marry us and whom our next-door neighbour, Clara, an Italian Roman Catholic, refused to sit next to, not because of religious differences but because someone had told her that he had had an unexploded bullet lodged in his spine since the war and she was afraid it might go off at any time and hit her.

He was generally a good vicar, but on that particular day he got very overexcited by some of the faces in the congregation. Jools Holland played the organ as I entered. I met Ade at the altar. And then the vicar took over.

'I see we've got Lenny Henry in the audience.'

That was his opener, and from that moment he veered off course into a small stand-up routine.

There were two types of people as far as my father was concerned: funny, nice people and 'stupid arses'. For most of the wedding, all I could hear was my father (who was an atheist) muttering loudly, 'Stupid arse! What's the stupid arse doing? Just get on with it, you stupid bloody arse!'

The vicar then moved on to the serious bit – the bit where he gives advice to the young couple starting out in the world. He talked to Ade and me about faithfulness and temptation and the dangers of kissing other actors and actresses during the course of our careers, and how challenging that would be for the other partner, the strain it might put our relationship under. I couldn't understand what had prompted him to see us suddenly as romantic leads. I knew Dawn would be laughing, and my father hadn't let up.

'*Stupid bloody arse!*'

The vows went without a hitch. We managed to say our bits without crying too much. Rik did the statutory 'Oh no, I can't find the ring' routine and, before long, we were walking out to Jools jazzing it up on the organ.

Happy, happy, happy.

The sun shone all day and we ate a delicious lunch and drank plenty of delicious Champagne in a marquee on the lawn.

My wonderful mother had pulled all this off without fuss or complaint, but then I do think weddings were more straightforward in those days.* We had a rest after lunch and speeches, and then everyone plus more came back for a party in the evening, and stayed in hotels organized by my brilliant mother. Dancing and drinking and general merriment until somehow, and reluctantly, Ade and I were decanted into my black Alfa Romeo Spider, and we drove away with the roof down to our first stop: a hotel in Chester that had a jacuzzi bath. In retrospect, yes, I must have driven over the limit, alcohol-wise, but breathalisers hadn't been invented yet. I was also three weeks pregnant, it later transpired.

SHUT UP, MUMSNET! My daughter was born happy and healthy – and still is.

So, how did all this come about? How come I'm waking up to a person I hardly even mentioned in the last chapter?

Well, a lot happened, let me tell you.

When the Comic Strip club eventually closed, we went on

---

* People now seem to be engaged for decades and plan their weddings for years, at extortionate cost not just financially, but to their mental health. My advice is to keep it simple; it's generally better just to make sure that it means something and that everybody has a good party. There you go. That's what I think, and you can put it in yer pipe and smoke it. You don't need monogrammed napkins or chairs with bows on or swans floating in a fake lake (now I'm talking to the weeping monster brides on reality shows). It isn't just actually all about YOU. It's everybody's day and that's the point. Feel free to puff away.

tour around Britain in a coach: Peter and Nigel, Rik and Ade, me and Dawn, Arnold Brown and what had become the house band – Rod Melvin on keyboards, Simon Brint on guitars and Rowland Rivron on drums. Rowland was a great drummer and a crazy man, while Simon and Rod were civilized and sat together making convivial conversation. The rest of us drank beer and played 'Who can stand on one leg the longest?' at the back of the coach, as it heaved us from venue to venue.

Usually, we would pull over in motorway services for the loo and lunch, but once we were driving through the back end of an industrial town up north and couldn't find anywhere until we came upon a rough pub in a run-down housing estate. We decided to go in. The boys put on their donkey jackets and working-class dispositions and, despite the odd look from the locals, we were served beer and a sandwich and seemed to fit in nicely. Then in came Rod and Simon – Simon in his favoured long black coat and fedora. He went to the bar as Rod sat down. He looked out of place. It was as if a drawing by Aubrey Beardsley had wandered into a Lowry painting by mistake.

Then the Aubrey Beardsley turned from the bar and said very loudly, in his wonderful gentle voice, 'Is that a dry sherry, Rod?'

The pub went silent. We'd been rumbled. We swigged down our drinks and were out of there.

The tour went relatively well and we played small venues up and down the country: arts centres, theatres, a working men's club and an old cinema in Glasgow where the seats had to be sprayed with disinfectant before the audience came in. We already knew each other well, but on that tour I felt we became a proper gang. I have to say that at this point, although I got on well with all the boys, there was no particular special spark between Ade and me. WE WERE JUST FRIENDS. Nothing to see here. Move on please, ladies and gentlemen. Thank you.

The following year, we were booked to go to Australia to perform at the Adelaide Festival and then some gigs in Melbourne and Sydney. It was this tour that meant Dawn had to give up teaching; it was comedy or education, and I hate to think what my life would be today if she had chosen the latter. I would probably still be sitting on a step in Chelsea doing the crossword and sprouting a small beard.

Going to Australia was like being paid to go on holiday. We stayed in proper hotels. We had our own rooms. We sunbathed by swimming pools, took trips to see kangaroos and koalas, I ate my first oyster, and we became fans of the Tanztheater Wuppertal, who were staying in the same hotel as us in Melbourne. We had a picnic at Hanging Rock and drank beer on Bondi Beach. We also had to perform shows in the searing heat – degrees-we'd-never-heard-of heat.

It was a busy old year, 1982. Before we even went on tour, Rik, Ade and Nigel had shot the first series of *The Young Ones*. Peter was originally going to play the part of Mike in the show but had fallen out with Paul Jackson, the producer and director. The problem with Pete was that he always had to be in charge, and still does. Pete had his own ideas and wanted to make films. Pete was, and still is, a man who decides what he is going to do and does it. He's incredibly persuasive, and managed to land a deal to make a series of short films for the soon-to-be-launched Channel 4. So a couple of months after returning from Oz, we found ourselves making *Five Go Mad in Dorset*, the first Comic Strip film, which was to go out on the Channel's opening night.

It was a low-key production. With all the budget going on the film itself, we actors came cheap. It was very home-made. We drove down to Devon together, picking other people up on the way, listening to our Walkmans in the back of the car and trying to stay calm when they chewed up our mix tapes. Once there, we stayed at Peter's mum's house, and slept in bunk beds and barns.

I had terrible tonsillitis for some of the shoot, and Betty Richardson was very kind to me, trotting up and downstairs with hot and cold packs to soothe my painful throat. My voice in *Five Go Mad* is pretty weird – halfway to Sandi Toksvig. When we went to Hope Cove, to film on the coast there, we stayed in basic holiday cottages, right on the beach and unbelievably damp. Bunk beds again for me and Dawn. It was like being on the greatest holiday with all your mates. Sleeping was the last on the list of priorities. There seemed to be no dividing line between work life and social life.

Having grown up there, Pete knew the South Devon coastline like the back of his hand. We shot in all his favourite secret and often almost inaccessible locations. The crews were small and the runners generally members of Pete's family. We didn't have Winnebagos or caravans or even an idea that they existed. No make-up trucks or wardrobe facilities. If you weren't filming then you lay about in the sun or hung around on set. Even if we weren't required that day, we generally made our way on to the set to watch stuff happening and consume the catering. Free food!

We all had the happiest time, mainly because we got given our first per diems. Per diems are basically envelopes full of money: an actor's daily allowance for expenses. And, because your accommodation and food are provided by the production, it is basically money for nothing. Or actually, money for drinking. As soon as filming had finished, we'd head for the pub. I was keen on getting to the pub, mainly because I was so good at pool. Nights ran into days, with limited sleep between the two. On several occasions during the shoot, the boys didn't actually get any sleep at all.

Channel 4 launched on 2 November 1982 at 5 p.m. Five million people tuned in to watch its first-ever programme, *Countdown*. Five and a half hours later, *The Comic Strip Presents . . . Five Go Mad in Dorset* became Channel 4's first-ever comedy show. Only 3.4 million people watched it, but it was about 3,399,700 more people than we'd ever had in an audience before.

The next day, several viewers called in with angry complaints about the irreverent spoof of poor old Enid, but it didn't seem to bother the Channel 4 bosses, who agreed to transmit the four remaining films in the series at the beginning of 1983 and commissioned a second series to be filmed later that year.

Although the films were Pete's babies, and he wrote the majority of them with Pete Richens, they were very much an ensemble effort. We all had the same sensibility and by then we were all beginning to know what we wanted to achieve. For me and Dawn especially, the work was a learning curve; we got a practical education in film: how to work with directors and film crew, what worked and what didn't. And there wasn't a sense that you had to fit in with what a committee of executives wanted. On the whole, we were left to our own devices.

A week after the screening of *Five Go Mad in Dorset*, the first-ever series of *The Young Ones* went out on BBC2. While the boys (Ade, Rik, Nigel and Alexei) became a cultural phenomenon, Dawn and I continued to work live, touring small gigs and fringe theatre venues throughout 1983. We had an agent, Maureen Vincent (still our agent today, she has single-handedly managed to keep the wolves from our door with patience and brilliant negotiation), and were forming our identity away from the Comic Strip.

We had a set that we could perform almost anywhere and required only basic facilities, i.e. a place where we could be seen by the audience. One of our first shows was performed to an audience just in front of the fireplace at the Chelsea Arts Club, all three or four of whom were, in fact, asleep. During another – performed to some directors' wives and, oddly, a Polish youth orchestra at the Nat Lofthouse suite at Bolton Football Club – we made the mistake of saying the word 'clitoris'. Cue gasps from the ladies present. We were virtually marched out of the building. The orchestra didn't understand any of the act at all, and the wives didn't like it.

One St Patrick's Day, we played to a full Irish pub in Kilburn on a tiny stage with only one microphone. We needed the microphone because the noise from the crowd was so loud, but only one mike isn't great for a double act. The punters were trying to have a conversation and we were an annoying distraction. We finished our act halfway through and left the stage. Nobody noticed. Next act on was Wacky and Zany Jim Barclay (arrow through the head), a regular on the circuit, whose finale was to place a large coin between his buttock cheeks then squat over a beer glass and drop the penny in. Nobody noticed him either. Tony 'The Guvnor's Cookin Tonight' tried a bit, realized it was hopeless, so packed in with his usual sign-off: 'Goodnight and may your God go with you.' By this time, everyone in the pub was facing away from the tiny stage. Suddenly there was silence. A person in the crowd sang 'Danny Boy' to huge applause and tears.

Still, we got paid. And that generally was the point.

Once we had established a little bit of a reputation, Maureen managed to get us our own small shows, Pentameters Theatre and the New End Theatre in Hampstead. This meant that we had to come up with an hour of material. Our other regular venues were the Latchmere in Battersea and the King's Head in Islington. By the time we were playing those venues, we realized that we needed a support act, and either John Sessions went on before us or we took Raw Sex (more about them later) along too.

Raw Sex allowed us time to change; they would fill in while we desperately pulled on a funny hat or our Menopazzi leotards. Oh yes, the Menopazzi Sisters were still part of the show and very popular, thank you. Their act now included juggling and quite a lot more flour. They were always the finale, so the mess could be coped with. They were also the bit that Dawn and I enjoyed most – even more than the audience. Totally covered in flour, a drum roll, huge amount of circussy preparation, a bit more flour, and then one of us would do a forward roll followed by bowing for the next three minutes. Thank you and goodnight!

In 1983 we took the show to the Edinburgh Festival, which was to be the only time that we would play there. Edinburgh is a showcase for new acts, particularly comedy acts, but Dawn and I spent most of our time at the Doris Stokes show. Doris was a famous medium and psychic and would speak to the dead relations of audience members. It didn't really matter to us whether she was for real or fake; she had to fill an hour by whatever means possible. First, she would go into a semi-trance. Then:

'I'm getting a "T". A "T". Hang on. What does "T" stand for, dear? Oh, he says they will know. So does anyone here know a "T"? No. You're going to have to help me a bit more, dear. Is it Tim or Tom or . . . ?'

Person in audience puts hand up. 'I've got a Sam!'

'Hang on, I'll ask him. Are you a Sam? Oh. Yes, he says, "I am Sam." I've got your Sam here, darling. He says he just liked a cup of tea. Did he like a cup of tea, your Sam?'

'Yes he did, Doris!'

'Then it is your Sam.'

Audience applause. She was a genius.

I'm not very good when it comes to chronology, and I can't quite work out how we fitted it all in. I asked Ade if he could remember 1983 and he seemed to think he had spent most of it in the pub with Rowland Rivron. This was no use to me at all. But then I don't ever remember feeling we were at work. Work and social life merged because we were young and always with our friends. Pub, film set, pub, pub, studio, pub, gig, pub, pub, pub, film set, film set, pub, pub, wine bar. There was only fun to be had.

In 1984, pub, pub turned into travelling round Dorset with my friend Ade looking for small cottages to buy. We weren't going out at this point but just loved driving in his huge Jaguar Mark X listening to Hank Williams and Emmylou Harris. He had an idea that he wanted to buy a cottage, and I thought I could buy it with him. In retrospect it seems a bit weird. But I really liked the Jag and I really liked being with him and that was it, I thought.

I hadn't been short of boyfriends in my young life. There was Joe 90, of course, and my first real boyfriend, Roger, who was tall and blond and a bit of a dish. Then there were the obviously slightly tarty times in Italy (no porn films, though, mind you!). I recently found all my diaries from the seven months I spent there, which make an eyebrow-raising read.

10 March 1977

After lunch, met Oscar outside and we walked. He asked me what was wrong and I said I was just pensive. In fact, I was wondering what the Hell I was doing going out with him . . .

After dinner, I set out for the Old Fashion to meet Roberto. Just outside the house, I got a lift from a Sicilian guy who I knew from the Old Fashion and he gave me a lift to Gambero Rosso, where I met Roberto.

At the Old Fashion, the small Sicilian guy had a private word with me and I agreed to meet him on Sunday. Roberto was rather suspicious.

Got a rather confused lift back to Via S Orsola with a policeman friend of Roberto's.

11 March 1977

Oscar is funny, he only wants to know about my childhood and what I do and what I'm thinking about. When he rings up he always asks what I was doing when the phone rang and what I've done all day. He knows I go out with Roberto which is one thing and I think he's getting the idea that I don't want to be his girlfriend just his friend.

12 March 1977

In the afternoon, again did little except eat digestive biscuits in milk. Roberto rang. I had forgotten to ring him at 1.00. Arranged to meet him at G. Rosso at 8.00. (Actually 3.30 but I heard him wrong.) Oscar rang at 7.30 because I'd said I might go out with him tonight. We spent hours on the phone in complete silence because he was upset that I was going out with Roberto. Was I in love with him? Why didn't I love him? etc. What a bore . . .

14 March 1977

At school I sat next to Ian, as usual. That gorgeous Turkish boy was there again wearing tight jeans and stars and stripes braces. CORR.

Oscar annoyed me. He asked me to find an English girl for him to talk to, to replace me when I go. And I hope I annoyed him by walking super quickly home and talking to him so he couldn't understand and then not repeating myself (I enjoyed that).

16 March 1977

Have just rung Roberto and he can't get out tonight but I'm meeting him tomorrow at 10.00 Alla Poste Pza Cardusio. So who can I go out with tonight? It might end up being Oscar unless I go and pick someone up at the USIS. I wish I knew the Turk better.

18th March 1977

Oscar depresses me and I want to hit him all the time and Roberto is too possessive and getting a bit heavy. Maybe he's just a bit too smooth.

Anyway, anyway. Back to 1983 and Ade. The only hint I had that I might like *him* quite a lot (my old brain is fairly dense about these things) was when a boyfriend and I split up, and his parting words to me were along the lines of: 'I don't know why you don't just go out with Ade, because you only seem to want to talk to him. You refer everything to him.'

I told him he was an idiot. I had no interest in Ade at all.

WE WERE JUST FRIENDS, ALL RIGHT? Nothing to see here. Move on please, ladies and gentlemen. Thank you.

On one of our jaunts in Dorset, the romance began and we had a kiss (I am blushing now and won't go into much detail, I'm afraid). A certain sort of knowledge was now had.

It was very easy. We were already such good friends. The hardest thing was announcing it to other members of the Comic Strip. It didn't feel incestuous, it just felt awkward. It felt like when Monica dated Chandler in *Friends*. Awkward. Dawn knew, of course. She said she had always been convinced that we should get together and was frustrated by how long it took us.

So, in the summer of '84 we made a Comic Strip feature called *The Supergrass*. We filmed it in Devon with the whole gang and then everybody had to know. We were holding hands under the table in the pub of an evening. We were sharing a room. And the plot of the film required us to kiss (the vicar wouldn't have had to worry), which we didn't seem to mind.

The only possible spanner in the works came when Ade crashed into my car. In those days, before he got responsible, Ade was forever having accidents. Within weeks of buying a beautiful old Ford Cortina off Dawn he had wrapped it around a lamp post in Soho. The council made him buy a new lamp post, which still makes us laugh. 'That's my lamp post,' he'll say, whenever we drive past it. In fact I think he owns two.

We were in Devon filming, driving back from a night out. Ade was in front of me in his huge Jag, and I was driving the car behind with Robbie Coltrane in the passenger seat. As we turned a corner to go uphill to the hotel, Robbie started shouting, 'He's in reverse, he's in reverse!' He had seen Ade's reversing lights go on, but I couldn't get my car in reverse quick enough and the Jag came back heavily into the front of my car. It fairly well crumpled the front, but it was still drivable. It was a tense moment. Ade was mortified.

The truth was, though, I loved Ade more than the car. Yes, more than my Alfa Romeo Spider. And I really loved that car! I had bought it with the very first bit of money I ever had. It cost £2,000, which was a FORTUNE. I should have done something sensible with the money, of course, but why would you? (Even now, when I hear myself telling my girls to do something sensible with any money they might have earned, there is a voice in the back of my head saying, 'Or you could just buy a really pretty car!')

My Spider was so damn cool. It was a head-turner. I wore a black hat and black leather jacket and drove it with the roof down. I still miss that car. I had to get rid of it eventually because when I was pregnant the lack of power steering became an issue. I swapped it for a newer red one, but it was never the same. I miss the smell of a classic car: leather and damp and engine oil. It's a heady mixture.

I learned to drive in an old banger in a field, and was allowed to drive my parents' car down the lane. So when it came to taking lessons I was fairly competent. My mother gave me a small sherry to calm my nerves before I took my test, and I passed it first time. Within a couple of weeks, however, I had smashed a tiny Honda the size of a biscuit tin – which contained me and three of my schoolfriends – into a tree and overturned it. The car was a mess, but no one was seriously hurt. It was horrible, but probably the best lesson I ever had. I have been lucky since and never had anything more than the odd scrape.

I love driving. I mentally pat myself on the back if I think I've taken a corner particularly well.

I love cars.

I believe I was the fastest-EVER female contestant on *Top Gear's* Star in a Reasonably Priced Car. If I had done one more lap, which I was offered, I know I could have beaten Simon Cowell. I was an idiot.

I like driving fast cars.

Mainly, I like beautiful cars.

Cars I would most like to own are the 1959 Bentley Continental, E-Type Jag, a 1949 Bristol 402 and an original Fiat 500. Meanwhile, Ade is probably happiest driving a Land Rover. He doesn't like my little Porsche. In fact he is happiest in a boat. So I like cars, he likes boats. I say potato, you say potato. I say tomato, you say tomato.

Nothing to see here, ladies and gentlemen . . . except the prospect of a long and happy marriage.

So we've got there. We are back. That's how come I am lying in bed, on honeymoon, with him. We are wearing matching His and Hers nightshirts that were given to us as a wedding present. Outside, the weather is terrible. It has rained constantly since we arrived and I think I have developed tonsillitis because I fell asleep in the jacuzzi bath of the hotel we stayed in on our wedding night. When I woke, the water was cold, the window was open and Ade had passed out on the bed. I'm not feeling at all well.

five

Dawn and I are sitting in Maureen Vincent's office. Maureen, who has been our agent for ever, and still is. Maureen, to whom we owe the longevity of our career, who kept us in the market-place both singly and as a pair and who, by never overpricing us (or indeed underpricing us), has kept us in the swim.

It is 1986 and she has called us in to go through a contract, a contract that is the most important of our career. We have been offered a series of *French and Saunders* on BBC2. Already, Dawn and I think we know everything about television, having done a series of the Comic Strip and a show called *Girls on Top*.

We wrote *Girls on Top* with Ruby Wax. It was our first attempt at writing a series.

Ruby had come from America and studied acting before

joining the Royal Shakespeare Company and then becoming a comedy writer. She is probably one of the funniest people alive. I can't remember speaking in the first few years of knowing her; just listening and laughing, afraid to interrupt for fear of being English and dull. Her life was being worked into a stand-up routine, and her brain was always ticking. Ruby on a roll is a wonder to behold; her take on life and people spins everything on its head. Her brain works so fast that sometimes she starts a story halfway through, as her mouth tries to catch up.

'Rubes, you have to start at the beginning. We don't know who you're talking about.'

'Didn't I tell you that already?'

'Your brain thought it, but your mouth didn't say it.'

When Dawn and I wrote with her, the characters that developed were just exaggerated versions of ourselves in that room: Dawn (as Amanda Ripley) trying to wrestle some kind of control and curb Ruby's excesses; Ruby (as Shelley DuPont) with no idea of political correctness whatsoever (and not really caring); and me (as Jennifer Marsh) saying very little, working out some comedy business I could do in the background while they fought it out. Jennifer Marsh was basically a moronic version of myself when I was twelve. She wore my twelve-year-old uniform: V-necked jumper, jodhpurs and jodhpur boots. I was very happy.

Ruby taught us a lot about writing, but the biggest lesson we learned was never to leave Ruby with a script overnight, or by the morning every line would be scrawled over and changed.

We taught Ruby how to say thank you.

To waiters, even though she would have sent the food back twice. 'Ruby, say thank you.'

To shop assistants and runners. 'Ruby, say thank you.'

Ruby wasn't really rude, but sometimes her brain didn't stop long enough for pleasantries.

Girls on Top was commissioned for Central Television and we

filmed it in Nottingham. Tracey Ullman starred in the first series (as Candice Valentine) and Joan Greenwood played our
landlady.

If Ruby taught us how to write funny, then Tracey was a lesson in how to act funny. She was by far the most famous of us,
having starred with Lenny Henry in *Three of a Kind*. She was the
first person we ever met who had Ray-Ban dark glasses. Proper
Ray-Bans. The most desired dark spectacles of the eighties. She
would arrive at rehearsals in a quirky hat and those Ray-Bans.

'Morning, Jen!'

I don't think Tracey could ever quite distinguish me from my
character Jennifer Marsh. And when she greeted me it always
felt like a verbal pat on the head.

'Hello, Jen! Aaaah! Isn't she sweet?'

We made two series of *Girls on Top*, and somehow in that
time I got married and had one or possibly two children. I con-
tributed almost nothing to the writing process for the second
series; I was pregnant and away in my head on baby planet.
Eventually, Dawn told me that if I didn't say anything, then I
wouldn't have any lines, which I accepted happily. In Series Two,
Jennifer Marsh was a bemused spectator of the battles between
the other two, while I planned a nursery.

The show was regularly watched by 14 million people, which
is staggering compared to today's ratings. But then there were
only four channels and it was put on at prime time. It is also possible that remote controls hadn't been invented then and people
were trapped, sofa-bound, with no choice but to watch it. In
certain episodes, however, it did have rather a stellar cast. Ruby
would rope in all her chums from the RSC, and the likes of
Alan Rickman, Suzanne Bertish and Harriet Walter had small
parts. Ian McKellen only escaped by the skin of his teeth.

Home for me and Ade was a top-floor flat above Luigi's Italian
delicatessen on the Fulham Road.

We had a basic rule: whichever one of us wasn't working was at home with the children. We have always made a point of not interfering with each other's work. And we never get jealous. That's the thing. If I work a lot, Ade thinks it's great, and vice versa. We keep the reason *why* we are working at the forefront of our minds. Making sure our kids are happy and having a nice life is always more important than anything, really.

From the beginning, the girls have always come first. But equally there has never been any question that Ade and I would put our careers on hold for them; we have always made a real point of keeping our home life and our working life separate. We don't take our work home with us. I mean, that would be quite hard anyway. We're not like actors who have to live apart for months and can't drag themselves out of character. We just mess about, make jokes and fall over to make ourselves (and hopefully others) laugh.

We have worked really hard to make sure that the girls live as normal a life as possible, and I hope we have largely achieved that. Though some things slip through. Once I took the girls to the cinema. When the film had ended and we were getting ready to leave, Beattie looked weary and said, 'Do we *have* to go backstage?'

I thought they liked going backstage, and always tried to make it possible if we knew someone in the cast of a show. We had gone backstage at *Joseph and the Amazing Technicolor Dreamcoat*, but I realize now that having actually seen the show, they couldn't help but find it a bit dull.

'This is the stage!'

In their heads: *Yeah, we just saw that when we were in the audience.*

'These are the costumes!'

Yeah, we saw those.

'Do you want to meet Phillip Schofield?'

'Will Gordon the Gopher be there?'

'No.'
'Can we just go home?'

When they were little they didn't watch us on television, simply because they were too young. Even once they were old enough they didn't see many of our shows, because we didn't sit down and watch them often. We were just Mummy and Daddy.

One of them came home from school one day and was looking at me strangely.

'What's the matter?'
'Are you Jennifer Saunders?'
'Yes, sometimes I am.'
'Because someone at school said that's who you were, but I said you were just Mummy.'

Ella told me the other day that when we went off to work or said we were going to the office, they always thought we were going to work at the Star and Garter Home for Retired Servicemen. We passed it every morning on the way to school and it looked like offices.

You don't realize how little you tell them. We really didn't talk about it at home.

In 2000 I was touring with Dawn. Our opening gig was at the Blackpool Empire. It's a massive theatre in a town that has seen better days. Growing up in Cheshire, we used to spend the odd day on Blackpool beach but mainly on the rides and in the arcades. I will do speed at a fairground, but I won't do height. I won't do the high roller coasters or anything designed to make you poo your pants, but I will sit on a wooden horse pretending to win the Grand National, and go on generally jiggly things, and the ghost train.

High rides and aeroplanes are the same to me. I look at them, and all I see is the things that could go wrong. Most of us *have* to go on aeroplanes sometimes – high rides you do not.

I once took my three girls on a waltzer, and the skinny rogue spinning the carts decided to give us extra spin. We were the only ones on the ride, so he gave us his full attention – spinning and spinning at such a rate. It was relentless. I started to panic and scream as I felt my little girls being pulled out of my grasp, but could do nothing as my brain was now flat against the back of my skull with the centrifugal force. It was only when he spotted a group of pretty girls waiting to get on that the nightmare ended.

So now I have crossed waltzers off the list. I am very happy on the 'It's a Small World' ride at Disneyland, and the spinning teacups. I'm also willing to look after everyone's bags and play slot machines.

So Dawn and I are in Blackpool starting the tour. First nights are always the most nerve-wracking. We had a very technical show which was two hours long and didn't have a support act. In order to give ourselves time to change, we had pre-recorded footage that came up on big screens (we also interacted with footage on the screens, so if something went wrong with the projectors we had had it). At the end of the show I was attached to a wire and had to run backwards up a screen showing a film of a huge Dawn. It looked as if I was being eaten by her. (I will do wires. I do like a bit of flyin'. Comedy flying is one of my favourite things. I think it ranks up there with a neck brace for funniness.)

As you might imagine, Dawn and I were nervous. We were getting ready in our dressing room, which was full of cards and flowers, and just after one of my frequent visits to the toilet my phone rang. It was a call from home. *How sweet*, I thought. *They've remembered it's our first night*. It was Beattie.

'Mummy, where's the Sellotape?'

The great thing is, I knew. I have an almost superhero-ey X-ray visiony way of finding things, and I will never give up. I will still be looking for the passport/keys/shoe/tiny-screwdriver-set-we-got-in-a-cracker-for-fixing-spectacles when others have fallen by the wayside or gone to bed.

I am really quite a tidy person now. You have to be once you have kids. For years, though, I was hideously untidy. My rooms always looked as if a huge laundry basket had exploded, and I dressed as if I had just been hit by the shrapnel. Once, when Dawn and I were sharing a house in Acton, we had a robbery and the police had to be called. On entering my room the officer was shocked and said it was one of the worst 'turn-overs' he had seen; all my possessions were scattered over the floor and mattress and it looked squalid – just as I had left it. He asked me if I thought that they had taken anything, and I had to pretend to take stock.

Had they taken the bed?

No, I didn't have a bed. Just a mattress on the floor.

The truth was, they hadn't been in there at all.

On the whole, you have to grow up when you have children. Ade and I would do the washing-up every night and were tidy and, above all, calm. My family was never noisy. Nor was Ade's. So we both like a bit of silence and calm; it doesn't frighten us at all. We would manage to get the kids up and off to school with relatively little fuss and then run the gauntlet of other mothers and escape before being press-ganged into a coffee morning or fund-raiser.

I always found it extraordinary how many women turned up late and in a panic, huffing and puffing, blaming the five-year-old, with a martyred air.

'Come on, come on, have you got your bag? No, well that isn't my fault. You should remember it. And now we're late!'

And then knowing looks to other mothers as if to say, *Nightmare, isn't it? Bloody kids!*

I mean, how hard is it to get two small children up on time, dressed, breakfasted and in the car without getting into a lather and dragging them into school as if you've just escaped Nazi occupation? And I'm not talking overstretched single mothers here, I'm talking Range Rover-driving women who obviously have a nanny!

I never enjoy going into schools. Ade is very good at it. Even as an adult, I would get butterflies in my stomach if I had to go in and speak to my girls' teachers, especially the head teacher. Best behaviour and say all the right things.

My own school life had been head down and get away with it. Don't get noticed, try not to cause trouble. I was generally quite afraid of getting into trouble.

One of my girls once said, 'Mummy, I don't know why you're so afraid of the teachers. They should be nervous of *you*.'

I don't think I ever recovered from Miss Dines. Miss Janet Dines.

Miss Dines was the headmistress of Northwich Grammar School for Girls. She ruled in a climate of fear.

She was tall and thin, always wore a black gown and had a large goitre (a swelling of the thyroid gland) in her neck. Her hair was kept short and neat. Being called to her office was a terrible thing.

One fateful evening, I had been to hockey practice and was outside school waiting to be picked up by my mother. Miss Dines and her sidekick, Miss Kirkpatrick, were just setting off from

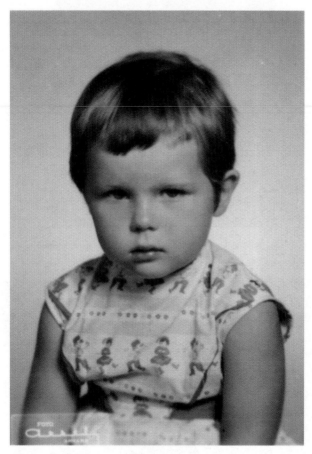

1. Podge.

2. Happy Podge.

3. Who was cutting my hair?

4. Just before I drowned.

5. My mother, brother Tim and me, on the golden sands of Littlehampton beach.

6. Picnic in Cyprus. My brother Peter is in the white carrycot.

7. Tim and me with Daddy, watching *Doctor Who*.

8. Test driving a very early eco-car. My brother Tim is on the bonnet.

9. All my heroes were cowboys or horses.

10. Two whippets, my great-aunt Mary, my grandmother Mooma and my posture.

11. Smart new mac and gloves. Riding school on a pony called Badger.

12. My mother looking slightly unhappy as the borrowed pony had just stepped on her toe.

13. Christmas morning. I wanted a tommy gun.

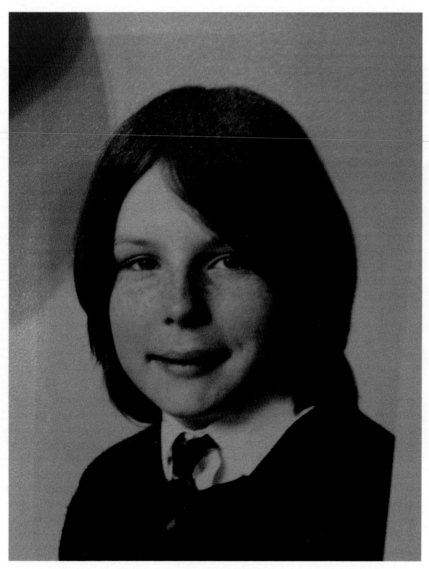

14. First year at big school.

15. Northwich Grammar School for Girls. I once volunteered to stand in for the goalie and made the mistake of being quite good at it and never got out. Helen Newman, who I was in Italy with, is back row, third from left.

16. Twelve years old and off to do some snaps with my snazzy Instamatic in my snazzy hat.

17. Mummy in the kitchen in Cheshire.

18. My parents in the swinging sixties.

19. I loved the martini shirt! My twenty-first birthday party in the cellar in Cheshire.
Dawn and me, lookin' a bit pie-eyed.

20. Theatre in Education. Peter (one of the only two boys on the course at the college), JoBo, me and Dawn. We performed to some poor schoolchildren. The opening number was 'Chattanooga Choo Choo'.

21. Dressed up to go out and stare at people on the Tube.

22. Very early Comic Strip club days. Yes, those were our stage outfits.

23. 1980s live show. A sketch that was based on my old headmistress Miss Dines.

24. The sublime Raw Sex: Rowland Rivron and Simon Brint, aka Duane and Ken Bishop.

25. Rik Mayall, Dawn and Alexei Sayle in a charming dressing room in Glasgow on the first Comic Strip tour.

26. Rik, Nigel Planer and Ade having a break during the filming of *A Fistful of Travellers' Cheques*.

school together (rumours were rife) to do their regular drive through Northwich to catch girls misbehaving, or not wearing the regulation red beret. Not wearing the beret was a crime punishable by death. She policed us in and out of school.

They saw me and – horror of horrors – I was still wearing my games socks. I stammered that I didn't know the sock rule. But I had to report in the next day.

Outside Miss Dines's office were two chairs. Girls wandering by would look sympathetically at you, crossing their fingers and wishing you luck. Those unfortunate enough to be sitting on the chairs had to wait for a green light to go on before entering. When it did, you had to be in pretty sharpish.

Miss Dines was sitting behind her desk, underneath which were the two black Labradors that would patrol the school playing fields at break-times.

– Why did I think that the rules existed? Particularly the uniform rules?

– Was I very stupid?

– Did I have eyes?

– Did I have a brain, because my silence on these matters would suggest otherwise?

– What was I going to do in future?

I felt sick and afraid. The school felt sick and afraid, and nobody seemed sicker and afraider than Miss Barnes, the deputy head. She was an older woman who behaved like a frightened budgerigar.

Every morning, there was Assembly. The whole school would gather in the hall, and often Miss Dines would be standing near the door, watching every girl go in – each of us hoping that the claw hand wouldn't land on our shoulder and pull us aside for some misdemeanour (laughing, untidy pigtails, whispering, inky cuffs, or just because you happened to catch her eye. You never wanted to catch her eye).

When we were all in, Miss Barnes would walk on to stage

and ask us all, in her tiny, frightened voice, to stand for Miss Dines, who would then stride down the side of the hall with her gown flying out behind her for effect. Once she was on the stage, she would say 'Good morning' and we would do a 'Good morning, Miss Dines' back. She would then sit down, and then, and only then, could Miss Barnes squeak for us all to sit.

One day, in the middle of lessons, the bell went. All classes were ordered into the hall. Nobody knew what was happening, not even the staff. Once the whole school was in, Miss Dines came on to the stage.

A girl had apparently been rude and sworn repeatedly at her.

This girl was dragged up onstage with a washing bowl and a bar of soap. Whereupon Miss Dines proceeded to force her to wash her mouth out.

There were some girls who didn't care, and faced her wrath. In my class, it was a girl called Jana Stenhouse, whose greatest triumph was running her knickers up the flagpole at the end of term. But generally, the girls and the staff were compliant.

On Sports Day, Miss Dines would take to the cricket pitch in full whites and a cravat (covering the goitre). We didn't play cricket at the school, but this was the traditional opening of the day – girls against staff. Miss Dines would stride out to the crease like a pro, patting down the odd divot, checking out the fielders, planning her boundaries and asking Miss Barnes (who was the umpire) to hold her jumper. One year she was facing a second-year girl who had been roped in to bowl. The very first ball left her hand at speed, went straight to the stumps and hit them hard. Everyone froze. The crowd was silent. Miss Dines made no move to leave the pitch. Under the pressure of Miss Dines's stare, Miss Barnes eventually piped up in a shaky voice, 'No ball!' and the match continued.

Shortly after I left, Miss Dines was taken to court by a pupil. This is part of the report. What is so bizarre is what was considered to be serious misbehaviour on the part of the girl.

Daily Mail, London, 13 November 1976

THE CLASSROOM TERROR
Head cleared as caned girl sobs in court
By James Golden

THE REIGN OF LYNNE SIMMONDS as a classroom terror ended when she was caned by the headmistress, a court heard yesterday.

Lynne, who had a history of bad behaviour, was sent to Miss Janet Dines for eating crisps during a maths lesson.

But the three whacks given to 14-year-old Lynne on her bottom landed Miss Dines, head of Northwich Girls' Grammar School, Cheshire, in court.

Lynne's parents brought a private assault and beating charge. They claimed that Lynne was punished unreasonably.

But after Lynne broke down weeping as she told of her classroom antics, the case was withdrawn and Northwich magistrates dismissed the charge against the middle-aged headmistress.

Lynne, who passed her 11 plus to go to the school, admitted a catalogue of misbehaviour when cross-examined by Mr John Hoggett, counsel for Miss Dines.

She said she told rude jokes in the scripture lessons while discussing moral and ethical questions.

She made remarks about teachers behind their backs and blew raspberries at them.

She told lies about having lost homework which she had not done and took a classmate's book without permission.

She stole a teacher's pen off her desk and offered it to a friend for a pound, and she disrupted the class.

Lynne was suspended for half a day by Miss Dines for the pen incident and her father gave her the strap.

She also admitted handing in a school project done by another girl, claiming it was hers.

But the girl – in hospital and temporarily blind – returned and Lynne was found out.

Then she was caught eating in a lesson and was sent to Miss Dines. The headmistress entered the punishment in the official book and told her she would be writing to her parents.

Lynne said that after the caning her bottom was sore for several weeks and she had been unable to sleep properly.

I knew girls who were caned so hard that the cane would strike the knuckles of the hand holding up their skirt. It beggars belief that a person was allowed to do this with no other adult present.

Dines was eventually removed from the school. My mother sent me a small article from the *Northwich Guardian* announcing her departure. The photograph was of three sixth-formers presenting her with her leaving present: a shotgun. How very appropriate.

In those days you got through school without much parental involvement. There was the odd parents' evening, but apart from that, parents were thankfully not encouraged on to the premises. That is how it should be. I wouldn't want to go home from school and have my parents know exactly what my homework is and how I've been in school that day. I wouldn't want my teachers to email my mother. I wouldn't want the school to send notes directly to my parents. I used to read all the notes from school on the bus and decide what they should and shouldn't see. I wouldn't want to go home and talk about school. For me, it was bus home, into house, throw down bag, eat sliced white bread and Flora marge, drink cup of tea, feet up in front of telly, then go and feed the animals. Clear head and do homework on bus the next morning, if listening to records had taken over in the evening.

I get the feeling nowadays that parents are expected to attend school more than the children. And why and what and where and why do some parents want to start up schools? Can you *imagine* if your parents started up a school? Would you – as their child – want to go to that school? No. You go to school to get away from your parents.

I'm sure most people don't want more choice. They just want a better school – a good school – that's quite close to where they live, and to not be required to enter the premises every other day and bake endless fund-raising cakes. Or is that just me?

I'm not a panicker. I think I get that from my mother. In fact, if there is a crisis, an air of calm comes over me. You may laugh, but I actually think I would be very good in a war, or if aliens landed, or in an energy crisis which forces us to be self-sufficient. I think I am quite resourceful. I made lots of successful dens as a child, am a good shot and learned early in my life that there are few things that can't be fixed with a piece of baler twine.

There is, of course, the possibility that I am a little bit *too* calm. When it comes to script deadlines and paperwork, I become rigid with the inability to tackle them. When I first met Ade, he was horrified that I would regularly put letters from the bank that had sat unopened for months straight into the bin.

A form of paralysis comes over me and I just can't read them. In our marriage Ade has become a martyr to the paperwork, the bills, the letters, the insurance, the credit cards, the banks, and I know I never thank him enough for it. I think if I hadn't met Ade I would probably be in prison.

I first got pissed off with the bank when the one I had my account with at college forced me to sell my red bike to pay off a £20 overdraft in my second year. If they'd just waited, I could have paid them! That's because the following year I had a good weekend job at the fire station. I cooked Sunday lunch for firemen. It was a job I had inherited from my friend Gill Hudspeth, and it paid about £20 a week, which was an unheard-of wage. The downside was that you had to get there really early and cook their toastie sandwiches as they were all waking up. They slept in their clothes, so it was all a bit stinky. I used to long for there to be a fire so they would get out of the kitchen area with their fags. I was usually hung-over, so the whole thing was a challenge.

Please let someone have a chip-pan fire so I have the place to myself.
Please, cat, get stuck up tree, or child, get head stuck in railings.

Each watch would buy the food for the lunch and so, until I got there, I had no idea what I would have to cook. And I didn't really know how to cook. Most things just got put in a roasting pan until they were the right side of burnt and then served up with Bisto.

But now, look, here we are in Maureen's office and the contract is on the table.

Maureen attempts bravely to hold our attention while reading out the details of the agreement, knowing full well that she is fighting a losing battle. We interrupt.

US: Maureen, Maureen. Do we get a pass?
MAUREEN: Can I just finish going through this and then . . .
US: Yes. Yes. But, Maureen, will we get a pass?
MAUREEN: Let me just get through this, loves.

A few weeks earlier, we had been called into the office of Jim Moir, the then Head of Light Entertainment (later the great saviour and reinventor of Radio 2) and told that the BBC was going to take the plunge and give us a series.

Actually, his exact words were, 'People I trust tell me you're funny. I'm going to take their word for it. I'm going to put my dick on the table and give you a show.'

Jim 'This is the wife, don't laugh' Moir was a lovely man from a different era. I don't think he ever read a script or came to watch a recording. In those days, executives made decisions and then let the people who made the shows just get on and do it.

The only time he ever did come down to a studio, he made a brief appearance, took me and Dawn aside and said, 'You two are my new Two Ronnies.'

Then left.

As Head of Light Entertainment, Jim had the job of hosting the Light Entertainment Christmas party every year. This was always held in a conference room on the top floor of the BBC. It was an event not to be missed, especially if you were a new-comer. It was always filled with real stars: the casts of *Dad's Army*, *It Ain't Half Hot Mum* and *Hi-de-Hi!*, Russ Abbot, the Krankies, Bruce Forsyth, Cilla and, of course, the Two Ronnies themselves. Everyone drank poor wine, ate appalling food and had the greatest time.

Light entertainment is different from comedy. Being com-missioned by LE meant that there had to be a certain amount of variety, i.e. music, in the shows. So every week we would have a singer and a guest star to fulfil the remit. I think it was a good thing. The shows were essentially live performance in a studio, and having a music guest made it feel like a real show. Even *The Young Ones* had to have a music guest.

MAUREEN: Have you got any questions before you sign this, loves?

US: Will we get a BBC pass?

MAUREEN: A pass?

US: So that we can just walk straight into the building and not get stopped.

MAUREEN: A pass?

US: Yes.

MAUREEN: Well, there's nothing in the contract specifically about that, but I'm sure it can be organized.

US: OK. But we will need one.

MAUREEN: Yes, loves. Are you going to sign?

US: Yes. But we will need one. We will need a pass.

MAUREEN: Yes. Note made.

We sign.

Six

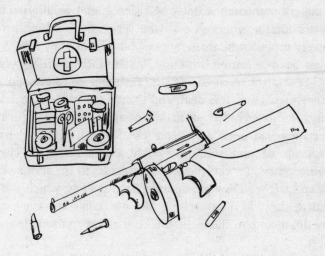

A couple of years later, Dawn and I are at the BBC. We have been given an office here, to write our second series.

The first series went out on BBC2 and was met with mixed reviews, as they say. But thankfully, in those days, the powers-that-be held their nerve and gave you a second chance. We were still learning, and the chances of getting it right first time were slim. Especially if, like us, you thought you knew it all and were not going to be told.

We had developed the French and Saunders characters, which was a plus. I was the misguided, bossy and generally cross one, and Dawn was the cheeky, subversive upstart. I was the one who thought she was a star, and Dawn was the one who managed to upstage me at every given opportunity. (Nothing has changed.)

We had decided to base the first series in a studio, as if we were producing our own variety show. 'Let the variety begin!' we would say, before introducing a troupe of dancers – led by the superb comedienne Betty Marsden – who would flap their way through a clog dance to the tune of 'Windmill in Old Amsterdam', accompanied by our house band, Raw Sex.

Raw Sex was Simon Brint and Rowland Rivron. They played a father and son, Ken and Duane Bishop. Ken (Simon) played the keyboards and was deaf, and Duane (Rowland) played the bongos and acted hideously drunk (often he was actually drunk). After they had been seen live, *The Stage* described them as 'musicians of almost indescribable sleaziness and technical incompetence . . . who reduced electronics to the status of the bow and arrow'. They were perfect for our show, which, we had decided, should be us looking like we didn't know what we were doing and producing something that didn't look like television.

We succeeded on both counts. It wasn't awful, but we knew it could be a lot better. In trying to make it simple, we overcomplicated it. There were some good sketches and characters, plus we had managed to persuade Alison Moyet and Joan Armatrading to be our musical guests. But there was also way too much faffing about and way too much bad dancing.

Still, we were learning.

For the second series, we got Bob Spiers on board to direct. Bob really knew what he was doing. Bob was a legend at the Beeb. He had worked on everything from *Are you Being Served?* to *Fawlty Towers*. He knew the studios inside out and, on a studio record evening, could genuinely boast that if we started at 7.30 p.m. we could be in the bar two hours later. As well as *French and Saunders*, Bob went on to direct most of *Absolutely Fabulous*, and rare was the time we were not necking a bevvy by 9.30 p.m.

He was fast and really clever. He never missed a shot or left a joke uncovered.

So, we are in our little room. Our little office room. I have arrived late, which is customary. Mobile phones haven't been invented yet, so I haven't been able to ring in with an excuse. Even if they had just been invented, chances are that Dawn wouldn't have one.

It took quite a long while to persuade Dawn to the mobile and I have never been able to persuade her to the computer. She doesn't use one. You can't email Dawn French off the teleovision. She is untouched by Google, Facebook and Twitter. I envy her that. My computer is the friend who knows I have to work but tries to tempt me to bunk off. It's the girl sitting next to me in class that puts her desk lid up and is trying to distract me with pictures of David Cassidy.

Stop it, computer! I know there are funny things on YouTube with kittens, and I know you have solitaire. And sudoku. And Angry Birds. But I have work! I have to do this thing. Leave me alone, or I will be forced to go back to the typewriter. That at least cuts out the printing stage. Printers who refuse to print and won't let you know their name. Printers who can't come online and run out of ink, even when there is ink in them. You know there's ink in them because you bought that ink, and it cost more than caviar. It has a cartridge of beluga fitted and it still refuses to print anything but light grey, so you end up just hitting it and hating it as it takes four sheets of paper through at a time and then gets jammed.

Yes, I might go back to the typewriter.

So, we are sitting trying to think up ideas.

Every journalist asks, 'How do you think up your ideas?'

And the answer is . . . You just think them. I suppose the real answer is by talking (not writing), and largely by playing. We play until we have something that works and makes us laugh. We play. We make up characters and voices and use people we have seen and lines we have heard, and then we play them into a sketch.

How comedy works is often misunderstood by some writers and producers. The phrase we most often hear is 'Can you two just stop messing about and get down to some work.'

They can't see that we *are* working! You don't just get there by working comedy out on a piece of paper and behaving yourselves. You have to take it as far as it will go, and then rein it back into something broadcastable. This is the fun of it. This is the point of it. You have to find the lines that don't just serve a purpose in the plot and are, to all intents and purposes, a 'joke'. You have to find the thing that really tickles.

I think Ken Dodd's tickling analogy – the idea that laughter tickles – is a very good one. It is that feeling that makes you laugh. The laughter is in the expectation as much as in the actual sensation. When Tommy Cooper came onstage, the expectation of the tickle was so intense that people would have to leave the room in paroxysms before he had even spoken a word.

I'm not saying that we ever achieved such heights, but that was always our ambition.

In our years working with various guests on *French and Saunders*, we soon came to realize that there are people with funny bones, those with none, and those who are simply nervous of being funny.

The guests with funny bones would always almost certainly accept the part, which was why we had wanted them in the first place. They understood the tickle. If someone hesitated, or wanted to see a script, we would be slightly dubious. When you have so little time to produce a show, the last thing you need is high maintenance. You want someone who wants to be part of the gang. That is why we so often had repeat guests: Alison

She was well behaved throughout and, despite having to have some minor plastic surgery, has remained our friend to this day.

There's one more star I need to mention in passing. It would be weird not to. Madonna. She who has adamantly refused to have anything to do with us.

We started asking Madonna to be a guest on the show very early on. Someone knew her publicist, who assured us that she was a big fan.

Marvellous.

We continually mentioned her in sketches and played her quite a few times. We were restrained at first, thinking that, hoping that – one day – she might be our friend (like Rowan Atkinson). After repeated snubs, we realized that our cause was hopelessly lost, and that, I'm afraid, made us quite cruel.

Madonna, Madonna, Madonna!

Why wouldn't you come on our show? We aren't crazies! We don't want your skin!

Anyway, back in our writing room. We would spend half the day talking and reading magazines, generally getting vague ideas and ammunition together. Nothing written down. Series Six of *French and Saunders* is a fairly accurate recreation of our writing process. That is my and Dawn's favourite series because it's so dangerously close to the truth.

You see, ideas don't just happen. You have to feed them. You can't do a decent poo if you haven't eaten anything. Apologies, dear reader, but it's the best analogy. We had to feed ourselves with gossip and trivia. All our writing was always improvised. The hard thing was writing it down, which we had to do for the production team. We would always attach a note at this point, assuring them that, although it might not read particularly well, it would eventually be funny. We promise!

By lunchtime, having exhausted ourselves making a list and calculating how long each sketch might have to be, we thought we definitely deserved a treat. Some nice food or maybe even a trip to a theatre matinee. We particularly liked matinees, with their guaranteed audiences of two ladies and a dog.

Occasionally, however, we went a little more highbrow. We once took in a matinee of David Hare's *The Breath of Life* – a two-hander, starring Maggie Smith and Judi Dench – at the Haymarket. Needless to say, the audience was full. We were particularly nervous because we were going backstage after the play to see Maggie; Dawn had met her doing a Dickens for TV, and they had got on well. We were so in awe of her and Judi that we were on our best behaviour.

DAWN: We must turn off our phones.
(*It is the twenty-first century, dear reader, and I have only just persuaded a reluctant Dawn to the mobile*)
ME: Yes, Dawn. I am turning off mine. It is off. If I can press any button, it will not come back on. Yes. Good. We are safe.

But such was our nervousness and the Power of the Dames that, a few minutes in, I leaned over to Dawn.

ME: I'm taking my battery out.
DAWN: Good idea. Look, I'm taking my battery out.
ME: My battery is out.
DAWN: My battery is out.

The play continued. In my head, I was still thinking about the battery and the phone.

ME: Dawn. I'm worried in case the electricity from the battery somehow transfers to the phone and switches it on.
DAWN: Yes, I'm worried about that too.

ME: I will give you my battery and you give me yours. Then I'll keep yours in my pocket and you keep mine in your pocket. But not near the actual phone.

DAWN: OK.

After the play, we went back to Maggie's dressing room. She thought the show had gone quite well, apart from the idiots who were whispering most of the way through the first half. You can't win.

Another treat we had lined up when writing was a trip to the Observation Room. 'Ah ha, what's that?' I hear you cry.

Well, the Observation Room was a glass box in Television Centre that was set high above one of the biggest studios. From inside it, you could watch whatever was happening on the floor below. There was a TV screen where you could tune into whatever was happening on the Ring Main. The Ring Main was internal TV, where anything that was being recorded or rehearsed in any studio could be viewed. Anyone, at any time, could watch you when you thought you were having down time, messing about, looking rough or picking your nose. But for us, it was fantastic. We watched studios being set up, rehearsals, actresses talking when they didn't realize that microphones were picking them up. It was a fountain of material. Oh, how we loved the Observation Room! We would take our sandwiches there. It felt naughty.

We once watched almost the whole of *The House of Eliott* (a period drama about the fashion industry of the 1920s) from the Observation Room and Ring Main. We couldn't quite believe how funny *The House of Eliott* was. We particularly loved how overdramatic the storylines were: 'How are we ever going to find any new buttons?' We went on to create 'The House of Idiot' for *French and Saunders* with – I have to say – almost pinpoint accuracy. We knew everything! We knew what they said when cameras were on, and we knew what they said when cameras were off.

The great thing about parodying TV and films in those days was that there was a fairly good chance that, if something was popular, then millions of people would have seen it. TV was a common, shared experience. Big films were obvious, but we did occasionally parody a director or a genre. Our favourites were actually always the less obvious ones: Bergman, Fellini and *Whatever Happened to Baby Jane?* We didn't have to do perfect impersonations as we were always French and Saunders within the parody.

If there was trouble, Dawn could always ask in the sketch, 'Are we going to do the accent?'

'No. It's just going to be my voice.'

Our parodies did cost quite a bit of money. Nowadays I don't think the budgets would be there to do them. *Misery*, *Lord of the Rings* and *Silence of the Lambs* were all shot on film and on location, with as much care as the original. Bob Spiers would often match the films shot for shot.

In Bob we had the best director, and in Jon Plowman we had the best producer. We had the best make-up and wardrobe, the best camera team – nearly all had trained and grown up at the BBC. Creatively it was the best place that we could have been. Plus, in those early days, the budgets were agreed in-house and were much more fluid. If we were doing a particularly expensive parody, say, or if we needed more wigs here or a special effect there, the accountant would see if he could nip a bit off Russ Abbot.

The BBC was more than a channel. More, even, than a production company. The BBC was a national resource. It trained and produced the greatest technicians in television, most of whom then eventually went on to work in the film industry. It was a centre of learning and creativity, with an executive culture that trusted the creative staff to do their job. It was the

DAWN: It's me.

ME: Who is me?

DAWN: It's me! Your comedy partner, Dawn French.

ME: What do you want?

DAWN: Can I come in?

ME: Yes. Come in. What are you waiting for?

(*It was the closest to a catchphrase that we
ever had.*)

Dawn enters.

She could be dressed as Pocahontas, or a vicar. And I could be
wearing my BBC turban and sweatshirt or be Jackie Onassis.
Dawn can be very surreal.

ME: What have you eaten today, Dawn?

DAWN: All I have had — and this is the truth —
is a piece of coal and a worm.

She once decided that she should enter with a huge human
ear attached to her back, which she was growing for 'The Giant'.
I love it when she introduces 'The Giant' into the dialogue.

DAWN: Jen, Jen . . . JEN!

ME: What?!

DAWN: You know The Giant?

ME: The Giant?

DAWN: Yes. THE GIANT!

ME: The one up the beanstalk?

DAWN: No, no, no, no. Not that one, you idiot! Not that giant, you fool! Why would it be that giant? Oh, I see what's happened here . . . do you think there is only one giant?

ME: Well . . .

DAWN: Oh, Jen. Oh, Jen. Oh no, how very sad. Jen, there's more than one giant. This one lives over the hill.

ME: The Jack and Jill hill?

DAWN: Yes. The Jack and Jill hill. Not the bean-stalk giant, you fool. Oh dear. Sometimes you are very naive.

ME: Does the giant know about the Borrowers?

DAWN: What?

ME: The Borrowers.

DAWN: The . . .

ME: Borrowers. The little people.

DAWN: Oh, Jen. Oh dear. How sad! You don't think there are little people, do you? Oh dear. They don't exist.

For so many years, we were allowed this playground and this dressing up. We could be men, we could be ABBA, we could be aliens, we could be Thelma and Louise.

We also managed to sign a contract guaranteeing us a certain amount of programming at the BBC.

'Maureen?'

'Yes, loves.'

'The contract.'

'Yes, loves.'

'We know it's full of stuff and everything.'

'Yes, loves. You don't want me to go through it, do you?'

'No. No. It's just, can you say what's really important, which is . . . Please can we have a parking space in the doughnut?'

The doughnut was the BBC building at the heart of Television Centre. It was circular, with a hole in the middle, and there were a few car parking spaces near the stage door.

'Do you actually want that in the contract?'

'Yes, please. We do. We just want to be able to drive in and park there when we are in the studio.'

'Right, loves. I'll talk to the powers-that-be.'

And we got it! I don't think Dawn and I were ever happier than on the day we were allowed to park in the doughnut. We were waved through a security gate and barriers opened.

It was notoriously difficult to get into the BBC, no matter how long you had worked there, no matter how well known your face was (unless you were a man in a white van, in which case you could enter at will, load up, and leave with an entire stock of props and costumes – with a friendly wave to see you on your way). But now we had parking rights. I never, ever tire of the thrill of entering the BBC.

It was the eighties. We had our own shows, got married, had children, wore shoulder pads, hung out with Bananarama, and consequently got fairly drunk on occasion. We wore baggy shirts buttoned up to the neck and high-waisted jeans. We discovered the Groucho Club and could actually afford the drinks. We took part in the *Secret Policeman's Ball* and hung out with the Pythons. This was in the days before celebrities had been invented: people just did their jobs and got cabs home. No hangers-on. No PRs.

Just look at Band Aid. Band Aid! You wouldn't be able to do that now. Bob Geldof just rang up a bunch of his friends, asked them to sing a song for starving Ethiopians, they said yes, put on a leather jacket, jumped in their cars, went to the studio or Wembley, had a few drinks, danced around a bit in the sunshine, had a few more drinks, had a laugh and then drove themselves home. But now, can you imagine? It would take about 4 million people about 4 million years to plan, and there would be absurd amounts of entourages and dressing rooms and Tweeting.

Not in the eighties.

In the eighties, life was bloody great.

In the words of Jackie and Joanie 'San Angelo' Collins, 'It's got lipstick, it's got sex, it's got men, it's got women and it's got more lipstick. It's true, we know, for we were there. For we are those Lucky Bitches.'

And we certainly were.

Seven

1991. The year we started making *Absolutely Fabulous*.

I had given birth to my daughter Freya the October before. When I was pregnant, Dawn and I hadn't really worked together much, and she had made *Murder Most Horrid*.

We have always felt that working apart is a good thing to do. I think that a lot of double acts have trouble because they rely too heavily on the partnership. If one wants to go off and do something, the other one gets bitter and jealous and unemployed. That has never happened with us.

Well, the unemployed bit has. And generally, that would be me. Mainly because Dawn has always been very employable – being the fine actress that she is – with a fierce work ethic. Plus, she gives very good presents.

I am always content 'resting'. I think it's my natural state. Never happier than when just pottering or daydreaming, and relying on Ade to bring in the beans.

I have been to auditions only a very few times, and found them to be cringingly embarrassing. I freeze up and become, frankly, moronic. You see, I'm not trained, and I have nothing to fall back on. I turn into the me who went to interviews at universities: silent and dull, with absolutely no prospects.

For film auditions, they now do a very modern thing of getting you to come in and put yourself on video, which can then be shown to producers in America. It's horrible. Acting out some nebulous lines, with all the other lines being read by the work experience child, to blank faces and a tiny camera (or probably nowadays someone's phone), for them to then ask you if there are any other ways you could do it.

Yes, there are lots of other ways I could do it, you idiots. Why don't you tell me what you want?

And all this for the chance of playing an English nanny, or witch, or 'best friend of', in a film that nobody will ever hear of.

I have friends who still suffer the humiliation of auditions. The stories they tell make my jaw drop. One was sitting waiting to go into an audition when the young director came out, talking on the phone, and said, 'I think we've basically already cast the part, but we're still seeing some people.' He then looked at her and indicated for her to go in.

Luckily, I have now done enough that people tend to know if they want me or not. Of course, auditions are necessary – yes, casting agents and directors, but treat people nicely, I beg of you. And young directors, please don't let your fear become rudeness.

(Oh, and of course do bear me in mind, dears, for any award-winning work you might have in development. Not the shit, just the award-winning stuff, please.)

*

Anyway, in 1991 Dawn and I had planned to do the fourth series of *French and Saunders* at the BBC. Studios had been booked for the end of the year, with director Bob Spiers in place. Bob Spiers – 'His Bobness' – was a comedy veteran, who had directed several of the Comic Strip films. He was a brilliant director and a hero.

Just as we were about to get down to writing it, Dawn and Lenny got the call they had so desperately been waiting for. There was a baby ready for adoption. This joyful news of course meant that Dawn would have to put work on hold. I imagined that the studios would be cancelled, and we would wait for a suitable time to get the whole thing up and running again. Whenever Dawn felt ready.

Then Maureen rang.

'Now, love, I've been putting my heads together and thinking vis-à-vis the studios and wondering if – rather than cancel them – there might be anything that you could possibly do?'

'Do?'

'Well. Write?'

'Write? On my own?'

'Yes.'

I was thrown into confusion. Write on my own? How could that happen? I had some gardening and some important sweeping planned, and possibly a holiday. But I could tell from her tone that this was serious.

I had a think. I had never considered writing on my own. I had a really big think. I told Ade what Maureen had suggested and he seemed to think it would be a good idea. I was aghast.

So I started to think seriously . . .

In desperation, the idea for *Absolutely Fabulous* gradually dawned on me. I thought about the character I had enjoyed the most on *French and Saunders*, the character for which I had done the most writing. She was the mad 'modern' mother that we had done in a sketch the series before; the ex-hippy with the sad, straight daughter. I could speak her easily, which would make the writing simpler (indeed possible). It was a starting point, at least. I mean, the sketch was about ten minutes long. *So*, I thought, *it's only got to be another eighteen minutes and it's a show . . .*

'Is it a sitcom?'

'Yes, Maureen. I think so.'

'Well, write a treatment and we'll get going.'

And that was it. We were on a roll. I wrote a few pages and showed it to some people. Jon Plowman liked the idea, and then I was sent around the Beeb to talk to various script people, who looked pretty confused and suggested that the characters should be more sympathetic, somehow.

Yes, of course I'll put some men into it, and yes, the daughter might need a friend. OK, I'll write it so normal people can relate to it.

But the great thing about a producer like Jon Plowman is that he ignores everybody: 'Just go and write it how you want to write it.' It was going to be on after the watershed on BBC2 anyway, so it was expected to have a bit of a kick in it.

I wrote the pilot in an A4 notebook and handed it in. That was the only time (in a show that ran for thirty-nine episodes) that I wrote a complete script on time. But then I didn't really know what I was doing. Various folk read it and suggested things: *Perhaps something should happen? Perhaps it should have more of a story?* But I had never written a story, or a plot. An 'emotional arc' was, and largely still is, a mystery to me. I had written sketches, so I suppose what I wrote was an extended sketch, with as many laughs as I could pack in over half an hour.

Half an hour isn't long, especially if you have to introduce the characters. A BBC half an hour is luckily the full thirty minutes, and if you're running over, you used to be allowed to run the titles over the last scene. Not any more! Now they seem to like to trail the next show about five minutes before the one you're actually watching actually finishes. Apparently, this is to stop people turning over, in case – by watching credits for those twenty seconds – they might actually believe that the whole of television was over, and their life might end.

It's not for me that I get pissed off. It's for all those people who work really hard on that show: the vision mixers, the cameramen, the costume, set and make-up designers. These people put their heart and soul into a show, only to have their credit scrolled past at a hundred miles per hour, in the tiny strip of screen you're allowed while the next show is being trailed.

I will stop now.

In the aforementioned *French and Saunders* sketch, my character's name was Adriana, but for the series I chose to call her Edwina, known as Edina. Edina Ronay was a fashion designer, so I think I took it from there. I actually love the name Edina. Her surname was Monsoon, because Ade had an alter-ego called Eddie Monsoon – a breakdown of Edmondson, obviously – and I thought it would be funny.

I decided that the daughter shouldn't have a friend, as that was the whole point. But I did want Edina to have a friend, and that friend would be Patsy. I just like writing two people. I'm used to a double act, and Edina and Patsy are the ultimate double act. They allow the other one to exist, they encourage each other's behaviour, and it normalizes it for them. On their own they are rather sad characters. Together they are a force.

Much has been made, over the years, of whether or not Edina was based on the PR guru Lynne Franks. Well, yes, there are elements of her in Edina. In fact, there are elements of a lot of people in her, but mainly me. Writing Edina was like writing a long, late-night drunken rant; things you think but could never say. She has no brakes, only an accelerator pedal, and keeps going till she crashes.

For a while in the eighties Lynne had done some PR for Dawn and me. We had got to know her as a friend. She was extraordinary. She did fashion PR at a time when we didn't really know about fashion or PR. Lynne PR-ed fashion on to the map; suddenly, it wasn't just the property of *Vogue* and *Harper's*. People were starting to get into designer labels, and many designers had their names emblazoned on the clothing, so everybody was aware of them. For years, we were all walking billboards. Lynne was into everything that was new: clothes, music, clubs. She was a whirlwind of zeitgeist.

PR was the perfect job for Edina because it meant that she didn't have to operate in just one area. She could do PR for anything, even though fashion was her passion. I had learned from Lynne that, when fashion designers give out samples of outfits, they are generally a size 10 (a lot smaller now), so I thought that this would be what Edina would wear. She would always be wearing the latest thing, with it never quite fitting. It could be fabulous and 'directional', but a little bit painful. Cutting edge, but cutting in.

Out shopping for Edina's costumes, the costume designer Sarah Burns and I would be in Harvey Nichols or Selfridges and the assistant would ask, 'What size are you?' We would have to answer that it wasn't relevant, because the clothes didn't really have to fit. That it was better if they actually didn't fit. Edina's wardrobe was either made or bought, because no designer would have really wanted to lend anything for it to look so hideous. I thought it was a miracle that any of them let us into their shops at all. The first time I met Christian Lacroix, I actually apologized to him. He appeared in one episode and allowed Edina to fall at his feet and then walk away with her still attached.

Edina's daughter, Saffy, and their relationship owed nothing to Lynne. That came from other people. Saffy is the bedrock of the show. She is the audience. She is the one who catches Patsy and Edina out and makes them feel ridiculous occasionally.

We auditioned for the part of Saffy (for the record I was extremely lovely and professional to everyone who came in, and provided Hobnobs). Jane Horrocks came in to read. She was brilliant, but completely wrong for Saffy. And when you find someone that funny, you don't want to let them go. I knew that Jane had to be in the show, so I adapted the part of Bubble, Edina's secretary, to accommodate her genius. Bubble was originally going to be a tall, blonde posh girl – clueless, but posh. Jane took it to a whole other level of stupidity that I could only ever have dreamed of. I know a lot of people wonder why Edina would put up with someone so stupid, inefficient and insulting, but, truth is, she needs someone to blame. And when you find someone that hilarious, you just make it work. Who cares? It isn't real.

Bob Spiers had worked with Julia Sawalha on a series called *Press Gang*. He really rated her, so asked her to come in. Julia is a fantastic actress with a level of concentration and focus that is frightening. From the moment she read the first line of a scene between Edina and Saffy, I was terrified. I found myself not being able to look at her. And I made Edina more and more ridiculous, just to deflect the fear. She was hired on the spot.

The casting of June Whitfield as Edina's mother was a no-brainer. In the pilot, she only appeared in a flashback, but I knew it had to be her. It had to be a character that was straight and normal and lovely on the surface, but with an edge. Just a little bit of madness. And this, to me, was what June had been playing all those years in *Terry and June*. The slightly downtrodden housewife, with a twinkle of knowing.

Edina was the result of a rubber-gloved, hands-off upbringing; delivered by forceps and raised in 1950s sterility. She was an only child who was deprived of attention and had been seeking it ever since.

All that was left was Patsy.

In the original script, Patsy was very different from what she eventually became. I had written her as a hard-nosed, hard-drinking journo. I had based her character on my friend Harriet

Thorpe, who had been at college with Dawn and me. Harriet is the perfect supportive friend. Whatever I tell her, she tells me that I am right, because I know best, and that I mustn't ever let anyone tell me that I don't.

If I'm having trouble writing – which is always (and I'm amazed she hasn't got bored of me yet) – she will say, 'Well, you shouldn't feel guilty, darling. And you know why? Because you're brilliant. And you're better than them. And they are bloody lucky to have you. Don't they understand that this is how you work? You can do this standing on your head. Don't listen to them. It will happen, because it always happens, and that's your genius. Fuck 'em. You don't need this! Just write it now. Write it and get it over with. Well done, darling.'

This became Patsy's purpose: to support Edina, no matter what. To tell her that she was right, and wonderful, and to hell with the rest of the world.

We offered the part to an actress who would have been brilliant as a hard-nosed journalist, but she couldn't do it, so we were stumped. Until someone – I think it was Ade – came up with the genius idea of Joanna Lumley.

I knew Joanna from *The Avengers* and *Sapphire & Steel*, of course, but she had recently been on a Ruby Wax show playing herself as an alcoholic actress at the end of her career. A 'has-been'. And she was hilarious. Jon Plowman had seen this too and his instincts are nearly always right. I rang Ruby, who confirmed that Joanna was brilliant and that I HAD to have her.

So a small room was organized, and Joanna came in to read a scene. This was really for her benefit, so she could see what she might be getting into, and have the opportunity to choose not to.

We read a scene that was set in a car, and so sat on two wooden chairs, next to each other. It was quite awkward. I couldn't really explain the character to her and had entirely forgotten my character. I became mute. Joanna has a lovely voice and a natural elegance. All I could think of suggesting was that perhaps . . . I don't know, but maybe . . . I don't know . . . but maybe she could have not such a *nice* voice? Maybe? I don't know.

For some inexplicable reason Joanna – and I thank God for this – accepted the part.

I rewrote Patsy for her almost immediately. Everything fitted into place. Joanna would talk about the sixties and her modelling days, and it became clear that Patsy had to be in fashion. I had no idea what a fashion director on a magazine did, but it seemed ridiculous enough that it was a possibility. A job that isn't really a job. That just involved pointing at some clothes and then going out to play.

On our first day of filming we were doing all the little outside bits for the pilot, which you do before you go into the studio. This is always quite hard, because you don't really have any rehearsal and haven't a clear idea of what will go before, or indeed come after, because so much changes when you go into the studio.

Joanna and I were in a big Jag, filming a conversation as Patsy and Edina go to Harvey Nicks. It was a little awkward because we were both just getting to know our characters; it's quite embarrassing acting in front of people sometimes.

Am I being funny, or does she just think I'm a fool?

Luckily, we had plenty of time to get through this because the supporting artist who had been hired to play the chauffeur had no experience at all of driving cars. At the beginning of every take, we would either go backwards or not move at all. If we did get going, halfway through a take he would jam on the brakes and we would fly off our seats. It broke the ice, and after a few post-filming drinks we never looked back.

Some of my happiest times have been sitting in the back of a car with Joanna, having conversations in character that just make us pee. She is a seriously funny person, and the joy is that she is not remotely precious. There was nowhere we couldn't go with the characters. For someone so beautiful, Joanna has no apparent vanity. She also likes a drink and a fag, so she was perfect for the show.

As a person who doesn't really smoke, I found it occasionally challenging. I had to smoke in a few rehearsals so that in the opening scene in the studio I didn't take a great big nervous drag and pass out.

I used to steal cigarettes from my parents' cigarette box. Yes, young reader, they used to have boxes filled with loose cigarettes that they would hand round at parties. I'd regularly grab a handful and go off with my friend Fif and smoke them. Well, puff them. I don't think we ever inhaled. The first time I inhaled was on a school trip in the fifth form and I nearly died. My friends had noticed that I was just puffin', and stood in a circle around me until I drew the smoke of an unfiltered No. 6 into my lungs.

Nice.

We smoked my parents' fags until there were no more left in the box. Then we took my dad's pipe and had a go with that. To this day, I can't believe my mother never noticed. I must have stunk of tobacco. But then she has always had the best attitude to discipline: if you are going to make a big fuss about something, it has to be important.

Anyway, anyway, back to *Ab Fab*.

We made the pilot and it went before the judges, who gave us a series. The only negative comment we got was from Robin Nash, then Head of Something at the BBC, who said that he didn't like seeing women getting drunk. Well. You're not really supposed to *like* them. I love them, and I love playing Edina, but I don't *like* them.

What I love about Patsy and Edina is that they give you a chance to say and do all the things you never really would. Eddie and Patsy can say the unthinkable. Eddie and Patsy can park on pavements, shout at people who annoy them, wear inappropriate clothing and fall over drunk in the street. They can be as cruel and callous as they like. They can be rude about celebrities, fashion and niceness, and they can be wicked to Saffy.

And yet, Saffy tortures her mother as much as her mother tortures her. Because actually, without her mother there, Saffy has got nothing to shout about and no identity of her own. She's defined by what her mother isn't and hasn't been, and in this way her mother gives her life a purpose, and that purpose is to be horrible to her.

The heart of the show isn't the drinking and smoking and partying. It's the painful *ménage à trois* of Eddie, Patsy and Saffy. The jealousies. The hatreds. And, most crucially, the need to be loved.

Eight

June 2002. I am sitting in a beautiful hall in the Senate building in New York, dressed in a white Ralph Lauren trouser suit, Philip Treacy hat with a Stars and Stripes scarf tied round the brim, and badges announcing that 'I Love NY' on my lapels. Joanna is next to me, and she is looking as much like Patsy as she can. Hair up, plenty of red lipstick and proper high heels.

We are here to be honoured with the Freedom of the City. It is Gay Pride week, and we are here to receive an LGBT award. No, dear reader, not a lettuce, gherkin, bacon and tomato sandwich award. Have you no sense or sensibility? I mean a Lesbian, Gay, Bisexual and Transgender award. Obviously.

*

The fact that our show had become a success in Britain and America was, to a large extent, thanks to the gay community. Edina and Patsy were gay-friendly. Edina longed for her daughter to be gay because that, at least, would make her more interesting. Edina's catchphrase – I do realize it's not an actual catchphrase like 'Where's me shirt?' – was: 'Darling, all my friends are gay. ALL my friends are gay.'

And yet I never anticipated Patsy and Edina becoming gay icons. I entirely missed the idea that these were divas, that they had the perfect mix of bravado and vulnerability – but then I never dreamed that the show would take off in the way that it did.

I have to point out, here and now, that I was not alone in the writing of *Ab Fab*. Ruby Wax played a huge part. In fact I credit Ruby with some of the show's funniest-ever lines. We needed a script editor, and I chose Rubes because no one can turn the world on its head like she can.

I would write the scripts in fear of having to show them eventually to Ruby. She was so brilliant, and I was afraid that they would be substandard. I didn't give Ruby long with any of the scripts, but it was always worthwhile. She would take them, read them, and then we would meet. I would see that the scripts were covered in her scribble. She would go through them, scene by scene, giving alternative lines and possibilities, and at some points just saying, 'I don't understand the next two pages but I guess you know what you're doing.' She gave me all her thoughts and I could take 'em or leave 'em. Ruby is never precious and I owe her much, not least for some brilliant lines:

'Skirts so high, the world is her gynaecologist!'

'These women shop for lunch! Labels are their only sustenance! Their skeleton legs in Manolos have worn trenches down the pavement of Sloane Street. There are just enough muscles left in their sinewy arms to lift up a credit card!'

Because of lines like these, *Ab Fab* took off.

The other person, apart from Ruby, whom I credit with teaching me how to write a script is Ben Elton. Ruby taught me how to build a gag, how to keep it going until the line was an extreme, to never be satisfied with 'quite funny'. Ben taught me that there is never a situation where a joke cannot be had: if you're in a restaurant, don't just write the dialogue, write all the jokes about restaurants as well. Never miss an opportunity. If you're in a shop, write all the shop jokes you can think of. Jokes, jokes, jokes. They can be subtle, but never miss the chance to shove 'em in.

Unwittingly, *Ab Fab* hit the zeitgeist head on, which was lucky really, on several counts. We were lucky that the fashion world seemed to be flattered to be insulted. We were lucky that audiences seemed to have as much fun watching it as we had had making it. And we were lucky that each and every one of the Js came with their own following: mine from *French and Saunders*, Julia's from *Press Gang*, June's from *Terry and June*, Jane's from the theatre.

Then, of course, there was Joanna. Every man of a certain age – any age, in fact – is in love with Joanna. And in the show she managed to look stylish and elegant, but simultaneously insane and debauched, without ever appearing less than beautiful.

To this day, I have not been out for lunch or dinner with Joanna without several old boys in red trousers and/or panama hats sidling up to our table. Joanna is a magnet for a certain type of gentleman who is sure that they have met before.

'Joanna.' (He doffs his hat.)
'Hello.' (She smiles kindly.)
'We've met before.'
'Of course. How are you?'
'Do you see very much of Ginny any more?'
'No. No, I don't.'
'Well, how lovely to see you.'

'And you. What a treat.'

'Will we see you in October?'

'I do hope so.'

'Do give my love to Figgy.'

'I will. How lovely.'

He moves away. This has made his day.

I say: 'Who was that?'

'Absolutely no idea . . .'

'Who's Ginny?'

'I have no idea.'

'And Figgy?'

'I don't know.'

Joanna has this ability to make everyone she ever meets feel special. And it's not put on. She is genuinely a good and kind person.

So, *Ab Fab* was a success, and the great thing about success is it means you can do more of what you're doing, make more of what you've been making. For that alone I couldn't have been happier. We had all become a family. There is no better feeling than going into a rehearsal room knowing that people you love will be there. Apart from the fact that there sometimes wasn't a script (small detail), it was incredible fun.

June Whitfield was a lesson in professionalism. She is meticulous, razor sharp and unpretentious. She knows how to do her job so well, but will never tell you that. She is always questioning – never knowing best and yet always knowing best. She has a firm grip on what she does, but with the lightest of touches. I was always aware that I should make sure that June had enough lines, only to find in rehearsals that she would slowly trim them back.

'Does Mother need to say this?'

'Whatever you like, June.'

A pencil line would be drawn neatly through the line. She

always knew that she could do more with less, and was never wrong. (That was not something I ever learned, as I yabbered my way through series after series. There were occasions when someone should really have shut me up.)

Jane Horrocks would brilliantly do anything she was told. I think that's the sign of a great actress. She never questioned the lines, just how I wanted her to do them. If it was still unclear, she would ask me to do them, and then do them the same way. For me this was perfect, because I don't really know how to schmooze actors into giving a performance. With less than a week to rehearse and record a whole show, we would have to accept that there wasn't time for motivation. We just had to say the line quickly and move around the furniture efficiently.

Some actors do find that hard. They can be thrown completely when they arrive in the studio sets, having before only had approximations in a rehearsal room. We had an actress in once who had to enter down the stairs and move around the kitchen table. On every rehearsal in the studio she would stop.

'What's the matter?'

'Is the table going to be there?'

'Yes, it is there.'

'It's just . . . well, in rehearsals it wasn't quite in that position.'

'It is going to be there.'

'So I'm going to have to walk all the way round it.'

'Yes.'

'So when shall I say my line?'

'When were you saying it before?'

'When I got to the other side of the table.'

'So say it then.'

'You still want me to walk round the table? You can cope with that, can you?'

'Yes. Just come in, walk round the table and say your line.'

It took five tries. She would come down the stairs and stop as if the table were blocking her path. I could hear Bob swearing through the headphones of the stage manager.

'Just tell her to fucking walk round the fucking table!'

'Bob's asking if you would mind terribly just walking round the table.'

Five times. She eventually managed it, but with a small head-shake of disbelief.

I like actors but prefer to have comediennes. Comic actors and comediennes know if they have been good. I once had an actor come up to me after a show looking really down.

'What's the matter?'

'Was I really awful? I mean, I'm sorry.'

'No, you were actually brilliant.'

He was shocked. 'But you didn't say anything!'

'That's because you were brilliant. Didn't you hear the laughs? If you were shit, I would have told you.'

Julia was always quiet in rehearsal. While I would be flapping away, enjoying Edina, thinking up new lines and messing about (working), she would wait. And wait. She would quietly read a book, sitting cross-legged in a corner of the room, waiting until we had finished, and then join the scene with devastating efficiency and effect. She could judge a scene perfectly and always had the right tone and energy. She knew precisely how to counteract the Eddie/Patsy cruelty.

There was one scene we shot in which Patsy was being particularly vicious to Saffy. She should have been aborted, she said. When she was little, they had tied her to the central reservation of a motorway to try and get rid of her. Suddenly, as we were speaking, I was struck by the sense that this might not be acceptable, that it might actually be *too cruel*. But Julia was adamant. She pointed out that it would only be unacceptable if Saffy was affected by it, and she wasn't. It didn't hurt Saff. It was just words. And the more they tried to hurt her, the stronger she became. This observation gave us free rein, and we never held back the viciousness again.

Every series we were allowed one trip away.

Our first trip in the first series was to the south of France, where Patsy and Eddie had a disastrous holiday in a gîte. Patsy's misery was compounded by the discovery that what she thought was cocaine was in fact talcum powder and that, while she imagined she was having a good time playing ping-pong only because she had sniffed 'the coke', that was actually a lie. She must have actually enjoyed the ping-pong. Which was a horrific idea to her.

By the time the second series came along, we had Morocco in our sights. It was the perfect place for old sixties birds to hang out. They would have spent some time there in their youth, taking drugs and sleeping with anyone who crossed their paths and still had a pulse. Joanna said she remembered parties where people would get so out of it they would end up just humping the furniture. It was for this trip that we came up with the idea that Patsy might once have been a man. She might have had a dodgy sex change op in Morocco that lasted only a couple of months before it fell off. Patsy could be any sex and any age.

In the next series, we went to America.

The Comedy Channel had bought *Absolutely Fabulous*. The deal had almost floundered when they proposed subtitles, just in case the Americans didn't understand what we were saying. This never happened, thank God. We signed the contract and, from that moment on, the Comedy Channel put the show out pretty much on a loop. At first, it was only the East and West Coasters who 'got it', but then we started getting fan letters from Ohio and Omaha. We were the crazy broads!

When it came to our attention that Eddie and Patsy had had

their own float at the Sydney Mardi Gras, we realized that the show was becoming bigger than us. The characters became more famous than we were. And with every series I wrote, I felt less and less in charge of the characters' destinies. It was less an exercise in which I decided what happened, more a case of pleasing those who loved the characters and satisfying their expectations. It was very weird.

Once the show became a hit in America, we naturally decided to go and film there. 'Door Handle' was the first episode in Series Three, in which Patsy and Eddie fly to America on Concorde in pursuit of the perfect door handle. During filming, we had to have bodyguards. Bodyguards! We didn't actually need them, but they were lovely.

For 'The End', the last episode in Series Three, we found ourselves back there again. At this point, Patsy has gone to work for a magazine in New York, and a lonely Eddie has gone to find herself on a retreat. Soon they realize that life without each other is pointless, and Eddie hires a helicopter to track her best mate down.

This was one of the most terrifying moments of my life. I am not great when it comes to flying and was put off ever going in a helicopter by Robbie Coltrane, who once informed me that there are seventy-two moving parts within the rotor blade system alone. That's seventy-two moving things that could go wrong.

So, as I got into the small chopper that was taking me to the building close to Central Park that Patsy was standing on the roof of, I was not filled with confidence. In fact, I was shitting it. It was a small, lightweight thing – a two-man copter – and at my feet there were clear panels, so I could clearly see the ground below.

WHY?

Added to the drama was the fact that the *News of the World* had sent out a journalist and a photographer to follow us. They wanted to follow us in a helicopter. Thankfully this was deemed dangerous and Jon Plowman reached a deal with them: if he gave them some exclusive photos, they wouldn't follow us. We wanted to avoid a mid-air chase at all costs.

We flew over Manhattan to the building where the film crew and Joanna were stationed on the roof. We were so close to the building that I could see the panicked faces of office workers inside. In order to get the shot, we had to hover close to the building – but just below the top – until the pilot heard 'Action!' over his radio, at which point he would rise up level with the rooftop, where I had to wave and mouth lines to Joanna.

It took so many takes.

Each time we dipped down again, out of shot, we would see people in the offices close to the windows, screaming and gesturing to us to 'Move back!'

'We are making a TV show!' I would mouth back to them, as if that would actually make any difference. Surely they wouldn't mind dying if it was on TV?

It was dangerous, and the thermals can be strong close to buildings. They had every reason to be screaming at the windows.

With just a *whoof* of hot air from below, we could all have died at any moment. Luckily, there was no such *whoof*. Even Trump Tower refrained from trumping, and we were safe. It almost certainly wouldn't be allowed to happen today. Oh no. Health and Safety, the ripples from 9/11 and just common sense would rule it out entirely.

Back then, near death was one of the perks of the job. And it has to be said that, when it came to the perks of *Ab Fabbin*, the slot machine kept paying out.

During those years, Joanna and I came to an agreement: if we were asked to do anything – anything at all – which involved a free flight and a guaranteed laugh, we would automatically say yes. Parties, promotional trips, flights on Concorde, chat shows, you name it. We'd meet at the airport, and from that moment on the fun would commence. An all-expenses-paid trip to the US was the best of perks. I mean, a business-class flight and five days in New York or LA? Only an idiot would turn these down.

'Not paid by the licence payers, I hope!' I hear you cry.

No, dear reader. No. Paid for by Americans!

We were never happier than when on a lovely flight to America. When you have a partner in crime, even work is fun. In Joanna I had found another double-act partner and, like Dawn, she was the best I could have hoped for. They might not look the slightest bit like each other, but, in reality, Dawn and Joanna are not at all dissimilar. They are both extremely nice to people and are endlessly making up for my grumpy sullenness.

When Dawn and I started out, appearing on chat shows was far from my forte. I had no idea what to do at all. They were basically my idea of hell. Didn't know what to wear, how to sit, how to be. Looked fat. Always wore a dress that was made of wool and far too hot. Couldn't think of a single interesting word to say. Wanted the ground to swallow me up. Stared at interviewer with beady, seemingly disapproving eyes. Inwardly panicked. Wanted to be liked. Ended up being immensely weird-looking and leaving comedy partner to compensate.

Knowing that I wouldn't – or actually physically couldn't – Dawn set an early precedent of doing all the talking. And she has been talking ever since. Actually, as I've got a bit older and a bit more confident, I've got a bit better at talking and being a real functioning person and things. I can even smile occasionally, so the pressure has been taken off her a little bit. We now do the radio occasionally, and I have to talk. And do you know what? I find it easier and easier. Sometimes I can honestly say I'm on a roll.

But during promotional trips to America, Joanna – like Dawn – often had to protect me from myself. She became a master in the art of taking over in interviews and not letting me say the one thing I shouldn't say.

'Jennifer Saunders, what do you feel about the success of *Ab Fab* in America?'

'Um. I really don't care.'

Here, Joanna would intercept, hand on my knee.

'She doesn't really mean that. What she actually means is . . .'

All the time looking me hard in the eyes and silently saying, *Speak no more, you idiot fool*.

Like Dawn, Joanna is also acutely aware of people's feelings. When we filmed 'Door Handle', the Four Seasons hotel gave us a green room – a base, as it were – in a two-bedroomed penthouse apartment. As the filming day progressed, it became clear that this room was up for grabs for the night, and Joanna and I were offered it.

It was spectacular and, much as we had affection for the Algonquin, where the Beeb had put us up, it was nothing, I mean *nothing*, compared to this. We took the offer. What happened next is an example of how similar Dawn and Joanna actually are. We had to check out of the Algonquin. We had to move hotel. Slightly embarrassing, but not really. Not really, if you don't engage personally with the transaction.

Not possible for Joanna, who, like Dawn, will compensate with presents and money, if all else fails. She tipped the guy on the desk so much money that he could have bought the hotel the next day. And probably did.

Dawn is incapable of leaving a room without saying goodbye to every single person in it. On the first rehearsal day of every series, she would make me sit down with her and compile a list of everybody we would have to buy presents for on the last day. It became a joke between us that, by the last series, Dawn would not be happy unless she had bought everyone a car.

DAWN: Jen, what shall we get the cameraman?

ME: A car?

DAWN: Yes. The producer?

ME: A house?

DAWN: Yes. The make-up department?

ME: Holiday to the Seychelles?

DAWN: Yes. And everybody else in the whole of the BBC?

ME: A nice bottle of Champagne?

DAWN: Marvellous.

We are incredibly similar in many ways, but different in even more.

Dawn is happy when her diary is full. She carries a big diary in her handbag and it is well used. She refers to it all the time. She remembers birthdays and anniversaries and notes down all her appointments for the year ahead.

I am happy when my diary is empty. I don't carry a diary, but put things into my laptop calendar if they are important and hope they transfer via the iCloud. Sometimes they do, sometimes they don't, usually depending on how much money I have paid to Apple to update my nearly-new-but-obviously-out-of-date software.

I am bad at remembering dates of birthdays, even those of my own children. But then I don't expect them to remember mine.

I begin to feel slightly claustrophobic if I have more than two or three things noted down per week. I like it clear. I don't ever really want to know what I'm doing next year. Or even next month.

Unless, of course, it's a ceremony honouring me at the New York Senate. That I quite like.

So, Joanna had rung me before we left and said, 'Darling. By the sounds of things, this is going to be quite a flamboyant affair.'

'Yes. I agree.'

'So let's not let them down this time.'

The time to which she was referring was a party we had attended in New York a while earlier to launch a new season of *Ab Fab*. We had arrived at the party looking like our normal selves, only to be greeted by huge, drag-queen versions of our characters. The party was spectacular, with a Champagne fountain. Camp and kitsch. It was everything Patsy and Eddie would have adored. We arrived as ourselves and made no impact at all as we came through the door. No impact. We were not noticed.

Eventually, when we made our presence known and were reluctantly allowed into the roped-off area, there were gasps of disappointment.

'Oh my God, it's them!'

We were too ordinary to live up to expectations. We had normal hair and normal clothes. We were the real mice that arrive in Disneyland to be greeted by Mickey and Minnie. We weren't like Minnie. We were small and brown and barely recognizable.

So, for the Senate trip, we decided to Go For It. To dress for it. To not let anyone down. It was Gay Pride, and we wanted them to feel appreciated. We would dress as close to the characters as we could. We felt this would do the trick. We could act up and be camp.

On the plane over, while sippin' the odd beverage, I casually mentioned to Jack Lum (calling everyone 'Jack' if their name begins with 'J' is something I picked up from Ben E. I really only use it for Joanna, who is Jack to me) that perhaps a speech of thanks might be in order.

'Do you think so, darling?'

'Well, something perhaps . . . something in the way of a thank-you.'

'Darling, I think we know how this will be, and I think we shouldn't linger. We will be Patsy and Eddie. I will do a few "Cheers, thanks a lot" and you will do "Thank you, sweetie darlings", then there will be some nice photos and that will be it. No speech. No bloody speech.'

More Champagne was drunk and more tiny meals eaten and then, as we were about to land, actual bottles of Champagne were thrust at us by hostesses and stewards. *We are Eddie and Patsy and we NEED more Champers.*

Back at the hotel, over a few bottles of vintage BA, we discussed our plan again and I agreed.

The next morning, Joanna and I arrived at the Senate in all our finery, with Jon Plowman, only to be greeted by men in dark suits. Politicians. Senators. Dark-suited and very serious. These were not frivolous awards at all; these were serious and political. My heart began to sink.

We had a small drinks reception with the Senate's Democratic Leader, before being taken in to the formal, austere hall where an audience awaited us. We hadn't really been able to speak about it, but we both felt that we had misjudged this. This was a serious do.

I was regretting the hat and the suit and the sheer amount of Stars and Stripes very much indeed. Everyone else was soberly dressed. The audience facing us were not gay people as we knew them. These were all dressed in shades of brown. Very lovely, but really quite serious.

The event kicked off with stories of brave gay people facing adversity.

We clapped.

Then a moving song by the sister of a gay man who had been murdered because of his sexuality.

We cried.

Then the life story of a transgender man – now woman – who had fought prejudice and actually become a senator. Speeches remembering those who had died of AIDS, or had survived and gone on to inspire others.

We were frightened.

'Darling?'

'What?'

'I think you may need a speech.'

'I haven't got a speech. You said I didn't need to make a speech.'

'Think of something.'

I was looking out at a sea of sweet but serious faces and, before I knew it, our time had come. The House Leader came to the microphone and began his Proclamation honouring me:

'Whereas, a great state is only as great as those individuals who perform exemplary service on behalf of their community, whether through unique achievement in professional or other endeavours, or simply through a lifelong commitment to entertaining and enlightening others . . .'

(*Oh dear.*)

'Whereas, Jennifer Saunders plays the self-promoting, twice-divorced working mother Edina in *Absolutely Fabulous*, a show that brings joy, laughter and warmth to New Yorkers because of the vision of her writing and the producers, performers and broadcasters involved . . .'

(*Ah.*)

'Whereas, Jennifer Saunders is also the creator of the critically acclaimed hit series *Absolutely Fabulous*; which has earned two International Emmy awards; five BAFTA awards; a Writers' Guild award; two Royal Television Society awards; and four British Comedy awards . . .'

(*Right.*)

'Whereas, Jennifer Saunders' generosity and humanity in her writing and performance have created characters that have great appeal to the Lesbian, Gay, Bisexual and Transgender communities, through their portrayal on *Ab Fab* in a positive and affirming way and demonstrating how they add to the texture of life . . .'

(*Should have had a speech.*)

'Whereas, it is hoped that Jennifer Saunders will continue to produce and write brilliant episodes of *Absolutely Fabulous* as well as act in the role of Edina for many years to come . . .'

(*Will do.*)

'Therefore, be it resolved that I, State Senate Democratic Leader Martin Connor, and the New York State Senate Democratic Conference, recognize that in Jennifer Saunders, we have an individual worthy of our highest respect and esteem; and be it further resolved that on this day, June 27, 2002, at New York's City Hall on the occasion of the LGBT Pride Award Ceremony, we proclaim Jennifer Saunders an Honorary New Yorker for today and for ever.'

(*Oh, Christ.*)

Joanna had her own declaration. And that wasn't all. He introduced Whoopi Goldberg, who was making a speech, yes, a SPEECH, about us, before we collected our awards. Whoopi made a wonderful, generous and very funny SPEECH, none of which I really took in, because I was now in full panic mode.

Stupid hat! Stupid suit! Stupid Stars and Stripes scarf! Stupid, silly us!

All we had was a 'Thank you, sweetie darlings' and a 'Cheers, thanks a lot'.

I stumbled to the podium and accepted the award with a mixture of 'Sweetie darlings, Bolly, sweetie. Darlings. Buggery bollocks' and trying to be serious. A tragic mixture. Joanna had more success with a bit of Patsy.

We walked away, feeling slightly ashamed, but also a little bit pleased with our Proclamations. We were Honorary New Yorkers. We had the pieces of paper and were proud.

We left the Senate building and were whisked by car to much more familiar territory: an *Ab Fab* lookalike competition in a gay club.

Thank God.

The music was loud, the men were very gay, and most of them were in costume.

We could relax. Drinks were necked.

We judged the lookalike competition, which was fierce.

The winner was a man whom had made himself into Saffy's best friend, Titikaka, a girl whom Edina had tortured throughout the series and whose plaits she had once set on fire. He won because he had serious detail, down to the scarring on the back of his neck. It wasn't a popular winner, obviously, but he was original.

The rest of the trip was a whirlwind: driving around the city in a limo with Debbie Harry, looking for a place to have fun; a night in Bungalow 8 with Graham Norton; a party thrown for us by Glenda Bailey, the editor of *Harper's Bazaar*. Joanna and I would always end up back at our hotel, spinning with drink and jet lag but nevertheless staying up late, just laughing.

At the Four Seasons suite, we lay staring out at the skyline, amazed by our good fortune. We watched the lights change colour on the Chrysler Building and played with the electric curtains.

New York was special.

We occasionally swung trips to Los Angeles, one of which I should run past you briefly, dear reader.

In 1996 we were invited to present an award at the Comedy Awards in LA. We were, of course, thrilled at the prospect of a free trip without the pressure of having to do publicity, and accepted immediately.

The Awards were organized by a chap called George Schlatter and his wife, Jolene. George had been the producer of *Rowan & Martin's Laugh-In* and was a big cheese, a big pro-doooosa.

Where would we like to stay?

We said the Hotel Bel-Air, as we had never been there. They liked the idea, and agreed, and we couldn't believe it! The Bel-Air is an old-fashioned hotel in a rich, lush suburb of LA. Set in its own gardens, it has a whiff of Old Hollywood about it. We were put up in one of the bungalows: our own two-bedroom space with a garden and pool just outside.

Oh yes. Result!

George and Jolene – she is small and blonde with the perfect country-singer beehive – were attentive. We were sent baskets of flowers and fruit and some muffins. The whole time we were there, George and his wife organized things for us to do. Jolene adored us. She adored and loved us so much that she once declared that she wanted to adopt us.

All we had to do was dress up once and sit through an award ceremony before going up to present one (to Kelsey Grammer, as it happened).

The table we sat on was filled with hopefuls and has-beens, none of whom ate or drank. This was a professional engagement for them, and alcohol did not pass their lips. Joanna made a comment about just having had breast surgery that seemed to go down quite well, but was reported in the British press as having been a disaster. JOANNA'S BIG BOOB! But actually all was fine.

Once we had completed the task of award presenting, we were to give a party. Not a big party, but a party at which Joanna and I could choose any guests we wished to have at our tables.

Anybody?

Yes, anybody.

I chose Carrie Fisher, Laurie Metcalf, Lily Tomlin, Mo Gaffney and Roseanne Barr. Roseanne had bought the rights to *Ab Fab* in America (which sadly nothing ever came of; American studios just don't go for smoking, drinking and swearing) and was a friend. Roseanne had once introduced me to Dolly

Parton, and would always be one of my favourite people for that fact alone.*

Carrie brought Ed Begley Jr. I hardly knew Carrie – just a little through Ruby – and the evening seemed stilted. Apart from Mo, I felt that all were there by order, rather than by choice, and I had no idea how to get the conversation flowin'.

Joanna, on the other hand, had selected a table of friends and had a lovely evening, chattin' and laughin', while, back on my table, I had become mute. I wanted to tell Lily Tomlin how much she meant to me and how influential her work had been, but instead just stared at my food. By the time I had stopped staring at my dessert, I realized that Carrie had actually gone,

---

* Let me quickly regale you here, dear reader, with my Dolly Parton story.

I was taken by Roseanne to Morton's in Los Angeles – a large restaurant beloved by the rich and the celebrated. Dolly Parton was there with her agent. I was jet-lagged and was being plied with wine by Roseanne, who was convinced that I should drink as much as Edina. I did. Was a little wobbly by the time we went over to Dolly's table. Dolly's agent left, so it was just the three of us.

I was impressed with Dolly and therefore fairly mute. At one point I went to the loo and sat there for quite a long time trying to think of any Dolly Parton song that I could sing to her. Luckily nothing came into my head, and I returned to the table.

By now we were the last left at the tables. Roseanne and Dolly had started discussing tattoos. Roseanne showed hers to Dolly: fairly basic shapes in black ink. Dolly said she had tattoos. First shock. Then she showed them to us. Second shock.

She opened her jacket. And there they were – not just her tits but her glorious tattoos. They were angels and flowers, shaded in pink and blue pastels.

I was gobsmacked. Her words, 'This will go no further, right?', were fully adhered to. Until I got back to the hotel. I had to tell someone, so I just about told everyone. I didn't want to wake up the next morning and doubt my own story. I had seen Dolly Parton's tits.

leaving only a small green pill on the chair on which she had sat. Essence of Carrie.

After the party, Roseanne took me and Joanna to the Comedy Store. This was where she and many of the greats had started out. We met Richard Pryor, who was quite wobbly and not at all well at this point. I didn't know what to say. He had been such a hero. Thank God for Joanna, who can always cope perfectly and made everything very easy. We stayed and drank and had fun, and the awkwardness of my dinner soon didn't matter.

Later that evening, on a bit of a high, we found ourselves being driven back to the Bel-Air. It had been our last night. We stopped at a traffic light and an open-topped car pulled up beside us. George and Jolene were sitting in the front! George was driving.

We couldn't believe it! What a coincidence! How marvellous. Here were lovely George and the woman who wanted to adopt us. We wound down the window.

We waved.

We shouted.

We screamed.

We waved.

The lights turned green, and George and Jolene drove on.

Their heads never turned.

They had already forgotten us.

We were past. Old news. Has-beens in their world.

We headed back to the hotel under no illusions.

You are loved as long as you are useful.

Good lesson.

Nine

In the days before Twitter* and email, there was writin' post-cards and sending faxes.†

Jack Lumley and I used to send each other endless cards and faxes, handwritten, illustrated with drawings and cut-out pictures from magazines. We were nearly always in character: I was Sandwich and she was an ageing actress in need of work.

* I have had to cut down a bit on Twitter because I found myself spending more time in a day trying to think up funnies for Twitter than for actual scripts. It's like having an audience that's always there, always waiting. There's always something more fun to do than write scripts.
† For the very young, a fax was like a printer, but the paper was on a roll and just kept coming and coming. Or, as Bubble would say, 'Lots and lots of very important paper coming out of the answering machine.'

Dear Jennifer Saunders,

Thank you for your nice letter – I think the nice photo you love of me is out of print now (such a rush!) but I'm sending you the original fan picture which I send to my fans for your dressing room.

You know I could help you in your career as I could get you into the papers and give you oxygen of publicity which has always helped me in my career, which has admittedly taken a bit of a dip just now. But I could give you hints and tips. Please write again if you want HINTS AND TIPS and photos. Just off on my hols in the sun so see you soon.

Please don't forget me,

Joanna Lumley

I have boxes and boxes of faxes. I have kept nearly every one to this day, plus every card and piece of paper and old menu that they were written on.

Dear Jennifer,

I expect you will be very excited to get this letter. Yes, it's me really writing to you myself – although as you can guess my life is *very* full and *very* busy. I like to let my fans know that I care about them.

About your film next year – although I am very busy and very much *in demand* I'm sure I can fit it in somehow. In fact any time at all would suit me fine – I don't usually play *small parts* but I do feel it might give your film more of a chance if it had a star name in it. Also I don't usually eat out with fans as it usually creates *havoc* in restaurants. But just this once it would be lovely to eat anything at all with anyone actually. As I expect you can guess I am quite a shy private person so please don't tell the *newspapers* where we are going!! Or they might send photographers and even journalists who might like to interview me. I must rush off now into another room – you can cut out my autograph and keep it if you like. Please don't forget to come on Saturday.

Sincerely yours,

Joanna Lumley, xxxx

All the way through these faxes are mentions of a film. I cannot for the life of me think what this film is, but whatever it was, it never happened.

Dear Jennifer,

I am hoping my new lips will look nice for your show. I can only afford to get one done at a time. I've gone for the top lip like Ivana Trump. Also I think the BBC should pay to have my chest reinflated. They went down a bit during an Air Ethiopia flight and one burst during a screenfight with Kate O'Hara but they'd look good again I'm sure. I'm just off to Canada to see a world famous surgeon about my neck. Also the hair looks nice and yellow and the graft hardly shows. I'm learning my lines on page 2 already. Please don't recast yet. We'll make your film a ting-a-ding hit.

Love from Joanna

Only someone as beautiful as Joanna could make these jokes. And her beauty secrets, I hear you cry? Have just a modicum of everything – a little food, the odd cigarette, a small amount of exercise – and then a really good drink.

Dear Miss Saunders,

The word on the woodvine is that you is about to start auditioning 'hopefuls' for your new series of *Absolutely*

Fabulous and would like to enter myself as you may remember I have worked with you in America givin interviews and helping you out with hair advice. PLEASE GIVE ME WORK AS I CAN HELP OUT with hair advice and looking natural. I also speak French in films and also work with Mrs Cath. Deneureveux as advice on hair and 'BOTOX'.

Give me work please.

You can reach me at this address. Meet me soon.

My beauty regime is . . . er . . . erm . . . Should drink more water. Should eat less. Should exercise more (but not actually kill yourself the first time you try or suffer injury that means you can't do any more). Remember to get your hair cut on occasion. Try not to bite ya nails.

Fax from 'Cherry Lyn', Laines due Pingguin, Sussex:

To Mrs J. Saundre, Star

Dear Madam,

I enclose a recent photo I have been a very busy model, never stop working, and hearde you was looking for talent, scouting I should say, I should coco!! I am up-to-the minute with goode dress sence and can bring fun to any session please will you give me this job as you can read on my cover photo sent in by my fan I am just the same! Always chirpy and can provide jersey skirt and earrings too I'm a professional but honestly times is hard madam. Give me work please send money.

I never sent Joanna money. I was immune to her begging.

Dear Madam,

Am available for high class modeling work as these recent Mario Testino photos will testify. Please let me know when you perpose to do a fashion shoot. I can bring wig and bobble hat if necessary.

Please send money up front.

Is you goin to Los Angeles in April or not? I am not sure we know what to do.

Please send pills.

I did of course send pills. I always has a few hanging about.

A great many of the faxes I sent to Joanna were informative and beautifully writed, apart from the odd begging fax . . .

Urgent! Official!

Needing money for trainin'. Wot have you left me in will??

Leave me all your money for trainin' or else I won't be any good and I am needin' some J-Cloths and some plugs cos they never comes with them on. So leave them me in your will! + jewels + money + house.

Please!

You'm very rich so do it!!

I WANTS TO ACT! I have written to others as well so don't feel special, yes alright,

Sandwich

. . . and the odd pleading fax . . .

Dear Jack the Bafta,

Well, it's that time of year again.

Do you think ya might be moseyin along on 21st to pick up another or are you going to China or are you dead?

I certainly is not going if you ain't – and will start backing out now –

I believe Gina Lhologrobidigillolloda is there this year with her mother so that might be fun.

Love J X

Jack Lumptious was often abroad, and I felt it my duty to keep her in the swing and up to date on all matters.

Dear Jack,

I told Alex Keshishian (Bless Ya!) that you had declined grace-fully the offer to 'do' Patsy in America. He duly passed the message on and reports that people are dumbfounded. People turning down the chance to have their own Series Network in US just doesn't happen, especially when they come from a small place like London. So, he says, they are likely to throw great wads of cash at you as punishment – they will try to break you down with loving words launched at your person – they will try and Velcro it to your body – they will try to make you eat it – millions of it – and then sign a contract.
Be strong!
On the other hand, they may accept the decision in a business-like manner and cast Bette Midler and Dame Diana Rigg.
Heigh-ho! Just kiddin'! I think we should treat *Ab Fab* as a bit of a Larry Doomer – if ya know what I mean. Ya don't wanna be Patsy après 50 – ya wanna be with big horses me thinkin'.
La di da!
See thee

Jx

Fri lunchtime
Dear Jack,

Have just returned from costume fitting at Angels for 'The

Piano'. And guess what! As I came out of the fitting room, who should be sitting there waiting to come in but Anna Paquin who played the little girl in *Piano*. I said nothing as was overcome and in awe of someone so little and in possession of an Oscar. My resemblance to Holly Hunter is uncanny. For she too is very small and petite and birdlike. It is rumoured that when they were shooting *The Piano* they wasted three days just filming a little piece of seaweed thinking it *was* Holly Hunter. She is the size of a very small budgerigar. She didn't have a caravan on set but a rather elegant birdcage where she could be placed for safety when not in shot. If the weather was less than clement, a lovely lace cover would be placed over the cage to protect her. When needed the director would open the little cage door and put one finger in on to which Holly would climb and perch on as she was taken on to the set. She was always shot very close to the camera to give the illusion of almost normal proportions. I admire her. It was only her perfect Scottish accent that persuaded Jane Campion to use her.

Blimey, I've got a horrible cold!

Harriet is coming over in a minute and we are going to torture each other about how fat we both are. Take Polaroid photos in size 10 bikinis and swear to not eat for ever and ever Amen.

Dawn went to a mighty celebrity gorgeous party at Elton John's house the other night. (I was invited, phew!, but couldn't go.) Many, many A-list celebs and high class entertainers were there plus PRINCESS DIANA!

1. Dawn said Elton mighty nice, good sort, kind boyfriend – who showed them around the house which used to be a real pop star's mansion but which got cleaned up at the same time as Elton and is now a shrine to beautifully ruched curtains. He has a specially made cabinet to keep his spectacles in.

2. Richard Gere was there – v. good looking but sincerely dull.
3. Tim Rice (who did lyrics to Elton's music for *Lion King*) with girlfriend of teenage years.
4. Jeff Katzenberg – ex Disney boss – staying with Elton and main reason for bash.
5. Sylvester Stallone – v. small – attached himself to Princess Diana – velcroed himself to her side. She complained to Dawn, who was unable to detach him.
6. Princess D – v. beautiful – relaxed. Girly.

Sylvester Stallone has a three-storey caravan at the stage at Shepperton! Mentioned that to Disney in passing.

Have had no word from Dame Judi or Dame Diana. Waiting in anticipation. Secretly hoping that it is Lady Dame Diana for gossip sake.

Have to go and see Sandra Bernhard show at the Royal Festival Hall on Monday night. Going with Ade, Ruby, Richard E, D and Len. Can't say I've ever liked her in anything I've seen except *King of Comedy* but Roseanne says she is a great actress and anything Roseanne says is alright by me. Richard E Grant is a friend of hers and says she has got a long way on a small amount of talent. She has aura of a huge star because she lives with an entourage – hair, make-up, secretaries, girlfriends, etc. She is desperate to be Patsy.

I have to work with D now – finish off the Dickens.

Still 3 episodes of *Ab Fab* to do before next week. Never felt calmer in my LIFE.

Great to talk w/ya yesterday.

Love ya

J XXXXX

★

Dear Jack,

Going Dutch appeals to me. Eating sugary cake and sweet liqueur is a charming pastime. And not having to display any character or personality that would make you stand out from the crowd is a very good way to live. Makes people very happy. Nice flat life. All day see horizon. Always horizon sometimes bicycle. Make jolly jolly life for Dutch people. We are very popular in Holland.

And cult in Brazil. Much mail and interview requests coming in now from Brazil where we are a *cult*. Just awaiting invite on first class airline to Rio and I'm off. Real mouse goes to Disneyland yet again.

They are making a film of *Ab Fab* in America with Jodie Foster and Courtney Love and have asked me to be the voice of an invisible pudding. I have agreed and think I can get you the 'mumbling invisible cigarette'. Oh yes!!

Jxxxx

Fax to Joanna when she was filming *James and the Giant Peach* in the US:

Dear Jack,

Got your fax. Hurrah, it works! I can start ripping pages out of newspapers and sendin' them to you.

I hope yer final make-up test goes well – and when did you ever meet a director that didn't treat actors like stop motion puppets? Eh?

I am not intendin' to move to Hollywood. I am not wantin' a house in Bev Hills and am only intendin' to sell the series format to Roseanne. Nothing more. Don't think you can get rid of me that easy, my dear. I intends to do me film come what may. (Am watchin' many episodes of *Martin Chuzzlewit* today with my dear friend Dawn French and so has to be talkin' like this, dear lady.) What mean ya by 'Mr Floppy (must he go)'?

No news from Jeanne Moreau, I has yet to write part for her and shall send it to her.

I am sorry that San Francisco isn't nice for you and don't apologize for being gloomy on the blower. When gloomy – ring me and moan. That is what I is here for.

Dawn and I are watching as many videos as possible in the name of research for our Xmas Special. Dickens, *The Piano*, Anne and Nick. I want Dawn to be Charlie Drake and we are trying to get Julie Andrews to be Christmassy with us in our finale Dickensian dance number. Heigh Ho. By gad!

Our Julia excellent in *Chuzzle*.

Damn! – you'll miss the comedy awards. Damn! You'll miss the Light Ent Party. But don't be too downcast, ya may arrive back in time for the *Noel's House Party* Celebrity Crinkly Bottom Christmas edition. And don't forget the Hearts of Gold Sunshine Variety Club Bravery Awards dinner. I've organized for you to be Guest of Honour.

The awful Michael Hurll Comedy Awards are giving June a life-time achievement award and wanted me to present but I've turned it down. Nothing on earth would drag me to that dreadful occasion again. I'm sure Roy Hudd will do it and much better too. Good old June!

Have you got Alan Bennett reading his diaries? Great stuff. I'll send them to ya!

So, babe. Don't forget to write your ghost story.

You are much missed and talked about.

J XX

Fax after fax after fax. No wonder I never got a script written on time.

Hi There!

Christmas seems far too close now. I just can't see time to do anything. We complete on the house in Devon next week and I can't foresee a time when I can go down there. Every day this week is Rehearse, Write, Shop, Sleep, Write, Rehearse, Shop, School Play, Write, Work, Rehearse, Studio, Shop, Shop, Light Entertainment Party.

Yesterday as I was driving through Richmond I said to Ade, 'I won't ever come shopping on a Saturday, it's a crowded nightmare of desperation' and he said, 'It's a Sunday!' What horror! Richmond used to be glorious on a Sunday, feeding the ducks on the river, strollin' along the river bank, a little antique window shoppin', church bells ringin', tower clocks a tickin', a little boatin', a little eatin' in local bistro, drinkin' in the Ducks Arms and sitting on the Hill on a bench dedicated to a dead pensioner, a'gazin' at London's most famous river view. But now! That ain't possible. WOT A FUCKIN 'ORRIBLE WORLD THIS IS! Heigh-ho!

Going to see *Oliver!* tonight with Ben and Sophie and all the girls, who are already great fans of the musical.

Saw a clip on the *Royal Variety Show* the other night (which had been edited to a mere 2½ hours. WHY!) and Jonathan Pryce seems to have decided not to make Fagin particularly Jewish – more actory sounding really. I suppose he may be worried after the trouble he got into for going a bit slanty eyed in *Miss Saigon*. But really! Will give full report tomorrow.

The tickets cost £27 each. Most W-End prices are now over £30. Maggie Smith is charging for *Three Tall Women* (play with Frances de la Tour and unknown tall woman by Edward Albee) a cool £35. A ticket. They apparently get a very executive audience. I think they should get shorter actresses and cut the ticket price accordingly.

Apparently executives and Americans are willing to pay – sometimes the price is just tagged on to their hotel bill and it is unnoticed. I expect soon it will be all inclusive and you'll get your complimentary tickets to *Three Tall Women* or *Cats*, right alongside the soap and shower hat.

I've had an idea that I think we should patent along with the bra radio mike. It is for Celebrity Airbags that come out of your steering wheel when you've had a crash. You could plunge your head into a huge cleavage of someone's out-stretched arms. I think it would do very well in the executive toys market.

There must be some other way to make money. This writin' thang is bloody time consumin' and borin'. Gotta go, babe. – work to do. See ya soon.

Lotsa love

XXXX

A brief word here about the *Ab Fab* film that never has been. You may see it one day. You may. Only the other day, I saw a G-Wiz and thought how funny it would be to have Eddie and Patsy in a G-Wiz car chase.

There's only one problem. I actually have to sit down and write the damn thing. Most frustratingly for me, it just doesn't seem to be able to write itself. It requires me to write it. And that is why it has never been written. Heigh-ho!

You never know. You just never know.

Dix

In my head, I'm multilingual. But in reality, I'm not. Basically I have just the one tongue. I travel the world thinking how great it is to have been born English; speaking English to foreign people who speak English. How lucky are we?

I do, however, speak a little Italian. I can order food and hold a small conversation. I have a brilliant, convincing Italian accent. So convincing, in fact, that all I have to do is say *Buongiorno* and I am engaged in long explanations and chats, during which I generally just nod and agree heartily. They think I'm a native, you see. They even try to guess where I'm from . . . is it Milano or Torino? Yes, I really do make a pretty good stab at Italian and have only once ordered testicles by mistake in a restaurant.

My French, on the other hand, is not such a success. This is not for want of trying; I have bought all the cassettes and I know quite a few words. But I just cannot, for the life of me, do the accent.

Absolutely Fabulous didn't go out in Italy. I don't think drunken old birds appealed to Berlusconi. It did go out in France, but it was never as popular there as it became elsewhere. Frankly, it went down better in Serbia. I know this because I get royalty cheques from Serbia, but very little trickles in from over La Manche.

It is possible that the French just don't find women getting drunk funny. Although, personally, I think it could have been the dubbing: I once saw an episode of *Ab Fab* dubbed into French in which Eddie and Patsy just seemed like normal French women going about their daily business. Patsy was particularly French: she didn't eat, she smoked and drank, and was fairly rude to people.

The show was, however, a cult hit with the gay community in France, and on the strength of that a producer wanted to make a film version. The French make films like we make TV. It's a big home market, subsidized by the government, and they churn them out. So they bought the rights and various story-lines and got on with it.

I thought no more about it, until one day Maureen called.

'Hello, love.'

'Hello, Maureen. How was your holiday?'

'Fine, love.'

'Golf?'

'No. Throwing myself down a mountain. Now, the French have been on to me about you possibly making an appearance in the film. You remember . . . They're making a film, love?'

'I had forgotten, but I have now remembered. Thank you.'

'Now I know this is going to be difficult, but they only need you for half a day . . .'

now, and we just laughed the whole way. And the only thing I had to do the next day was sit in a crowd for ten minutes and then fly home again!

In my room at the Ritz, I found a pair of silk pyjamas on my pillow – a present from the film company. Cherry on cake.

Could this get any better? Answer: actually, no. And it didn't. No.

The six o'clock wake-up call the next morning brought us back down to earth and regretting the gin. But at least I awoke in silk.

The weather was cold, and we were taken – not whisked – bleary-eyed to the set in a minicab, deposited in a small office and told to wait. For some reason, I started to become nervous. We waited, and waited, until eventually the producer and director came in and told us that everything was wonderful but they were still dressing the set – and left again.

I shouted after them, 'Remember, NO LINES!'

We waited.

Someone came in with some jewellery that Jean Paul wanted me to wear. I thanked them. It was lovely. And actually I was allowed to go home with it. Nice perks, but I had peaked at the silk PJs.

We waited, and I had a little make-up applied.

Then the director and producer came back in. They were nearly ready for me.

'To just sit in the crowd?'

'Yes. Next to Catherine Deneuve.'

'Pardon?'

'Would you mind sitting next to Catherine Deneuve?'

'Er . . . no.'

They left again. Who, in their right mind, would object to sitting next to Catherine Deneuve. She is a goddess. I worshipped Catherine Deneuve. I mean, it's CATHERINE DENEUVE.

I was just arranging how Abi could subtly take a photo of me with Catherine Deneuve when the director appeared again, holding a small piece of paper.

Would I mind saying a few words with Catherine?

He handed me the piece of paper. It had a few lines of script on it.

I looked at Abi. Abi looked at me. Lines. OK, it was only four lines, but, dear reader, in French! My heart stopped beating and I turned into an ice cube.

Catherine DENEUVE (à Jennifer SAUNDERS): Absolument prophétique!

Jennifer SAUNDERS (à Catherine DENEUVE): Littéralement fabuleux!

Catherine DENEUVE et Jennifer SAUNDERS (*en choeur*): Absolument fabuleux!

Patricia font un scandale et volent le sac aquarium.

Jennifer SAUNDERS: Je vais me réveiller, elles vont disparaître . . .

Catherine DENEUVE: Vous les connaissez?

Jennifer SAUNDERS: On a été présentée.

There are some fairly complicated words in there, I'm sure you'll agree, dear reader. Some words with accents and one especially nasty word with a hat on.

Abi quickly became a CD for practice purposes, and we tried the lines again and again. But I couldn't get them! And, if I tried them with the accent, I simply brought up phlegm.

Suddenly I was called on to set.

'But . . . I . . . haven't really . . . had enough . . . time.'

*

On set I was introduced to Josiane Balasko and Nathalie Baye, who were playing Eddie and Patsy. They both looked hilarious and we talked a little, I think. I can't really remember because all I could think about was the lines. The only thing we had done all morning was wait, and now time was going too quickly.

I spotted Deneuve sitting in the director's chair at the side of the set. She was immaculate and stately, cigarette in one hand, espresso in the other. Gay satellites circled her, replenishing cigarettes or coffee and attending to the hair, which was a magnificent hair-sprayed helmet of a do.

I thought about all the films she had made in her lifetime. Deneuve. The face that, by doing nothing, says everything. The actors she had worked with. Delon. Mastroianni. The directors. Buñuel, for God's sake!

And now she was going to have to say a few lines with a fool.

Finally, I was introduced. She was, of course, perfectly charming and funny, and spoke flawless English. I attempted conversation as we were taken to our seats on the set. I made the decision not to look at her as we said the lines, just in case mucus came out. I really didn't know what was going to come out of my mouth when the time arrived.

That time arrived all too soon.

The lights came up on the catwalk, and the models walked down through water and a heavy rain effect. It was beautiful.

Action!

French Eddie and Patsy storm the stage and the camera comes round and pans across the crowd to Catherine and me. We start the actin' and the speakin'.

CATHERINE: Absolument prophétique!
MOI: Abberlabbermo fabberlo!
CATHERINE et MOI: Absolumenti fabbala dabbala!
MOI: Chervay moo revery san dispatchketchup.
CATHERINE: Vous les connaissez?

MOI: La plume de ma tante.

AND CUT!

MOI: How do you think that went?
CATHERINE: I think we may have to go again.

And so we did. Again and again until finally I must have said it in a way that they thought they could do something with (or perhaps they had given up altogether). But by then it was getting late, and Abi was looking at her watch and then looking at me. We were in danger of missing the flight home. Even private jets have slots apparently and can't just take off and land willy-nilly. We had to go. The fear of seeming rude to Ms Deneuve by rushing off was nothing compared to the terror of not making it back for the show and having to face Dawn.

We air-kissed and 'au revoired' ourselves into a small waiting car driven by a very young runner from the film, and were then hurtled through the streets of Paris at such speed that we both had visions of a certain famous crash in an underpass.

I will never understand why, on film and TV sets, it is often left to the runner to transport the actors about. These young-sters must have only just passed their test.*

Anyway, we made it on to the plane with seconds to spare. We flew back and, within an hour, I was in much more familiar territory.

---

* I also can't understand how they get the insurance. As an actor you pay over the odds for insurance. I once asked a broker why that was, and he said it was in case we were transporting famous people around in our cars. Like Laurence Olivier, for instance. I thought if I was transporting Laurence Olivier around in my car, I would probably be arrested, as he has been dead for some time.

'Good evening, ladies and gentlemen. We are French and Saunders!'

'I'm Jennifer Saunders.'

'And so am I!'

When the film of *Absolument Fabuleux* eventually came out, I was amazed to see the scene still in it. And with my voice. I think. I took a good deal of confidence from this.

Then, in 2005 . . .

'Morning, love.'

'Good morning, Maureen.'

'Now, there's a part in a French film come up.'

'Really?'

'It's filming half here, half there, and you wouldn't be needed the whole time. The part is an English woman.'

'Right.'

'Now, you *would* have to speak French.'

'Well, I can do that. I speak French.'

'I thought you did. So that's a yes, is it?'

'Yes.'

In my head this was going to be the perfect vehicle to break into the world of films. I could have a nice sideline going in European movies. I mean, if Kristin Scott Thomas can do it!

For this film, they were going to give me a dialogue coach and send me tapes of the script being read in French. Perfect.

It was called *L'Entente Cordiale* and starred Christian Clavier, a very funny man who speaks only a little English. And Daniel Auteuil, an extremely well-known French actor. I was told by Patrick, my make-up artist, that Christian is a 'king' in France and that both he and Daniel had been given the honour of being allowed to have holiday houses in Corsica. They are very particular in Corsica and apparently you have to be chosen, or you run the risk of having your house set on fire and being generally terrorized off the island. I fantasized that, if I ever got in trouble in Corsica, I could call on one of the two 'kings' to help me out.

Both men are quite small, so I resigned myself to the fact that I was going to look like a great big bear beside them. Heigh-ho.

The film was a comedy, and for the life of me I can't remember the exact plot (if I ever knew it). But my character was an English woman who helped them along in the caper.

The whole crew was French, as were most of the actors, with a few English exceptions. Shelley Conn and Sanjeev Bhaskar both had parts. Shelley had to speak Hindi and French with a Hindi accent. She spoke neither, but pulled it off. Or, at least, I believed she pulled it off. It sounded like the right kind of noise to me.

We shot in various locations around London – from Mayfair to Tooting – and it all seemed jolly. Plenty of laughter and messing about. I mean, there were the odd moments when I had to repeat a line or I didn't know when to come in with a line because they were speaking so fast in French that it was impossible to follow. It would suddenly just go very quiet and I would notice everyone looking at me before the director shouted, *'Coupé!'* And there was the odd occasion when they would all be looking at me because they simply hadn't understood what I had said, but then neither had I.

In Paris, we shot some scenes in the Jardin des Plantes, which is a garden with a sad zoo in it. I had a quick look at the reptile house and even the snakes looked sad.

I had been taught to play the cello – or at least fake it well – and I had to make serious woman-playing-cello faces. This was even harder than talking in French. Long strokes with the bow and a bit of wobbly hand on the bridge. Serious face, eyes closed, slight shaking of the head to denote impending ecstasy. This went on for a whole morning.

Thank God for lunch.

The great thing about French film sets is that they always

break on time for lunch because the food cannot be kept waiting. The catering is a wonder to behold compared with what
I'm used to. Normally, there's a truck and you all queue up in
dribs and drabs to get a plate of something meaty or salady and
a jam roly-poly with custard. You then take it to the 'bus', which
is a double-decker adapted for the purpose, and eat it with the
crew. Or you go back to your rabbit hutch if you want to be
alone and have a quick nap afterwards.

In France, it is different. Everybody breaks at the same time
and then eats together on laid-out tables. You are served a
three-course meal, and wine and beer are available. Moderate
drinking is in fact encouraged. The food is delicious and the
whole affair is very civilized. Being allowed a modicum of alcohol doesn't seem to slow down the afternoon at all; in fact, I
would say it rather oiled the machine.

When my involvement in the film came to an end, I knew I
would mostly miss the lunches.

I 'completed my part' in the middle of the countryside, about
an hour from Paris. There was much kissing and giving of
presents. I was unsure what accepted practice was, present-wise,
so I just took a leaf out of Dawn's book and gave big and plenty.
Much more kissing ensued, and telling me I'd been fantastic and
how much they were looking forward to seeing me again at the
premiere and what a party we would have . . .

Months went by. Months and months. I heard nothing. No party
invite arrived. Occasionally I would bump into Sanjeev in London.

'Heard anything about that French film?'

'No.'

'It must be out soon.'

'Yes. I would have thought so.'

'Perhaps we have been cut out and they're too embarrassed
to tell us.'

We laughed.

★

A full year went by and eventually I googled the film. *L'Entente Cordiale* had been released and we had both been dubbed. They had been too embarrassed to invite us to the party. My voice had been replaced by a quite hard but precise French voice, and she had struggled to make the words match my movements. I might as well have just opened my mouth sporadically like a goldfish for the whole film. The effect would have been the same.

So that was it. Kristin Scott Thomas could breathe easy. I air-kissed my foreign film career goodbye.

Eleven

I am sitting in a cabana down by the sea in the south of France, in April 2004. It is a little striped tent in the grounds of the Hôtel du Cap-Eden-Roc. I am not alone. Sitting next to me is Rupert Everett and, opposite us, a nervous Japanese journalist.

It is a press junket and every journalist is allowed less than two minutes in the tent to ask their questions before a PR person comes in and tells them their time is up. They are then moved to another cabana, with another member of the cast. This one is talking *way* too slowly.

'Hello, Mr Everett and Miss . . . [he looks at his notes in his shaking hand] . . . Saunders.'

'Hello.'

'How are you?'

'We are very well.'

'I want to tell you, we are big fan in Japan . . .'

PR: 'I'm sorry, your time is up.'

Japanese man then shakily packs his notebook away, bows and is replaced by a Swedish one.

PR: 'You have two minutes!'

It had begun with a call from Maureen a year earlier.

'Hello, love.'

'Hello, Maureen. Good morning!'

'How are you?'

'I'm very well, thank you. How was your holiday?'

'Very nice.'

'Were you throwing yourself down a mountain?'

'No, golf. Couple of things, love. Would you please get round to sending me back the various contracts that you are still in possession of. Are you in possession of them?'

'Er . . . not sure.'

'I'll send them to you again (*small sigh*). Now secondly. A voiceover for a cartoon.'

'Yes.'

'It's a DreamWorks thing.'

'Yes.'

'It's the follow-on from the *Shrek* one. Did you see that?'

'Yes. Yes, I'll do it.'

'The other cast are Antonio Banderas, Eddie Murphy –'

'Yes.'

'Mike Myers, Cameron Diaz –'

'Yes.'

'Julie Andrews, Rupert Everett, John Cleese –'

'Yes.'

'Would you have any interest, love?'

'Yes. Yes, I would like to do it.'

'Fine. So that's a yes?'

'Yes.'

'It would require you to sing.'

'I can sing.'

'Yes, I thought you could. I'll let the various folk know.'

Back in the cabana, the Swedish journalist takes too long to get her notebook out of her bag.

'So, what was it like working together?'

PR: 'I'm sorry, your time is up!'

We shouted after her as an Italian took her place, 'We didn't actually work together!'

And that was the truth. In the whole of the *Shrek* process, I was never in a studio with any other actors.

The director was Andrew Adamson, a gently spoken New Zealander with long, blond hair. He was a fan of *French and Saunders* and *Ab Fab*, which was how I had come to be considered for the part.

In the first meeting, he had shown me the initial artwork for the Fairy Godmother. It wasn't quite how I had imagined she would be, based on my own physicality. She appeared to be quite short and dumpy and rather old. Heigh-ho.

It was from these drawings and the bits of script that I had to find a voice for her. Which, as it turned out, was basically my own voice, with a bit of Joan Collins thrown in for good measure. I really only have two voices that I can do well: Sandi Toksvig and Joan Collins. I can do Felicity Kendal at a push.

Sometimes, when I do a part, I have no idea what the voice is going to be until the director says, 'Action!' I genuinely have no clue what will come out of my mouth. And, once you've started with a voice, you then have to remember it for the whole show.

But then I'm not technically trained, you see. I'm sure real actresses have a much better method.

In *The Hunt for Tony Blair*, one of the final Comic Strip films, which we made in 2011, Peter Richardson asked me to play Margaret Thatcher. OK, I can do that. Then he said, 'But it's film noir and set in the 1940s, so, actually, Maggie is based on Gloria Swanson in *Sunset Boulevard*, although I want her to look like Bette Davis in *Whatever Happened to Baby Jane?*' This is Pete's bonkers-ness, and also his genius.

I was flummoxed. John Sessions was in a scene with me and I practised a bit with him before shooting. John, who is an expert at all voices and impersonations, looked at me and said, 'Drop the regressive "r".' I now had nothing.

On 'Action!' I really thought this was going to be the moment I was found out. I have spent my entire career waiting for the tap on the shoulder.

How has she got away with it for so many years?

Why, she's no good at all!

Fingers would point. Laughter. Cruel laughter.

Gotcha!

But luck was on my side. What came out of my mouth was deemed satisfactory and I got away with it. All I had to do was try to remember the voice from scene to scene.

The Fairy Godmother was altogether simpler. Andrew would read in all the other parts and hold up pictures. Until I eventually saw the finished film, all I could imagine was the other characters speaking in a soft New Zealand accent.

The recording was done in lots of separate stages. The script would change as the animation was built up. But in all of these stages it was only ever Andrew and me. I never met any of the other actors until Cannes.

Often, in a recording session, Andrew would ask me to be more animated as I said my lines. But surely I'm just the voice? Not quite. The whole thing was being recorded on film, so that the animators could add my physicality to the character's movements.

In the final session I realized, to my horror, that the Fairy Godmother explodes. Explodes! I know that she was the baddy, but this did seem a bit harsh. It seriously reduced my character's hope of appearing in any future films. This didn't seem fair at all. Why would she explode? Couldn't she just limp off or repent?

I made them record the line 'I'll be back!' just before she popped, but it was never used. This was always going to be a one-off.

In the cabana, I thank God that I'm sharing it with Rupert. At least we can have a good laugh. I have known him, on and off, since college. He went there to train to be an actor, and I remember him looking languid in the coffee bar and generally refusing to take anything seriously until he was expelled. Rupert always looks as if he has just thought of the wickedest thing to say and is about to spill the beans. Which he often is.

We get a break occasionally and have a look around the other tents. Julie Andrews is being lovely and gracious in her slightly larger cabana. Rupert shouts in, 'I hope you're asking her how she got here. She travels by umbrella you know!'

Eddie Murphy seems to have the biggest tent and is surrounded by an enormous entourage of agents, family, security, PRs and children. I saw him arrive. A convoy of people all trying to organize other people, who are trying to be important and organize the organizers. And there are some people who don't seem to know why they are there at all. They may have just got swept up in the crowd at the airport and found themselves there by accident.

I arrived at the Eden-Roc with nobody and immediately regretted it. I had a beautiful room with a balcony set over the rocks, and a view of nothing but sea. As soon as I saw it, I thought, *What an idiot!* This was going to be amazing and I had no one to share it with. I called Ade and said he had to come immediately. But he was busy, so I told Ella, who was just sixteen, to get on a plane, and she did.

Sometimes you need someone to walk around staring at people with. Plus, the fact that she was sixteen gave me a great excuse to walk up to actors I'd never met before in my life and tell them that she was their biggest fan.

I mean, Jack Black was there. And Cameron Diaz, with Justin Timberlake as her date. What's not to stare at? Melanie Griffith, Angelina Jolie. HELLO?

It was all a glamorous fantasy.

Out of my window, I would spot the occasional paparazzo scuttling like a crab across the rocks, trying to get pics of the stars. Long lenses were trained on the swimming pool in the hope of catchin' a famous pair of breasts. Mine, it turned out, were of no interest at all. I could have walked totally naked on to the balcony and shooken me booty, but all lenses would have remained pointing at the pool in the hope of catchin' Jennifer Aniston in a bikini.

'My name is Olga.'

'Hello, Olga.'

'Miss Saunders, what was it like singing in the film?'

PR: 'Your time is up!'

A word about singing here. I can sort of sing, but what I'm better at is impersonating singing. Actually, they are not impersonations. They are impressions. I can give the impression that I am singing. I can basically sound like someone singing. I can sound like Cher or Mary Hopkins or Alanis Morissette. I can't sound like Celine Dion, but did once try and, I have to admit, it was one of the worst impersonations EVER.

For *Shrek* I knew it would require slightly more than an impression. I had two songs to sing. I wondered if I could get away with a Rex Harrison-ish talking-singing. But no. They wanted The Works.

They had sent me a guide for the two songs, sung by a professional singer. She was really very good. She could easily have passed for a Disney heroine – Mulan or Pocahontas, perhaps. She could even have been Ariel in *The Little Mermaid*. Class.

And the song – 'Holding Out for a Hero', made famous by the gravelly-voiced Bonnie Tyler – was terrifying. It had a couple of notes that were mountainously high.

I had a singing lesson. Just the one, but it taught me one invaluable thing, which I shall now impart to you. When thinking of a scale of notes, don't think of the high notes as being 'up' and the low notes as being 'down'. Think of the whole scale as a road ahead of you with the high notes further away and the low notes closer. Use more breath for the further away ones and don't stick your face in the air to sing higher. This was a revelation and gave me some confidence, at least. Talent would always be limited.

Singing lesson down, I knew that there was only one other thing that I required and that was Simon Brint. He had done all the music for all our shows, live and on TV, and had somehow made me and Dawn sound good. He had told us when to come in and when to stop singin', when to sing higher and when to sing lower, and was always tactful, even if it was disastrous.

I asked for Simon, and he was allowed to stand near me on the recording day.

When the backing track started in my earphones, I would look to Simon to start me singin'.

'*Somewhere after midnight in my wildest –*'

He stopped me.

'Jen, I think perhaps you've started just a little flat.

We practised some more.

'Go again.'

'*Somewhere after midnight in my wildest fantasy, somewhere just –*'

I was stopped again. Not actually singing the right tune this time, and a little late in.

And so it went on. With the patience of a saint, Simon saw me through the whole song line by line. And sometimes word by word. The geniuses in the booth somehow stitched the whole thing together and, lo and behold, I COULD SING.

Simon is no longer with us. Very sadly, we lost him in 2011 and I miss him every day. He was a beautiful soul, a quiet genius and a very dear friend.

Thanks to him, everyone seemed happy with the singin', but I didn't see the results until the screening in Cannes. Sitting in the booth with Rupert, I could talk about the process, but having not yet seen the film, I was getting a little nervous. The rest of the cast had already been to premieres in Los Angeles and New York. The thing you realize about a job like this is that people are not paid a fortune for the work. They are paid it for the endless publicity. They will take up to a year out travelling the world, promoting a film. The fact that I didn't is probably the reason that 'I'll be back!' never made it into the final cut.

Wherever Rupert and I went, Julie was never far behind. We were the English contingent, and we clung to each other like barnacles. Every morning, when I was having my make-up done, I would get a call from Julie's assistant.

'Julie is wondering what you're wearing today.'

I must admit that my options were limited. I had some tops and some trousers and some ill-advised shoes (polka-dot peep-toes) that I had panic-bought at the airport. Luckily, I discovered that Cannes is relaxed – I only needed smart things for the actual red carpet.

For me, as always, that meant Betty Jackson. Thank the Lord for Betty. She's a fashion designer who has won every award going; she designs real clothes for real women; and she's now a close friend, as I've said. If it weren't for Betty, I would never go to anything at all.

If an event loomed, I would fax Betty at extremely late notice.

HELP! A charity fax for . . .

Dear Miss Botty Jockson,

I'm sure you must be fed up of receiving unsolicited mail – and now faxes – from deserving causes, but we feel ours is special. It deals with a very serious problem that simply won't go away by ignoring it. So please don't rip this up, please go on reading.

HELP! is a charity that is concerned with the problem of obesity and weight excess in performers and actresses who, through no fault of their own – other than overeating and having heavy bone syndrome – find themselves in possession of lovely clothes that simply do not fit and cannot be expected to fit in the very near future. 'So what?' you might say. 'What the hell has that got to do with me?', and you'd be right up to a point; but you can help. Many of these so-called actresses have important celebrity do's and Royalish functions to attend in the next couple of weeks – occasions at which they, or someone very nearby, might be photographed by the paparazzi or better, and wouldn't you like it to be your clothes on the edge of that frame? Imagine opening a Sunday supplement and seeing that inevitable full-page colour feature of Joanna Lumley with one of our beneficiaries wearing one of your sleeves just creeping into shot. Well, this could well happen.

There is one very needy case we have on our books at the moment and that is Jennifer Saunders, Joanna Lumley's wacky sidekick in *Absolutely Fantastic* (also known as Dawn

French). She finds herself in the all-too-familiar and tragic position of having a pair of velvet trousers that are far too tight and a trip to Milan (as well as a subsequent fashion award ceremony) looming very large on the proverbial horizon. The government turned her down flat when she asked for assistance and no grant is available for one in her position, but that's the world we live in! So we turn to you. Can you help her? Could she come to your shop and get a lovely new outfit (an HP scheme is presently being run by HELP!) for Cannes or have new trousers? You are our last hope, although of course there is always Edna Ronda or Jaspar Carrot, who have been very good to us in the past with Fergie.

Please call on 081 948 — or fax before 4 p.m.

We think you are marvellous and just sorry.

Yours in anticipation,

Sandwich

Betty would reply, horrified by the thought of having to dress such a minor star, but would eventually acquiesce.

HELP! A charity fax for . . .

Miss Backy Jettson,

Thank you for responding so promptly to our desperate request. Miss Saunders is thrilled that you are able to provide her with suitable outwear befitting a minor celebrity of her short standing. She hopes to be able to repay you in some way – a ticket to the next Torvill and Dean four-hour ice spectacular perhaps? – or simply an auto-graphed postcard (for a small charge), whatever! – just let me know.

The tabard-style dress that you described over the phone

sounds perfect and very befitting. She'll look great in anything frankly, as long as it's not a bias-cut Lurex boob tube
with matching chaps and Beatle cap, but there are very few
of us could get away with that these days. The 'midi' was
always my favourite but that's me (and 'less about you', I
can hear you mutter). We trust you implicitly and know, of
course, that you know best in most things.

Thank you. We think you are marvellous and are very
sorry about everything.

Yours,

Sandwich

Quick note from Jennifer Saunders (actress)

Dear Mrs Jickson,

Is it entirely necessary for me to be measured? I have a very
good set of figures from the BBC that they took in 1984. I
am an actress so ya must understand the fear that the
words 'total shaper' and 'tape measure' induce in me.
However, I suppose you have a job to do. Heigh-ho!

Betty always comes through, despite the fact that I know she
sometimes despairs at my dress sense.

For this particular red carpet moment, I was wearing a lovely
tiered black chiffon dress and felt great. It was a wonderful
night. Everything was organized beautifully, without panic or
fuss. We were all loaded into black limos, and snaked our way
to the centre of Cannes.

Maureen had made it out for the screening, so I had an entourage of two.

We drove together to the carpet, but once out of the car, I
was Rupert's date. Having him on my arm meant that the
photographs were basically of Rupert and the top of my head.

He is ridiculously tall and, even with my high-heely spiky shoes on, I barely reached his shoulder.

Light bulbs, light bulbs, flash, flash, flash.

Red carpet, red carpet, red carpet.

From my limited experience, the red carpet at Cannes is extremely civilized. Not like the nonsense you see at the Oscars. None of the 'Who are you wearing tonight?' and 'Where are your jewels from?'

Joanna Lumley once pointed out to me that the red carpet is the new beauty pageant. Everyone must look lovely, behave, be polite and cry when they get the crown. But surely, despite this, these people are supposed to be grown-ups!

I saw an actor being interviewed on the red carpet at the Emmys who actually made the camera look at his Tom Ford socks. A rich man showing us his free socks. Thank God always for Helena Bonham Carter and Björk. Why is everyone forced to give such a shit?

Inside, it is just an ordinary cinema and you sit in ordinary cinema seats. I was sat next to Ella on one side and – for heaven's sake – Julie Andrews on the other. I was nervous anyway about seeing the film. I was singing in it. And Julie Andrews wasn't singing in it, on account of the fact that poor Julie Andrews can't sing any more. Which doesn't seem at all fair, really.

When my first song started, my palms were sweating. When it was over, Julie leaned over and said, 'Well done.'

'Thank you.'

When my second song started, I was perspiring heavily and trying to make jokes all the way through. But Julie was extremely gracious. She patted my knee.

'You did very well. Well done.'

I had the Mary Poppins seal of approval.

*

After that, it was mainly partying; not the 'just get drunk and shout a lot' kind of partying, but the 'quite glamorous, wish I had a camera with me' type of partying.

At one point we were all transferred to Paul Allen's yacht.

Paul, by virtue of being one of the co-founders of Microsoft, is hugely rich. When I say 'yacht', I mean 'super yacht'. Not a yacht with a sail. An oligarch yacht, times two. A Russian doll of yachts. Within the main bulk was contained every size of craft, from sailing boats and launches down to jet skis. I believe there was even a submarine on board. And a swimming pool as big as the sea that it was sitting in.

There were hundreds of staff in ironed shorts. There was a music studio and a cinema. And, when we eventually got on board, it had more seafood on it than I had ever seen in one place before. They had trawled the oceans and dumped it on silver platters, with a little piece of lettuce.

The party was in full swing. Ella and I toured the yacht and stared. It was one of those times when what you want to say – 'This is too much. This is obscene. I mean, really' – is different from what you actually say, which is, 'This is bloody amazing.'

We saw a titchy person who turned out to be Angelina Jolie attempting an oyster. The oyster nearly ate her. She is very small. We met Melanie Griffith, who was guarding Antonio Banderas like a squeaky Rottweiler. She didn't let him out of her sight all night.

All the decks were elegantly arranged with party people – some cool, some just gawping like us, but all slightly overcome by the sheer wealth.

I had met Paul Allen before.

Every year, before the world altered and even millionaires started to count their small change, Paul Allen would throw an enormous, extravagant party. Ruby went once – to Venice – and came back full of extraordinary stories of masked balls, tabs in every cafe in St Mark's Square, and flotillas of gondolas full of the Great and the Good.

I had been invited too, it turned out, but had not understood why someone called Paul had sent me a weird box with a Venetian mask in it. I'd given it to one of my children to wear.

However, when the mini explorer's suitcase with the Alaska invite in it arrived, I was more clued up. A four-day, all-expenses-paid trip to Alaska? Oh yes! Ade, we are going.

The flight – which left from Luton airport – was basically a big jumbo jet with a few sofas and a bar in it. And passengers who had very nearly all, at some point or another, been in *Hello!* magazine. Musicians, actors, film directors, Jerry Hall. We arrived in Alaska and were transferred to a giant cruise ship. It wasn't pretty. It was a floating apartment building, but Paul had hired the whole thing. For four days we sailed past glaciers and whales, stopping occasionally for trips out on a canoe or to see bears. We paid for nothing.

His reason for this was to get people from different areas of expertise to meet each other and network. At breakfast, you could be sitting next to a conservationist or a geneticist, a singer or an actor.

Paul Allen, a geek with a tummy, would basically have much rather been a rock star than a computer genius. One night, there was a big party during which he got up and jammed with the assembled rock stars, the Dave Stewarts and co. It was like the whole trip had been a big old excuse for Paul to have a jam session.

Back at the hotel, Ella and I ventured into the *Vanity Fair* party, which turned out to be just like any other party. Low lighting, loud music and not much to eat. So we went back to the room and went through the goody bags. *Shrek* slippers, T-shirts, iPods. A decent haul.

I imagined what it would be like back on the yacht, the sun going down and Cannes twinkling in the distance like a small tiara. I considered myself very lucky. *Shrek* had allowed me to dip into another world and have a good old stare. Not a world I want to live in, but thoroughly worth the jaunt.

Twelve

I am now sitting on a boat at sunset, floating down the River Ganges, looking back towards the ghats of Varanasi.

There are two musicians playing. One on a small, light drum, and one on some kind of oboe called a shehnai that is ear-piercing and playing music that would appear to have no melody or beginning. And, regrettably, no end.

Lying near the musicians is Goldie Hawn. She is politely tapping her hand along to the non-existent beat. Next to her is her assistant, Teri Schwartz, a tall, handsome American wearing a good pair of khaki chinos. Next to me is Ruby Wax. And this is all her fault.

It is October 1997. A few months before, I had received an overexcited call from Ruby.

'Jennifer, we have to do it.'

'Do what?'

'Didn't I tell you?'

'No, Ruby. Start at the beginning.'

It turns out that Ruby had met Goldie in LA. She had already interviewed her for her TV show, so they knew each other, and Goldie had told her about a film script she had been trying to get written. The first script that had been done wasn't right, and now she was looking for new writers.

'We can do this, Jennifer. Jennifer, this will not take us more than a month. Not more than a month, Jennifer. Will you talk to Goldie?'

'Errr . . .'

'She's calling you tonight.'

Goldie called. She explained the plot of the movie she wanted written; it was about a woman whose husband dies and who wants his ashes scattered in India. This takes the woman on a voyage of self-discovery at a time when everything is changing in her life and she has lost a sense of purpose. Goldie, at this time, had just turned fifty.

It was to be a comedy.

On the surface, this seemed like a piece of cake. The only thing that Ruby and I hadn't introduced into the equation was that we had never written a film script before.

This was to be a factor when, a year later, we were still at it.

Even today, Ruby and I will meet and discuss writing the film. One day, it will happen. It will be done.

We met Goldie on one of her trips to London. We sat in her hotel suite and she regaled us with stories of India.

One story was about a disabled Indian journalist she knew and admired. He had once dived into an empty swimming pool and broken his neck and was now in a wheelchair. She told us the story of how she had once been at his house when his mother was there too. They were talking and a Barbra Streisand record was playing.

He then looked at her and said, 'Goldie, will you dance with me?'

She said, 'No, I can't dance with you, I'm not strong enough.'

The mother said, 'Yes, you are, Goldie. You are strong enough.'

And they lifted him to his feet and she held him up as they danced to Barbra.

Goldie was visibly moved as she told us the story. When she left the room to have a pee, Ruby turned to me with a look of disbelief.

'Jennifer. I think she wants that story in the movie.'

She was right. And we did try.

We started writing. We worked out some good characters and a whole world for Goldie's character to exist in, in San Francisco.

I had become obsessed with the idea of writing a film about the menopause, and so that became my focus. Ruby wrote about the modern-art world and the character's youth in the 1960s. We wrote pages and pages, about characters upon characters, and it was the length of two feature films before the words 'ashes' and 'India' were even mentioned. Because the truth was, we didn't know anything about India. Neither of us had ever been. We were quite happy in our little modern-art and menopause world, and couldn't really see the point.

To this day I can't believe we didn't just write what Goldie wanted. She wanted a lovely film about a woman who goes to India, looks gorgeous and finds herself. We could have done that and it would have taken a month. What were we thinking?

Goldie's frustration eventually turned into plane tickets. She, Ruby and I flew first class to India along with her assistant, Teri.

The trip was for ten days. Our first stop was Mumbai, where

we would be staying with a friend of Goldie's, who was called Parmesh.

She met us at the airport. As we queued to go through customs, we could hear a voice shouting and just see a hand waving above the crowd.

'Goldie Hawn! Goldie Hawn! This way! Goldie Hawn!'

We eventually found Parmesh and Goldie explained that Ruby and I were travelling with her. From that moment on, we were 'Goldie Hawn and her team! Goldie Hawn and her team!'

Mumbai airport was chaotic and hot, despite the fact that we had arrived late at night. I could see Ruby was suffering from culture shock. As we headed to the car, she gripped my arm.

'Jennifer, don't look, half-man, half-skateboard coming up fast behind us.'

Parmesh was extremely rich. We were taken from the airport in an air-conditioned Mercedes to her beach house. The house was heavily guarded and fenced, and we were greeted by an army of servants. Cases were taken to rooms, and Goldie and her team were served drinks. In her manic way, Parmesh could not do enough for us. At one point she decided we should have caviar. She snapped her fingers.

'Caviar for Goldie and her team! Caviar!'

One of the men serving shook his head, but Parmesh wouldn't relent; she knew that she had caviar left over from her daughter's wedding, and we were to have it – at four o'clock in the morning. Now! Caviar!

The staff went off shaking their heads, but duly arrived back ten minutes later with a huge lump of the stuff. Parmesh invited us to tuck in. We tried, but the spoons wouldn't enter the fish eggs. The caviar was deep-frozen. Parmesh tried, but it was like concrete.

'I'm sure it's fine. We'll just wait. I'm sure it's fine. It's fine. We can eat this. It's fine. I'm sure it's fine.'

Thankfully, Goldie was tired, and we were eventually allowed to go to bed.

Next morning we were woken by loud acid-house music which the staff had thought we might like, and for the next few days we were given the Parmesh air-conditioned tour of Mumbai. It seemed a source of annoyance to Parmesh that Goldie could not be separated from her team. We were taken to Bollywood sets and air-conditioned hotels where she had arranged for Goldie to be sold some jewellery. We drove past slums and mind-rasping poverty, past (and I'm sure sometimes over) thin dogs and thin people scraping a life from the streets.

We once asked a woman who was travelling in the front of the car how she felt about the poverty. Did she feel awkward, being so privileged?

'No,' she said. 'You see, the problem is they are just lazy. They could work if they wanted to, but they don't want to.'

At one point Ruby said to me, 'I never thought it would be like this, Jennifer.'

'What did you expect?'

'I thought it would be like the Caribbean.'

One night there was a party at Parmesh's. She had invited the rich and famous of Mumbai to meet Goldie (not her team). It was a hot night. Every night was a hot night. A few nights before, we had been invited out for dinner in a nearby house. We were expected to get there at midnight and food was not served until two o'clock in the morning, when it was about half a degree cooler.

Back at Parmesh's party, Ruby and I – dressed in almost nothing – were sweating. When we went out to join the party around the pool, we were amazed to see nearly all the guests in designer clothes. We weren't shocked because they were designer; we were shocked because most of them came from the winter collection. Leather jackets and trousers and high leather boots.

Why weren't they expiring? Ruby and I were losing hydration at gallons a second and these people appeared cool and calm, done up head to toe in Dolce & Gabbana.

Parmesh smothered us with hospitality, but by the time we had got over our jet lag and it was time to leave, Ruby and I were glad to go. We needed to lose the air-conditioning and smell India. Our next stop certainly opened the nostrils.

We flew to Varanasi, a city further north in Uttar Pradesh. It is one of the oldest cities in India, and one of the oldest continuously inhabited cities in the world. It is also the holiest of the seven sacred cities in Hinduism and Jainism, and Hindus believe that if you die in Varanasi you will achieve salvation. It is, in effect, its spiritual centre.

If we wanted culture shock, this was it. Varanasi is a riot of colour and smells; it buzzes like a beehive. The streets are jammed with rickshaws and taxis, and the alleyways leading down to the river are crowded and alive. Because it is traditional to burn dead bodies on pyres by the river and then scatter the ashes on the water, there is always a slight whiff in the air of barbecued corpse; often we would pass families in the streets carrying a stiff relation down to the water's edge. I saw a corpse strapped to the roof of a car that was driving towards the town; the blanket that was covering it had blown free and just the dead old feet were poking out over the windscreen. (I think there's something rather good about that. My grandmother Gan Gan always said she didn't want any fuss at all when she died and would be quite happy to be put on the bonfire.)

In Varanasi we began to understand India a little, and Ruby became smitten. After an awkward moment with some lepers on our first day, she was hooked. One day, she and I were in a taxi being taken back to the hotel when the driver stopped at a crossroads. He turned and spoke to us.

'OK, if we turn left, we go to Rajasthan and Pakistan, and if we go right, we go to Nepal. Where are we going?'

We chose straight on, back to the hotel, please. But at that moment I could understand how so many hippies and travellers get stuck in this place and never come home. We could have gone anywhere. And the truth is, it somehow felt very safe.

Now we are on the boat, and it is one of our last nights in Varanasi. Goldie's assistant, Teri, is not looking well.

Teri came to India with all her own food. She had a large suitcase full of ready-made meals. She was, she said, on a diet – but I suspect she was actually just a little unwilling to eat native. She was tall and robust but also a little nervous.

One day, when we were having our palms read by a man down by the ghats, I picked up a bottle of water that I assumed was mine and took a few big swigs. When I looked at it, I realized that it wasn't mine. It was water, but murky water, and the inside of the bottle was green with algae. I had drunk Ganges water; water that contained every kind of human and animal excretion, dead bodies, spat-out toothpaste and soap. Plus anything else that might have slopped in upstream.

I showed Ruby.

'Jennifer, you are going to die.'

I stayed calm, but was dreading the night ahead and what might come out of either end. It seemed inevitable that something would occur. Then, as we were all walking back to the street to find a rickshaw, an extraordinary thing did occur.

Ruby and I were walking some way behind Teri and Goldie. We saw them stride past a thin slip of a dog that was coiled up at the side of the road like a snake. As they passed, it stirred, uncoiled and, in one quick movement, leaped up and sank its teeth into Teri's bottom. Having committed this act, it then sauntered off down the street, leaving Teri in shock.

She had been bitten by a dog. IN INDIA.

We rushed back to the house of the fortune teller (who had somehow missed this event on Teri's palm). Teri took down her trousers and let us examine the wound. Yes, it was a bite, but no, it had not broken the skin. Trousers up, we went in search of a rickshaw to take us to our hotel, where we could get more advice. My drinking-of-the-Ganges-water had taken back seat to this full-blown emergency.

We could only find one rickshaw and the driver told us all to pile in. He was a thin man pedalling an ancient rickshaw with four very well-fed women in the back. Uphill. The journey got slower and slower, until eventually Ruby got out and decided to push. And now another extraordinary thing occurred. A passing cow, with exceptional hornage, butted her up the bum. I mean, what are the chances?

Back at the hotel, Teri – who had grown paler and paler on the journey – went to her room and took medical advice. This was a woman who previously would never even take a head-ache pill.

I, meanwhile, went to my room and drank a bottle of whisky. My mother had always said it was good for killing things, so I took her advice. Apart from a cracking hangover, I never suffered any repercussions.

I was quite pissed when we were summoned to Teri's room later. She was standing there with a Sikh doctor who had been recommended by the hotel. Teri came towards us and whispered, 'Does this guy look like a doctor to you?'

When we had all agreed that he did in fact look like a doctor, she was happy and proceeded with the consultation.

The doctor was going to order the anti-rabies drugs, and for the rest of the trip, poor Teri had to inject. That evening, she wasn't well. I think she was in shock. India had risen up and bitten her in the ass, Ruby pointed out.

Goldie told us that she had given her some of her own antibiotics in case it helped.

'Antibiotics for what?' we asked.

'Cystitis.'

Really?

The world had, for one day, gone totally bonkers.

To get to our next stop – Delhi – we took a small Sahara Airways plane from Varanasi. It was a rickety old plane, and because neither Ruby nor Goldie is a happy flier, I was forced to be strong. Ruby gripped my hand with a tight claw, and I told her it was going to be fine. The turbulence was strong and we started bouncing, but no one else seemed particularly concerned. I think it's always a good idea to examine the face of stewards for any flicker of nerves. But everyone seemed happy.

I don't like flying. Never have. This is odd, mainly because I am the speed-junkie daughter of an RAF pilot. But the truth is, I simply don't understand how an aeroplane stays up in the air. And I feel slightly afraid that every negative thought I'm having will be unscrewing a small rivet in the engine. Positive thinking, positive thinking. Dawn has a different method of keeping herself alive: she imagines a pair of hands holding the plane up all the way to its destination.

About half an hour into our journey, the turbulence seemed to be getting worse. I looked out of the window and all I could see ahead of us were mountains of monsoon clouds. Huge grey mountains.

Plane very bouncy by now. Ruby drawing blood.

The pilot came over the speaker to reassure us in a jovial and calming manner.

'Ladies and gentlemen, as you are aware, we are experiencing some strong turbulence. I have been trying to divert, but I'm afraid that there are monsoon clouds in front of us and monsoon clouds to the side, so (*small chuckle*) we must just carry on and resign ourselves to our fate.'

There was a moment's kerfuffle from Ruby and some shouting,

but all settled down and we bounced our way to Delhi inside a storm cloud.

I have never been a fan of people who applaud when a plane lands (it is mainly done by Italians, I think), but when that pilot landed that plane, we were cheering and giving a standing ovation.

We stayed a few days in Delhi. At the hotel, I got faxes from Ade and the girls. I don't know what Beattie had been reading about India.

27 October 1997

Dear Mummy,

It's quite cold in Devon. Nothing is really happening and it's quite boring.

It took us six hours to get from London to Devon!! There was lots of traffic and daddy got very angry. I bet it's very hot in India with all the cows walking around eating people's potatoes.

We are going down to Chagford today so we can see how Eddie is getting on.

(p.s. I miss you) xxx love Beattie xxxxxxxx

And from Ella:

27 October 1997

Dear Mummy,

I am missing you loads! Daddy is missing you to.

Beryl was sick in the car on the way down to Devon, I'm not really surprised though because it took 6 hours to get to Devon, because of some stupid road works. We were patient and entertained our selfs with sweets.

I hope you are having fun and aren't to tiered. And I can't wait to see you again. Floppy is going to have his teeth clipped soon. But whisky and beryl are fine.

Keep in touch
Lots of love from

Ella xxxxOOOOxxxOOOxxx
Ελλα (in greek)

Ade sent a fax explaining that he hadn't really been that cross in the car.

I did miss them. And Whisky and Beryl are dogs, by the way, the Border terriers we had at that time. Whisky was named by Ade, and Beryl was named after my comic-strip heroine, Beryl the Peril. Beryl was often sick in the car. We used to try to cover every available surface in old towels, but she would still manage to throw up down the back of a seat, or once into the holes by the automatic gearstick. She was probably more afraid of messing up the lovely clean towels.

After Delhi, we took a train north to Rishikesh, 'the gateway to the Himalayas'. Rishikesh was where the Beatles hung with the Maharishis, and it is considered the centre for all types of yoga and indeed yogi.

We visited Hindu temples and Buddhist temples. It felt so different from the chaos of Varanasi and the smog of Delhi. The Ganges powers through the town, fresh and cold, and there is little traffic. Mainly, the whole place is overrun with monkeys and cows.

Our job on this trip was to take in the atmosphere and come up with ideas for the film. We tried. We really tried. On the surface, it all seemed so simple. We had a story, and now we had the basis of plenty of funny material, and Goldie was pretty straightforward. I still can't believe we made our lives so complicated. We were already two months past the month that Ruby said it would take.

From Rishikesh we drove for one night further up into the Himalayas, where we stayed in a small hotel. It had a few rooms and beautiful views out over the white water of the Ganges in the valley below. No other guests.

In the evening, Ruby and I joined Goldie in a moment of reflection and meditation in a beautiful room overlooking the gardens. Now, I like a bit of reflection and meditation and I'm not impartial to a bit of yoga, occasionally, but Goldie wanted us to 'ommmmmmmmm'.

With her.

To 'ommmmmmmmm'.

Ruby 'ommmmmmmmmmed', but I just couldn't find the 'om' in me.

Ruby looked at me.

'Jennifer, om!'

I look back on it and wonder why I couldn't 'om'. I feel the whole project would have worked if I could just have raised one decent 'om'.

Poor Goldie Hawn.

Thirteen

The Laws of Procrastination have been the bane of my life. The laws that say 'Don't panic!', that say every second not spent doing the task is 'thinking time', time spent 'getting ammunition'. After all, how can you write without having things to write about? Get out there and experience life! Unfortunately, in my case, that really just involves taking the dog for a walk, sweeping, or watching *Flog It!* and anything with 'Antiques' in the title.

Take my first day of writing this book, for example. To start it, I took myself off to our cottage on Dartmoor. It was raining heavily outside and the sheep in the field in front were tucked under thorn trees, out of the wind. There is no Internet in the cottage and no television and it is very quiet (save for the weather). All I could do was write. There wasn't even a view to distract me; it was as if I was inside a cloud.

When I arrived in the morning, I discovered that there were dead flies all over the floor, so I had to hoover for quite a while. This was entirely necessary because – according to the Laws of Procrastination – you cannot start work if there is an obvious job undone. And that job can be anything from tidying all yer drawers to washing everything in the whole house, including people.

I suctioned up every dead fly, some cobwebs, some crumbs and some coffee granules. If it hadn't been for the rain, I might have headed out and hoovered the field.

I had brought my phone with me for emergencies, so, after the clean-up, I did feel that I deserved a couple of games of Bejeweled (a terribly addictive time-waster), one round of Scrambler (time-wasting, but good for the brain and the offset of dementia), and I did some very important texting before putting the phone on silent and opening the computer.

I had very nearly put my fingers on the keyboard when coffee came into my head. I always write best on coffee. So I thought it necessary to make some. Just black coffee. Coffee with milk makes me feel sick. So just a cafetière of black coffee. Marvellous.

I sat back down at the table with my computer open and allowed myself just a little time looking at my screensaver, which is a picture of my grandson, Freddie Furlong. He is only nine months old as I write, and very lovely. Before I knew it, I was looking at photos of him on my phone. I have literally hundreds of him, but with the self-discipline of a master of self-discipline, I eventually found the strength, after half an hour, to put the phone away, face down on the table. Face down and on silent. I will NOT be governed by the phone looking at me and ringing me up and taunting me with useful apps and the possibility of Twitter.

Drank some coffee. Had a little think.

I now had Twitter in my head. Just had to check my 'Followers' count. I didn't Tweet because I thought someone who knew

me and knew I should be writing would see that I had been distracted and have a go at me later.

I put Twitter away. Pushed phone away again. The taunting,
teasing devil phone.

I needed to move away from it. So I had a wander with my
mug and looked out of the window.

Had quite a long think about sheep's wool and lanolin and
how it used to be in lots of hand and face creams when I was
growing up, until they discovered that it encouraged hair
growth. That was discovered too late for many a hairy-handed,
bearded woman, unfortunately, but now it's about as welcome
as parabens in beauty products.

Then the door of the cottage burst open and in came Freddie's dad, soaking wet and holding out some lunch for me that
he had brought up from the house. Home-made crab cakes
and salad. Good Lord! I wasn't going to have lunch. I was going
to work right through lunch. I hadn't got any food in the cottage
because food can be distracting, and my reward for working was
going to be a nice supper. I was going to work till six and then go
back to the house and have a glass of wine and supper.

'You don't have to eat it. I just thought you might like some,'
said Dan.

'Oh well, since you've come all the way up here,' said me.

'How are you getting on?'

Dan could see I was some distance from the computer.

'Really well. It's a really good place to work,' said me, con-
vincingly.

'You might want to light a fire.'

'No. I'm fine.'

I thanked him for the totally unnecessary food, and he left.

The crab cakes were delicious and I necked them quickly. I was
very hungry, as it turned out. I was anxious not to waste any
more time, but while eating the salad, I found a very small slug.

It seemed quite well, despite being covered in yoghurt dressing, and I let it roam free around the bowl. It was a fascinating slug with an interesting face.

As I watched the slug, I felt the temperature of the room drop and I thought to light a fire before getting down to writing. Yes. To light a fire. No point starting and then getting cold and then stopping to light a fire. Light it now. Do it now! So I did.

I tried to light it quickly, get it going and then not sit and watch it. That takes some willpower. I found that willpower after a mere twenty minutes, when I managed to tear myself away and returned to the table.

The slug was now on the table and not looking at all well. It had dried slightly and curled into a ball, like the inside of a winkle. I felt very guilty because I had quite liked the slug.

I picked it up and put it outside the door, into the rain. Perhaps it would revive. It seemed to uncurl and, for a moment, there was hope. But then the rain just pounded the poor slug and turned it into mush.

An unspecified time later, with not a single word written, I got up from the floor by the glass door I'd been peering through, only to discover that I had been sitting there so long that I had got terrible pins and needles. I was forced to hobble about for quite some time until my dead legs relented and I could return to the computer.

This is actually PATHETIC. And not only does it drive other people mental, but it also drives me mad. I want that feeling of having done it, of having signed it off, of pressing Send on a whole document of writing that has been done on time.

I try to pretend that this is the way it has to be. This is the way I work. Last minute means it has energy and life and, to a certain extent, this is true. With a sitcom. Handing it in late does mean that there is less time for other people to poke their noses into it, but it really has always been living by the seats of many pairs of pants.

27. Ade and me in Australia with the Comic Strip. We're not actually going out at this point.

28. Cheer up! In the Caribbean on holiday with Ade while our wedding is being organized.

29. 11 May 1985. Wedded.

30. The reception. My father actin' the fool with a make-up brush, with Dawn over-actin' the fool behind.

31. Rik, my god-daughter Cordelia, me, Ade and Robbie Coltrane on the ground.

32. My agent Maureen Vincent at our wedding.

33. At the wedding. Robbie Coltrane and Jools Holland. What a lovely couple they made.

34. Honeymoon. Photo taken by camera on timer, not by chambermaid.

35. Ade and me with Ella when she was just one year old.

36. Dawn and me as Anne and George in Five Go Mad in Dorset.

37. Peter Richardson, the man behind the Comic Strip.

38. *Girls on Top*: Dawn, Joan Greenwood, Ruby Wax, Tracey Ullman and me. I've got my Mr Bean face on.

39. Now that's what I call lighting!

40. The Menopazzi Sisters. Please note tassels on back of leotards.

41. This photo needs no caption.

42. Live tour in 2000. Dressing room at Hammersmith Odeon, doing phone interviews.

43. On tour. Make-up removal on coach.

44. Madonna!

45. 'Braveheart'. Never happier than when in a chest wig and beard.

46. 'Star Wars'. Me with my girls Ella, Beattie and Freya as very cheap supporting artists. Note beard but no chest wig. What a howler!

47. *Ab Fab*, France. Joanna Lumley and me on a break from filming.

48. Ah, the sixties! Joanna, Zandra Rhodes, meself, Lulu and Britt Eckland.

49. In New York. Hideously overdressed to receive LGBT award.

50. With Graham Norton at the International Emmys. I'm sportin' a huge flower given to me by Anita Pallenberg.

51. Edina with God (Marianne Faithfull) and the Devil (Anita Pallenberg). Both are actually goddesses.

52. In Varanasi with Ruby Wax.

53. Trying to amuse Goldie Hawn in Delhi.

54. With the divine Catherine Deneuve. Abberlofabberlo.

55. During *L'Entente Cordiale*. Serious face.

56. At *Shrek* screening in Cannes with the ridiculously tall Rupert Everett.

57. En route to baldness.

58. Bald.

59. Ella's wedding. Dan, her husband, standing to my left.

Yet I have seemingly got away with it.

There has never been a show that couldn't be made because the script wasn't written. Although it's been close a few times. Especially with *Ab Fab*.

I've written on the train on my way to London on the morning of a read-through. I've dictated scripts to my kids to write down as I'm driving. I've sat up all night writing till I'm hypothermic and the word count is at a standstill and I can hear the dawn chorus.

Birds tweetin' means time is almost up.

It's really not a good way to be. Detrimental to one's health.

There was one time, however, that I really didn't get away with it.

Dear reader, I am now going to show you the faxes that passed between Goldie and her assistant Teri, and me and Ruby, after our return from India in 1997. These were faxes.

Pre-India visit, we were pretty chipper. We had written a chunk of the beginning of the film. We had changed the title from 'Ashes' to 'Baby Love' and changed Goldie's character's name from 'Goldie' to 'Baby'. The premise was good: she loses her husband but finds herself.

Jennifer, we can do this in a month!

FAX TO: Goldie and Teri (upon their return)
FAX FROM: Jennifer Saunders

Dear Miss Goldie Hawn and Miss Teri Schwartz,

Thank you and goodbye. Words that should have been unshipped from my mouth in the Departure Lounge, had we not somehow missed each other. But as Ruby – yes Ruby! – said, 'It means the circle is not closed, it was meant to be!' I agreed. We are both a little changed.

I hope your trip back was happy and un-gruelling and turbulence free. I did have to somewhat resign myself to my fate on BA due to a woman retching into sick bag behind me *all night long*. There's never a healing spirit around when you want one.

London was a shock – very cold and a natural fog thicker than the pollution in Delhi. Extraordinary. I stood at a station to get a train to Devon and my fingers turned into Pop-sicles – too many suitcases, too few clothes and Popsicle fingers.

In Devon, crisp leaves were falling from the trees – sounding like heavy rain – echoes of the Glasshouse.

India was extraordinary.

Missing you already.

Swami Jen xxxx

Yes, India was extraordinary. But it wasn't a holiday! It had a purpose. To make us write. WRITE. Write the story Goldie wanted . . .

FAX TO: Jennifer Saunders
FAX FROM: Goldie Hawn

Got your uplifting message – yes, back home with *all* the trimmings! I fade daily at 2 p.m. and drift into uncon-sciousness.

The trip was a step in time! And I had more fun and laughs. My spirit spins back to numerous moments shared, so free, so unencumbered.

You are a fine woman, Mrs Jennifer Saunders. And will make an exceptional swami in your next life.

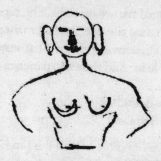

Can't stop thinking and '*dreaming*' of the final musical number. I did it for Kurt in the kitchen and he laughed *hard*! It's brave and really good.

The sun is shining in my meditation room and illuminating all of my sacred artifacts from previous visits. Let it shine on you too.

Love you.

Miss the laughs.

Goldie

We did have laughs. Plenty of laughs. And the musical number was something that Ruby came up with for the end of the film. I think it began with some flies on a cowpat in India, and the flies are doing something like a Busby Berkeley number. Then the camera pulls back to reveal a full Bollywood production on the ghats in Varanasi, with even the dead rising up from the pyres to join in. I think that was the gist. Goldie loved it. So now we had an ending. We had also been given some pretty clear notes from Goldie on what she wanted to see in the script and what we needed to do.

The script was too serious and her audience would definitely expect it to be quirkier. She wanted the character lighter. She said that there was no point in her playing a WASP. She wanted the character to be alone at some point and to have to rely on the goodness and spiritual nature of India. She repeated the story of the disabled friend to us; the one she had managed to dance with. We were under no illusions any more. That story had to go in. We had to get the cripple in. And time and patience were running out.

FAX TO: Jennifer Saunders
FAX FROM: Teri Schwartz

We think about you and the trip all the time – what a time we had! Goldie and I thought – how about a date, a goal if you will, for the script to be sent to us. How does Dec. 15 work? It would be great to have it to read by the 15th, before the holidays while the experience is still fresh and bubbling in your memory.

Look forward to hearing from you.

Love and good cheer

Teri

Oh dear. I have a deadline. I don't like deadlines. I don't like them at all.

FAX TO: Teri Schwartz
FAX FROM: Jennifer Saunders

Dear Teri,

All faxes received and understood by we the newly enlightened.

Good idea! Ruby back today and we will restart the progression.

Dec 15th v. good date – mainly because it is before Xmas and to clear the desk before the festivities would be excellent and also I'm taking the kids to N. York for 5 days on the 13th which I had set in my mind as a deadline anyway. So full steam ahead etc etc.

OK. So – we will press on – pull up our slacks and give the brain a bit of oil and the computer a bit of a good old poundin'. Tinkerty tonk.

Jennifer x

I don't know why I decided to write to them as if I was Bertie Wooster. It's not good though, is it, dear reader? These people were paying us. Paying us! They had taken us to INDIA. And now I was trying to be blasé and cheery and tinkerty tonk. And did we oil our brains and pound the old computer? Heigh-ho and tonkerty tonk, no, we did not. And I am ashamed to say it goes on and on.

FAX TO: Teri Schwartz
FAX FROM: Jennifer Saunders c/o The Slow Brain Trust

Dear Teri,

I'm so sorry I didn't call you back last night but there was a momentously important football match on. Manchester Utd (my team) v. Juventus (Italian champions). We won, which is the only reason I can write today with a sharp nibbed pen without stabbing it into my thigh! I then came up to the office and worked late – YES I DID – and wrote some good bonsai jokes.

My fax no is 0181 332 —. You can pester me on my fax and on my phone. I know you are probably very furious waiting for more paper offerings and I am dotting the 'i's' and crisping up the next batch. I hope you like the opening.

Jx

Please bear in mind that we are just days off the deadline. Did I pound the computer? No, I didn't. I watched football. Now, it is true that I do take my football extremely seriously. Manchester United has been my team since I was at school. And this *was* an important European match. But even I am shocked at the nerve. 'I hope you like the opening'? They had read the opening before! All we had ever sent them was the opening. The bonsai jokes were four pages in. All we had was the opening . . .

FAX TO: Teri Schwartz
FAX FROM: Jennifer Saunders

Dear Teri,

I know you're expecting it and it is coming – I had a slight rethink – it was turning into a Bergman film and Ruby is back this week and I *really* want to go over things with her. *Please* forgive. I am sending you the first few pages so you see something is in existence and it may be a hint of the style etc. A canapé for you.
    More soon, I promise.
    Please still like me.

    Your Jennifer

Please still like me! Pathetic. I am PATHETIC.

They have had a morsel and a canapé and I should now be shot. They get nothing more before Christmas and it becomes fairly tense. I mean, Christmas is always busy and there's so much to organize, and I did have the trip to New York planned with the girls. Actually, it was a lovely trip. Just me and the girls staying in a penthouse suite at the Four Seasons, which I had got for free courtesy of *Ab Fab* Perks Ltd. We climbed up the Statue of Liberty, skated in Central Park and ate epic breakfasts at the Plaza, but my fingers never touched a keyboard once.

After New Year, I had a phone call from Goldie, who told me to come to New York. She had to be there for a few days and we were to bring all the writing we had done and stay there until we had finished the script.

As it happened, Ruby couldn't make it, so I went there alone.

I thought, if the worst came to the worst, I could write it on the plane.

FAX TO: Miss Goldie Hawn
FAX FROM: Jennifer Saunders
DATE: xx January 1998

Dear Goldie,

My flight gets into New York JFK at 11.40. It is British Airways. Later than I thought due to British-Summer-Winter-Greenwich-Meantime and gaining and losing hours at whim it seems.

Happy to pick up the cost of flight through my company – we owe you that much by now at least *I am sure*.

Spoke with Ruby today; she gave me enough notes over the phone to keep me re-writing non-stop this weekend.

Look forward to seeing you on Monday.

Love
Jennifer

Unfortunately, the writing-on-the-flight plan was foiled by free Champagne. The flight cost so much, it seemed a shame not to enjoy it. And so I did. I was feeling very nervous when the announcement came that we were about to land, so I started desperately going through my excuses in my head. If, during my life, I had spent half as much time writing as I have making excuses for not writing, things might have been very different indeed.

Now, I am good at bullshit when I need to be, but I had a definite feeling that I was about to be found out. It was an almost out-of-body experience. Dead man walking. I hadn't done the work. I had drunk Champagne.

I wished Ruby had been with me. She would have written on the plane and she would know what to say to Goldie.

Her apartment was many, many floors up, on top of a

building overlooking Central Park. Little did I know, as I took the lift up, that I wouldn't be taking it back down again any time soon. Goldie was suitably disappointed by the lack of script and was fairly stern. I had brought her no pages. Nothing printed at all. The little I had was in the laptop. I had not done my home-work and I was to be kept in until I did do it.

I sat at my computer for three days. I didn't go out. I wasn't allowed out.

My work was checked at regular intervals and I was fed and watered and allowed toilet breaks. Goldie stationed herself where she could see me, and always between me and the door. Sometimes she sat at the door. I was going nowhere.

If Goldie went out, she didn't leave me a key.

I wrote and wrote.

After three days, the routine loosened up a bit and I was taken one evening to see *The Lion King*, which had just opened on Broadway. I had been a good girl and I got a treat.

I wrote some more and Goldie added things all the time. She did try to introduce the cripple gently into the script, but I knew that my life wouldn't be worth living if Ruby read it. We already had too much going on.

By the end of the week, the script had filled out. I was just writing to order, which is how it should always have been. The problem was, we weren't cutting anything as we went and the script had become an epic. A seven-hour epic. It was three different films: a film about a woman coping with grief, a film about a woman coping with the menopause and a film about how hilarious India can be. A couple of days later, we were almost done and I was allowed another treat. I was taken to see Eartha Kitt at the Café Carlyle. Eartha was marvellous. She was seventy-one and did a full backbend over a chair in the finale.

Goldie was very kind – is very kind – and she is a huge star. Being out in New York with her jolted me back to reality. She wanted this film to work because she was fifty and roles for women of that age in Hollywood are rare. Meryl Streep and Diane Keaton had them covered. This was a very personal film for her as well; it was about so much that she loved in India. This woman has a meditation room. She gives great 'om'. This film was to be an expression of Goldie.

After five days, I was released and allowed to come home.

FAX TO: Goldie Hawn
FAX FROM: Jennifer Saunders
DATE: 22 January 1998

Miss Hawn!

Have just come up to the office and picked up your fax. The builders are in here at the moment so I am working from the house – where the telephone is broken – ho hum! There is a new number in the house which is 181 408 —.

The feeling is mutual re our time in New York. All good – all progressing.

Freya was off school today and put on *The Lion King* video and it bought back to me how breathtaking that show was – I am determined to get the kids to it somehow.

It was such a joy – and thank you for NY – nicest kick up the ass ever had.

Speak soon

Love Jennifer

Yes, the kick up the ass had worked to a certain extent, but now the script was a mess. And neither Ruby nor I knew what to do with it. Plus, it had been going on so long that other things in our lives had begun to take over and take priority.

FAX TO: Goldie Hawn
FAX FROM: Jennifer Saunders
DATE: 28 January 1998

Goldie, Goldie, Goldie!

Please excuse errant behaviour. When I spoke to you at the weekend I forgot I had a pre-standing filming commitment for 3 days this week. As it turns out it's these 3 days and they are rather long – my mind was elsewhere.

Today however I get back at a reasonable hour and will do the computer print fax thing.

Rest assured that every spare moment I am ensconced in Winnebago with portable.

Apologies. I will consider myself stared at angrily.

Love J x

FAX TO: Goldie Hawn
FAX FROM: Jennifer Saunders
DATE: 1 February 1998

Dear Goldie,

I faxed you some pages late on Friday so you should have up to page 94. If not let me know as my machine often puts them through in clumps and I was not here as it was faxing.

I have read through it and it is not good. *I know* it is not good – soulless and no direction but I am pressing on to the end and will go back then.

Anyhow – I'm ploughing on and can't apologize enough for last week.

Lesson is always limit your availability even to very old good friends or get stuck for 6 days in the most extremely horrible conditions – no discernible organization or heat source or part. Ugly place, ugly costume, ugly face – ugly actress by end of week.

So cross. *So* angry. So sorry.

Don't hate me. Hate self enough for all our needs.

Will drink bottle of whisky and give this 'looking for Ravi' stuff some semblance of writing.

Think of you hourly.

J x

FAX TO: Jennifer Saunders
FAX FROM: Goldie Hawn
DATE: 7 February 1998

Darling girl,

Call me and send me what you have got. You owe me some pages this Monday. Let me know what you think and we can discuss it.

I love you and think of you and because I have these sentiments I refuse to let you rest! Work! Work! Write *shit* if you have to, just WRITE!

XXX

FAX TO: Goldie Hawn
FAX FROM: Jennifer Saunders
DATE: 9 February 1998

Baby Delivery Report for Attention of Mrs Hawns (eventual mother)

Monday, February 9th a.m. Labour now reaching third stage and progressing speedily and satisfactorily. Head showing and surrogate mother's pushing hard now – much dabbing brows and screaming. Small whisky administered for pain-killing purposes.

Full urgency of situation appreciated.

Baby well over-due and must get out by end of week to increase chances of survival.

Forceps at the ready. As soon as it's out it is yours to breastfeed. It is a heavy one with a light-weight personality – much like its surrogate mother's.

Yours Drs Sandwich & Johnson.

We did give birth to a baby of sorts: a mess of a baby weighing in at eighteen pounds. It was sent to Goldie, and then Ruby and I were summoned to LA. We were put up in a lovely hotel in Santa Monica which was close to Goldie's office. We met with Goldie several times, sometimes at her house and sometimes in her trailer on the set of *The Out-of-Towners*, which she was filming with Steve Martin.

We were in her trailer talking about the main character.

'You see, I think she needs more . . .'

'. . . jewellery.'

I looked at Ruby and Ruby looked at me. I had now lost the plot.

We went back to the hotel.

We walked on the beach and Ruby did some rollerblading. We sat by the pool and drank. We went back to our rooms and got a note to say that Teri would be ringing us. I went to Ruby's room.

Ruby took the call.

It was brief.

'Hello, Teri.'

'Hi. Listen, Goldie wants to know . . . Is there *any* way you can get the cripple into the village?'

Ruby repeated the line to me and I shook my head.

It was over.

No further correspondence.

Well, that is, until recently, when Goldie and I met in London and found that, all these years later, it was actually possible to laugh about it. Just. Only just.

fourteen

I blame the chickens. The mesmerizing chickens.

When you own chickens, they defy you just to feed them. They draw you into their little world of characters, rivalries and absurdities. It is the most addictive soap opera.

You wake up thinking chicken: wondering if the Light Sussex has been allowed on the perch that night, or whether the crazy bantam with the headdress is still being bullied by the Wyandotte. Will the Rhode Island Red ever lay an egg? Will the ex-battery hens ever be fully accepted? Most importantly, will Kat and Alfie ever get back together again?

★

Explanation. In 1999 Ade and I moved the family from Richmond to Devon. It was a quick decision and one that we have never regretted.

For years, Ade and I had been looking for a small place in Devon, somewhere close to Peter and Marta Richardson, in the area we knew and loved from making the Comic Strip films with them.

I saw it first in *Country Life*, where it was described as a 'Small Gentleman's Manor'. Ade was not exactly a small gentleman, and it was further north on Dartmoor and bigger than the weekend cottage we were after. But I liked the look of it. I rang up the estate agent, who said it had been taken off the market. Yet it still wouldn't leave my head. I hadn't even driven past it, but there was something about it that I just loved. It is a traditional granite Devon longhouse that would once have been a farm, perfect for small gents and indeed a small family. A few hundred yards from the moor.

As luck would have it, it came back on the market. We viewed it on a misty, damp Dartmoor day in the autumn, when the rain dripped from trees that were heavy with lichen. The view was obscured by a cloud, and the stream that runs right by the house was a torrent. Every surface was covered in thick, beautiful moss. Inside, the house was atmospheric. We were suddenly in a Thomas Hardy novel – the new folk pushing in on old ghosts. We were drawn in.

We bought it, dear reader. I have never been sentimental about houses; I've always felt that I could move on and start anew very easily (a hangover from my childhood, I suspect). But I honestly don't think we could ever let go of our Devon house. It is the house that the girls think of as home.

We moved there permanently because we felt that the girls – Ella, in particular – needed the freedom that Devon would provide. She had expressed the desire to run on the moor and ride ponies. We didn't realize quite how keen the others would be. We were anxious, particularly, about Beattie, who was very happy in Richmond. We needn't have worried.

US: We're thinking of moving to Devon.
BEATTIE: OK.
US: OK?
BEATTIE: Yes, if we can do it quickly.
US: But won't you miss your friends? I mean, you've known most of them since nursery.
BEATTIE: Most of them haven't been my friends for quite a long time, actually.

Freya was easy too. So that was it.

We then set about creating our own menagerie. Ade went from being a man who could only just about tolerate a small dog to a man enjoying two dogs, a few cattle, a small herd of sheep, ponies, a rabbit and the crazy cast of chicken *EastEnders*.

We lived on 'Devon time', time that can make hours pass in mysterious ways. Some days, I would take the girls to the school bus, get home, muck out a stable, and then it would be time to pick them up again. Sweeping, pottering in the garden and day-dreaming whiled away the hours.

The girls all rode and had ponies and enjoyed the same freedom that I had had when I was growing up. If one of them had said, 'I am going for a walk up on to the moor for an hour or so on my own,' I would almost certainly have said, 'No, that's not safe.' But if they were going up on to the moor on a large, some-times unpredictable animal, my response was more relaxed: 'Of course you may!'

The lanes to the house are narrow and, although there is a farm and another house close by, it is off the beaten track. The loudest noise you will hear is the mooing of cows, or the occa-sional tractor. Apart from friends and locals, no one knew we were there, or indeed cared. Why should they? Which is why I was so very cross, in fact enraged, when the *Daily Mail* decided to send a helicopter over the house to get some pictures. The minute I saw it, I knew, and my heart pounded with fury as it came low and flew round and round. What I really wanted to do was go out and flick 'V's and throw things, but I managed to contain myself.

Another time I was out with one of the girls in the lanes. She was on a pony and I was on a bicycle, and we were heading back to the house. We turned a corner and saw a car blocking the lane a little way ahead. It seemed odd and, as we got closer, a man leaped out of the driver's side with a big camera and started snapping. We couldn't get by, so had to turn and run away and hide until he had gone.

I was FURIOUS. I wanted to punch him. Eventually, when we thought he had gone, we made our way back to the house. I told Ade, who set off on a hunt for him, but couldn't find him. We imagined he had left. But then I saw him in a field, sneaking around the house, snapping and snapping.

I saw red, shouted, and yes – as a person of my generation does – flicked the 'V'.

That was the pic that appeared in the papers: Grumpy Rude Person. In the *Mirror*, it was the photograph that they ran on the Letters page with one person saying that it was *outrageous* that I should behave like that, that I should have more respect and act more graciously. After all, it was BBC licence fee payers' money funding my wages!

The reason I was angry was that Ade and I don't play the publicity game. We don't do premieres and red carpets and self-promotion. Up until then, the papers had left us pretty much alone. I don't want people knowing where I live, and what that photographer in the lane was doing was making it less safe for my children. I don't want creeps hanging around.

There. Said it. I did actually say it forcefully to a poor *Daily*

Mail journalist at a press thing some time later. He looked chastened and said that he would pass it on. I don't get angry often, but when I do, I really do. (I didn't flick the 'V's that time though, dear reader.)

Anyway, anyway. A few years after we bought the house, my parents uprooted from Cheshire and moved nearby. My father had retired and, on their own in the Grange, they felt that they were rattling about in it a bit. They had been regular visitors to our place and loved the area, particularly the people.

There is something special about our part of Devon. I think this is because it is that little bit far enough from London that it isn't overrun with commuters. None of the locals feel the need, therefore, to be insular. People are interested in you and pleased that you like the place; you are left alone but, subtly, your every move and sighting is being noted.

My parents bought a house close to the village and set about creating another beautiful garden. It is just above the cricket pitch, and in the summer their gardening was accompanied by the gentle crack of leather on willow and, on one memorable occasion, the not-so-gentle crack of Ashley Butler's Achilles tendon (it could be heard half a mile away). The years in the Air Force had made my parents experts at organizing a social life, and within a short time they had a close group of friends.

My brother Simon moved to the area too and became the landlord of the local pub. He really is the greatest facilitator of other people's good times, with the Joanna Lumley-like ability to have in-depth conversations with people he has never met. They always seem to know him.

Simon was living with my parents when my father fell ill with cancer. He was an incredible support for my mother and a steadfast nurse to my father.

In typical style, my father kept his extraordinary good humour throughout his illness. Thanks to his wonderful GP,

Pete, and local nurses, he was able to die peacefully at home. We sent his ashes up in a firework from the top of the hill in front of their house. It seemed appropriate for a man who loved to fly.

He is much missed, but often quoted in the family. His jokes live on with my girls. He would always lick his knife at the table, because they weren't allowed to – 'Nappa just licked his knife!' – or steal food off their plates when they weren't looking. He was a wonderful father and much-loved grandfather. This is the reading I chose for his funeral:

> The only life worth living is the adventurous life. Of such a life, the dominant characteristic is that it is unafraid. It is unafraid of what other people think . . . It does not adapt either its pace or its objectives to the pace and objectives of its neighbors. It thinks its own thoughts, it reads its own books. It develops its own hobbies, and it is governed by its own conscience. The herd may graze where it pleases or stampede where it pleases, but he who lives the adventurous life will remain unafraid when he finds himself alone.
>
> Raymond B. Fosdick

After we had moved to Devon we didn't abandon the London life. I was still doing the odd *Ab Fab* and *French and Saunders*. I would go up to the smoke regularly on the train. It generally *was* a race even just to get to the train, because getting to Exeter is a forty-minute journey, plus you have to take the parking and ticket-buying into consideration. I would leave twenty minutes for it. If Terry Wogan was on the radio before I hit Whiddon Down roundabout, I knew that I was certainly going to miss the train. I would have to start thinking up my excuses.

I never really planned to write a television series set in Devon. It just happened. The contributing factors were the following. Firstly I was full of disbelief that nobody had done a TV series based on the film *Calendar Girls*. Secondly I was sick of seeing the country portrayed on TV as being only full of people who were either 'oooh arrr!' or 'I say!' and nothing in between. Thirdly I had been struck by what an extraordinarily difficult situation widowhood is. Fourthly I had met Sue Johnston at my brother's pub and decided that I had to work with her.

Eventually, *Jam and Jerusalem* was born.

I wrote the pilot episode alone, but the rest of the series I wrote with Abi Wilson. I had first met Abi on a documentary that I was making about dance – as you do. She was working for the production company and we got on well. After that Abi would write to me occasionally, wondering if I needed anyone in a PA capacity or anything. When she sent me a letter saying that she was now working at the Money Channel, I knew we had to get her out of there.

It was 2000 and Dawn and I were about to go on tour. I thought it would be good to have Abi there as 'general factotum', which was, in fact, her initial job title. Dawn insisted on a formal interview and we demanded to see all her O-level certificates and swimming badges. All her paperwork was in order and she passed with flying colours.

By the time *Jam and Jerusalem* came along, Abi was my PA and general factotum. She had the same passion for the show and the subject matter as I did, and she is – goddammit – a bloody brilliant writer.

Everything about that show made us happy. The cast was made up of many brilliant women – Sue Johnston, Pauline McLynn, Joanna Lumley, Dawn French, Rosie Cavaliero, Suzy Aitchison (June Whitfield's daughter), Doreen Mantle, Maggie Steed, Salima Saxton, Sally Phillips – and a couple of wonderful men, Patrick Barlow and David Mitchell. Mandie Fletcher directed and Jo Sargent produced: also wonderful and also brilliant (so in fact everything was not just wonderful, it was also brilliant).

The setting was North Tawton in Devon, and if we weren't filming, we were sitting in my brother's pub, where Pauline would give us all a quick flash of her tits before calling it a night. Which was lovely. I've added lovely to the mix.

At first, I wasn't going to be in it, but as I was going to be there every day anyway, it seemed a bit silly not to be. I also managed to get most of my family in it, and horses and dogs.

It was such a happy show. We made it to try and show a good community – a funny community – where, basically, people make the best life being who they really are. Where young people and old people sit together in the pub. Where life isn't about money and position. The complete opposite of *Ab Fab*, but much closer to the world I was living in.

I miss that show. Shows are like families. You become very close very quickly, call each other darling, and then it's all over. I miss all the families.

I wish the BBC had given us another try. They cancelled it just as the ratings were getting good. The cast even offered to do it for less money. But no. Thumbs down from some twat in a meeting.

Heigh-ho.

The main problem for me, not doing *Ab Fab* any more, is that I no longer have a voice to say the things I shouldn't say.

For example: on the airbrushing of photographs. Yes please, if it's my face. If it's going to be my face almost actual size and taken very close up on the front of a magazine that is going to be in supermarkets and newsagents, then yes please, I want to be airbrushed. I don't let strangers that close to my face under normal circumstances. They keep their distance and see me in a nice light. I want a good photograph. Everyone knows it's just a photograph.

On the set of *The Life and Times of Vivienne Vyle*, a show that I wrote with Tanya Byron about a daytime confessional talk-show host, was to be a giant, blown-up photo of me. A photographer was sent to the rehearsal room and snapped me quickly in the wig. I was a bit worried because she didn't seem to have any heavy lights or, indeed, any expertise. But I thought they must be putting an effect on it. A filter. A graphic effect. Something.

I walked on to the set the first day and there was my face – fifteen foot high, at least. They had not put any effects on it. It was shiny and open-pored and creviced.

I screamed. It was airbrushed.

The writing of *Vivienne Vyle* had come about when Tanya had sent me an idea. We had first met in 2005 when Dawn and I asked her to be a guest on a series of *French and Saunders*. Tanya is a psychologist and had a show called *The House of Tiny Tearaways* on television, which we loved. In it, she dealt with children's various eating and behavioural disorders. We got her on to *French and Saunders* to give us that same treatment: to show where our behaviour was going wrong and how we should, to all intents and purposes, grow up.

We were nervous that she would find it all a bit too silly; she did, after all, have a proper job, she was Dr Tanya soon to be Professor Tanya, and we were just ridiculous people who hadn't even managed to write a script for her. She was, thankfully, more professional than us and had managed to devise her own script. Her job in our show was, along the lines of her show, to stop us regressing into silly childish behaviour and if necessary to intervene. I was Brigitte Nielsen and Dawn had one of her finest moments as Jackie Stallone. Tanya did a great job and only admitted afterwards that she had been in fact 'shitting it'. Her words, I promise you, not mine.

After that Tanya and I kept in touch and became friends. Her job fascinated me. Psychology is the best character study. I learned that pseudo dementia can simply be brought on by constipation (something to remember, and why I always have some prunes handy), and that I would probably not be good at her job because I'm a little low on empathy. I belong to the 'Just pull your socks up' school of thinking.

One day she plucked up the nerve to send me the idea for *Vivienne Vyle*. It was an idea she had had for a character, a day-time talk-show host along the lines of Jeremy Kyle, whom we were slightly obsessed with. Tanya had never written a comedy show before and was very naive. She arrived for the first day of writing, sat at the desk and got ready, fingers poised on the keyboard. How I laughed. That's not how you write comedy, you fool. You have to talk aimlessly for days, read magazines, go shopping and have quite a lot of lunch.

She soon got the idea.

Back in the chicken run there's been a bit of a disaster. Baddy fox has been and there may have to be a total recast.

fifteen

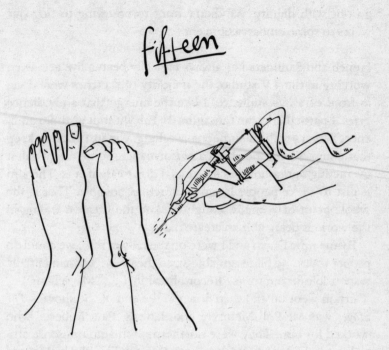

Dawn and I are in a tattoo parlour. In Auckland. She is in another room and sounds in pain.

It is 2009, the last leg of our final 'Still Alive' tour. We've been driving past this tattoo parlour with its bright neon sign every night, en route to the theatre. I don't know how it happened, but Dawn and I seem to have had the same idea at the same time. We had been trying to think of something to do to mark the end of the tour and, in effect, the end of the act.

For some reason – which on occasion we now regret – we had decided that, as we were 'getting on' and it was unlikely that any TV company would ever be able to provide us with a budget for another full *French and Saunders* series, we should go out with dignity. We didn't want to be trying to flog our wares to some embarrassing end.

French and Saunders has always basically been a live act. Even working in the TV studio, the majority of sketches were done in front of a live audience. I like the energy that an audience gives. I particularly can't imagine *Ab Fab* without a studio audience. When you hear someone laughing, you just want to keep that going. So you heighten a performance. Some might call it overacting but, as long as it works, I don't care if it is. The aim is just to make people laugh as much as possible. That is the whole point of comedy. Laughter. And the greatest feeling in the world is being able to create that.

By the time Dawn and I were on the telly in 1983, we could do proper tours and fill reasonable-sized theatres. The man initially responsible for our tours ('Record-breaking' . . . 'Marvellous' . . . 'Curtain went up and then down at the end of the show' – *The Stage*) was Mr Phil McIntyre and, latterly, Paul Roberts, who worked for him. They were northern, with a no-nonsense attitude and a lifelong commitment to Everton FC. Phil had toured *The Young Ones*, but wasn't really a theatre man. Up until then he had just toured heavy metal bands, so we were a piece of cake. Just Raw Sex, a few props, and some bangers and streamers before the interval, please.

We had a fairly fantastic time. It felt a little bit like rock 'n' roll. We had a coach and roadies. We stayed up late drinking, and keeping an eye on Rowland, who could be wild. In those days he drank a lot, but was banned from drinking (as I was) before or during a show. Afterwards he could get as pissed as he wanted.

He transgressed a few times. But only once did he make me so angry that I pushed him up against a wall with my hand on his neck and gave him an ultimatum.

'If you ever, and I mean EVER, do that again, you are off this tour.'

We did sometimes have to lay down the law.

One morning, both boys were late getting on the coach, and Dawn and I laid into them.

Paul Roberts looked up.

'Hey, lads . . . The bitches have turned.'

The bitches have turned. We had this printed on our tour jackets. It became the 'The Bitches Have Turned' tour.

Paul could always come up with a great phrase. One night on the 2000 tour he came into the dressing room a little puffed up and excited.

'Well, can I just tell you ladies that we have a special guest in tonight. I think you'll be rather pleased, as it is in fact The Cher herself.'

Indeed we were quite excited. We love The Cher. She actually once came to a recording of *Ab Fab* and I had had a feeling I had met her before.

'Oh yes. The lady herself is in tonight. Shall I organize for her to come back for a little drink?'

'Yes.'

'Marvellous. Ho ho. The Cher.'

Paul is normally a cool person. He is good-looking and charming. But he kind of lost it with The Cher.

She came backstage after the show. She's an old rock 'n' roller who doesn't mess.

Paul was ready with the Champagne, but Cher wanted a beer. This only increased his awe of her. He produced a beer, wearing a look of 'There you go, chap' on his face.

As we talked, he hovered, and we could tell he wanted to say something to The Cher. Probably along the lines of 'I think you're bloody great, and you're so normal, and I'm a big fan.' Eventually, he butted in.

'Nice belt, lady!'
That then became the catchphrase of the tour.
NICE BELT, LADY!

I actually love being on tour.

Every night is different. Sometimes it works; sometimes it doesn't. Quite often something crucial goes wrong. But it is always funny. And the best thing of all is that it keeps your ego in check. Because you can't ever expect or believe the applause. You have to earn it. You have to justify it. People have paid a lot of money and have often come a long way to see you; the very least that you can do in return is work hard for them. Because you are only ever going to be as good as your last show; and that, more than anything, keeps you on your toes.

The other thing about touring is that you are living in a little bubble. For weeks and weeks, everything is done for you. You are checked into hotels, your cases are taken care of, you're fed and entertained and absolutely everything is done to ensure you get on that stage in the best possible nick. Or, at the least, that you get on that stage.

I used to think that it was odd how, on film sets and in studios, the actors are fussed over the whole time; they just sit and have teas, coffees, newspapers and food brought to them, and they are constantly accompanied by a runner. Now I realize that this is simply practical. The production team want all the actors in one place, where they can see them, so that if they are required on set they can be got at quickly. You can't have actors wandering about, willy-nilly. They must be confined. And the same applies to being on tour: you have to be kept in sight at all times.

It is a strange life, and not one that partners or friends really fit into. A bubble. There was an unfortunate moment when Rowland brought his girlfriend of the time along. She was called Wendy, and she was the lead singer of Transvision Vamp. It threw us all into a spin. We had our nice routine worked out – who sat where on the bus, what we ate, what we talked about – and Wendy had her own ideas.

No, Wendy. Wendy, Wendy, Wendy. No. Lovely as you are. No.

It is hard when you go back to normal life too: it takes a while to settle back into family routine. Javier Bardem once said that the hardest thing about working away from home for months was returning home and being expected to fit back in straight away. You gradually acclimatize. It's a bit like winning a goldfish at the fair. You take it home in its little bag of water, but you don't immediately tip it into the tank. First you float the bag with the fish in it in the tank so that the temperature equalizes. Then, after an hour or so, you release the fish.

Often too much is expected of you when you are still in the bag.

To be honest, Dawn and I always did relatively civilized tours, and by the time we had children, we would organize small breaks and sensible travel arrangements so that we could get home as often as possible.

We did girls' tours.

No, we won't do Glasgow and then Swansea the next night, Paul. We would like to work our way down the country in a relaxed and pleasant manner, please, with a couple of nights off every now and then. (Crew love it though. They like nothing better than a 'get out' late, a drive through the night with no sleep, and a 'get in' the next day fuelled by Red Bull.)

So, I love working live. I love theatres. But with one exception: I just don't like doing plays. I should point out, at this point, that I have only ever done one play. But it just wasn't my thing.

Dawn loves plays, loves acting in plays, and is bloody good at it. It is just not for me.

The only play that I did was one Dawn and I did together. It was called *Me and Mamie O'Rourke* and was written by a friend of ours, Mary Agnes Donoghue, famous for having written the film *Beaches*.

It was a good play. It had Robert Ackerman directing – very

good – and a designer called Ultz. What's not to like? It was about two Los Angelean women who are both having relationship trouble. At one point they wonder if their deep unphysical friendship might not actually be repressing a secret lesbian desire for one another, and attempt a kiss. I kissed Dawn every night. Still. What's not to like?

It was just the fact that, during the play, I never came offstage. Once I was on, I was on for two whole hours. The play was sort of funny, but not our kind of funny. It was theatre funny. And I had to be in the same place, night after night. I had to leave home just as the children were being put to bed and the possibility of a gin and tonic was being mooted, and go to the theatre.

When the play opened and the lights came up, I had to be standing there on the stage. My opening line was out across the audience: 'Goodbye!'

It was a gift for the funnies in the stalls.

'But we've only just got here!'

'Goodbye! Will Dawn be on soon?'

I dreaded it.

During the performance – looking drab in bad dress and wellies for the WHOLE play – I had moments when I had to sit at a table and read magazines about guns and murder. Which I found interesting, to the point of actually reading them and not coming in on cue quite often. One night, I actually fell asleep and woke to find, not just the audience staring at me, but the rest of the cast as well.

Not my forte, it has to be said.

OK. Back in the tattoo parlour, Dawn and I have had some thoughts. I thought that perhaps we should have a tattoo of a gravestone with 'F&S RIP' on it. We could have it on our bottoms.

Dawn thinks maybe something a bit prettier. Something written, perhaps. We really can't make up our minds, so the nice tattoo artist – who, it would appear, has practised mainly on himself – says he will work up some suggestions. He is young, with no idea who we are. I don't think he can really understand why these two old people have come in. He sets to work, his piercings jingling as he does so.

He is back with a design. It is pretty. It is our names, multi-coloured, in flowery writing. We both look at it, and then at each other.

ME: What do you think, Dawn?
DAWN: What do you think, Jen?

We both know what we think.

ME (*to the boy*): How long would that take to do?
BOY: A couple of hours.
DAWN: Mmm, it is lovely.
ME: But do we have that time, Dawn?
DAWN: No, Jen, I'm afraid I don't think we do.
ME: No. Listen. I think we just want something a bit smaller, as we don't have the time.
DAWN: But it is lovely, and if we had the time . . .

He brings us a hefty folder containing just about every design of smaller tattoos imaginable. We flick through it. They still seem quite big. Eventually, we turn a page and see a little star. A little dark star. We like the star. It is small.

ME: And Dawn, it is in black ink and my friend who removes tat-toos says that black ink is the easiest to remove, should we ever want to.

We point to the star. We decide to have two stars each. We are going crazy now!

Dawn will have them on her wrist and I will have them on my ankle.

We are separated and worked on by different tattooists. Dawn is squeaking a bit in pain. Turns out the wrist is an even more sensitive place to be tattooed than the ankle. Some minutes (and quite a lot of blood, it seems) later, we are done.

We are pleased. We think we look quite cool.

We have tattoos. Who'd have thunk it?

Our very last night in Auckland was the end of the act.

It's funny, but Dawn and I were actually less emotional than some other people were about it. You still have to go on and give your best.

As the show finished, we were bombarded with flowers and chocolate. It was kind and appreciative, and I know we are going to miss the thrill of that live work. And that feeling – that incredible feeling – when your audience are having fun. That they are enjoying you enjoying what you're doing and – most crucially – enjoying each other.

I honestly think that that is what audiences have been buying into all these years: they have been buying into our friendship. They love that we love each other. And they love that we have fun together. The fact that we make each other feel good makes them feel good, which makes everybody happy.

Nowadays we have a show on Radio 2 that brings us together on high days and holidays and gives us the opportunity to sit together and think up funnies.

The real reason that Dawn and I were not so emotional when the act ended was because we knew that we would always have the friendship. And we do. If I want to have laughs and play, I just have to go to her house. We still have the same kind of fun that we always did, only without the audience. There is nothing I enjoy more than meeting Dawn for lunch and simply talking and talking. Death is the only time limit we have on that.

Sixteen.

After the Australia and New Zealand summer 2009 tour with Dawn, and retiring 'the act', I had planned a year off. A year of just living and experiencing life and thinking what to do next. I'm here to tell you that didn't happen. Instead I got breast cancer.

I had always had regular mammograms and was aware I was overdue my latest, but only by about seven months. That October I spent a few days in Spain with my old friend JoBo, who had just been through breast cancer treatment. We sat by her pool and talked about it, and she showed me her scars. She had had chemo and radiotherapy and had kept both breasts. She had come through.

JoBo – who could embellish any story into a drama – was very matter-of-fact and, I thought, stoical.

One of her doctors once told JoBo that he thought she must be in denial because she never broke down. She said she was just 'getting on with it', which I understood and thought was admirable. Sometimes she would come into London and we would go out shopping or to a gallery. She would arrive at the house with her bald head, but then, in the car, before going out in public, would pull what looked like a dead cat out of her coat pocket, fluff it up and pull it on to her head. The wig made her look weirder than just being bald, but it was hilarious. She was remarkable throughout, and I never heard her complain.

So, on returning home from Spain, I knew I had to book my mammogram, or 'mammoliogram', as Edina would say.

I don't know why I always find it so hard to get around to organizing these things. It's a phone call and then an hour at most of your time, but I would always put it off and put it off.

Eventually, I found myself at the clinic. At this point, can I just say that I will never understand why they make you take off your clothes and put on a gown that does up at the back. I can't do bows on my back. I can't reach my back. And I'm not sure about you, but my tits are at the front.

I put them in the boob press. Never an entirely pleasant experience, but over soon enough. Off I went, confident that they would be clear. They always were. I had no family history of breast cancer. I had breastfed, which I sort of thought exempted you.

Next day was a Saturday, so I was surprised, and in fact still in bed, when my GP rang. Odd. He said that something – a small lump – had shown up on the mammogram. My heart started to thump. It was a very small lump, but would I go in and see him?

When?

Now.

OK . . .

Ade was away rehearsing for a panto in Canterbury, so I was on my own. I lay there for a while and settled it in my head. Time seems to move slowly at moments like these. I wanted to think everything through; it was something quite serious but, like all illness, it was also a bit of a bore.

Oh, please don't let me be ill . . . I haven't got time to be ill! I have no time to sit in hospitals! I have work and children and I want to do stuff and be in control of my own life, even if that just means watching Homes Under the Hammer.

In his office, my GP, Martin, tells me all the facts. It's tiny; so small a lump it's only just big enough to have been detected. (I was surprised they found anything in my breasts at all. They're still big now, but back then they were HUGE. I had always worn a DD-cup bra, but in truth, and having watched Gok Wan's *How to Look Good Naked*, I knew I was at least an F.)

My doctor attempts to find the lump by hand, but fails, and we conclude that the lump must indeed be really small.

So all is good. But I need another mammo, just to be sure, and then I'll need to see a surgeon.

Yes, yes. I will.

He seems to have thought of everything, which is great. There is a plan. Marvellous. Here's the plan: mammogram. See surgeon. Biopsy. See surgeon.

The surgeon's name is Mr Gui (pronounced Gooey). A funny name, yes, Jennifer, but totally the best man. Good. So that's that. There's a plan.

Am I OK?

Yes, I am.

Good. Anything I'd like to ask him?

Well, yes. I've had a problem with my shoulder. An ongoing pain. Could he recommend a specialist?

Your shoulder?

Yes. I really need to get it sorted.

He gives me the name of a man to see. Good. You see, my thinking was that I really did need to get that sorted as well, and why waste a trip to the doctor? In for a penny, and all that. And you're taking the time off anyway.

I left his office with numbers and appointments and then sat in my car for a while to take it all in.

At home, I set about telling my family. I had been quite glad – in a way – that I was on my own, so it wasn't necessary to start putting other people's minds at rest immediately. I had time to get the story straight in my own head. I told Ade I was fine, that we'd know more after the next screening, and that I was happy and reassured by the doctor. Telling other people is actually one of the hardest things, because you don't want them to worry, but you also don't want them to find out from someone else. So I would always say it like this:

'OK. I've got something to tell you, but just remember that it has a happy ending.'

Cancer was like having a job without having to do any work. Someone else does the planning and you just have to turn up. Everything is mapped out for you.

Ade was calm, which I like. The last thing I wanted was to have to deal with someone else's shit, to have to be the rallier.

When I gave birth to my girls, it was always reassuring that, no matter how much pain I was in, or screaming or near-death throes I did, I could look at Ade, sometimes nodding off, sometimes reading or making a cup of tea, and think, *Well, it can't be that bad. Ade doesn't seem worried* . . .

I tried to have my last two babies at home. Succeeded with the first, Beattie, who was born just above Luigi's Deli on the Fulham Road and grew up on some of the finest Italian baby food known to man. Not so easy with Freya, who refused to be born. Hours and hours I bellowed in the bedroom, to very little effect, with a midwife – determined Freya would be born before she went off her shift – sticking her fingers in and trying to dilate me by force. So painful. More bellowing, more gas and air.

At one point, Ade left the room to find one of the girls on the stairs outside.

Looking slightly worried, she said, 'Daddy, is there a dragon in the house?'

'No,' he said. 'That's just Mummy.'

The dragon was eventually taken to hospital and relaxed with an epidural.

So, I was back at the clinic to have yet another scan, in the gown that does up at the back so everybody can see your pants as you walk along to the mammogram room.

The results, plus me fully dressed again, thank God, were then sent post-haste to Mr Gui.

He was studying them as I walked into his office. It seemed there were now two small lumps in the left breast, but he was reassuring. They were small and could have been there a long time. No rush, but let's operate quite soon. Why don't you go now this minute and have a biopsy?

So I did.

I was now slightly regretting that I had neglected to bring anyone with me for these appointments. Not just for support, but to share the story and have a laugh with.

To do the biopsy, the doctor used ultrasound to locate the lumps and then, guided by that, he plunged an enormous needle into the breast to extract a tissue sample. Not at all pleasant, but being able to watch it happen on a screen was fascinating.

I also have to declare at this point that I am pathetically competitive, even when there's no one to compete with. My family long ago banned me from playing board games. I will negotiate winning even before I begin to play Monopoly. If I go bankrupt, I have to be lent money so I can continue with the game and eventually win. Equally, I want to be the bravest. I will not complain unless it's absolutely killing and, at the same time, I want the doctor to feel happy and will attempt to make them laugh, if at all possible.

So, back to the biopsy.

DOCTOR: Tell me if this hurts.
ME: I certainly will.
DOCTOR: Anything yet?
ME: I didn't realize you'd started, ha ha.
DOCTOR: You can have more local if it's painful.
ME: No, no, I'm fine. Would *you* like some painkiller? Ha ha.
DOCTOR: OK, I'm putting the needle a bit further in now.
ME: Actually, yes. Yes, a bit more if it's going. Sorry. So sorry.

When the results of the biopsy were in, I had an appointment to see Mr Gui at the Royal Marsden. Ade was by now giving his Captain Hook in Canterbury, so I took my friend Betty with me.

It is very sobering to be in a waiting room with people you know are a lot worse off than you. Sitting there, I couldn't fall back on my default behaviour of 'make light, make jokes'. I knew I was lucky. It had been caught early and the prognosis was good.

We sat with Mr Gui and a breast nurse. Breast nurses are fantastic people. If ever you need to talk about your breasts, they are at the end of a phone.

'After this appointment, you may like to speak to one of the breast nurses.'

'Yes, I will. Thank you very much.'

Mr Gui had the results of the biopsy. As expected, it was cancer, but it didn't appear to be fast-growing. Hurrah! So he had a plan of action. Double hurrah!

The two lumps were quite deep in the tissue of the left breast, which was good because when he operated, he thought he could remove enough healthy tissue around them without having to remove the breast. This is the only time I have been thankful for enormous knockers. So this meant that the left breast would be considerably smaller.

'I see.'

'Basically, it would be reduced, and lifted.'

'I see.' I'm quite interested now.

'If I do that, would you want the other breast done at the same time?'

'Or . . . ?'

'Have different-sized breasts. Or have the other one done at a later date?'

'Are you mad?'

Mr Gui drew it out for us on a scrap of paper. It was very basic. One big tit and one small, pert, lifted tit. Doing both at once would mean a longer operation and recovery time, but that was what I wanted and, as far as I was concerned, Mr Gui was a god.

I could feel Betty getting anxious that I wasn't thinking through all the information I had been given, and instead was just getting overexcited at the prospect of a tit lift. Which I was. This was a result.

Betty, however, was brilliant. Trying to stem my rising hysterical pleasure, she explored all the options, and the advantages and disadvantages of each. What happens to the nipple, etc., etc. (By the way, it's always worth taking someone with you to appointments. They will ask questions and get the facts when you're just trying to be brave and not a bother, and they will remember things later when your mind is a blank.)

A couple of weeks later, I was in hospital waiting for a breast-lift – sorry, lumpectomy.

I had only ever had one anaesthetic before, and that was for a back operation many years previously. We were living in Richmond and I had just started recording a *French and Saunders* show. Outside our house was a car parking place covered in too much gravel. Thick, unstable, stupid gravel.

Ade had a lovely Moto Guzzi motorbike parked there, and every time I pulled in fast to park, the gravel would shift and his bike would crash over. The last time it happened I was too embarrassed to go in and tell him, so I attempted to pick it up myself. While straining, I felt a distinct popping sensation in my back followed by pain. A lot of pain.

I had slipped a disc, but decided I didn't have time to have a slipped disc and soldiered on. We were taking the kids to Euro Disney with our friends Betty and David and their children, and I wasn't going to miss that. However, it was a mistake. The Runaway Train and Thunder Mountain took their toll on my spine and I had to go and see a doctor, who prescribed intensive physiotherapy and some pretty fabulous painkillers.

I was fine. I could record a *French and Saunders*, no trouble.

Yes, I was fine. I was fine until just after we'd recorded a Pan's People sketch with Kathy Burke and Raw Sex. I jumped off the raised stage on to a concrete studio floor wearing some 1970s high heels. That totally did it. The protruding disc was now crushed, and bits were floating about inside and jabbing into any nerves they could find.

I was put to bed with more painkillers and a pile of pillows under my legs. I looked like a dead beetle and was told not to move.

Days came and went. I was supposed to be rehearsing the next week's show, but I was totally incapable and drugged to the eyeballs. However, I was still convinced that I would be able to make it to the studio on the night. At one point, through a druggy haze, Dawn and the director appeared at my bedside with Geraldine McEwan in tow. Surely not. Miss Marple in my bedroom and I hadn't even showered or hoovered?

She had been brought to me so we could rehearse a sketch

for that week. What must she have thought? She was in the bed-room of a drugged-up dead beetle who couldn't see the lines, let alone read them.

I didn't manage to get in for that studio recording, and Dawn managed far too well on her own. I made a slurred phone call to Dawn that was played to the audience over a PA in the studio. Tragic.

Back to the matter in hand.

Before I was ready for the operation, there were two more procedures. They had to locate my main lymph nodes, so one could be tested during the operation. This is done by visiting a nuclear facility that is situated behind lead walls in the hospital. You are injected with radioactive stuff (slightly unclear on the exact details here, as you can tell), then everyone leaves the room and a scanner traces the movement of the stuff as it finds the lymph nodes (you get the gist).

Then, in another facility, thin wires are put into the breast so that they touch the lumps. This is done using ultrasound, and the wires are used as a guide for the surgeon. So I went home the night before the op looking as if I had been impaled by two E strings in a bad guitar smash.

I wasn't feeling quite so clever this time.

DOCTOR: Tell me if you need more local anaesthetic.
ME: Yes I do. Thank you.

No more messing about.

I am very nice to the anaesthetist when she comes in to see me on the morning of the op to go through the procedure and get me to sign all the forms. So many forms. Sign here, please. Check all the details. Is this you? Date of birth? Profession?

Profession. Always a hard one. I used to put 'Actress'. Then

'Actor'. Then 'Comedienne'. Then 'Actor/Writer'. Now I just put 'Entertainer' and hope I'm not asked to make balloon animals.

I'm especially nice to the anaesthetist because someone once told me that it doesn't matter so much who your surgeon is. It's the anaesthetist who keeps you alive. Get the best one.

Mr Gui then arrives on his rounds, followed by a phalanx of nurses. I'm due for the op that morning, so he has come to give me a pep talk and mark me up. I open my gown, and he marks up my breast with a rather sharp felt-tip pen. This is possibly more painful than anything that is to follow. He draws small-ened tits on present large tits freehand. He's no Picasso, and I pray he's more skilled with a scalpel. I am reminded that surgeons are called Mr because in the early days they weren't doctors, but actually butchers brought in to do the chopping up.

I am reassured by all the nurses, who love Mr Gui and say he really does the very best 'cuts'.

A few hours later, my time has come. I am walked in gown and hospital slippers down to the lift and then down to the theatre. I am shocked to learn that the lovely cocktail of drugs called the pre-med is no longer given. Damn. I was looking forward to that. No pre-med? What is the world coming to?

Here goes. On to the operating trolley and straight to needle in arm from the anaesthetist, whom I am still being very nice to, and out for the count.

Seventeen

So, chemotherapy . . .

Stay with me, dear reader.

The first thing I had to do was to meet my oncologist, Professor Paul Ellis. Ade couldn't make the first appointment due to Captain Hooking, but a timely oil spillage then came to our rescue. Someone had leaked diesel oil under the massive panto tent in Canterbury and it was deemed unsafe to perform, due to the fumes. I presume there was the possibility that, if a child dropped a cigarette butt, it could turn into a giant Peter-Panny fireball. So he had a few weeks off.

Paul Ellis explained in beautiful detail the reasoning behind chemotherapy. My cancer was hormone sensitive and HER2 positive, so I was going to have Herceptin as well as other drugs. He did some small sketches on a scrap of paper. From the drawing, I understood that there were some spiky things that needed small hats. Then he went through all the different options of drugs I could have and the various courses of treatment. I made a good face and attempted a question or two, but all I wanted to say to him was, 'Listen, you don't have to do this. I will be happy with the option you choose. I trust you.'

It is the same with my agent, Maureen, and contracts. She knows that it is pointless going through the fine detail with me. Fine detail, to me, is white noise.

'I won't go through the whole thing with you, love, because I know it bores you. Any questions?'

'No.'

'Do you just want to sign where indicated?'

'Yes, I do. Thank you.'

So Paul decided on a six-month course of treatment that we all agreed sounded the business. Six months. I made a note on the calendar. Six months and then back to normal. Job done.

Before the 'off', I had a portacath fitted. This allows the drugs and whatever else to go directly into a vein. It was quite different from what I imagined. I thought it would be like the top of a carton of fruit juice, but no, it actually sits completely under your skin and the needle is then stabbed through into it, which means there is never any trouble finding a vein. Marvellous! All this required was a small operation, which gave me the chance to see Mr Gui again, and the anaesthetist, whom I was again extremely nice to.

Port in place, and the chemo began.

The first one *is* a bit scary, because you have no idea how you're going to feel. I had my own little cubicle, and Ade and the girls came along to keep me company and have a look.

The clinic offered me a thing called a cold cap, which is a helmet you wear that is extremely cold – freezing, in fact – and can prevent a good deal of hair loss. I gave it a go, but losing my hair was not a real worry for me. I've spent a good portion of my adult life in wigs of one kind or another. Most people don't really know what my real hair looks like, and are shocked to find out that it's not red and curly.

A little detour about wigs here. There are acrylic wigs, the kind you can get in department stores, which are obviously not made from real hair and are attached to an elastic net – pull-on wigs. But wigs made from real hair are painstakingly constructed by specialist wig makers and made to order. Every individual hair is knotted on to fine lace. The first fitting you have involves having your hair pinned down as flat as it will go and having layers and layers of cling film wrapped tightly round your head. It's not a good look. The hairline is drawn on to the cling film before the whole thing is removed and used as a template. Then a huge box of dead hair is produced, of every length and colour imaginable, and the selection process begins.

It's not actually dead people's hair – which is what I always used to believe it was. Or nun's hair. It is just people's hair that is cut off and sold. So, basically, poor people's hair. The hair is then knotted on to lace by tiny people with tiny fingers and excellent eyesight. It takes weeks. The hair is then cut and treated like normal hair. It's hairpinned on to yer head, and the lace at the hairline is practically invisible and stuck down with glue. There you go. Just so you know.

Anyway, with a very cold head, it's time for the saline drip, some paracetamol, some antihistamine and then the big boy: a huge horse syringe of red liquid that's pushed in through the port. Then more saline. Then wait. And what comes is like the most enormous hangover you've ever had in your whole life; it's like a night on mixed spirits, wine and grappa. It's a real cracker. It's a humdinger.

When we left, I was walking very slowly, and clutching a large bag of various pills and anti-sickness medication, which worked brilliantly. I never felt sick. I was lucky. And the steroids they give you keep you fairly buzzy for the first few days. They tell you to keep active, so I swept the patio ceaselessly.

The following night, Dawn and I were booked to appear at the Palladium – no, I'm joking! It was actually the Albert Hall, for the Wainwright/McGarrigle Christmas show. As we knew Rufus Wainwright and loved the whole family, it seemed like a fun thing to do. I can't remember exactly what it was that we did, but I expect it involved dressing up, showing off and listening to some wonderful music. As it turned out, it would be one of Kate McGarrigle's last shows as she sadly died of cancer the following year. She was unwell that night but extremely brilliant and brave, and it put what I was going through into perspective.

From one day to the next, you never really know how you're going to feel: some days you can go for a long walk, the next you get breathless after a few steps. Sometimes you stay in bed; sometimes you just have to get up. It is the most frustrating thing: you have the perfect excuse to just lie abed, but you can't because you feel like you should make an effort.

Freya was still living at home and was an absolute stalwart. She checked I had taken all my drugs and even had to administer the odd injection. I don't mind injections, and I thought I was quite good at them, but, as it turned out, I could give them to anyone or anything as long as it wasn't myself. Mainly, I could give them to sheep and lambs.

One year in Devon, when we still had our sheep, Ade had decided to put them to ram, with the aim of having lambs by Easter. The only slight problem was that he had failed to realize that the dates of Easter change every year. Thus the lambs started to arrive a month earlier than he expected, and he was locked away in Fame Academy for Comic Relief. So I had to do all the lambing. Lambing is satisfying and enjoyable but bloody tiring and involves giving injections of antibiotics to the lambs that are struggling. I got pretty good at it. Big needle, tiny lamb? Yes. Tiny needle, own huge bum or thigh? No.

The weird thing is that I came to quite enjoy my visits to the clinic. If you're me, having treatment is a fairly good thing: your life has a routine and a pattern. You do what you're told, and I find that quite liberating.

I had the same wonderful nurse every time. Joel was funny and a sharpshooter with the needle; bullseye every time, and no fuss and nonsense.

Friends would drop by with papers, and I had a rota of company keepers.

I came to like my big white chair. I had given up on the cold cap. It was painfully cold and looked funny. It's hard enough making your way to the loo with your drip stand in tow, without having to wear what looks like a spaceman's riding hat as well.

My hair had started to thin so I cut it short, and then shorter, until we all knew it was time for the clippers to come out. Freya shaved my head.

I had always been certain that I had a pan head, all flat at the back. But lo and behold, my head actually had a shape. I looked quite cool and felt great. I found myself stroking my head a lot. Finally Ade and I had matching hairdos.

My make-up artist and friend Christine Cant and hairdresser Beverly Cox had, between them, lined up various wigs and fake lashes, so I was well provided for on that front. Like JoBo, I always had a little acrylic wig that I could pull on, which didn't look half bad under a beanie hat. Luckily it was winter, so I just wore hats all the time if I went out.

Ade is a good hat-wearer. Why don't more men wear hats? I can't bear it when I watch the news and see bald reporters standing outside in the sleet with their collars up and a bare head. Wear a cap! Ade has got into caps recently. Caps, hats and glasses. If he doesn't, he says he looks like an onion.

I didn't keep my cancer a secret. It was just private. All my friends and the people I worked with knew, and I think the press probably did too. I just like to think they were being respectful. Yes, I actually do believe that's possible.

I have great girlfriends and family who rallied round and who I am incredibly thankful for. Because of course there are times when it isn't possible to stay positive, times when you feel completely bloody shit. There are times when you just want to cry all day. The chemo is accumulative; you have to think of it as medicine, but it is also trying to kill you.

My lowest point came when I had lost all my hair; every eyelash, every pube, every follicle was empty. Your periods stop and you have no hair. There's very little for a girl to do in a day! It was then that I got a terrible rash all over my face. They think it was a reaction to the Herceptin, and it was horrible! I felt like a great big overgrown baby with pimples all over my face. A big, horrible, red-faced baby.

So, feeling like hell and not wearing anything like my best underwear, I went to see a dermatologist. I thought it was pretty obvious, but still she asked me what the problem was. I pointed to my face.

'Is it anywhere else?'

'No, it's just on my face.'

'But it's nowhere else?'

'No.' Quite angry now. 'It's just on my face.'

'Would you strip off so I can have a look? Just go behind the screen.'

Strip off? I am incredulous. But I do as I am told and go behind the screen, wanting to cry. Why does no one ever specify what they mean by 'strip off'? Even when I have a massage, I'm never sure what to leave on and what to take off before they cover me with a pie crust of towels. And at the doctor's, it's a nightmare! Does she mean just take off your jumper, or does she mean take off everything but leave your bra and pants on? Or does she mean *everything*? Why aren't people more specific? Why must it be left to the embarrassed individual to have to ask? And I'm wearing a wig. Do I take the wig off and go out bald, or will this be too shocking? I decide to remove it. I don't care if she's shocked.

'Shall I keep my bra on?'

'Yes. If you like.'

If I *like*? I want to keep all my clothes on. I would like to keep all my clothes on! *I don't know you, and I don't want to be here.*

Suddenly, the screen gets pulled back and she's looking at me in my very poor bra and pants. She circles me and then gets me to stand in a better light and looks again at the strange baby. Am I on *Candid Camera*?

'OK. Get dressed now.'

'Thank you.'

'It's just on your face.'

I can't answer because it would make me cry. I am silent until I leave.

She gives me some steroid cream for my FACE. Which I take and apply to my FACE and which clears it up slowly from my FACE.

Just after Christmas, I get a call from Maureen.

'Hello, love. Just to say, I think I may have taken your name in vain. I hope you don't mind. It's just I was talking to Judy Craymer. You know, love, the producer of *Mamma Mia!*'

'Yes, I know.'

Of course I knew, but I couldn't understand why Judy herself would be interested in having anything to do with a person who had ripped the piss out of the *Mamma Mia!* film as mercilessly as I had.

I recalled Sue Perkins as 'Judy' in the sketch, and wondered what Judy really must have thought . . .

JUDY/SUE: The genius I had was thinking of ABBA . . . and

then friends called and said, 'Hey, Judy, you've got to make it into a film!' And so I did!

Judy had taken it all with a great sense of humour, thank God.

'Mamma Mia!' may be my favourite of all the parodies we ever did. At a time when we had retired the French and Saunders act, we were suddenly given this gift by Comic Relief. I had of course been to see the film, and walked out knowing that I could not go the year without somehow wearing Meryl Streep and her dungarees.

We had a fantastic cast: Joanna Lumley, Sienna Miller, Alan Carr, Miranda Hart, Sue Perkins, Mel Giedroyc, Matt Lucas, and Philip Glenister, who was a revelation as a comic actor. He was playing Pierce Brosnan and had noticed that, in the movie, Pierce is generally leaning on something – a wall, a door, a tree. And when there was nothing close, he would simply lean on his own hand.

The whole thing was a joy. We honestly didn't want it to end! We would happily have gone on and done the whole film. I wished it could have become my job for the rest of my life – just singin' and dancin' and messin' about. I wouldn't care if no one ever saw it, because sometimes that's not the point; sometimes, when something you're doing with people you really love really works, it's enough. It's like being in the best game of pretend that you had when you were a child, but with huge, need-to-pee laughter.

So.

'Judy is looking for a writer for a new project.'

'Really?'

'And I told her you might be interested.'

'Right. What is it?'

'It's a musical based on the music of the Spice Girls.'

'Maureen. Ring her up now and tell her I want to do it. Don't let her get anyone else.'

'Right, love. Will do.'

'Tell her what I'm going through, but assure her that my brain is fine.'

Of course my brain wasn't really fine, but I didn't realize that until months later when my brain was actually fine.

I met Judy, and liked her, and shared the same vision for a Spice Girls musical. We also shared a love of martinis, which made everything even more pleasant. I hadn't stopped drinking during chemo; I just thought that alcohol in the old bloodstream was the least of my worries. But of course, and yes, thank you, I do realize . . . DO NOT TRY THIS AT HOME.

Judy was patient as I went through the treatment and the accumulation of chemicals took its toll. My nose was constantly dripping, due to the lack of nasal hair, and often bled, which was less than lovely. I felt breathless if I exercised and had little in the way of an immune system. I felt chemical. I felt like a chemical.

The midpoint between treatments is the lowest point for your immune system and it is recommended that you avoid people you might catch something from. It was at one of these low points that I went to Canterbury to see Ade in panto. I got in a slight panic. The tent was vast and hot and filled with germ-ridden children. It was a cauldron of mucus. But I had planned for this and had in my bag a white mask as often seen modelled by Michael Jackson and forensic pathologists, so I wore it. Feeling ridiculous but safe.

When the six months was up, I was relieved. But strangely I knew I would miss the routine. I would miss my hours in the white chair. I would miss laughing with Joel. I would even miss my portacath.

The radiotherapy treatment kicked in immediately, so I could put off my medical-institution cold turkey for a few weeks.

What they do basically is blast the affected breast with X-rays to kill off any stray, unwanted cancer cells that have managed to survive everything else that's been thrown at them.

It is incredibly precise, and you have to lie still in a lead-lined room as they align you with the machine, using a tiny dot of a tattoo that is between your breasts. You have to breathe rhythmically as the rays are delivered in pulses on the out breath, so that they don't affect your heart. (I can now hear doctors screaming, 'That is not how it works, you idiot! Didn't you listen to the explanation?')

The nurses leave the room and seal the massive doors.

And then the voice starts. A calm, soothing woman's voice.

'Breathe in, breathe out, breathe in, breathe out . . .'

I do as I'm told.

'Breathe in, breathe out, breathe in, breathe out . . .'

I had always believed that I would be impossible to hypnotize. I just don't think my brain cuts out easily.

Doing research for *Ab Fab*, Abi and I once went to a woman who was famous for taking people back into their past lives. She had been on TV and taken the likes of Phillip Schofield back to – in his own words – seventeen something. It was regression. Or Soul Freedom Therapy, as she called it.

We went up to her flat, which was predictably cream-coloured and full of candles. We were upfront and told her that we were only there out of interest; we were curious to see what might happen.

I was actually excited about who I might once have been, because there are times when just being who you are isn't enough. I want past lives, and I knew that Edina definitely wanted them too. Abi was there as my witness, and to pull me back from the brink if it all got a bit hairy. There was a time in my second year at school when we put a girl into a trance on the playing fields and couldn't get her to come round. Teachers had to be called. I didn't want that to happen. I didn't want to get stuck in Cleopatra's time with nothing but handmaidens for company.

She was a nice woman, with a perfectly normal voice. I sat on her comfortable sofa and closed my eyes. Then I heard a different voice. It was still her, but this was her regression voice, slower and deeper and frankly silly. Without opening my eyes, I just knew that Abi was desperately trying not to laugh. I was trying not to laugh.

She attempted to take me to a lovely beach where I could hear the waves gently lapping on the shore – a place where all the cares of the world had disappeared and I felt relaxed . . . so relaxed . . .

'The most relaxed you've ever felt . . . and now I want you to feel sleepy . . . you're drifting off . . . OK, now I want you to find a place to be and I want you to imagine looking down at your feet . . . you are somewhere else . . . take time and look around . . . where are you?'

'I'm still here. Sorry.'

I opened my eyes to see her disappointment and Abi in the grip of laughter suppression, trying not to catch my eye.

'Sorry.'

We tried everything. We tried dimming the lights and lighting more candles. We tried lying on the floor on my front and on my back. We tried Abi not being in the same room. Eventually, I was so embarrassed that I put myself firmly on the lovely beach and beyond, faked a shiver, and allowed her to cast off a demon spirit that had become attached to me.

What we didn't try – but should have tried – was a voice saying, 'Breathe in, breathe out, breathe in, breathe out,' because within thirty seconds of the door closing and the voice beginning, I was always asleep, and sleeping wasn't the point because then I wouldn't be focused on my breathing. At least twice every session, I would be woken by the klaxon alarm. The heavy doors would open and the whole process of alignment would have to start again.

Even now, just writing the words, I can feel my eyelids droop and a heavy sleep coming upon me . . .

'Breathe in, breathe out, breathe in, breathe out . . .'

KLAXON!!!*

* It's probably not done to thank people before the end of the book, but I must insist.

Thank you, Joel, my nurse; Mr Gui and Professor Paul Ellis.

Thank you, Betty, Tanya, Christine and Abi, for your support throughout and asking all the right questions.

Thank you, Ade and the girls, for keeping it normal and helping with injections. Particularly Freya, who was living at home at the time and was the best friend and the bravest person of all.

Eighteen

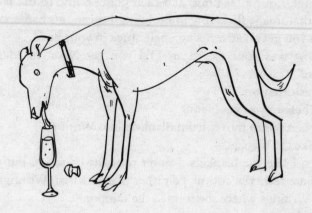

When my hair eventually came back, it came back with a vengeance. It came back *everywhere*. Every tiny hair follicle – even the ones you thought were extinct after years of plucking and shaving and waxing – erupted into life. I started going over my body with a magnifying glass and a pair of tweezers. My face was a fuzz.

My head hair grew back thick and steely grey and looked quite funky – until my addiction to bleach kicked in again.

It was midsummer when it started to regrow. I had gone to stay in the south of France with our friends Betty and David. Tracey Emin was having a birthday party nearby, and we were invited. She's a great character, Tracey. I went to her retrospective show at the South Bank, *Love is What You Want*, and it was wonderful. I tell you, what that woman can do with a blanket is nobody's business! (Except of course it is.)

In one room, there was a big screen playing an animation of one of her drawings, a drawing of her masturbating. It was on a loop, so it looked pretty frantic. At the side of the screen was an attendant, an oldish man in a blue uniform sitting on a chair. All he had to look at was the screen. Day in, day out, shift in, shift out, hour after hour, and then going home to the family with that image flickering in his brain. I mean, it's bad enough when you get an advertising jingle stuck in your head.

'How was your day, dear? Did you get Neon or Masturbation?'

'Masturbation.'

'When do you get Neon?'

'When Susan moves from Blankets into Writings.'

'I like the blankets.'

'Yes, I like the blankets. I never thought I'd say it, but they really are rather beautiful. I'd rather Blankets than Writings.'

'Is Writings where she framed the tampon?'

'Yes.'

'Yes. I think I prefer Blankets.'

Tracey is often at Betty's house in the summer and we have, on occasion, got stupidly, beautifully drunk. One time, we were in the pool singing one minute and then passed out the next. I woke up on the bed still in my wet swimsuit. And then Ade walked in. Hours had passed and he announced that the rest of them were off to get something to eat in Cassis. I refused to be left out and was going to prove that I wasn't *really* that drunk, actually.

I got dressed. Well, I thought I had got dressed, until I was seen by the others. I still had my swimsuit on, but had pulled on a couple of pairs of leggings (with my shoe still inside one of them), a shirt, a dress and a jacket. But I went to Cassis. I wasn't going to let the fact that I was decidedly wobbly and walking inside my own leggings stop me. I'm afraid that I recall little else of the evening, dear reader.

Tracey, meanwhile, had passed out and wasn't seen till the next day. Lightweight.

Anyway, before we set off for the party, I had to make a decision about whether to wear the old wiglet or not. It was so hot that I took the decision to ditch it and go with the light sprinkling of new growth that had appeared.

It was a terribly glamorous party in a restaurant on a beach, and the photographer Richard Young was there snappin' the arty crowd and me. I didn't mind, because Richard is one of the good guys. He's a gent. During the party, he came up to me and asked if I wanted to hold back the photos of me because my breast cancer hadn't been made public. I had a quick think, but told him it was fine. There was no way I wanted to go back to the wig.

The pic went in the papers (with lovely Richard Young, unprompted, giving all the proceeds to a breast cancer charity) and for a few days it was news. And then, just as quickly, it was over. Though I did fear that, from then on, I would always be referred to as 'Brave Jen' . . .

Brave Jen's Cancer Hell Secret

All Clear for Brave Jen

I made a statement via Maureen that just said I had caught it early and now it was gone. Surprisingly, I got lots of correspondence from people telling me that it was a reckless statement and that cancer is never gone. That I was only in remission and it could come back at any time. I was being told off for being positive! And for giving a false impression, apparently. I didn't care. As far as I was concerned, it was gone and the chances of it coming back were – and are – really small. You move on.

And I did. I was out and about again.

Bear with me while I briefly explain the final part of my treatment. I have to do this, because it is relevant to the story I will tell next. I sense you're tiring, but delay switching off the light, or making a cup of tea, or putting the Kindle under the sunlounger and reapplying the cream, because it won't take long.

I had started taking the drug tamoxifen, which prevents you ever having any oestrogen ever again. This basically means it plunges you into the menopause in one fell swoop. It's fairly brutal and you go through all the accompanying side effects: hot flushes, weight gain; a sense of mourning for lost youth, sexiness and somehow the point in anything.

I did become depressed, and this is how I know . . .

Ade and I had wanted to go away on holiday in the late summer. I had said I would book somewhere but could never quite get my head together to do it. Eventually, Ade said that he would do it. I was pleased. We decided to go on a tour of the lakes in northern Italy: Maggiore, Como and Garda. This sounded good. Ade took care to show me all the places we were going to stay, and I approved everything. It looked idyllic.

Was I happy?

Yes, I was. What could possibly be nicer?

We flew to Milan, hired a small Fiat 500 and drove to our first stop on the trip: a lovely hotel that I had seen on the Internet, and approved of, on the shores of Lake Maggiore.

The weather was heavenly. We drove through the town of Stresa, towards the hotel. There were lots of hotels on that road. I thought the first one was going to be ours, but it wasn't.

Evil Jennifer started to feel awful and shamed and shut up, thank God.

In the museum in Bolzano there are the mummified remains of the 5,000-year-old man who was discovered beautifully preserved under ice in the Alps. They have his thin, contorted, leathery body and all his artefacts on show. It is a truly fascinating thing to see. So the fact that I couldn't get enthused about him was a real sign for me that all was not well. I love a corpse. I love a bit of gruesome. As a teenager, I lay in bed at night in my bedroom with blue walls and a red ceiling (I had decorated it myself) and terrified myself reading Dennis Wheatley novels. I would lie awake wondering how long it would take me to draw a pentagram on the carpet if the devil came to visit. Oh yes, I love a bit of gruesome. I would actually like to go back to Bolzano in my real mind and see the 5,000-year-old man again.

I wish I had read more books. I am ashamed to admit that I don't read much. I'm not even a good skimmer. I just don't read huge amounts. I *am* still partial to the odd murder, however. I have read the complete works of P. D. James and Patricia Cornwell. Thankfully, Patricia is fairly prolific, so I always have a good murder for the holidays.

When friends say, 'Have you read the latest so-and-so?' I just say, 'Yes. Marvellous.'

'Not as good as their last though.'

'No. Not as good.'

The truth is, I have probably never heard of so-and-so.

Ade is a great reader. He reads novels and history books and almanacs and books about words and books about books, while I sit in bed next to him playing Jumbline on the iPad.

After Bolzano, we stayed a night in Verona and then flew home. I recognized that what I had felt was pretty awful and not normal. Crying in the bath is not normal. Not for me, anyway.

It was Tanya Byron who put me straight.

'I think you might be depressed.'

'No. I'm just angry all the time.'

But of course she was right, as she generally is about these things. It was all about chemicals and hormones and the general lack of serotonin, which is what you produce when you're happy. Actually, if you want to know about these things, it's probably best to surf the Interweb and not rely on anything in this book. In fact, don't rely on this book for anything. Just be totally safe and don't ever quote me.

So I went and got help and got some little pills which opened the curtains again and exiled Evil Jennifer.

Some time later, I did an interview for the *Radio Times* and talked about the after-effects of chemo. This interview, unbeknownst to me, was then translated for the Foreign Press, before being retranslated back into English. I would like to share it with you.

Jennifer Saunders has announced candidly about adversity from abasement afterwards her analysis for breast cancer.

The 53 year old humerous entertainment singer pronounced her menopause was triggered by Tamoxifen, a drug since to women after operation for a cancer to cut a risk of it entrance back. It had left her feeling vexed as good as incompetent to get out of bed.

'You accept that "I wish to go to bed and beddy-bye forever." You feel fagged out as it creates we feel depressed.'

She pronounced her husband, Comic Adrian Edmondson, had additionally been influenced by her condition. She joked in a repository interview: 'Ade was essentially

vibrating in a residence a alternative day as good as
pulled a sheepskin over himself.'

'I said, "Why dont we spin a heating on?" And he said,
"Because you're prohibited all the time. And thereafter
cold. And thereafter hot. And thereafter sweating, as
good as thereafter not sweating."'

Of 6 months chemotherapy she endured, Miss Saunders said, 'You only courage your teeth as good as bear it.'

It was a single of her most appropriate friends, clergy-
man Tanya Byron, who done Miss Saunders realise she
was pang of depression.

'I'd say, "The accomplished apple is adjoin me. Everyone abroad is amiss about everything," and she'd say,
"No darling, I anticipate that ability be depression."'

Read the abounding account with jennifer Saunders
in the Christmas bifold affair of *Radio Times*, on auc-
tion now.

I had been thinking about one thing all that year. I wanted
another dog. I missed Whisky and Beryl. It is odd living without
animals. Living without children and animals is even odder.
Talking to a dog is like talking to yourself, but without the sense
that you're going mad. You talk to the dog, and then you reply
for the dog, and whole conversations can be had and decisions
made without anyone else present.

'Now, where did I put my handbag? Can you see it, Beryl? Is
it upstairs? Oh no, there it is! Yes, there it is, you stupid woman.
It was staring you in the face! I am not a stupid woman, and this
may well be the early onset of dementia, so less of your lip,
Beryl. Now, do you want to come out with me today and I can
give you a walk on the way back? Yes, I do. Good. Come on
then! What are you waiting for? I'll need to get out some cash,
but you can wait in the car, can't you? Now, where are my
shoes?'

I was in the park one day and heard a woman severely telling someone off:

'It is just ridiculous how you behave! I mean, what do you think you're doing? Why don't you listen to me? You can't just run off, because you'll get lost! Think about that. Think about it. Think! I'm just so disappointed in you. It just can't go on, or I don't know what I'm going to do. Maybe we just can't come to the park any more. How would you feel about that? Hmm? Now, come on, we're going back to the car.'

I eventually saw her as she walked by me. A woman in a Barbour jacket and wellies, towing a disgraced-looking spaniel.

I'm not that bad. I do realize that they don't speak English.

I wanted a dog. I needed a dog. It's strange to go for a walk without a dog. In the country, if you see someone walking on their own through a field, it looks a bit weird, unless they're wearing Gore-Tex and have a map around their neck. But a person walking alone in normal clothes in the middle of nowhere makes you wonder what they're up to. If they have a dog, it's perfectly clear. They are walking the dog. Nothing suspicious about that.

I spent hours googling dogs. It seems to be popular to have cross-breeds at the moment, especially something with poodle in it. Labradoodle, Jackapoo, Cockapoo, Lhasapoo, Pugapoo, Poopapoo. And then there's just Poo.

All these dogs look very adorable as puppies, and of course you'd be seduced by them. So I made myself look at pictures of grown-up Poos. Old Poos. And that made my mind up. I wanted a whippet. Nothing with 'poo' in it at all.

You can't beat a poo joke. Although, when I was growing up, my family had a different name for it. We called it a fourth. Never knew the reason for this until recently. It came from my grandfather, who was a don at Christ's College, Cambridge. The college is built around courtyards, of which there are three.

Off the third one is a toilet, so visiting the lavatory became known as 'going to the fourth'.

My father was retching one day as he came into the kitchen.

'Cat's done a huge fourth in the bath!'

Sorry to take you there, dear reader, but I thought it interesting.

I got Olive, a blue whippet, as a puppy and have never regretted it. She is a real friend and comes everywhere with me. She is well behaved in meetings, eats chips, likes to catch squirrels, and will wear clothing, wigs and scarfs for comedy purposes without complaint. She has her own Twitter site, which is nothing to do with me (that's perhaps slightly creepy). She has appeared on television and is generally recognized more than I am these days.

Once, I was standing on a train platform with her coming back from Devon to London when a woman approached and said, 'Hello. I know you, don't I?'

I looked up and she was talking to Olive. She then looked up at me.

'I know who you are too, but this is the one I wanted to meet.'

So, life is good again. I have a job writing a musical, a documentary to make about horses, and I have a dog.

Onwards.

Viva Forever! was a great job, and I feel lucky to have had it.

It was also a huge learning experience. Musical theatre is like no other world. Compared to a play, a musical is like a juggernaut. Nothing is simple. Music is complicated. Even the casting is complicated. Every part has to be covered by someone else, understudies and swings, and under-swings and over-studies, roundabouts and see-saws.

We did workshops and I discovered it is such a joy to be in a room with people who can just sing. Really sing. And actually dance. Dawn and I have spent so long pretending to do these things, and you watch so much TV with contestants on talent shows trying to be good at these things, you forget there are people who actually can do them. And are brilliant at them.

Choosing which Spice Girls songs to use was the hardest part because somehow they had to add to the narrative. They had to be part of the story. The Spices had a lot of hits, but not a huge oeuvre (I try to use the word 'oeuvre' as often as I can, as it adds pretention to a sentence, I find). Oeuvre.

One of the nicest parts of doing the musical was meeting up with the Spices again. I knew Emma Bunton the best as she had been in *Ab Fab* a few times, part of my oeuvre, and when it came to explaining the storyline to them and playing the songs, she came to the meeting with Mel C. Also one of my favourites. My other favourites are Mel B and Victoria, and Geri is definitely my favourite. They sat and listened as I read out the storyline, and then Judy would play the songs in the relevant places – or in fact most of the time turn the air-conditioning on and off because she got her remote controls mixed up.

What I love about the Spices is how much they loved being Spice Girls. As they listened to the songs, they would reminisce and on occasion actually cry. When the Spices are together there is a great energy, and that happened on the opening night. They were a gang again.

Despite all their ups and downs they remain fiercely loyal to each other and to the Spice Girl legacy. Even Victoria, under all the stiff fashionista carapace, is still a Spice at heart.

It was a great night, and Judy threw a party that might go down in history as being the best party ever.

The reviewers killed the show, for the moment. Judy had been warned that they would go for it even before any had seen it. I think some are still bitter about *Mamma Mia!* being a hit despite their efforts.

But I feel sure it will be back. Brighter and better, and we will all be flickin' the 'V's.

Nineteen

'Are you filming this, Fer?'

I am in my mother's garden and we are laughing as she is being strapped on to a stretcher and put into an air ambulance. I am filming it on my phone. We are amazed that the helicopter managed to land in her garden. She made me film that too, as it landed and the rotor blades blew all her plants flat.

It is August 2010. I had a phone call less than an hour ago. I could tell it was her, and that she was distressed, but I couldn't make out what she was trying to say to me. It seemed like nonsense. I tried to calm her. Somehow, I knew it must be a stroke.

'Mummy, I think you've probably had a stroke. You've had a stroke, Mummy. Sit down. I'm coming now. Just sit down.'

I ran to my car and drove fast to her house. I probably should have called the ambulance then and there, but I just wanted to get to her. She was waiting at her door when I arrived a few minutes later. I took her inside and made her sit down.

Once she was sitting down, she became calmer.

I called 999 and described her symptoms over the phone. She seemed to have lost some movement in one arm, but her face wasn't lopsided and she could manage a smile when asked. But her speech was decidedly all over the place.

While we waited for the ambulance, she tried to speak. She slurred words that had nothing to do with meaning. But, rather than get frustrated, my mother began to laugh. Family default mode.

Every time she tried to say something, it became like a game of charades, and every time I tried to guess the word, we laughed.

'Mummy, the ambulance is coming and I think we should pack a bag for you. Where are your nighties?'

She pointed upstairs.

'In the donkey.'

HUGE laugh. The donkey turned out to be the chest of drawers.

We laughed until the tears streamed down our cheeks. When the first medics arrived, they must have thought we were mad. Either that, or that I was incredibly heartless.

How old was my mother? they wondered.

I am afraid that I have always been bad at dates and ages and birthdays. I barely know how old I am. I couldn't think how old she was, and nor, at that stage, could my mother. We settled on seventy-eight. This was wrong. She was actually seventy-seven.

They decided to call the air ambulance and save my mother the long road journey to Exeter. Somehow, it managed to land on a small stretch of lawn between her vegetable garden and shrubbery. The crew was amazing and my mother incredibly brave. I realize that I have inherited her ability to be an unfussed, uncomplaining patient. The only thing she can't tolerate is being treated like a fool.

She was loaded into the helicopter, smiling at the paramedics. When it had left, I went and got all her necessaries from the donkey and sped to the hospital in my car, where my mother had been disembarked and was now in the Emergency Department.

I have come to rather like hospitals. I like the fact that there are definites in hospitals. That there are lots of people there, all knowing what they can do and what they should be doing. I used to think BBC Television Centre was like that, but don't let me get started on that again. I think that the only similarity between the Beeb and the NHS is the number of bad management decisions that have caused them to lose sight of their original purpose. In the BBC's case, making TV programmes. In the NHS's case, saving lives and making people better. I'll shut up now.

My mother had many tests and scans, all of which were inconclusive. No one seemed to know how or where it had happened. No clot was visible. We thought it might have had something to do with the fact that, when she had been mowing her lawn on a ride-on mower a week or so earlier, she had become trapped under a low branch that had pushed her head back as the mower moved forward. It had taken her a while to get her foot off the accelerator. This theory was dismissed, although I personally think it's still a possibility. One moment she was sitting on the sofa watching the racing, the next she had woken up and realized she couldn't speak. She had had little movement in one arm but had managed to press a speed-dial button on her phone that had put her through to our house. Thank goodness we were there.

They kept her in hospital for a week or so while they completed more tests. She was then sent home. At home, she made a remarkable recovery. The thing that takes the longest time to return is confidence, but she is now back to her old self, with a little bit of forgetfulness thrown in. There is still the odd 'donkey' – which causes convulsions of laughter – and numbers occasionally elude her. When she first came home, we realized that the only number she could remember was twelve. She would get up at twelve, meet people at twelve, have supper at twelve, and everything cost twelve pounds. She wasn't allowed near a chequebook for months.

She is a strong and remarkable woman, my mother, and I thank God that I was in Devon, that she managed to press the one button on her phone that rang me and that I was in to take the call. I could have been sweeping. There have not been many times when she has ever asked for help, and even now I know she doesn't actually use the stairlift that we put in for her, because it takes too bloody long.

A month or so before this, Ade and I were in our kitchen in London and got the greatest, happiest phone call from Ella. Her boyfriend, Dan, had asked her to marry him, and she had accepted. Little 'Ella Bella Bing Bong Fish Can Fly' was going to get married. The girl who had arrived looking like a little cross kidney bean had grown into a beautiful young woman and was going to get MARRIED! The girl who had once just wanted to wear a kilt and do Scottish dancing very, very fast, the girl who frightened us slightly in her Marilyn Manson phase, the girl who still bounces on the trampoline with her sisters, who has her own version of how the world works – Ellapedia, where all the facts are made up by herself – was going to marry the best person she could marry. Dan Furlong. Ade and I love Dan. He is a builder and a joiner and a man who can put his mind to anything. He is also a brilliant washer-upper. That makes him actually perfect.

They wanted to be married in the local church and have the reception on the lawn in the house in Devon. They didn't give us an awful lot of notice and we were quite glad of that, because it meant we just had to get on with it and focus on what was important. Church. Dress. Booze.

Like mother, like daughter.

OK, I might go a little bit Pippa Middleton on you now. We had a big tent on the lawn filled with tables and benches, and flowers done by a friend of Dan's mum. Soft roses and wild-flowers. And candles. Most of my preparation time seemed to be spent going backwards and forwards from IKEA and Trago Mills with car loads of candles, blankets (in case it got cold) and cheap umbrellas (in case it rained). Ade ordered all the booze and the band for the party in the evening, and the cars to and from the church. My brother Simon brought some barrels of beer to add to the booze and agreed to act as MC. Fittingly, my little butler-like brother grew up into a perfect publican. He is still the best host, not least because he has an encyclopedic knowledge of most things and is never short of conversation.

We had a posh hog roast, which was Ella and Dan's request. I nearly insisted that they had posher food, but luckily most of my bossiness was squashed, and the whole thing was better for it. I concentrated on candles and pots of geraniums for the garden.

Ella and I went and found her a cool, glamorous dress in London that she wore with her battered cowboy boots. She looked sublime. Dan wore a tweed suit.

The vicar, Anthony Geering, who was the vicar from Chagford who had conducted my father's funeral, came out of retirement to marry them. He definitely wasn't a 'stupid arse'. He was the very best of vicars. The Church of England should never have retired him without first cloning him and sending him out as an example of how vicars should be. (Bear in mind, I am talking as a hedging-their-bets agnostic.) He put the congregation at their ease and told them they were free to move about and get closer if they wanted, to see all the good bits. No one was confined to pews behind pillars. He made it inclusive and emotional, meaningful but never solemn, and we all left the church on a high.

The sun shone all day. We were lucky, because it had rained solidly the week before. Once the tent was up, the water had poured like rivers off the roof and on to the lawn. Again, lucky that there is almost no grass at all on our lawn and it is just thick moss, which absorbed the water like a sponge.

Back at the house, after the church, we continued on a high, fuelled by Champagne and beer and the sense that something wonderful had happened.

Ade made a speech that had us all in tears. He barely got through it himself. There is nothing more likely to make Ade emotional than talking about his daughters. He loves his girls with a passion, and they love him. He has been an extraordinary father.

Ella is a musician, which she gets from him, and he taught her guitar and piano. At home, the house is always full of music. Ade has taught himself to play virtually every instrument with a string, and the trumpet too, and Ella has his talent. He has a library of songbooks, and the music they play ranges between country, folk, rock and Christmas carols. There was a time when I attempted to play the guitar and sing along with them, but quickly realized I was majorly outclassed. Now I only do it if I am really sure of a harmony. I have seen the odd smile pass between Ella and Ade when I join in. They have pointed out that I can sing the tune that is in my head, which doesn't always match the tune of the actual song, and that my timing has always been up the spout.

I think this must be where a lot of *X Factor* auditionees go wrong. When you're singing along to a CD, you can't actually hear what you are singing. Singing unaccompanied is a whole different kettle of fish and some talent is required.

Beattie is now a fully fledged comedy girl. She started doing comedy at university. She went to Manchester and did the same course that Ade and Rik and Ben had done all those years ago. In her second year, she invited me and Ade up to a comedy night. She was performing in a double act with her friend Rose Johnson. Yes. A female double act. We thought it was an amazingly brave move, and we sat in the audience not quite knowing what to think but just praying that she was funny. And, lo and behold, she was. They were both hilarious, and she has never looked back. The comedy group grew to be six girls called Ladygarden (explain that one to yer grandparents), and they took shows to Edinburgh and did gigs around the country and a bit of telly. Beattie now has an agent and a TV sitcom under her belt. She is still doing live gigs with the two remaining Ladygardeners, and they call themselves the Birthday Girls. The word 'proud' doesn't even go halfway to expressing how we feel. She has a beautiful nature, is kind and self-deprecating, and a demon on the Xbox. So, so PROUD.

Freya is the youngest and is studying fashion at university. From a very early age, she wanted to do fashion. Although, if anyone asked her what she wanted to be when she grew up, she would look them in the eye and say, 'Gorse bush.' That had the desired effect and shut them up. Her godmother is Betty Jackson but I don't think that influenced her early years. From the age of five, every birthday or Christmas, Freya would gather up the wrapping paper and disappear to her room with a roll of Sellotape. Half an hour later, she would appear downstairs in a perfect outfit, a wrapping-paper outfit. Dress, hat and shoes.

There is little more enjoyable than sitting having supper and getting Freya to do her impersonations of the girls she worked for when she did magazine internships. We are always on at her to write it down – 'It's funny, write it down' – but I know that in her head she's thinking, *Yeah, yeah, that's what you do, parents. I am different.* And she is. She is determined to make her own way and has Ade's work ethic to help her.

*

Just when you think life is good, it gets better. Ella announces that she is pregnant, and eight months later I am in the delivery room with her and Dan and the midwives.

When they called, it was because Ella had thought she was quite close and was having contractions at regular intervals. But when I arrive, she is still in bed talking coherently. I know – but don't have the heart to say – that it might be quite a while yet. There is far greater pain to come. About eight hours of pain later, Freddie Furlong is born. I realize I am prejudiced, but Freddie was beautiful then and has grown even more divine since. I mean, even the midwife said he was 'scrumptious'.

We are grandparents.

If we are not talking about Freddie, we are looking at pictures of Freddie. I now have pictures only of Freddie on my phone. If Freddie is in the room, we stare at him, and when he is taken out, we revert to looking at photos of him. He is a little king. When I look at him, I know with conviction that he will never be able to do any wrong in my eyes.

He has two doting aunts who both confess to having womb ache. Ade always said he never really wanted a son and was happy with his girls, but I'm sure that he has already ordered Freddie a season ticket for Exeter City Football Club and is planning boat trips. I imagine that one day, when Freddie is of age, he will come to town and take me to the Wolseley. I will have white hair, a stick and possibly some furs. I will introduce Freddie to the waiters and tell them that if he is ever in, they must furnish him and his chums with the finest Champagne.

So there you have it. Life moves on. The girls are happy. Ade is happy with his work and music. I am happy pottering about and have got back into the horsey world.

By sheer accident, I have become an Ambassador for British Showjumping. This happened because, on the Radio 2 show that Dawn and I have, Dawn mentioned that she had been invited to the Badminton three-day event with her daughter. That's normally my sort of thing, and I was vociferously jealous. Maria Clayton at British Showjumping heard this and wrote to me, inviting me and a guest to Hickstead that year. I took Judy Craymer, who had in her youth been a showjumper. By the end of the day, having met most of our old heroes, including Harvey Smith, we were both made Ambassadors. We handed around the Ferrero Rocher and were thrilled.

It's like stepping back into my sixteen-year-old self's jodhpur boots. We have been to events with the Olympic gold medal winners Nick Skelton, Ben Maher, Scott Brash and Peter Charles. I carried the Union Jack ahead of the team at the international jumping at La Baule. I am actually almost living out a daydream.

Recently, I have bought a horse. This came about because I made a documentary called *Back in the Saddle* in which I took up riding again. In fact, it wasn't going to be about me taking up riding again. It was supposed to be me just looking at all the horsey events pre-Olympics, but bloody Clare Balding interviewed me and asked me if I was going to give it a go, and because I can't refuse a dare, I said yes.

Completely out of shape and not having ridden for years, I was put though my paces by showjumper Tim Stockdale and event rider Piggy French. Tim gave me a two-hour jumping lesson after which I thought I would never walk again. My privates felt like they had been sandpapered in preparation for redecorating.

Piggy put me over cross-country jumps that startled me at first. But they both gave me confidence, especially when they pointed out that I didn't have to worry about the fence: the horse would jump it, they said, so I didn't have to. Growing up, most of my ponies wouldn't jump very well, and my friends and I had more fun pretending to be ponies and jumping the fences ourselves. I was a marvellous showjumper with my own legs.

At the end of the documentary, they arranged for me to jump

a small course at a big event. I was nervous and therefore very bad-tempered about the whole thing.

'Listen. I did not say that I would actually do this. AND, if I do this, I don't want people watching. AND I don't want it announced on the tannoy. AND all this is still only "if" because I might not actually do it . . .'

They had given me a lovely big horse called Jack, and eventually, despite the amount of people surrounding the ring, I went in. It was twenty jumps, but I had warned them that I might only do five. The buzzer went and I started jumping. Jack knew exactly what he was doing and had learned the course better than me. I was slightly encumbered by the amount of body protection I had to wear for the insurance – back protector and exploding jacket – and looked like the Michelin Man on horseback. After a few jumps, the tannoy kicked in:

'AND IN THE RING NOW . . . JENNIFER SAUNDERS!'

From that moment on, I had a running commentary and cheers from the crowd every time I got over a jump. I couldn't stop now. My plan had been foiled, and I had to go on and complete the course. Jack jumped a clear round with Huffy Puffy Sweaty Jelly Legs on his back. It was GREAT.

I felt that Jack deserved the huge amount of Pimm's I consumed after that.

Back to the point. Making the documentary, I had been over to Ireland and met a horse producer, Richard Sheane, who buys the best young horses from all over Ireland and brings them on before selling them to the top riders. He knew Piggy. Some time later, he called me up and told me he had a horse I might like and that it would be a good horse for Piggy.

The thought of being a three-day-event horse owner was exciting. A bit like a grandchild. All the joy, but you don't have to do the mucking out.

Piggy and I went to Richard's place in Ireland, and he showed us some horses which Piggy tried out but wasn't totally convinced by. So he took us over to his other yard where there were some really young ones and one that did catch our eye. He was called Aubane Boy. Piggy rode him and liked him, and I knew I had to get him when Richard told us that his stable name was Freddie.

He is at Piggy's yard now, learning his trade.

I've been terribly lucky. I have a wonderful family and very nice friends. I AM lucky. I've had fun. So much fun. I've been paid to muck about. And the best thing is that it feels to me like there's much more fun to be had. I hope so. I really hope so. And by fun, I mean work. Here comes my 'old person' rant. It amazes me how many of the young today just want to be famous. To be a celebrity. Because the absolutely very last thing anyone should want to do is end up in the celebrity swamp.

There are too many celebrities! The fallen, the has-beens, the lucky, the untalented, now all writhing around in the same shallow, stinking swamp, pissing in the same water. And yet we can't take our eyes off them. We love watching the wallowing of the second rate. If those mags were full of brilliant minds, we wouldn't care. We would have NO INTEREST AT ALL. We don't want glamour; we mostly want the gutter.

You hardly hear anything from the talented ones any more. What ever happened to Juliette Brioche? Or Michelle Pfifferfefferfeff? Where are they now? And the one with all the gums? Meg Ryan! Are they too old now? Have Meryl and Helen cornered the market in wrinklies?

Can I also just say, while I'm at it, that I'm fed up of film posters of pretty girls and boys, running around with guns, being plastered on the side of buses? If they were holding cigarettes instead of guns and smoking nonchalantly, they would be banned. If they had a fag in one hand and a glass of wine in the other, they would be shot!

Where be the double-cream film stars of ye olden days?

They have been replaced by skimmed milk and yoghurt adverts.

What is it with yoghurt adverts? What is this strange yoghurt porn we have to put up with? Have you ever *seriously* got yourself into a slinky nightie, in the middle of the day, closed the curtains and reclined on the sofa with a pot of yoghurt?

YOGHURT.

It will take you, at most, two minutes to eat and that includes licking the lid. And then you will put the pot down on the floor with the spoon still in it, so it tips up and smears on your carpet. It's over. What are ya going to do then? You are going to feel a fool. A great big silly, soppy, stupid fool. You're going to hope that nobody, especially someone you know, comes to the door.

'What are you doing? Why are you in your nightie? Why are the curtains closed?'

They barge past you into the sitting room, because they're expecting to see a lover. How sad, when all that's there is an empty pot of yoghurt.

Yoghurt and chocolate. That's what women want, apparently. Oh yes. That's what we all want.

'Don't tell my husband, but I'm seeing a yoghurt and he doesn't know about it.'

'A Müller Light?'

'No. It's a full-fat Fruit Corner.'

'Jesus! Be careful.'

'He'd have a fit if he knew.'

'Is it serious?'

'No, no . . . well, I don't know.'

'I had a thing with Cointreau once.'

'Really?'

'Yes. I look back at it now and I don't know what I was thinking. Have you ever been tempted by Baileys?'

'No, never. The occasional chocolate mousse, but no, it's the Fruit Corner.'

'What would the kids think?'

'Oh, I don't think it would affect them. They know I've had the odd Petits Filous on occasion.'

What's HAPPENING?

D'you know, I think I might just be too tired to keep up.

I'm too old now to fool the world with a new profile. You'll just have to take me or leave me. I have no Pinterest, no Instagram, no Facebook. I'm bored of Tweeting, but fear the baying mob.

That is my reality now. No virtual status. No avatars in virtual sites.

I DON'T WANT TO BE LINKEDIN. I have spent my whole life trying to be linked out.

I don't want to have to get there first, see it first, be the first to have it, know about it before anyone else. It's like the news nowadays. Why are they always reporting what people *might* be saying, what decisions *might* be made? Why can't we wait? We're not babies who need to be told that supper is nearly ready, or what's going to be on the next page of the book. Shall we guess, children?

Everybody's leaking these days.

I know I certainly am, but maybe that's just my time of life.

So what else? 'What's next?' I hear you cry. The truth is, I don't know and, do you know what, I like it that way.

There is no Plan.

I'm off now, to do some sweeping. I thank you, dear reader, for your patience.

The only person to blame for this book of mine is Clare Balding.

Yes, she of all the talking during the Olympics. Yes, she the one whose family are all animals.

Well, it's her fault. I went to her book launch party and, after a few Sauvignons, was charmed and flattered by her editor into submission. It's all Clare bloody Balding's fault. Please send all your thoughts and comments about this book to Clare Balding. Unless of course they're really nice, in which case send them to me.

If you are standing in a bookshop and have accidentally picked me up (as it were), I can guess what you might be thinking: *Oh no! Not another celebrity autobiog by someone cashing in on TV fame!*

But let me tell you . . .

Yes! That's exactly what this is.

I realize they're everywhere nowadays. Like a disease. But a lot of books out there are by babies. Biebers and Tulisas. They've only been awake a couple of years. Next we'll have tiny foetuses writing books.

The thing that this one has going for it is that I am really quite old. I have also met quite a few celebs, which is always a good sales point. I was told to stuff it with celebs and royalty and a touch of sadness.

If you've had cancer, then milk it. You don't hit the best-seller lists by holding back. Don't spend too much time talkin' 'bout your family. Nobody except you is interested in the old grannyparents. If you've touched the skin of royals, then make those two seconds last a chapter or two.

OK, I have met the Queen once and Princess Anne. I also met Prince Charles and praised his chutney. Camilla laughed, but he didn't hang around.

There are *thousands* of books out there, dear reader. Thousands of books. Mis mems, happy mems, chick lits, chick knits, cookbooks, diet books, cookbooks, cookbooks, food, diet, food, food . . .

Gwyneth Paltrow, for God's sake.

'Recipes that make you look good and feel great.'

I actually bought Gwynnie's book, thinking it would be funny and a good tome for fun-poking, but ended up loving the pictures, buying chimichurri sauce and stocking the fridge with cilantro. Which is actually just coriander. Who knew?

Special thanks to:

Ade, for marrying me

Ella, Beattie and Freya, for being my children

My mother, Jane, and father, Tom, for giving me a childhood full of freedom and laughter

My brothers Tim and Simon

My brother Peter, whose life was far too short

Dawn French, for years of friendship and fun

Betty, Harriet, Tanya, Christine and Abi, the girls who helped and supported me through my 'brave time'

Very special mention to Freya, for actually being very brave

JoBo, for the stories

Maureen Vincent, for her patience and all the work

Abi Wilson, for all the extraordinary help and sharing so many adventures

Joel Rickett, my editor, for persuading me and holding his nerve

Chloe Fox, for steering me through

Gemma Feeney

Mary Lou North and Cindy Cull, for making Devon possible

Mr Gui and Professor Paul Ellis, whose great care got me through the 'mis'

Joel, my nurse

Jon Plowman

Bob Spiers

Jo Sargent

Simon Brint and Rowland Rivron

Jack Lumley, June Whitfield, Julia Sawalha and Jane Horrocks

Ruby Wax

Jan Sewell, Christine Cant, Sarah Burns and Rebecca Hale, for all the face paint and dressing up

Peter Richardson, for the break

All the Comic Strippers

All the Jam and Jerusalemers

All the Vivienne Vylers

The two Sallys in New Zealand

Goldie Hawn

Judy Craymer

Jayne Astrop and Kay Perry

Olive

Index

Index

BONKERS

'Jennifer Saunders's fans – which as far as I can tell means pretty much
everyone – will be unsurprised to learn that *Bonkers* is a lot better
than all right . . . It's written with affecting candour' *Guardian*

'Fabulous. A great read. A touching, honest and laugh-out-loud memoir
from one of our most-loved comedians' *Woman & Home*

'Sends up the genre while providing all the key ingredients: family history;
early struggles; major influences; full CV; brushes with death (a cancer
scare); and a cast of A-list walk-ons. Her no-nonsense approach to life off
camera is endearing and her clear-eyed view of herself (as a procrastinat-
ing party girl) is hilarious. She is especially good on the horrors of
Hollywood. If only all celebrity autobiographies were this funny'
Mark Sanderson, *Daily Telegraph*, Books of the Year

'Sharp, poignant, life-affirming' *Sunday Mirror*

'As honest as it is uplifting' *Daily Mail*

'Coruscating' *The Times*

'Reads like a series of comedy sketches. Saunders never takes
herself too seriously and can be uproariously funny and, yes,
truly "bonkers"' *Financial Times*

'An endless stream of funny anecdotes . . . regaling the reader
with entertaining (but never bitchy) stories from her own brushes
with the world of celebrity' *Irish Independent*

'Laugh-out-loud moments and touching too. In a market filled with
woe-is-me self-obsessed celeb memoirs, Saunders has produced a
refreshingly funny and uplifting read' *Irish News*

'*Bonkers* is Jennifer at her best: funny, generous, clever and
self-deprecating. Full of personal anecdotes, *Bonkers* also
contains a hilarious and very recognizable description of
procrastination, Saunders-style' *Diva*

Both Rebecca and the bed were looking more and more tempting by the moment.

Angus desperately needed some air. Or a cold shower. Maybe both.

"What would you like to do first?" he asked her, trying to distract himself from his thoughts.

Make love with you, she thought. *Now wouldn't that shake him up?*

But instead she said, "I don't know." Rebecca turned her face up to his, the shining soul of innocence. "Why don't I just put myself in your hands, and you can take it from there?"

Angus wondered if there was a special place in heaven for detectives who resisted temptation when it came in such pretty wrappings. Ever so lightly, he brushed a wayward hair behind her ear. It was all he would allow himself.

"Becky, you've got to stop saying things like that. A man can be noble for only so long."

Dear Reader,

Have you noticed our special look this month? I hope so, because it's in honor of something pretty exciting: Intimate Moments' 15th Anniversary. I've been here from the beginning, and it's been a pretty exciting ride, so I hope you'll join us for three months' worth of celebratory reading. And any month that starts out with a new book by Marie Ferrarella has to be good. Pick up *Angus's Lost Lady;* you won't be disappointed. Take one beautiful amnesiac (the lost lady), introduce her to one hunky private detective who also happens to be a single dad (Angus), and you've got the recipe for one great romance. Don't miss it.

Maggie Shayne continues her superselling miniseries THE TEXAS BRAND with *The Husband She Couldn't Remember.* Ben Brand had just gotten over the loss of his wife and started to rebuild his life when…there she was! She wasn't dead at all. Unfortunately, their problems were just beginning. Pat Warren's *Stand-In Father* is a deeply emotional look at a man whose brush with death forces him to reconsider the way he approaches life— and deals with women. Carla Cassidy completes her SISTERS duet with *Reluctant Dad,* while Desire author Eileen Wilks makes the move into Intimate Moments this month with *The Virgin and the Outlaw.* Run, don't walk, to your bookstore in search of this terrific debut. Finally, Debra Cowan's back with *The Rescue of Jenna West,* her second book for the line.

Enjoy them all, and be sure to come back again next month for more of the best romantic reading around—right here in Silhouette Intimate Moments.

Yours,

Leslie J. Wainger

Leslie J. Wainger
Senior Editor and Editorial Coordinator

Please address questions and book requests to:
Silhouette Reader Service
U.S.: 3010 Walden Ave., P.O. Box 1325, Buffalo, NY 14269
Canadian: P.O. Box 609, Fort Erie, Ont. L2A 5X3

MARIE FERRARELLA

ANGUS'S LOST LADY

Silhouette® INTIMATE™ MOMENTS®

Published by Silhouette Books

America's Publisher of Contemporary Romance

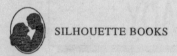

SILHOUETTE BOOKS

ISBN 0-373-07853-6

ANGUS'S LOST LADY

Books by Marie Ferrarella

MARIE FERRARELLA

lives in southern California. She describes herself as the tired mother of two overenergetic children and the contented wife of one wonderful man. This RITA Award-winning author is thrilled to be following her dream of writing full-time.

To Rocky,
67 furry pounds of
completely unqualified
love

Chapter 1

"Do you know who I am?"

She'd startled him. Angus MacDougall was just opening his office door, ready to call it a day—a hell of a long day—when he found the woman standing in his doorway, her hand poised to knock.

Recovering quickly, he took a step back. Some of the weariness that cloaked him began to slip away as he studied the woman. Interest stirred. Unconsciously, Angus straightened his six-foot-three frame.

With her trench coat hanging open on either side of her, the woman had a windblown, wet look from head to foot. And she seemed a little off balance until he realized the lady was wearing only one shoe. But though she looked dazed, like a game show contestant stumped for the prize-winning answer, at first glance she didn't appear to be hurt or bruised.

Angus smelled a setup. Okay, he was game for a riddle.

Riddles came with the territory, especially if one of his friends was looking to play a trick on him.

His lips parted in a minimal smile. "No, who are you?"

Angus wasn't prepared for the look of dejection that entered her eyes at his response. And certainly not for the depth of disappointment that he saw there. The woman paused, as if trying to shore up some inner resource before she replied.

"No, I'm serious." She moved closer to him, so close that he could smell the rain in her hair and on her skin. And the faintest whiff of something else. Smoke? He wasn't sure. Her eyes scanned his face, a dying ember of hope glimmering faintly there. "Do you know me?"

She was pretty, even with her hair plastered to her face. Dry, she might even be beautiful. He would have remembered if he'd ever met her. He rarely forgot a face, and hers would have been etched on his brain.

It was a trick.

Leaning out into the hall, Angus looked around to see where the person responsible for this was lurking. Probably hiding in a doorway, he guessed. Everyone knew he had a weakness for damsels in distress. This one had all the earmarks of one. Maybe a little too much so, now that he took a closer look. Whoever had put her up to this had overplayed his hand.

A quick scan of the hall told him there was no one else there. A smattering of doubt began to surface, but he ignored it for now. Angus turned his attention back to the woman.

"Okay, I'll bite. Where are they?"

"They?" she repeated, confused.

"They. He, she, whoever put you up to this." Angus looked out again, with the same results. Nobody. When he looked back at her, the woman's expression remained unchanged. The uncertainty within him spread out a tiny bit more. "This is a joke, right?"

The air and the light seemed to go out of her at the same time. She looked as if she'd just lost her best friend. The words slid past her lips in a whisper that bordered on defeat.

"Then you don't know me."

Any other time, Angus would have been more patient with her. But today had been a hell of a drawn-out day, stitched haphazardly onto an even longer night. A night in which he had sat up with Vikki and a bellyache that wouldn't go away. Small wonder. Vikki had consumed enough junk food for three seven-year-olds her size.

Running on coffee the consistency of mud, and several lukewarm burritos, Angus wasn't in the mood for elaborate games played at his expense, no matter how inherently sexy the lady might be.

Gently moving the woman back, Angus stepped over the threshold, his hand on the doorknob.

"No, lady, I don't know who you are," he said wearily. "Now if you don't mind, it's been a damn long day." The day's events flickered through his mind like an old-fashioned silent movie. "The kind that makes me want to turn in my license and my weapon and get a nine-to-five job with insurance benefits and a fat pension plan at the end of the line."

He'd been thinking about it more and more lately, ever since Vikki had turned up in his life. He didn't have just himself to consider anymore.

But deep down, he knew he really wouldn't want to change his life. The thought of a nine-to-five job by any name still chilled him. Angus had had security and turned his back on it before it permanently anesthetized him. That was the danger with security. It dulled the soul.

Angus shut the door behind him and heard the lock click into place. What he needed right now was a little time to unwind. That and a tall, cold beer. He tried to remember if there was any left in the refrigerator.

The woman remained where he had moved her, looking for all the world as if she intended to stay there, not out of any sort of stubborn perverseness but just because that was where she was.

He had seen hopelessness before. It was there, in her eyes, though she seemed to be struggling against it. Struggling and losing. Against his better judgment, Angus paused, waiting. She still made no effort to go.

"I'm leaving," he announced, as if the fact might not have registered. Angus turned squarely to face her. What did he have to do, *push* her into the elevator? "The game is over, so why don't you just go home?"

Looking back later, he figured that was the moment she'd actually hooked him. The woman turned her eyes— eyes that were as close to violet as anything he'd ever seen—up to his.

"I can't."

The two ends of the conversation, such as they were, just didn't seem to be fitting together. "You can't what?"

"Go home." She fit her mouth around the word. Home. It had no substance for her, no texture. No feelings. Nothing. "I can't go home."

Angus wondered why, but told himself he wasn't going to get sucked into this. He had enough real cases to keep him busy. That, and Vikki. After six months, he was still getting used to her. And, he knew, she to him.

"Well, then maybe you should go somewhere else." Turning, he took a step toward the elevator.

And stopped.

The look in her eyes seemed to be holding him in place.

Even without facing her, he could feel her eyes on him, silently entreating him to stay.

Surrendering to the curiosity that was as much a part of him as breathing, Angus gamely turned around again. "All right, why can't you go home?"

She wasn't going to cry, she wasn't, she thought frantically. It was just that she felt as if everything was caving in on her. And she didn't even have the vaguest idea what that "everything" was.

It was the void that frightened her most of all. The huge, horrible nothingness that threatened to swallow her up if she let it.

She pressed her lips together hard, hoping that would somehow keep down the hysteria that was building within her. It made her chest ache to hold back, but at least she wasn't crying in front of a stranger like some pathetic fool.

In her world, there were nothing but strangers. Even *she* was a stranger, she thought helplessly.

"Because I don't know where home is." Her voice hitched, threatening to break. She pressed her lips together again.

Angus peered into the woman's face. He thought of himself as a pretty good judge of people. He saw the struggle for control going on in her eyes.

And then he knew.

His voice was kind, gentle, as he lightly touched her shoulder. Angus felt like a heel adding to her anguish. "This isn't a joke, is it?"

A ray of hope flickered. She wasn't even sure why. There was something in his voice that reached out to her, gave her comfort. She shook her head in reply. Her lashes were moist and she blinked, pushing the strands of wet hair out of her eyes.

"I wish it was a joke, but I really don't know where home is." She raised her eyes to his face again. "Or who I am." There, she'd said it out loud. Fear leaped in and spread webbed fingers through the void that was wrapped around her. "I don't know who I am," she repeated.

It didn't seem possible. "Just like that?" Angus had certainly heard about people getting amnesia, but the only time he'd ever seen it happen was on some movie-of-the-week. He'd never come across anyone with it in real life.

Until now, he amended. *Amnesia.* That would certainly explain the lost, waif-like quality he detected about her.

The woman nodded. Damp, dark blonde hair fell into her face again. She brushed it aside mechanically.

"Yes, just like that." At least, she assumed that it had come over her suddenly. She couldn't swear to anything with even a grain of certainty.

"What happened?" Sympathetic now, his tone was the one he used whenever he comforted Vikki after she'd had one of her nightmares.

Frustration filled her, barely manageable. "I don't know. I came to in an alley. The rain woke me up."

This wasn't the kind of conversation that should be conducted in a hallway, Angus thought. It looked as if he wasn't through for the day after all. He knew that Jenny would stay with Vikki until he got home. His seventy-year-young, motorcycle-riding neighbor had all but adopted Vikki as her granddaughter. Angus dug his key out of his pocket and unlocked his office door.

"C'mon back inside. Let's talk about it."

Reaching inside for the lights, Angus switched them on and gestured for the woman to enter. He followed, closing the door behind him. She stood beside the chair as if she wasn't certain what to do.

"Sit down," he urged gently.

Obeying, she sat down on the very edge of the chair, her hands gripping the armrests.

It was a bare-bones office. The walls were painted a neutral beige, with a couple of file cabinets placed against one and a good-sized window directly opposite. There were two doors off to one side—behind one was a tiny bathroom, behind the other an equally tiny darkroom. The room was dominated by a wide, well-polished desk that stood in the center. The view was great. When the smog and the fog weren't jockeying for position outside his fifth-floor window, he could see the ocean.

She'd pulled herself together again, he noted. Rigid, she was perched on the edge of the chair like a hunted bird that was ready to take flight at the slightest unfamiliar sound. And she was shivering.

"You look like you could use a cup of coffee."

Without waiting for her answer, Angus went to the closet-sized bathroom and filled the coffeepot with water. Placing it on the hot plate, he switched the coffeemaker on. All he had left was instant.

Could she use coffee? she wondered, watching him. Did she like it? Did she even drink it? She had no idea. Frustration gurgled through her like water from a freshly dug well, flowing out into the dirt. Creating mud.

"Thank you," she murmured. It wasn't for the coffee, it was for his thoughtfulness. For letting her stay for a little while when she had nowhere to go.

Angus nodded, then looked at her over his shoulder as the water began to brew. She was clutching her hands together in her lap like a schoolgirl waiting to have detention assigned. He looked on either side of her. "No purse?"

She looked down before answering, as if she hoped that one might magically materialize. It didn't.

"No. Nothing. Except for this." Shifting in the chair, she dug into the pocket of the trench coat. When she withdrew her hand, she was holding a small business card. It was stained and bent. And his.

Angus frowned, taking the card from her. He looked it over. There was nothing written on the back to indicate who it might have come from.

"Where did you get this?"

If she knew that, maybe she'd know who she was. She struggled to keep the despair from engulfing her.

"I don't know. I thought maybe you'd given it to me." She let a shaky breath escape her lips. "That's why I came. To see if you knew me."

Steam was rising from the glass pot. Angus measured out two teaspoons of coffee, put them into the mug, and watched the hot water he poured over the granules turn dark.

"How did you find me?" It would seem to him that if she had amnesia, she wouldn't know her way around.

"I asked directions. I don't know how long it took me to walk here."

A half smile curved her mouth. Angus found it completely captivating. It took him a moment to focus on the conversation.

"I guess people don't like to stop to talk to deranged-looking women," she finally said.

She didn't look deranged, just wet. And frightened. He glanced down at her foot. "Maybe the fact that you're wearing just one shoe had something to do with it. Where did you lose it?"

Embarrassed, she moved her bare foot behind the other one. She shrugged, hating this helplessness that held her prisoner. "I don't know. When I came to, I only had one on."

He nodded, then remembered he'd already poured the hot water. "How do you want your coffee?"

"I don't know."

The words haunted her. She'd been repeating them over and over again in her mind. Fresh tears threatened. She *didn't* know. Not her name, not where she lived, not even something as simple as how she took her coffee, or if she took it at all.

She looked as close to battle fatigue as any soldier he'd ever seen. The lady was perilously close to breaking down.

"We'll try black," he said soothingly.

Crossing to her, Angus handed her the mug. The way she wrapped her hands around it, he knew she was seeking warmth from it more than sustenance.

"Maybe you should get out of that," he suggested, nodding at her coat. Rather than having kept her dry, the coat was sealing moisture in around her. "I've got an old sweatshirt here someplace."

Angus began opening the drawers in his desk. The third one yielded a faded blue sweatshirt and an old W-2 form he had thought was missing. He placed the sweatshirt on the desk in front of her and made a mental note to file the form.

"You can change in there if you want." He indicated the tiny bathroom.

The coat was beginning to feel dank. She rose and took it off. But rather than go into the bathroom, she merely slipped the sweatshirt over her blouse. The sweatshirt was several sizes too large for her and the sleeves hung down well past her hands. It accentuated how lost she felt.

Huddling in the sweatshirt, she sat down again and picked up the mug. Her fingers were half buried in the sleeves.

"Thank you." The words were far too inadequate to express the gratitude she felt. As long as she could talk to him, she didn't feel so alone. Or so frightened.

She looked more like a waif than ever, he thought, studying her. There was a red mark on her forehead he hadn't noticed before. Angus stepped closer, his eyes narrowing as he gently moved her hair aside. Part of a scab that had just begun to form was torn away. "You're bleeding."

"Am I?" Her fingers fluttered along her hairline. Now that the rain wasn't washing over her, she could feel a thin, sticky line forming just over her right eye. She winced slightly as her fingers came in contact with it.

The headache buzzing around her temples amplified twofold.

"Wait." Angus caught her wrist, drawing her hand away from the wound. "I've got a first-aid kit. Let me clean that up for you. The last thing you want is an infection."

Self-conscious, she began to demur. But by now her energy was almost completely depleted. She let out a small puff of air. "I'd appreciate that."

The small red, white and blue box Angus pulled out from beneath the bathroom sink was battered and well-worn. It had been old even when he'd gotten it, left behind by the previous occupant of the office, an accountant who—according to the building maintenance man—was accident-prone. Angus placed the metal box on the desk, flipped open the rusty lock and took out what he needed.

"This might sting," he warned her just before he applied the antiseptic. She winced again, and he flashed her an apologetic smile. "Sorry."

"That's okay." Wanting to fidget, she forced herself to remain perfectly still as he worked. "It's nice to feel something besides cold and bewilderment, even if it is pain.''

Angus wiped away the peroxide residue. ''Must be rough,'' he empathized. ''Not knowing.'' He knew it would have had him climbing the walls.

Yes, it was, she thought. Extremely rough. ''I feel like I'm a void,'' she told him. ''A huge, gaping, endless void.'' She sucked in her breath again as Angus pressed the ends of the Band-Aid against her wound.

''Can't say I know what that feels like, but it must be hell.'' Angus stepped back to inspect his handiwork. It would do for now, he decided. ''I think that'll be okay.'' He closed the kit.

Her neck aching, she lowered her head again. She felt awkward. Awkward with herself. With the situation. With imposing on this man. This wasn't right.

Taking a deep breath, she rose to her feet. She offered him a brave smile and her hand. ''Thank you.''

Angus looked at her hand, his own remaining at his side. ''Where are you going?''

She lifted her shoulders helplessly, then let them fall. She had no destination. ''I don't know, but I've imposed on you long enough. And since you don't know who I am—''

Her voice trailed off as she turned toward the door. What more was there to say? He didn't know who she was. That made two of them.

Angus hustled to get between her and the door. She couldn't just walk out of here, he decided. Not if she had nowhere to go. ''That doesn't mean I can't help you find out.''

''How?'' And why would he want to if he didn't know her?

Angus smiled to himself. Maybe she hadn't finished

reading what was written on his card: Angus MacDougall, *Private Investigator*.

"Well, the best place to start is the police station." He took her trench coat from the back of the chair and offered it to her. "It takes twenty-four hours before a person is officially declared missing, but that wouldn't stop someone from calling if they were worried because you hadn't turned up where you were supposed to be."

She flushed as she took the coat from him. "Do you think so?"

Angus helped her put the coat on over the sweatshirt. "If *I* thought you were missing, I'd certainly be calling every place I could," he assured her.

As he took her arm to guide her out the door, her limp caught his attention. With only one high heel on, she was off-kilter.

"Hold it." Returning to his desk, he opened the bottom drawer and deposited a pair of running shoes on top. They were his, an old pair he kept in the office for emergencies. Running helped him clear his head. "I know they're pretty large, but if we stuff some paper in the toe, they'll do in a pinch." He smiled at her. "At least there are two of them."

Grateful, she put them on, then glanced in his direction. "Any chance of there being a hamburger in your desk?"

It was the first hint of a smile he'd seen on her lips and it lit up her face. "No, but I think something can be arranged."

When they walked out of the building, the rain had temporarily stopped. Angus took the break in the weather as an omen. Stories handed down from his ancestors had been vivid enough to make him believe in omens, both good and bad. This one was good.

Angus guided her to his car. There weren't very many left in the lot. The nine-to-fivers had gone home an hour ago.

"It takes a little while to warm up," he explained as the vintage Mustang refused to start. His hand, large and sturdy, swept over the dashboard, as if coaxing a response from the vehicle.

Like a lover stroking his mistress, she thought. Her eyes widened. Where had that come from? Did she have a lover? Was there someone really waiting for her?

He saw the startled look. "What?"

Embarrassed, she looked away. "Nothing."

The engine caught. It had taken only three tries. Vindicated, Angus nodded in satisfaction.

"See, what did I tell you? If at first...." As he guided the car from the lot, his eyes shifted to her face. The solemnity wrenched at his heart, and he made a promise he had no way of knowing if he could keep: "It's going to be all right."

Like a child assured that there were no monsters under her bed, she wanted to believe him. Wanted to, but was afraid to. "Do you think so?"

He had absolutely nothing to base his assurance on. But that didn't stop him. In his estimation, she needed to hear the words.

"Sure I do." Leaning over, Angus covered her hand with his own in a mute gesture of comfort. Her hand felt like ice. "I know a few guys at the precinct. They'll be able to help you."

She sat looking straight ahead. It began to drizzle again.

Angus thought he heard her whisper, "I hope so," and squeezed her hand again before he withdrew his.

That made two of them, he thought.

* * *

"I'm afraid I can't help you." Detective Al Biordi looked at the man he had once served under in naval intelligence, and at the woman Angus had brought in. Noting the devastated look on her face, he quickly added. "It's not a matter of not wanting to. It's a matter of not being able to. No one matching your description has been reported missing." He pointed toward the computer he had just spent the last fifteen minutes poring over. The program he had accessed had yielded nothing. "Not here, or in any of the nearby states."

She began to protest that she hadn't been to any other state, then stopped. How did she know that? Maybe she had been. Maybe whatever had happened to her had happened somewhere else and afterwards she'd somehow managed to get here.

The ache in her head increased several notches and the hamburger Angus had gotten for her lay like cold lead in her stomach.

"Maybe nobody knows I'm gone," she said quietly. Or maybe, she thought, nobody cared.

"Exactly. All this means is that you probably haven't been missing for very long." He glossed over the word *probably*. The detective's expression softened. "Maybe this amnesia thing just happened in the last few hours."

Angus nodded. It was more than possible, given the state of her attire. Well, there was nothing they could do for tonight.

"Will you excuse us?"

Before she could answer, Angus ushered Al aside. He wanted a word with the man alone.

It was only necessary to take a few steps away from her within the crowded squad room for their voices to be lost in the din. Still, cautious, Angus glanced back at her to make sure that their words didn't carry.

She looked so small and lost, he was tempted to return to her, take her into his arms and just hold her. For a second, he almost gave in. Common sense intervened.

Angus turned to his friend. "All right, now what do we do?"

There wasn't a whole lot Al could suggest. "You can come back tomorrow and check with me then."

That still left them to deal with now. "Meanwhile? She's got no place to go, Al."

Al shook his head. If he had a dime for each person he'd come across that had no place to go, he would have been a rich man by now. The county was filled with them. He motioned Angus over to his desk.

Taking a pad out, he began to write. "I can give you the address of a homeless shelter that'll take her in. It's nearby." Finished, he ripped off the page, offering it to Angus. "It's the best I can do."

"Yeah, I know." Angus took the address from him. "Thanks."

Absently, he tucked the paper into his pocket and turned around to look at her again. She was watching him hopefully.

He didn't like the idea of just dropping her off at some shelter, but it really wasn't his problem, he reminded himself. It wasn't as if he didn't have anything else to occupy his time. Mrs. Madison was counting on him to come through with the evidence she needed to substantiate her claim that her husband was being unfaithful. And there was that little matter he had to clear up for Hogan, plus a background check for Dynamic Aerospace due by the end of the week.

If that wasn't enough, there was a certain miniature blue-eyed female who was only just now beginning to trust him—and she was waiting for him in his apartment.

His plate was definitely full.

His eyes slid over the woman's heart-shaped face, lingering on each feature. Her expression tugged at his heart.

Hell, he had nothing to feel guilty about. He'd done everything he could for her. He'd brought her here and stayed while she gave Al her statement. He'd even given her his sweatshirt and his running shoes. On top of that, he'd fed her. Nobody could fault him if he drove her to the shelter and just went on with his life.

No, it really wasn't his problem. Angus heard himself sigh. *She* wasn't his problem, just a stranger who had wandered in off the street.

A stranger who just happened to have his business card in her pocket.

Where the hell was she?

God damn it, he'd looked everywhere. If she was dead, she should have been here.

Why wasn't she here?

There'd been a story on the news this morning about the body of an unidentified female being found, but that was in Westminster. There was no way she could have gotten up there in her condition.

He was sure he'd gotten her. It wasn't a clear shot, but when his gun had discharged he'd seen her stumble. He had hit her, he bet his life on it.

He *was* betting his life on it.

If it hadn't been for those firemen, he would have been able to go after her and finish the job. He hadn't been able to wait them out. The others had been waiting for him. The others, who couldn't know about this snag.

A string of obscenities echoed, following him through the empty, crumbling parking structure as he returned to his car.

What the hell was he going to do if she was still alive?

Chapter 2

Angus was still arguing with himself fifteen minutes later, as he turned his car down Main Street.

He glanced at the woman before looking back at the road. It might have helped assuage his conscience if she'd talked, if she'd gotten on his nerves or even unreasonably lashed out at him because he was her only available target in this newborn world in which she suddenly found herself. Then he might have felt justified in leaving her at the homeless shelter.

But she didn't do any of those things. She didn't lash out, she didn't get on his nerves. She didn't say a word once she got into the car.

What she did was sit perfectly still in the passenger seat and silently watch the rain flirt with the windshield wipers as the storm temporarily slacked off and debated its options for the remainder of the evening.

Without saying a single word, the woman who had unintentionally wandered into his life without warning or preamble had succeeded, just as unintentionally, in making him feel like a heartless bastard because he was abandoning her. Never mind that she didn't know him and he didn't know her. None of that mattered right now. He was the only name, the only face, Angus reasoned, that this woman knew.

And what was he doing? He was foisting her off on the first homeless shelter he came across.

Pretty damn heartless, that's what his father would have said, looking down his hawk-like nose at him. Not that his father knew anything about hearts—just about assigning guilt. His father had been born without the vital organ in place. That was supposed to be one of the things that made Angus different from his father. He was supposed to have one.

His conscience continued to nag him as he brought the car to a slow, reluctant halt by the curb directly in front of the shelter.

It nagged even harder as he took a good look at the building. Squeezed in between a vacant store with a jagged, horizontal crack running the length of the front window, and a pawnshop that sported both dust and items in its show window that were undoubtedly older than the woman beside him, the homeless shelter looked woebegone and forlorn. Whatever color it had once been painted had long since been worn away by the endless parade of lost souls who had crossed the threshold with hopelessness as their only traveling companion. The only bit of color evident was the graffiti scrawled over the gray metal door. When he made it out, he winced at the sentiment that had been spray-painted there.

Angus felt like a hypocrite for trying to smile at her. "This is it."

She turned to look at the building and slowly nodded.

Angus couldn't shake the feeling that he was the head gladiator releasing the Christian virgin into the lion-filled arena.

"You'll be all right?"

It was a dumb question, Angus berated himself. How could anyone be all right in a place that reeked of despair? What was he doing, bringing her here? She didn't belong in a homeless shelter. She wasn't a homeless woman. She was a woman who had misplaced her home along with the rest of her life.

Fighting against the shiver that threatened to take possession of her, she pressed her lips together, then answered, "I'll have to be."

A feeling of being disembodied, of floating just outside herself, played over her as she placed her hand on the car door latch. Looking at him one last time, she forced her mouth into a smile. He'd gone out of his way for her when he hadn't had to. She was grateful to him for that.

"Thank you."

Angus had no idea what she was thanking him for. But the fact that it might be for bringing her to this forsaken place burned away the last bit of his detachment. Whatever distance he'd been trying to nurture died a quick, ignoble death on Main Street, between Fairview and Langhorn.

He couldn't let her go in there.

Leaning over her, Angus quickly pulled the passenger door shut before she had a chance to get out.

Obviously confused, she looked at him quizzically. "What are you doing?"

It was perfectly clear what he was doing, he thought. What wasn't clear was why—and he was still working the reasons out in his head.

"You're not staying here," he told her with finality.

Part of her felt like a prisoner who'd just been given a stay of execution. But stay of execution or not, her current situation was still very much up in the air.

"I've got nowhere else to go." The hollow sound of the words mocked her.

Nowhere to go. No home, no one waiting. What if that were all true? Not just temporarily but for always? She didn't think she could bear that.

"Yes, you do."

He said it with such conviction, the protest temporarily evaporated from her lips.

Glancing in the rearview mirror, he found his way still clear. Angus pressed down on the accelerator and pulled away from the curb. He wanted to get going before he changed his mind or, at the very least, decided to have it medically examined.

You would figure that a thirty-year-old guy with his background would have gotten hard-nosed by now, Angus thought. Or at least callous enough not to succumb to a pair of sad violet eyes, no matter how incredible they looked.

Especially when the owner of those eyes wasn't even batting them at him seductively.

Seduction he knew he could have handled. Easily. It was the fear, the vulnerability he saw within those eyes that had delivered the knockout punch. A technical knockout.

He'd been TKOed—and she'd never even lifted a hand.

"Where are we going?" she finally asked.

"My place." Making a U-turn, Angus didn't look at her as he answered. He didn't have to. He could feel the waves of her apprehension crowding into the front of the car between them. "It's not what you think," he assured her quickly. "I just couldn't leave you in a place like that."

He wouldn't have left his dog in a place like that, if he'd had a dog.

She felt herself wavering between relief and uneasiness. But she had to trust somebody. And there was just something about Angus MacDougall that told her he was a good choice.

Choice. As if she had any.

Stifling a soft sigh, she dragged her hand through her tangled hair. "Won't your wife mind if you bring me home without at least warning her first?"

Was that genuine concern, or was she trying to feel him out for information?

Angus smiled to himself. Maybe he *had* been in this business a bit too long. He might not be hard-nosed, but he was certainly getting cynical.

"I don't have a wife." He slanted a look in her direction. The woman had stiffened and was trying not to show it. He took no affront. For all she knew, she could have wandered into the office of a homicidal maniac who happened to give out business cards. "I do have a daughter, if it makes you feel any better. Her name's Victoria. Vikki," he amended.

Vikki, at seven, had opinions on almost everything, most of all on matters pertaining to her. Dealing with her was a bit like trying to find his way through a minefield without losing any limbs.

Angus felt, rather than heard, the woman's sigh of relief. "It's not that I don't trust you, it's just that…"

He spared her the agony of trying to find the right words.

"Yeah, I know. I'd be the same in your situation." He flashed what he hoped was an encouraging, sympathetic grin in her direction before looking back at the road. "But you have to sleep somewhere, and I figure you might as well do it in a place where the sheets are clean and no one'll get in your face with questions you can't answer yet."

He couldn't possibly know how grateful she was, she thought. Whether he realized it or not, he was giving her a lifeline to cling to. Someone familiar to hang onto. His was the only face she knew.

She blinked and tears formed in the corners of her eyes. "You're being very nice."

Angus shrugged. Gratitude always made him uncomfortable. It wasn't anything that he'd had even a nodding acquaintance with when he was younger. He'd never learned how to handle it.

"Just maintaining good client-private investigator relations." The confused expression on her face registered after a beat. "That was my card in your pocket," he began to explain. "That means that someone I've dealt with sometime in the last year and a half must have given it to you."

He noticed that she took out the card again and turned it over in her hand.

"How do you know that? The time, I mean. Why a year and a half?"

Pressing down on the accelerator, he made it through the yellow light. The car behind him braked suddenly, its tires squealing.

"Because before then, I didn't have business cards. Just an ad in the business section of the phone book. Maybe if I run some names past you, one of them might mean something to you." He kept the names of all his clients in a small navy bound book that he carried with him in the back of his car. You never knew when a name or a number might come in handy. "That's all it takes, some-times." He spared her another look. She seemed to be relaxing just a fraction. He congratulated himself on the progress. "Just something to trigger your memory."

If only it were that easy. Her mouth curved in a smile. "Are you always this optimistic?"

He grinned as he turned into the parking lot closest to Harris Memorial's emergency room. "Always." He winked at her. "I consume a lot of sugar."

She seemed to become aware of her surroundings for the first time since they drove away from the shelter. She stared at the building, then at him.

"You live in a hospital?"

Angus came around to her side of the car and opened the door, then stepped back. "I'd feel better if you were checked out." Maybe he'd been presumptuous, but there was a reason for that. "I don't really like that cut above your eye." Actually, he was more worried about the pos-sibility of a concussion, but she had enough on her mind without having to hear that.

She hesitated, looking at the squat section of the hos-pital that faced the lot. "I don't have any money."

He wasn't rolling in it, either, Angus thought. Mentally, he juggled a few bills that he knew he could put off for a few weeks.

"Don't worry about it." Shutting the car door, he took her arm. Angus nodded toward the entrance, silently coax-ing her. "We'll put it on the tab."

She took a few steps forward, but when the electronic door yawned open, she remained where she was, standing on the outside.

"I don't know if I'm up to this. Won't they want to know things, like my insurance company, my social security number, an address?'' She looked at him pointedly. ''A name?''

Was she remembering something? Angus searched her face for an indication that she'd tapped into a memory. But there was nothing. ''Anything coming back to you?''

She hadn't realized that she had just rattled all that off. ''I sounded as if I'd just been through this before, didn't I? Checking into a hospital, I mean.''

A look of concentration came over her face, but her efforts seemed to be in vain. Her disappointment was almost tangible.

Whatever she had just said must have popped up in her mind without preamble. Sighing in frustration, she shook her head.

Angus refused to let that daunt him. Or her. Taking her arm again, he led her through the opened doors.

''I guess we'll just have to keep you talking until something does come to you. As for what we tell the hospital,'' he said as he approached the emergency room sign-in sheet and picked up the pen, ''let me take care of that.''

He signed her in as Jane Reilly.

It felt as if an eternity had dragged by before she was finally free to leave the hospital. Standing just outside the emergency room, she took a deep breath. The air smelled of rain. She absorbed the familiar scent like a dry, greedy sponge. Absorbed, too, the sight of Angus's car. It looked like an old, beloved friend to her. Technically, she supposed it was.

He read the signs correctly. ''You hate hospitals?''

''I just don't like getting poked and prodded.''

''Can't say I blame you.''

Getting in, he backed the car out of the spot.

''Who's Jane Reilly?''

The question caught him off guard. "Just someone I once knew."

He aligned his car with the security box and tapped out the security code number he'd been given by the outpatient registration receptionist. The striped pole slowly rose in a crooked salute, allowing them to pass.

No, that wasn't fair, he thought. Jane Reilly was far more than just someone he'd once known. She deserved better at his hands. Even if, ultimately, he hadn't fared better at hers.

"Vikki's mother," he murmured. The barrier fell back into position behind them as he waited for a dark green van to pass.

He'd said "Vikki's mother," not "my ex-wife." The woman looked at him. The warm smile had faded. His jawline was just the slightest bit rigid, as if he'd braced himself against the onslaught of memories. At least he *had* memories, she thought enviously.

"You weren't married?"

Nothing wrong with her mind, Angus thought. Her question roused a bittersweet sensation within him. He wasn't closemouthed, but he generally wasn't all that talkative either. Not about some things, anyway. Tonight was different, though. For some reason, he felt the need to talk.

Maybe it was because talking to her didn't matter. This wasn't anything she'd be likely to remember once her own memory returned. It wouldn't be important enough to her. Not the way it was to him.

"No." His voice echoed back at him within the car. He hadn't realized how sad that word could sound. "She never wanted to get married." He'd asked her three separate times before finally giving up. He shouldn't have given up so easily, he thought ruefully. "Marriage was too conventional for her."

If the name belonged to someone else, there might be complications if she used it. "Won't there be some sort of a problem, my using her name?" she asked.

The bittersweetness mushroomed, threatening to swallow him up. Angus reminded himself that it was all in the past. Nothing he could do to change that, or any of it. There was no point in agonizing.

The feeling wouldn't leave.

Eyes on the road, he shook his head. "None that I can think of."

He sounded different, distant. Had she tread on something she shouldn't have, or was that just her imagination?

Because she was desperate for some kind of answers to at least this, she pressed on past a point that had a No-trespassing sign.

"Where is she now?"

Sometimes he wondered that himself. Other times, he let his imagination take over. "Scattered to the four corners of the world."

He could almost visualize it. Jane had been so vital, such a free spirit. It seemed appropriate somehow, thinking of her gliding on the wind.

The woman beside him was silent—trying to understand, he guessed. "She died six months ago," he told her. "I didn't know until after she was cremated."

No use in going over that terrain, either, he told himself. There was nothing to be gained.

"You didn't stay in contact with her?"

"No."

He'd damned himself for that a thousand times. If he'd remained in touch with Jane, if he'd insisted on it, then he would have known about Vikki. More than that, he would have been part of her life from the beginning instead of jumping into fatherhood feet first, seven years after the fact.

"That was my fault." He accepted the blame readily, even though he could have argued that Jane would have done something about the situation if she'd wanted to. "When Jane refused to marry me after I'd asked her a third time, I became angry and severed all ties with her. By the time I finally cooled down again, she was gone. Vanished without a trace."

Vanished without a trace. Was someone saying that about her even right at this moment, the woman wondered. Struggling against the despair the question brought in its wake, she looked at Angus.

"Didn't you try to find her?"

It wasn't hard to guess what was going on in her mind. Angus smiled.

"You're probably thinking I can't be much of a private investigator if I couldn't even find one small, very pregnant woman. And you'd be right. Except that I *didn't* try to find her." And that was something he was still trying to make his peace with. "Pride got in the way."

Angus shrugged, wishing he could as easily shrug away the guilt. "And then I guess I just got too busy. Too busy to think about her."

Which was a lie, but it was one he'd needed to tell himself at the time. It had taken the sting out of missing her. Some of it, anyway.

The smile that curved his mouth was rueful. "I didn't even know I was a father until six months ago when Jane's best friend came to see me. In one hand she had a letter from Jane. With the other she was holding on to Vikki."

"That must have been a shock," she said. "Instant fatherhood."

He laughed then, and there was something very comforting about the sound. It was rich, bracing, and seemed to surround her, locking the world out rather than sealing her in.

"Something like that," he finally said.

She knew nothing about this man. And yet, she had a feeling that Angus was a good father. That he cared. After all, he'd taken it upon himself to help a stranger—how much better he must have been with his own flesh and blood. "How's fatherhood working out for you?"

"All right." He thought about it for a minute, wanting to be honest with her. With himself. "Slow. Some days are better than others. Vikki's still feeling me out."

He knew Vikki missed her mother fiercely. And there were times, when she held her head just so, that he could see Jane within the little girl. That was when he missed her most of all.

Angus pulled himself up abruptly, looking at the woman in the passenger seat. Amusement worked its way forward. "Hey, aren't we supposed to be trying to piece things together about *you?*"

She shook her head slowly. "There aren't any pieces to piece together about me." A shy smile slipped over her lips. "And I guess I just wanted something to fill in this gaping void in my head. If I sounded as if I was trying to pump you, I'm sorry."

He waved away the apology. "Nothing to be sorry about. And you're wrong, you know."

"About what?"

"About there being no pieces to work with." She was looking at him as if she expected him to pull a rabbit out of a hat. There was no rabbit—but there was hope. "We've got some pieces," he assured her.

Just as they turned into his garden apartment complex,

the sky above the car suddenly lit up. An angry bolt of lightning streaked across it. Several beats later, a crack of thunder loudly announced that the short honeymoon between man and weather was over. The storm was back and it had brought the heavy artillery.

"Well, there's one piece," she agreed. "I don't have a concussion."

He pulled his vehicle into its assigned space in the carport.

"Besides that." He could see she was waiting for him to elaborate. "To begin with, your clothes are designer label." Uncertain surprise entered her eyes. "I didn't have anything to read when the orderly took you to be x-rayed," he explained. Since she hadn't had any need of her clothes at the time, he'd examined them for drops of blood, tears or any other clues. That included reading the labels. "That means you either earn a good living, or your family has money."

There was another explanation. "Or my husband does."

He was pretty certain they could rule that out. "No wedding ring." Angus pointed to her left hand.

She looked down at it as if seeing her hand for the first time. Spreading her fingers, she held it up. "Thieves?"

In reply, Angus took her hand in his. It felt icy, even though it wasn't cold inside the car. She was scared, he thought, and he did his best to set her at ease.

"There's no indication that anything was pulled off." He drew her attention to her finger. "No scratches, no cuts—thieves are rarely gentle, especially when they're afraid of getting caught and they're in a hurry—no marks or even a tan line that suggests a ring has ever been on your hand."

Releasing her hand, he continued with his catalog.

"Your complexion's healthy, you have no split ends, your fingernails aren't broken or chewed and there are no small, white crescents on the nails, all pointing toward the fact that you're in reasonably good health and well-nourished. Furthermore, there's a slight callus on the inside of your right index finger, but not on your left." He traded hands, taking the other in his. "That would indicate that you're right-handed," he concluded. "See?" Angus smiled into her eyes. "Pieces."

Pieces. Tiny pieces, but pieces nonetheless. Would they somehow work themselves into a whole? Or was that all she was ever going to have—just fragments of what once was a life?

With effort, she pushed aside the thought before it overwhelmed her. "Now can you read my palm and tell me who I am?"

"That'll take a little longer." Angus glanced at his watch. It was later than he'd thought. It was almost nine. Two hours past when he'd said he would definitely be back. He'd called home from the police station to say he was going to be late, but that didn't negate the fact that he'd gone back on his promise to Vikki. "Oh, God."

His groan evoked guilt. She'd kept him away from home and he had a life of his own to lead. Everyone did, except for her. "I'm sorry."

She was, he thought. Despite the situation she found herself in, she could still think of someone else. It came automatically. He took it as a good sign. Angus smiled at her as he got out.

"Next time you lose your memory, try to do it in the morning. It'll fit my schedule better." He saw the bewildered look enter her eyes. He guessed he wasn't his sharpest at this hour. "My turn to be sorry. It was a joke. Now you can see why stand-up comedy was never a viable alternative for me.''

He had a nice smile, she thought. The kind of smile that crept into your subconscious, arousing trust. It felt as if he cared. The thought heartened her, even though she knew that, logically, there was no reason in the world why this man should care about the dilemma she found herself in. She was as much of a stranger to him as he was to her.

But for some reason he didn't feel like a stranger.

She looked toward the artfully arranged row of garden apartments. Which one belonged to him? And his child, she reminded herself.

Someone else whose life she was interrupting. ''Will your daughter be asleep?''

Angus led the way to his apartment, which was located on the ground floor. The door faced the carport, but the bedroom windows looked out onto the center of the complex. At night, the peaceful sight almost made him forget the frantic hum of the life that swirled just outside the manicured landscaping. It was worth the price he paid each month.

He grinned at her question. Though Vikki talked as if she were seven-going-on-forty, she had the constitution of a whirling dervish. Even if that whirling dervish had been up half the night with a bellyache.

''It's highly unlikely. Vikki hardly ever seems to sleep.''

After unlocking the door, he gestured for the woman to walk in first.

She did, and found herself immediately under the scrutiny of a petite, older woman dressed entirely in black leather, with hair that resembled the color of a ripe, pink grapefruit.

Jenny Marlow made no effort to hide her interest in Angus's companion. She took full measure of the woman before turning her attention toward her neighbor. She'd regarded him as her unofficial son from the day she discovered his profession.

"Well, it's about time you got back, MacDougall. I was beginning to think I was going to have to move in." Brushing seductively against him as she traded places with Angus, she wrapped her long, bony hand around the doorknob. "Lucky for you, my biker club doesn't meet tonight." The wide, amused grin uncovered a space where one tooth was conspicuously missing. Jenny maintained that a spill from the back seat of a Harley had been responsible. "Bringing your work home with you now, are you?"

Angus shoved his key into his pocket, along with his hand. "She needed a place to stay." Now that he thought of it, his neighbor was a far more suitable roommate for the woman than he was. "Jenny, would you—?"

Jenny read him like a book with large print. Fluffy pink hair fluttered from side to side as she adamantly shook her head.

"Sorry, can't help you. Got my grandson and his friend camping out in my living room right now, sleeping bags and all. Walking hormones, that's what they are." Jenny winked at Angus, opening the door. "She'd be better off here, trust me. You, at least, are a gentleman."

She paused as she regarded the woman one last time. "Got a heart as big as a swimming pool," Jenny confided. Her eyes glittered with sex and mischief as she looked at Angus. "Give him a tumble myself, but he's too old for me." Jenny punctuated the declaration with a loud laugh.

"No question about that," Angus agreed. "Way too

old.'' He looked toward the back. Vikki now occupied what had once been his den. ''Vikki asleep?''

Jenny snorted. ''You wish. She's in her room, playing with that damn hand computer game you got her. We had pizza,'' she suddenly remembered. She saw him reaching into his pocket and shook her head. ''My treat. There's a slice or two left in the refrigerator.''

Her eyes shifted again to the woman. ''I'd suggest you feed it to your guest here and fatten her up a little so she qualifies for a shadow.''

Jenny let herself out. ''Call me if you need me.'' She nodded at Angus's companion. ''It was nice meeting you, honey.''

The door closed, and the woman asked, ''That's your neighbor?''

He laughed at her tone, understanding it perfectly. ''Something else, isn't she?''

But Jenny was already forgotten as he regarded the woman before him. How did it feel, being a walking question mark? He wasn't sure he'd know how to handle it. He'd always been the type who had to know things, who had to get the answers, figure out the mystery before anyone else did. Not knowing who he was would have driven him crazy.

''You know, we're going to have to come up with a name for you,'' he told the woman, ''until we find out your real one.'' Crossing to one end table, Angus picked up the telephone book, then handed it to her. ''Why don't you look through this and see if any name appeals to you, while I look in on my daughter?''

He walked out of the room, thinking how strange it still felt saying that word. *Daughter.* Six months, and he still hadn't quite gotten used to it.

But he was getting there.

And maybe eventually, he thought as he heard the pages of the phone book rustling, so would the mystery woman.

Chapter 3

He knocked softly but received no answer.

Easing the door open slowly—mindful of the fact that even at the tender age of seven, Vikki guarded her privacy—Angus looked in.

He found his daughter sitting cross-legged on her bed, her eyes intent on the screen of the game she held in her hands. With her hair—dark blonde like his—falling into her face, she appeared oblivious to his entrance.

Angus knew better. Vikki absorbed *everything* that went on around her, like a proverbial sponge. In that, he supposed, she was a great deal like him. The nonchalant, spit-in-your-eye independent streak, so incongruent with someone so young, was something she got from her mother.

It wasn't easy, being the father of a precocious seven-year-old. Especially since he hadn't had seven years to work up to it. Days like today didn't help. She'd been sick last night. So sick that she'd actually allowed him to hold her and give her sympathy—something she'd yet to do of her own accord when she was well. There was very little else he could do for a bellyache that came from eating too much junk food. So he'd stayed up with her and held her and read her favorite story to her over and over again until he could recite it from memory, the way she could.

When he'd left this morning, he'd promised her that he'd be back early. Instead, he'd been exceptionally late and probably lost the headway he'd made last night.

But then, he hadn't counted on a woman with amnesia wandering into his office.

The fortunes of war. He doubted Vikki's seven-year-old worldliness made room for things like that yet.

Since she didn't acknowledge him, he made the first move. "Hi."

Vikki didn't reply. She didn't even look up. If he'd been his own father, he would have walked out. But Angus *wasn't* his father, and it was precisely the memory of those austere, stark days—when it had only been the Colonel and him, moving from base to base—that kept Angus in the room. Kept him there searching for a crack, an opening he could widen enough to wiggle through. He wasn't about to let Vikki shut him out the way the Colonel had shut him out. The way Jane had. Vikki was his and they were going to communicate.

He leaned against the doorjamb, watching her. Vikki's thumbs flew across the buttons as she battled to keep the earth safe from yet another alien invasion. She had great hand-eye coordination, he thought. The Colonel would have liked that.

Angus tried again. "Heard you had pizza."

She caught her bottom lip between her teeth and

pressed down harder on the right-hand button. Another alien bit the dust, he judged.

"Yeah."

Her answer was preoccupied. She might be young in years, but she was all female. And she was making him pay for breaking his word. Angus crossed to her bed.

"I didn't mean to be this late, Vik." He knew she liked him to call her that. It made her feel grown up.

Vikki's eyes momentarily left the playing field. They were accusing when they met his, the accusation masking the hurt just beneath.

Seven-going-on-forty, he thought again. A child shouldn't have to mask anything. Shouldn't know *how* to mask anything. In his opinion, Vikki knew way too much too soon, and he wasn't sure if that was really such a good thing.

He sat down on the edge of her bed. Vikki went back to playing her game. And to ignoring him. "I got caught up in a case. It couldn't be helped."

Her thumbs never stopped moving. "Did someone shoot at you?"

That seemed to be the only excuse she was willing to accept. Sometimes, she was positively ghoulish. Angus sighed.

"I think you watch too much television." He was going to have to talk to Jenny about that again. The woman had a weakness for movies about private investigators. Hollywood was giving Vikki some very strange ideas. "I've never been shot at, Vik. I don't handle those kind of cases. You know that." He had explained what he did at length when she first entered his life.

The look Vikki spared him was one of disappointment. "If nobody was shooting at you, then you could've come home."

He wasn't about to spend what was left of the evening arguing with her about it.

"I did. Just later than expected." He meant for that to be the end of the discussion. Rising, he nodded toward her door. "We've got a guest."

Her face became animated. She discarded the game as if it were nothing more than a candy wrapper, and scrambled to her feet. "A dog?"

It was familiar ground. Angus had no use for dogs himself, but if getting one meant so much to Vikki, he knew he was going to have to look into it. He wondered if there was any place that let you test-run owning a dog. The way he figured it, he'd already committed himself about as far as he was willing to, without seeing exactly what he was getting himself into.

"No, a lady."

"Oh." Exuding annoyance, Vikki picked up her game and went back to eradicating aliens. "Why'd you bring her here for?"

Very patiently, he removed Vikki's hands from the game. Over her protest, he shut it off and put the game on the bookshelf above her bed. "I brought her here because she has nowhere to go."

Vikki forgot to pout about the game. "She's homeless?"

Noting the barely contained enthusiasm, Angus decided not to disillusion Vikki for the moment. "I guess, in a way."

"And dirty?" Anticipating the sight of someone she considered really interesting, Vikki made it to her door ahead of her father.

Angus shook his head. The way Vikki's mind worked baffled him completely. Weren't little girls supposed to be neat and clean—or was that a thing of the past? He had never had a sister, or even a female cousin, but the girls he had known at the various bases he'd lived on had never had an affinity for dirt or flying bullets. Certainly not the way Vikki did.

And Jane had been unconventional, but nothing like this.

Vikki rushed out, heading toward the small living room. She stopped short when she saw the woman Angus had brought home with him. Her first reaction seemed to be disappointment. It shimmered across her small, oval face like a spring rain. And then she saw the white dressing taped slightly askew on the woman's forehead.

Hope sprung eternal.

"Did someone shoot at you?" Vikki held her breath, waiting for the right answer.

"No," Angus dismissed. This bloodthirstiness of hers was getting out of hand. About to say something else to his daughter, he almost didn't hear the soft, awestruck *yes* whispered behind him. Turning, he looked at the woman, positive he'd imagined the word. "Did you say something?"

"Yes." Her eyes opened wide, she was the personification of disbelief. "I said *yes,*" she repeated.

Like a woman moving through the languid waves of a dream, she gingerly touched the wound, then winced. It was still there, still real.

And she remembered how she had gotten it.

She raised her eyes to Angus's, just the tiniest shard of a memory catching the light, flashing through her mind before disappearing into oblivion. There was nothing before it, nothing after it. It existed autonomously. But it was there.

"Someone shot at me," she told him. Even when she said it out loud, it didn't sound plausible.

But she knew it had happened. Shutting her eyes, she could relive that one split second in time. Hear the gun discharge, feel the pain as something—the bullet—grazed her.

"Who?" Angus demanded. If Vikki's question had triggered something, maybe he could push that something a little further, make her remember more.

She pressed her lips together, trying to summon an answer. The fragment broke up until it was just so much dust. And then it was gone. Nothing took its place. "I don't know."

Vikki's blue eyes were huge with admiration. "Real bullets?"

That wasn't a cut on her forehead, Angus realized, that was a graze. The woman had been grazed by a bullet. He hadn't noticed it when he cleaned up her wound—and he felt like an idiot. But, despite the romantic notions attached to his profession, flying bullets didn't immediately jump to mind.

"It looks that way," he told his daughter. He ruffled the tousled blonde hair fondly. He noticed that she didn't jerk immediately away this time. Yes, he was making progress. "Also looks like you scored the first point."

Eyebrows drawn together, Vikki turned her small face up to his. "Huh?"

Affection nudged at his heart. She looked exactly her age. Seven, and not a minute older. "She lost her memory."

There was renewed wonder in her eyes as Vikki looked at the woman again. "You don't know who you are?" Her young voice hummed with awe.

At least *someone* was entertained by her dilemma, the woman thought, smiling at the little girl. "No, I'm afraid not."

That was the key word, she thought. *Afraid.* She was afraid that this condition would remain forever. Afraid that no one would turn up to claim her and take her back to her life. And afraid that she would never remember what that life was.

The grin made Vikki look like a miniature of her father. "Cool."

The woman found that she *could* laugh at Vikki's response. *Cool* wasn't the word she would have used to sum up her situation, but somehow, on the little girl's lips, it seemed like the right one.

Ever pragmatic, Vikki asked, "What am I supposed to call you?"

The fact that Vikki was interested in addressing her at all told Angus that his daughter had tentatively accepted the woman's presence in their home. Maybe she even identified a little with the woman, he thought, because for a long time, she didn't have a place to call her own, either. From what he gathered from Jane's letter, the life she and Vikki had led was pretty nomadic.

He glanced at the telephone book he'd given the woman before going into Vikki's room. It was sitting back on the side table, closed. Had looking at it proved too frustrating?

He began fielding Vikki's question for her. "We were just—"

"Rebecca." Even as she said it, as her tongue wrapped itself around the name, it felt right to her. Sounded right.

Rebecca.

Her name was Rebecca.

She'd found it on the second page in the telephone book. As soon as she'd read it, she'd known. It was her name. She waited for more, for her last name to attach itself to Rebecca in her mind. But just as with the earlier fragment, nothing more had followed.

Angus looked at her. This was beginning to feel promising. "Is that the name you picked?"

She shook her head. "I didn't pick it. It picked me. My name is Rebecca."

She remembered, he thought. She remembered her name and that someone had fired at her. The pieces were beginning to come together.

"Rebecca what?" Angus pressed.

Her smile was almost shy. And damn appealing. But he banished the thought as soon as it came. This couldn't get personal. He was just helping her in his professional capacity.

Yeah, right, by bringing her home with him. Very professional.

"I don't know."

Angus curbed his impatience. After all, they were making progress. The doctor at the emergency room had told him that most of the time amnesia was just a temporary condition. Dropping a dark curtain over everything was sometimes the mind's way of coping with an intolerable situation.

Like being shot at.

"You're doing great." He was the soul of encouragement. "Maybe by morning, the rest of it'll come back to you." Though she nodded, she looked extremely tired. Small wonder, considering the kind of day she'd had. "Until then, I can offer you some cold pizza, an old football jersey and a bed."

Vikki's head immediately jerked up at the mention of the last item. Suspicion clouded her small features. "Mine?" she wanted to know.

She'd had little when she came to him. Maybe that was

why she guarded everything she had so jealously. Still, it was a trait he didn't particularly like. He wondered if it was ingrained, or if, given enough time, he could break her of it.

"No, mine." He placed one hand on Vikki's shoulder, his eyes on Rebecca. "I'll take the couch," he added before Vikki had the chance to ask anything that might embarrass Rebecca.

He liked the sound of her name, he thought. *Rebecca.* It had grace, poetry. It suited her.

Rebecca had other ideas about the arrangement. "I can't put you out like that. I'll take the couch."

She glanced at it. The tan-and-brown sofa looked well broken in, comfortable for a night of TV viewing. But for sleeping? She had her doubts. Still, she couldn't take his bed. He had already done far more than most people would.

Angus tried diplomacy. "We'll flip for it," he proposed.

Vikki rose on her toes, tugging on Rebecca's arm. Securing her attention, she announced matter-of-factly, "He cheats."

"Not this time," Angus promised, raising one hand as if he were taking an oath. The significance of his daughter's statement hit him belatedly. He looked down at Vikki. "And how would *you* know if I cheated—not saying that I do, mind you."

It was all too obvious for Vikki. She sighed and recited in a singsong voice, "Because when you want me to win, I do."

Leave it to a kid to take all the complications out. "That could just be luck."

Vikki was unconvinced. "Mom said people make their own luck. Especially you."

He had already discovered that Jane had talked a lot about him to Vikki, telling her stories about him to fill a void and make up for the lack of his physical presence in the little girl's life. A fact, he thought with a touch of bitterness, that Jane had been responsible for. The upshot was that the little girl had come to him knowing a great deal more about him than he did about her. The sum of his knowledge had been contained in Jane's letter.

He saw no point in contending Vikki's assertion. Not in front of a third party. "Let's table this for now, okay?" Raising an eyebrow, he looked in Rebecca's direction. "So, pizza sound good to you?"

She had no idea whether she liked pizza or not. She only knew that she was hungry.

"Food sounds good to me," she confessed. The hamburger he'd gotten her had finally managed to settle in her stomach, and now it wanted company.

Angus walked into the small, narrow kitchen and opened the side-by-side refrigerator. A pizza box, marked extra large and wedged in slightly askew, took up the entire second shelf. Easing it out, he set the box on the only clear space on the counter and opened it. There were only two slices left.

He looked at his daughter. Coming up to his waist, she was barely forty-five pounds. "It's a wonder you don't explode. Where do you put it all?"

"Jenny ate most of it," she said defensively. "She said she needed energy so she could ride her bike." A broad, proud grin chased away the defensive look. "She took me for a ride."

His eyes narrowed. "Tonight?"

Vikki nodded.

Damnit, it was one thing for Jenny to risk her own scrawny neck, he thought, struggling to bank down his anger. It was another when she risked his daughter's. He'd warned Jenny the last time it had happened about taking off with Vikki like that. When it came to his daughter, he wanted to play it safe.

Looking down at her face, he had a feeling that Jenny alone didn't shoulder the blame for this joyride she'd taken. He'd already learned that Vikki was an expert when it came to coercing and manipulating.

"Vikki, you know what I told you about riding a motorcycle."

Rebecca's eyes widened in disbelief. "That old lady rides a motorcycle?" She'd thought Jenny was kidding about the biker club.

Angus grinned at her stunned expression. "Better not let her hear you calling her that. Jenny's liable to leave tire marks up and down your body to show you just how young she is." He was exaggerating, but not by much.

Vikki was less interested in defending Jenny than in setting the record straight about the older woman's mode of transportation.

"It's a hog," she informed Rebecca proudly. "Jenny says she's taking me to San Francisco the next time she goes up there."

Maybe he was being overly cautious, but if he didn't say something, he had the uneasy feeling that he'd come home one night to find that his daughter and his neighbor had just taken off.

"Well, unless she's planning a trip in about fifteen years, I'd say you're going over my dead body. Now wash your face, brush your teeth and get into bed," he instructed. "You stayed home from school because you were sick, remember? That means you need your rest."

Vikki frowned, but she knew it was useless to protest. Angus could only be pushed so far. She knew the limits.

"Okay." Dragging her feet, Vikki started toward her room. Pausing, she looked over her small shoulder. "'Night, Angus. 'Night, Rebecca."

Rebecca smiled. "Good night, Vikki."

"Good night, Vik." Angus took out two plates from the cupboard overhead. "I'll be in in a few minutes to tuck you in."

Vikki didn't want Rebecca to think she was a baby. "You don't have to." With that, she disappeared.

"I *want* to," he called after her. Angus shook his head, closing the cupboard door. "She's every bit her mother."

And he'd loved her, Rebecca thought with a touch of envy. What did that feel like, having someone love you? Loving someone in return. Did she know? Was there someone she was in love with? It didn't seem like the kind of thing a person would forget, and yet she'd forgotten everything else.

Rebecca swallowed her impatience. It wouldn't do any good to torture herself like this.

She nodded toward the rear of the apartment. "She's very bright."

She'd get no argument from him on that score. Vikki, with her old eyes and her even older deportment, had astounded him from the first.

"That, she is." Opening a drawer, he looked for two sets of knives and forks. The rest of the silverware, along with a number of dishes, were in the sink. Jenny's neighborliness didn't extend to doing dishes. Not that he blamed her. It wasn't something he relished doing, either. He usually got around to it when there was nothing clean left.

"Why does she call you Angus?" Picking up napkins from the counter, Rebecca followed him to the small table that stood in front of the window. Black venetian blinds were tightly drawn, keeping out any prying eyes. "Shouldn't she be calling you Daddy?"

He laughed as he tried to imagine that. The word belonged in the mouth of a little girl comprising sugar and spice, not hot chili peppers.

"I doubt that's ever going to happen. Vikki calls me Angus because that's the way her mother referred to me. I don't think she'd be comfortable calling me Daddy yet." He shrugged. "Maybe someday. Besides, I've got a feeling that calling me Angus makes her feel that Jane's still around in some way."

Rebecca studied him for a moment. For the first time since she'd walked into his office, she really looked at the man she'd sought out. There was a kindness to him, a kindness that went beneath the good looks and quick, ready grin. It wasn't just in his eyes, but all through him.

"That's very understanding of you."

Angus shrugged again. "I don't know about understanding, but I've got great survival instincts." His eyes swept over her. It amused him that right at this moment, they both had the same amount of information on her. That gave them a bond, however slim. "My hunch is, so do you." She'd run from her assailant, whoever that was. And had hidden well enough to give herself time to come to him.

He blew out a breath ruefully as he looked at the bandage. "I should have realized that was made by a bullet."

Someone had shot at her, Rebecca thought yet again. Even though they had missed, the realization chilled her. What could she possibly have done to make someone want to come after her and shoot her? Another wave of gratitude washed over her, drenching her in the emotion. She was here, with him. Safe, instead of at a homeless shelter where whoever it was who had robbed her of her memory could get another crack at her—and maybe, this time, succeed in killing her.

She repaid him the only way she could, by absolving him of any guilt or embarrassment. "Why? Do people shoot at you often?"

The question made him laugh. "No, not at all, much to Vikki's disappointment." Vikki would probably take him in for show-and-tell if he showed up with his arm in a sling and a fresh bullet hole somewhere on his person. "I grew up on a military base. My father was an avid gun collector. There was nothing he loved more than hunting, except for maybe the military."

Hungry for a feeling of family, she crept a little further into his life. "Did you go hunting with your father?"

"No." It had been a major bone of contention—his refusal. But it was something Angus had staunchly stood by, even when it meant being ridiculed. "I couldn't see how shooting small animals could be called a sport unless *they* were armed as well." A quirky grin flittered across his lips. "That didn't sit too well with my father. I think he would have related quite well to Vikki's bloodthirsty streak." Angus rolled the thought over in his head. "It's probably where she gets it from."

Rebecca looked down at the pizza on the plate he set in front of her. "I can't eat two slices."

He had a hunch she could eat not only two, but several more as well. "Lady, I didn't want to say anything, but I've heard your stomach rumbling more than once since we left the police station. Trust me, it can handle two slices of pizza easily."

Trust him. Yes, she realized, she did. She really did. Was that a mistake?

Her head began to ache again.

Rebecca looked at his plate as he threw out the empty pizza box. "What are you going to eat?"

Setting the box by the trash container, Angus took another look inside the refrigerator. Success. He lifted a carton and held it aloft for her benefit. "Leftover Chinese food."

"Don't you have anything fresh?"

"A can of tuna," he recalled. Or at least, he thought the can was still in the tiny pantry. "I'm not sure how old it is, but it hasn't been opened."

Rebecca shook her head, amused. "I mean like vegetables, fruits, things like that."

"Why?" He sat down across from her again. Ignoring the plate, he started eating straight out of the carton. "Do you remember being a vegetarian?"

"No. Maybe." She shrugged, frustrated. "I don't know."

He saw the furrow forming along her forehead. Without thinking, he leaned over and smoothed it with the tips of his fingers. He saw something flitter through her eyes, but couldn't identify it. He smiled, dropping his hand.

"Don't worry, it'll come to you. Just give yourself some time. Right now, I think you need to eat and then just relax. Get a good night's sleep. From all indications, you've had one hell of a day."

Realizing he'd forgotten them, Angus rose to get two glasses. He wondered if Jenny and Vikki had consumed all the soda in the refrigerator, or if he had just missed seeing the cans when he'd looked inside.

"Could have been worse," she allowed.

Opening the refrigerator, he glanced back at her. "How?"

The slight smile on her lips went very quickly and very unexpectedly straight to his gut.

"I could have not had your name in my pocket."

Chapter 4

Angus turned around slowly and looked at Rebecca, her words playing themselves over in his head.

Though the sentiment behind them touched him, it also put the burden of discovering who she was squarely on his shoulders. It wasn't that he minded the burden. Technically, he'd already accepted it when he'd decided to bring her home with him. But what if he failed? What if he couldn't discover who she was? What if he couldn't unite her with the life she'd misplaced? What then?

Suddenly, though he'd always been able to philosophically shrug things off and roll with whatever punches life delivered, Angus wanted very badly to succeed.

But until he did, he didn't want Rebecca pinning any wings on him. Not when there was a chance that those wings might ultimately fall off.

Setting the soda-filled glasses on the table, he straddled his chair and faced her. "Yeah, well, I'd hold off counting my blessings on that score if I were you."

Was he being modest, or was it that he was just un-comfortable accepting her gratitude? Rebecca couldn't tell. Maybe she wasn't any good at reading people, she thought. It was frustrating, not knowing even that much about herself. But that wasn't his fault. If he'd turned her away, God only knew what she'd be going through this evening.

"How can you say that?" She set the last slice of pizza down and looked at him. "You've already taken me in, fed me." A glimmer of humor entered her eyes. "Given me your shoes."

Rebecca glanced down at her feet and wiggled one foot back into one of the large running shoes that seemed de-termined not to stay on.

Angus watched as the shoe swallowed up her foot. "You do look a little like you're auditioning for the Ring-ling Brothers circus." He laughed to himself. "I have to admit, I never thought of my feet as particularly big until now."

Compared to hers, his were huge. Cinderella, that's who she made him think of. Cinderella without the glass slipper. Except he meant to reunite her with more than just her shoe.

"We're going to have to do something about that in the morning." They weren't that far from a small shop-ping mall. She'd undoubtedly feel better about herself if she looked less like she'd been on the receiving end of an accident.

Where did she begin to thank him? she wondered. He seemed to be thinking of everything, and acting as if it were no big deal. Though she really couldn't remember, Rebecca had a feeling that Angus was not typical of his gender.

"See, that's what I mean. You're taking care of me and

you don't have to. I'm very grateful to you for that." The smile in her eyes reiterated her words.

Listening to her, he'd finished off the last of the takeout without realizing it. Angus laid aside his fork and pushed the small carton closed.

"You do have an upbeat way of looking at things." Leaning back, he paused to measure his distance from the trash container, then tossed the carton. It sank in easily. "Maybe you'll rub off on Vikki."

"Why?" The little girl hadn't struck her as particularly unhappy. "Is Vikki usually down?"

"No, not down," he amended. "Just old. Very old." He thought about the life she'd had before she had entered his. Jane had traveled on both sides of the Great Divide, working at a number of casinos in Atlantic City and Las Vegas. "She hasn't had much of a childhood, moving from place to place with Jane."

In an absolute sense, Angus supposed that Vikki's childhood echoed his. He'd had no roots, either, no sense of belonging to anyone or anything. It wasn't really accurate to say that he'd had the Colonel. He'd only been one of the Colonel's accessories, less valued than his medals and certainly less liked than his prized gun collection.

"Everyone should have a crack at being a kid once," he said softly.

There was something in his voice, she thought. Sympathy? Or was it something else? Wistfulness perhaps? She couldn't quite pin it down, but somehow it generated an intimacy between them, a closeness she couldn't explain even to herself.

"Especially when they're the right age for it." She knew she was prying, but she couldn't help it. She wanted at least some of her questions answered. "Was there any reason Jane moved around so much?"

Rebecca was asking him something he'd asked himself a dozen times or more. Always with the same answer. He didn't know. Jane had made her living as a blackjack dealer by choice. The same choice that could have led her in a host of other directions. Most notably into his life and into his arms. But that was the path she had chosen *not* to take.

He shrugged carelessly now. "A fever of the blood, I guess."

"Restless feet—" she agreed, then stopped as abruptly.

He saw the look that crossed her face. Was she remembering something else? "What?"

"Someone said that to me once." Each word emerged slowly, as if it were being held up and carefully examined before being released. Rebecca raised her eyes to his face. "Someone I knew."

She looked too tired to be prodded at length. Angus lifted an eyebrow, silently posing the question.

Rebecca understood and shook her head. "I don't know who." She sighed, wrapping her hands around the glass of soda. Some of the fizz drizzled lightly on her hand. She hardly noticed. "You have no idea how frustrating it is, not knowing anything about myself." Her eyes met his again as she sought to make a connection. Being here with him made her feel not quite so alone. "It's like I'm locked up in this little room and I can't even find the door, much less the doorknob."

She was right, Angus thought. He had no idea how frustrating it was, but he could guess. "It's a little like—"

Rebecca nodded, anticipating the comparison. *"Alice in Wonderland."* Surprise shot through her. "Don't ask me how I know that."

"I won't." He laughed and then it was her turn to silently ask for an explanation. "I was just thinking that the state you're in is like having a box of surprises left on your doorstep. You just never know what might pop out next.'' And the irony of it was that she was as much of a surprise to herself as she was to him.

That was one way to look at it, she guessed. It occurred to her that he seemed like somewhat of an optimist himself. She liked that. ''More answers, I hope.''

He hoped so, too. He saw doubt begin to creep back into her expression and instinctively tried to block it. ''It'll happen.''

If he said so, she thought. It was all she had to hang on to.

It smelled like him, Rebecca thought.

As soon as she had entered Angus's bedroom, she'd detected the faint, pleasant scent of his aftershave floating through it. The scent had a soothing quality.

Soothing, and yet, in a way it stirred her.

Or maybe that was just her state of mind, she reasoned. If she let go of the tight hold she had on things, agitation immediately threatened to take over. She wanted all the pieces to be fitted together. She had no patience with waiting while minute fragments were being slipped into place.

With nothing to base it on, she still had a hunch that she'd never had patience in an abundant supply.

Rebecca turned around as Angus went to take something out of one of the bureau drawers. She was beginning to grow fidgety. As soon as he left the room and closed the door behind him, she was going to be alone again. And she didn't want to be alone. But she couldn't very well ask him to remain, either. Not without sounding as if she was making him an offer.

Like a child resisting bedtime because she is afraid of

the dark, Rebecca looked for something to talk about—
something to keep him here just a little longer.

She seized the first idea that came to her. "Um, listen,
I don't want you to think that I'm asking you for a free
ride."

It was right where he'd remembered, Angus thought,
taking out his old high school football jersey. He shook
it out before placing it on the bed. Number 17. How many
years since he'd worn it? He couldn't remember. He
didn't even know why he kept it. If anyone had asked
him, he wouldn't have said that he was a particularly sentimental person. But Angus supposed that he had to be.
There was no other explanation for his holding on to the
jersey this long.

Her protest caught his attention and he looked at her.
"As I recall, you didn't ask for anything."

Yes, she had. Just by being here tonight, she had, Rebecca thought. And it wasn't fair to him.

"I intend to pay you," she assured Angus with conviction. A gut feeling told her that she didn't accept charity. "I don't have anything now, but I must have a job in
my other life. As soon as I get back to it, I'll pay you for
all your trouble."

It was an odd word for her to use, he thought. He hadn't
thought of her as trouble. Just someone who needed him.
It also occurred to him that he liked being needed. Maybe
it pointed to some sort of latent vanity in him, but he had
to admit that he liked that need acknowledged as well.

"No trouble," he said, but noticed that she didn't look
convinced. "I consider it a mental challenge." He caught
himself wanting to push back a stray lock that threatened
to fall into her eyes. Surprised by the impulse, Angus
shoved his hands into his back pockets instead. "Right

now, you're the most interesting case I've had in a very long time.''

"There, you said it," she responded. "I'm a case. People who ask you to take on their cases pay you for that service. For your expertise." She looked at him, determined to lay a claim to some sort of integrity. "I want to pay you."

Her lips fell a little short of forming a pout as she stated her intent. Those lips held his attention a moment longer than they should have. Maybe even two moments. Angus roused himself, moving his gaze to her eyes. Just as lethal, he thought. He couldn't win.

"Like you said, once you get back to your life, you can write me a check." He turned down her covers, deliberately turning his back on her at the same time. It felt just a wee bit crowded in the room for him. And a wee bit too warm.

"Angus?"

Very carefully, he smoothed down the comforter, just the way he did for Vikki. "Hmm?"

She licked her lips, grabbing on to her waning courage before it disappeared entirely.

"What if I *don't* have a job?" When he turned around to look at her, her awkwardness increased. When she was herself, was she good with words? Because right now, she felt terribly clumsy and inadequate at framing her thoughts. "In my other life, I mean. What if I was fired?"

That was the least of his concerns. "We'll work something out," he promised. He nodded at the jersey. "Now get some sleep, okay?"

Rebecca picked up the green-and-white jersey and held it to her, as if just holding it could give her a measure of comfort. "Okay."

She was struggling with her fears again, he could see

it. Angus felt for her. Pausing, he reached for her hand. He meant only to squeeze it, one human being silently offering comfort to another. But the look in her eyes made him think of Vikki the first time he ever saw her. She'd been trying to put on a brave front, but it was evident that she was very afraid of this new world she suddenly found herself in. Afraid and lost.

Before he could think it through, or think to stop himself, Angus inclined his head and brushed his lips against the hollow of Rebecca's cheek.

The softness nearly undid him.

Like squeezing her hand, the friendly kiss was meant to give comfort, nothing more. It wasn't intended to open any doors, or to link itself to anything else.

It wasn't meant to. But it did, all the same.

Something happened in that small measurement of time. A spark had been set off, telegraphing itself across an invisible line.

Yes, something had happened.

Something wondrous.

Quivering inside, Rebecca stared at him as she touched her hand to her cheek. Her fingers lightly glided along the tiny spot where his lips had made the slightest contact with her skin. She was lost, not only in time and space—but also for words.

Angus, too, had felt something just then—sympathy, empathy? Desire? He wasn't sure just what. Maybe all of the above. Maybe it didn't even have a name. It didn't matter. What mattered was that he suddenly found himself wanting to hold her.

But he couldn't allow that to happen. He wasn't about to scare her or have her thinking the wrong thing. And he wasn't about to start anything, either.

Angus deliberately backed away from her, from the

feeling that had prompted his action in the first place. He was still backing away when he bumped against the door-jamb.

The contact grounded him. "I'll see you in the morning."

Still feeling a little dazed and disoriented—something that was beginning to seem like second nature to her—Rebecca nodded, repeating the word as if it were a faith-healing chant. "Morning."

Angus lingered for just a moment. It was all he would allow himself.

"I'll be right outside on the couch if you need anything." He nodded toward the living room. "Or think of anything."

"Thanks."

But all she *had* to think of, Rebecca thought ruefully as she closed the door behind him, were the events that had taken place since this afternoon. Everything else before then didn't even exist for her.

Like a white knight riding to her rescue, Angus MacDougall vividly dominated every thought Rebecca could call her own.

"Are you going to go back inside and read her a story?"

Angus's heart felt as if it had jackknifed inside his chest. Swinging around, he realized that he'd almost backed into his daughter. She was standing less than a foot away from his bedroom door.

Rebecca's bedroom door, for the time being, he amended.

Angus pinned Vikki with a stern look. She was supposed to have been in bed and asleep at least half an hour ago. "What are you doing out here?"

Vikki looked unwilling to give him an answer. She rocked on her toes, stalling. But he continued waiting, and she finally said, "Wondering if you were going to read to her."

With one hand on her shoulder, Angus guided his daughter back to her room.

"She doesn't need me to read her a story." Angus pushed open Vikki's door. "And what are you doing still up?" As if to negate his observation, Vikki scrambled into her bed. For the second time that evening, Angus found himself tucking covers around his daughter. "I swear Vik, you pop up more often than a jack-in-the-box."

Vikki's eyebrows came together in deep concentration. "What's that?"

"You don't know what a jack-in-the-box is?" Just went to show him how out-of-touch he was with the world of the nineties' child.

Her hair swung back and forth around her face as she shook her head. "I know what an inside straight is," she countered proudly.

She was Jane's, all right. Angus skimmed his finger along her nose. "You don't need to know that," he informed her. "And I'll see if I can scare up a jack-in-the-box some place and show you what one looks like."

He paused, mentally digging beneath the layers to see what this was really about. Unless she was sick, like last night, Vikki usually remained in bed once he'd tucked her in. Was she jealous because he'd brought someone else into the apartment? He couldn't see how that was possible, but then, he wasn't a precocious seven-year-old, either. Maybe she thought he'd paid too much attention to Rebecca, and not enough to her.

Angus tested his theory. "Would you like me to read you a bedtime story?"

A spark of light danced through her eyes before she lifted one shoulder in studied nonchalance. "If it makes you feel better to read me one."

She was still feeling him out, still trying not to become too attached. It didn't take a genius to see that the death of the only parent she'd known had left its mark on her—made her afraid to care. Angus was determined to wait her out.

That meant playing along with her game. "It would make me feel wonderful to read you one."

"Okay." This time, she didn't succeed in keeping the shine out of her eyes. She wiggled beneath her covers, staking out a place for herself. "How long is she going to stay here? Rebecca," Vikki clarified, as if there was a need to.

He hadn't given it that much thought. As long as it took, he supposed, although he was counting on it not taking too long. He didn't want to risk disrupting what he was so carefully trying to build between Vikki and himself: Trust.

"We'll take that one step at a time."

It wasn't the answer she expected. "Are you going to help her?"

Yes, he was going to help Rebecca. But, having been left out of every decision the Colonel had ever made, especially the ones that had affected him, Angus knew the value of making Vikki feel a part of what was happening. "Do you think I should?"

Vikki looked up at him, the tiniest bit of surprise in her eyes. And then it receded, as if she took Angus's question about her feelings as her due.

"Yeah, I guess so." Then, because the heart that she was struggling so hard to protect was large, sympathy played across her face. "It's pretty terrible, huh? Not remembering stuff."

"Yes, it's pretty terrible," he agreed. He tried to put it into terms she could understand. "What if you couldn't remember anything—not your favorite flavor of ice cream, not your birthday?" He looked deeply into her eyes, delivering his best card. "Not anything about your mom."

Vikki shivered. It would be awful if she couldn't remember Momma. "You'd better help her."

She really was a terrific little girl, he thought. He grinned at her. "I'll let her know you said that. I'm sure she'll appreciate it." Angus looked at the shelf over Vikki's bed. He had been steadily adding books to her small library. Books had been what had sustained him when he was her age. Books and a vivid imagination. "Okay, what do you want to hear?"

In response, Vikki pulled down the small, worn book her mother had given her. It had traveled almost as many miles as she had, and looked every bit of it. The grin on her face was positively impish as she held the book out to Angus. *"How about Whose Shoes Are Those?"*

He groaned, taking the book from her. "Aren't you tired of that yet?"

Her head moved from side to side in solemn denial. It was her very favorite story in the whole wide world. Because Momma had read it to her every night. "Nope."

Angus's sigh was deep and resigned. Bracing himself for wading through the sugary tale yet again, he opened the book to the first page. "Okay, lie back and close your eyes."

He waited until Vikki did as he said. Giggling, she snuggled farther under the covers and squeezed her eyes tightly shut. "Ready."

He wished *he* was, he thought as he began to read—from memory.

Rebecca dreamed all night.

She dreamed long, dark dreams that frightened her and made her struggle for consciousness. But sleep kept a tight hold on her, refusing to allow her to surface, to open her eyes and banish the shadows that hung over her like a death shroud.

Something or someone was chasing her. Gaining on her. Threatening to take her life away.

Fear ripped into her with a serrated knife, leaving jagged wounds.

When she finally managed to wake herself up, Rebecca was shaking. She felt as if she'd been running for miles. Fleeing. And not escaping.

Drawing a deep breath, she sat up and dragged her hand through her hair, trying to steady her tangled nerves. The scent that clung to the jersey, bringing Angus vividly to mind, helped to calm her down a little.

It was a dream, only a dream. Comprised of all the small, inner fears she'd experienced yesterday. Nothing more.

Or was it?

Was she remembering something, something that had happened to her?

Absorbed, shaken, it took her several beats to realize that she wasn't alone in the room. That someone was watching her.

She jerked when she became aware of Vikki in the corner of the room. Her hand spread over her pounding heart, as if to keep it from leaping out of her chest. "Oh, Vikki, you scared me."

Vikki moved closer to her. "I didn't mean to. You were making noises."

She was surprised she wasn't screaming and waking up everyone on the block.

"I'm sorry. Did I wake you?" It didn't look likely. The little girl was completely dressed. If she'd just woken Vikki up, she would still have been in her pajamas or nightgown.

Vikki shook her head. "You have a bad dream?"

She could still feel her heart throbbing in her throat. "Lots of bad dreams."

Vikki saw nothing unusual in that. "Momma used to have them, too. She said daylight made them go away."

Beginning to calm down, Rebecca smiled at the girl. "Your momma was a very smart lady."

The approval pleased her. One of the fences between them came down. Vikki returned Rebecca's smile. "Yeah, she was."

It was daylight now. The sun streamed in through the window as if yesterday's rainstorm was only a figment of her imagination. Rebecca looked back at Vikki. "How long have you been sitting there?"

Time meant very little to her. It was something that only grown-ups seemed to worry about. "Since Angus left. He told me to keep an eye on you." She said it as if she'd been entrusted with a special assignment.

There was a clock beside the telephone on the night-stand. Rebecca looked at it, her vision still blurry. It was ten after eight. Something vague and formless registered. She had a feeling that it was late. Was she an early riser? Or was it just that she had to be in to work early?

The same void she'd endured yesterday met her.

Rebecca sighed. "Did I say anything in my sleep while you were sitting here?"

"Uh-uh."

So much for that. Rebecca threw back the covers and swung her legs out of the bed. "Where did your father go?" The slim shoulders rose and fell carelessly in response. "Do you know when he'll be back?" The question drew the same silent response. Rebecca tried again. "Have you eaten yet?"

Watching her intently, Vikki shook her head.

At last, something to do besides just exist. "Okay, I'll make us breakfast."

Getting up, Rebecca looked around for the shoes Angus had given her. They were haphazardly kicked off, one on top of the other, on the floor beneath the window. If possible, the shoes looked even larger than they had the night before. She decided to go barefoot.

"There's only Chinese food and ice cubes," Vikki informed her.

She'd forgotten about his empty refrigerator. Rebecca smiled ruefully as she tugged the sheet and comforter back into place on the bed. She reached for the pillow and fluffed it up. "That's a little more of a challenge than I can manage."

"What is?"

Still holding the pillow to her, she turned around at the sound of his voice. A sense of relief flooded her. He was back.

"Making breakfast out of ice cubes and leftover Chinese food."

Angus had walked into his room, guided by the sound of their voices, assuming that there was no need to announce himself. His assumption had rewarded him with a rich view of a very enticing long leg as Rebecca had reached over to smooth out the comforter. His grip on the bag almost ripped through the paper.

"No need. I brought a Jingles breakfast." He indicated the bag that he was holding from the fast-food restaurant. He was surprised he was capable of forming whole sentences, seeing as how he'd almost swallowed his tongue.

In all the time he'd had his lucky jersey, he'd never seen it look this good. The edge of the shirt flirted with the tops of two incredibly firm thighs, leaving it to his active imagination to fill in what was being covered. Angus had to concentrate so that he didn't drift off completely and sound like some blithering idiot. It wasn't easy.

Rebecca seemed oblivious to the effect she was having on him as she came forward. She looked at the bag he'd brought back with less than high regard. "Wouldn't it have been easier just to go to the store and get some eggs and bread?"

She was making noises like a typical woman. That was a good sign, he thought. His mouth curved. "The bread part might have been, but you obviously have never seen me with a frying pan."

She took his disclaimer as a sign of modesty. "You can't be that bad."

"Oh, yes, he can," Vikki testified, moving in between them. It wasn't evident to Angus just whose side his daughter was on.

Rebecca capitulated. "Okay, as long as you do the shopping, I'll take care of making lunch."

Vikki regarded her with awe and a little wariness. Home cooking wasn't something she was accustomed to from either parent. "You know how to cook?"

Something else she hadn't thought about, Rebecca realized. She did now—and smiled.

"Yes," she declared happily, as if this piece of information were a long-lost friend. "I know how to cook."

Chapter 5

It was getting way too warm for him in this room, Angus thought. He seemed to be feeling overheated a lot since Rebecca had come into his life.

Leaning out into the hall, he picked up and produced another, much larger bag in an effort to liberate himself from the situation and from thoughts that were growing increasingly less professional. Who would have known that Rebecca could make an almost threadbare jersey look so damn good?

As he deposited the shopping bag on the newly made bed, Angus's attention crept back to her legs. Like a man on the verge of self-imposed abstinence, he allowed himself one last, long look. The view only got better.

He cleared his throat. ''Not that I don't think you look fetching in oversize shoes and rumpled clothes—'' and especially the jersey, he thought, but since Vikki was at his elbow, he kept that part to himself ''—but I picked up a few things for you before I stopped to get us breakfast.'' Luckily, there was a store right across from the fast-food restaurant that wisely opened its doors at eight, beating out the competition and amassing a loyal clientele.

Vikki was familiar with the store he frequented because of its proximity, hours and reasonable prices. *Steven's* was one of her favorite places to go. The toy area to which she always dragged him had more than a few things to snag her attention.

''Anything for me?'' Vikki looked at him with large, hopeful eyes.

He knew better than to forget her. ''Yeah, I got something for you, too.''

Vikki peered hopefully around him into the hall. ''A dog?''

He had his own personal Johnny One-Note, Angus thought. Owning a dog was getting closer to becoming a reality with each passing day.

''No, a new book.'' He produced it from the shopping bag. It was a storybook about five puppies and their new owners. At least it was *about* owning a dog, he thought, watching Vikki's face for her reaction.

''Oh.'' Vikki took it from him. Her disappointment faded a little when she saw the puppies on the cover. A small smile nudged its way to her lips. ''Thanks.''

''You're welcome.'' His fervent hope was that if he continued bringing her books, eventually he'd find something that would spark her interest enough to make her forget about the current favorite he had to keep reading over and over again.

He stole a glance toward Rebecca, wondering what she thought of his purchases. He'd gotten her a soft blue-and-white pullover and stone-washed jeans. Angus wasn't quite sure how to interpret the bemused expression on her face.

She held the pullover up against her. Angus had made it sound as if it were no big deal for him to buy these for her. But it was. It was a very big deal. It made her feel less like an inconvenience and more like a person.

Rebecca raised her eyes to his. "How did you know what size to get?"

She had obviously forgotten that he'd looked at the labels in her clothes at the hospital. Angus decided that she might not handle it well if he brought that to her attention.

"I've got a pretty good eye for details. I've been at this business for a while."

"What, dressing women?" she asked as a ribbon of amusement wound through her.

"No, just observing them." He looked at his daughter. Vikki appeared to have taken root where she stood. "C'mon, Vik, let's give Rebecca some privacy so she can take a shower and get dressed. Meet you at the nearest breakfast burrito when you're ready." Angus winked at Rebecca before ushering Vikki out and closing the door behind them.

With the new clothes clutched against her, Rebecca stood staring at the closed door. The flutter his wink had created was still threatening to take over her stomach. It took her a moment before she finally turned and went into the bathroom. A shower would seem like heaven right now.

"I guess you really do have a good eye."

Rebecca's words preceded her as she walked into the kitchen. Without thinking, she tugged on the hem of the pullover. It just barely came to her waist. The clothes he'd purchased were her size all right, but they seemed to be cut a little smaller than the stained clothes she'd discarded last night.

"They're a little snug," she allowed, "but I can move around in them."

Angus gave her an appreciative once-over. "Yes, you certainly can." The jeans *were* a little snug. In his estimation, that made the fit perfect. The clothes she'd worn yesterday hadn't allowed him to realize just how shapely she was. These left no doubt. She had the kind of body that lingered on a man's mind and teased his senses into rigid attention.

The look in his eyes made her feel warm, alive. She savored it, even though she figured he was only being kind. "I really don't know how to thank you."

His hand filled with napkins, Angus grinned as his eyes skimmed over her again. "You just did." Looking at her was certainly payment enough for his efforts. He gestured toward the table. "C'mon, breakfast is getting cold."

She sat down beside Vikki, who had nearly polished off her share. "We could always take out a lamp and warm it up." As the words left her lips, Rebecca's eyes widened; pleasure laid a comforting hand on her shoulder. "They use lamps to keep these warm, don't they?"

"They use lamps," he repeated. It was a silly little piece of miscellaneous information, yet she looked like a child with a new toy at Christmas—joy stamped on her face. She had remembered something she'd known before. "See, it's coming back."

"This time tomorrow," she said hopefully, "I might be able to remember everything."

He had a feeling she was being unduly optimistic. He didn't want to see her crushed. "Don't get ahead of yourself. Besides, even if it does all come together, there's still that small matter of someone shooting at you."

"A mugger?" Vikki offered, stealing a bite out of his egg sandwich.

Angus broke off half and gave it to her. "Maybe," he allowed, seriously considering the suggestion. His eyes shifted toward Rebecca. "Or maybe someone you know. You don't want to waltz back into a situation that makes you a sitting duck."

"Ducks don't sit, they float," Vikki corrected him.

Rebecca saw him suppress a grin. "My mistake," Angus conceded.

"All right, what do we do next?" Rebecca desperately wanted to be doing something more than just waiting for assorted bits of information to come drifting back to her.

"After breakfast," Angus told her, letting Vikki have the remainder of his sandwich, "I'll check in with the police to see if anyone has filed a missing person report on you yet."

Yet. It was the key word she was hanging on. *Yet* meant someone was going to—if not now, eventually. And that meant that she belonged somewhere, with people who cared.

"And if no one has?" It was a possibility Rebecca didn't want to entertain.

He'd already thought about that. "Then we go for a long drive."

Rebecca stared at him. Did that mean he just wanted to play a waiting game? Though she was grateful for everything he'd done up until now, this was her life they were talking about. And she was missing it. She couldn't just sit here—or in the car—and let that continue.

She wiped off the oil that had oozed onto her fingers through the red-and-white wrapper. "I don't mean to be telling you your business, but shouldn't we be doing something besides that?"

"We will be," he assured her. "We'll be looking. Actually, you'll be doing the bulk of that." Because she didn't seem to be following him, he elaborated. "I'm going to try to retrace your steps from my office to that alley where you said you came in. Maybe we'll come across something that'll help us find out who you are."

"Can I look, too?" Vikki piped up, as if she fully expected Angus to agree. She looked stunned and hurt when he didn't.

"Only at the television screen." And he qualified that. "And only if Jenny isn't watching some blood-and-guts movie on a cable station."

He didn't like the idea of imposing sanctions. Jenny was basically a good-hearted woman who had taken instantly to Vikki. But Vikki was his daughter and he felt he had to protect her from some things.

She squirmed in her seat, pouting. "Angus, I don't want to have to stay home."

There was no room for discussion on this. "And I don't want to have to worry about you when I'm out on a case."

Her lower lip stuck out even farther. "But you said nobody ever shoots at you."

"They don't," he agreed amiably, then pointed out, "but somebody *did* shoot at Rebecca."

That reminder only made Vikki more fascinated with the possibilities that the adventure held—and more determined to go with him. "You think he could still be there, waiting for her to come back so he can jump out and—"

"That's enough, Vikki." Angus cut her off sharply before she said something that would upset Rebecca. It was a wonder Vikki didn't have nightmares with a vivid imagination like that. Angus pushed back his chair. "Now, if you're finished, let's go over to Jenny's."

She left her bottom planted right where it was. "I could be a help," Vikki protested.

"Yes, you could." Her face brightened. "And the biggest help you could be to me right now is setting my mind at ease that you're safe."

Angry storm clouds gathered in her blue eyes. "I don't want to be safe. I want to be with you."

She probably didn't mean that the way it sounded, Angus thought—that her choice was to be with him. But just for the moment, he allowed himself to believe that's what she meant. "And I want to be with *you*, Vik. But not when I think it's dangerous for you to be around."

"*She's* going," Vikki said accusingly, jerking a thumb at Rebecca.

"I have to," Rebecca told her gently. She had no idea why she knew, but she understood the wrenching agony of feeling left behind. "But I'm the one who might make it dangerous."

"Then go away." Vikki's mouth shut in a firm, angry line.

Rebecca looked at Angus. "Maybe I'd better—"

It was the last straw. He wasn't about to allow his life, or anyone else's, to be dictated by a child. Even a child he'd grown to love very much.

"You, stay here," Angus instructed Rebecca. "You, come with me." Taking Vikki firmly by the hand, he pulled her from her chair and ushered her out of the apartment. The silence they left behind was deafening.

Guilt nibbled at Rebecca, making her forget her own situation for the time being. Angus and Vikki shouldn't be arguing over her, she thought, as she got up from the table. Mechanically, she began clearing the dishes. From what Angus had told her, father and daughter were just beginning to form a bond, just beginning to become a unit. A family. She had no right to jeopardize that.

But if Angus wasn't there to help her, who was?

Rebecca dumped the empty wrappers into the garbage. She bit her lower lip, trying not to give in to the lost feeling that was reaching for her again. Running on automatic pilot, she turned the water on and began washing the dishes.

Angus was still trying to frame an apology when he walked back into the apartment. Vikki had gone to Jenny without another word, giving him the silent treatment—which, though easier on his ears, made him feel guilty instead of annoyed.

That's because he cared, he reminded himself. When he'd been a child, his not speaking had never had any effect on *his* father. The old man had actually seemed to prefer it that way. If they didn't speak, they didn't see the hundred little ways that they differed. The bottom line was that the old man hadn't cared, and *he* had. And still did.

Things would work themselves out eventually, he thought with an inward sigh.

Right now, his immediate problem was Rebecca and her lost identity. More immediate than that was apologizing for Vikki's rudeness. She didn't need a child mouthing off at her and telling her to *go away* when she was in such a precarious, vulnerable state.

"Listen, I'm sorry about—" Angus stopped abruptly when he saw what she was doing. "Why are you washing dishes? We ate out of paper cartons."

Paper cartons that were no longer on the table, he noticed. The table was actually cleared, as was the counter. He hadn't been gone that long; how fast did this woman work?

Rebecca shrugged carelessly as she rinsed off another

plate. "Because they're in the sink." She lined the plates up neatly on the rack.

He didn't want her to think that she had to do that. "I was going to get to them."

She looked over her shoulder at him, an amused smile playing on her lips. It made her beautiful, he thought. "When?"

It took him a second to gather his thoughts. If he wasn't careful, he'd be the one acting as if he had amnesia. "Someday."

That had a nebulous sound to it. "When the board of health comes by to condemn them?" She nodded toward the dishes drip-drying in the rack. "I found something green on one of them."

"That's food coloring," he said defensively. "Vikki was experimenting with it the other day. Wanted to see if she could dye the plate."

Vikki sounded like a handful. And just right for Angus. "Uh-huh. Well, it still needed to be cleaned." She placed the last plate on the rack, angling it to fit. Angus *really* didn't like to do dishes, she thought. "There, done."

Because there was no towel around, she quickly wiped her hands on the back of her jeans.

"Thanks." Angus realized he was staring at her hands as they brushed against her back pockets—and very tempting bottom. He drew his eyes away. "You really didn't have to do that."

"Yes, I did," she countered. Then, before he could protest further, she added, "I think I like to clean. It seems to help me calm down."

He laughed. "Then you've *really* come to the right place." He scanned the area, looking at it through a stranger's eyes. It did look a little as if a tornado had made a pit stop here on its way to Oz. "This place will positively anesthetize you if you give it a chance."

Rebecca pressed her lips together, wondering if she should butt in. After all, Vikki was none of her business. But the dispute had occurred because of her, she reasoned, and in a way that did make it her business. "Do you think she'll be all right?"

"Yeah. She has to learn that she can't always have her way."

It was a struggle for him, she thought, being authoritative with a little girl. She could tell he didn't like saying no to her. "But most of the time, she has you pretty well wrapped around her finger."

The laugh was self-deprecating. "Is it that obvious?"

"The love is, yes. Most men would have trouble taking a seven-year-old into their lives, daughter or not." He looked surprised. "I'm guessing," she added. She was, but it was a guess based on instincts she was just beginning to rediscover.

"I don't know how most men would react—I only know what I believe. Every kid deserves to have their parents love them."

He said it with such solemn feeling that she had to ask. "Did yours?"

Her question must have told him that he'd talked enough, she thought, maybe even too much. After all, it was her life they were trying to piece together, not his. He changed topics. "Are you ready to go?"

It stung a little, but she accepted the rebuff. She'd probably ventured too far, she told herself. But it was all a learning process for her.

Rebecca nodded in reply. There wasn't anything *to* get ready. She spread her hands before her. "Yes. What you see is what you get."

What he saw, Angus thought, turning to open the door, was more than enough to satisfy any man.

The next moment, he upbraided himself again for letting his mind wander. He wasn't going to be any good to Rebecca if he allowed himself to veer off the track and start thinking of her as anything other than a client.

But it was hard to think of her in neutral terms, not when she smelled this good, looked this inviting.

As he got into the car, he noticed the concerned look on her face. Angus started the car and backed out. "What is it?"

"Vikki's last words keep replaying themselves in my mind," she said. "You don't really think that whoever was after me might still be there, do you?"

So, he'd guessed right. Vikki had gotten to her. "No, that's straight out of those movies Vikki and Jenny like to watch. I left Vikki behind because she'd ask a million questions. If I was busy answering them, I might miss something." His answer seemed to satisfy her. She relaxed a little beside him. "*If* we find the place again," he qualified.

And that, he knew, was a big *if.* But at the moment he had nothing else to go on if the police hadn't received a missing person report on her.

Rebecca kept pace with Angus as they left the police station, trying to harness the impatience she felt inside her—like a rodeo mustang pawing the ground, eager to shoot out of the stall, yearning to be free. She had prepared herself for this, for there not being any news on her. Had told herself chances were slim to none that a missing person report on her would turn up.

Still, she'd gone into the station hoping.

Angus could feel her frustration. It mirrored his own.

"It could still happen," he told her as they both got into his car. "Someone could still file a report on you."

"Why later? Why not already?"

He could sense that she was trying not to let her voice break.

He went over the reasons. "Everybody who knows you might think you're somewhere else, *with* somebody else. Signals get crossed, messages get misunderstood." There was a whole host of possibilities. None that she liked, he noticed. "Maybe you were on your way to catch a plane for a vacation. Everyone thinks you're away and won't wonder where you are for a couple of weeks."

"Or there is no one in my life," she said, studying her nails.

He didn't believe that for a minute. "Someone as beautiful as you are has to have someone in her life."

The certainty in his voice surprised her. As did the pleasure it created to hear him call her beautiful.

"You don't," she pointed out.

He laughed as he made a left turn onto a busy street. The car behind him came up too close. Angus pulled ahead, noting its license plate, just in case. He'd developed a knack of reading things backward. "You saying I'm beautiful?"

Rebecca felt color—or maybe it was just heat—creeping up her neck to her face. She didn't want to sound as if she was flirting. But that was exactly the way it *did* sound to her.

"No," she said quickly, then tagged on, "but you're not exactly something that only a cat would drag in."

He flashed an amused smile in her direction. "Thanks."

She wondered if she was normally this flustered, or if it was something new. "You know what I mean."

Angus let her off the hook. "Yeah, and you're wrong. I do have someone." He caught the look she slanted him. "I've got Vikki."

There was no reason why she should let that mean anything to her. For all Rebecca knew, ring or no ring, she might be married. Yet there was no blocking out the glimmer of excitement rippling through her. "Nobody else?"

He shook his head. "Don't need anybody else. Don't have time for anyone else," he added.

And he didn't. After Jane, there had never been anyone he'd allowed to mean anything to him. He'd never let things go that far. Just casual encounters and not many of those.

"But *you*,—despite the fact that there's no ring or a tan line to indicate that there'd ever *been* a ring—might very well be married or engaged or at least spoken for." And he would do well to remember that, Angus thought.

Spoken for. It was a quaint saying and it appealed to her. She had no idea why.

Rebecca thought about what he said, but there was nothing to link to it. No feeling, however vague.

"I don't think so," she finally said. "I mean, wouldn't it be something that I would somehow feel? If you love someone, doesn't it somehow slip beneath your conscious layer? Leave a mark?"

It had with him. More like a wound, though, than a mark. But she hadn't meant it that way. He smiled to himself. "Well, I know one thing you are."

"What's that?"

"A romantic." He glanced at her. She was looking at him with those wide eyes of hers, decreasing the space between them within his car without moving an inch. "Watch the road," he instructed, nodding toward the window on her side. And he would do well to follow his own advice, he told himself.

As he drove, Angus gauged how far he thought Rebecca could have walked in the rain yesterday, given the circumstances. The radius turned out to be larger than he'd first estimated, but he was determined to cover it.

None of the areas he slowly passed by stirred any sense of recognition within her. After a while, they all began to run together. Rebecca sank back in her seat. The constant tension of being alert had left her exhausted. "I'm sorry. I just can't seem to remember."

He nodded. Maybe it had been a long shot after all. "You were probably too disoriented to really notice where you were." He tried one last avenue, though as far as he knew, there were no alleys there that came close to her description. "Look, we've been driving around for a long time. Why don't we take a break, get a cup of coffee, start fresh later?"

Rebecca read between the lines. "You don't think we're going to find it, do you?"

He wasn't about to encourage a feeling of hopelessness. "I wouldn't be in this line of work if I wasn't an optimist. Didn't you read the fine print on my card?" He deliberately kept his expression sober as she shook her head. "It says *Miracle Worker*. It's not a title I take lightly." He saw her smile struggle to the surface. "There, that's better."

Silly though it seemed, she did feel better. He *made* her feel better.

"Thanks, I—" Her eyes widened as the site on the opposite side of the street registered. "Angus, wait. That's it." Excited, she pointed past his left shoulder. "Over there. I think—" She didn't think, she knew. "Yes, that's it."

Angus pulled over to the right, grateful that there was no car behind him now. As a matter of fact, traffic along the street was nonexistent. This was no longer the popular area it had once been.

He took a good look at where Rebecca had indicated. "That's the ground floor of a parking structure." Small wonder that he hadn't been able to find it. He'd been taking her to alleys. "That's where you woke up?"

Everything she could remember had turned into one huge blur. "No, but I remember—I remember running through here." She felt it more than she remembered it. "This is where the car was, the one that tried to run me down."

Angus pulled away from the curb and made his way to the structure. It wasn't used very much anymore. Parking was free now that the mall that it had once serviced had lost more than half its stores. Businesses had gone elsewhere, to more popular, better traversed areas that catered to an upscale clientele. A few bargain discount stores, as well as some of the lower quality fast-food restaurants, had moved in to take their place.

All in all, it wasn't a very memorable place.

How had she come to be here? he wondered. "Are you sure this was the place?"

"I—I think I am," she confessed. The feeling of certainty was gone. She wouldn't have been able to swear under oath that this was where she'd been, but subconsciously the area nagged at her, taunting her to remember.

Angus parked in a space, cutting off the engine. Rebecca didn't move. Fear suddenly draped over her, immobilizing her. "Why are we stopping?"

"You weren't driving when you were here," he told her. "*If* you were here, you were on foot. So we're going to walk." He rounded the trunk and opened her door.

"Maybe something else will come back to you." He took her hand, coaxing her out of the vehicle.

Feeling foolish, she got out and looked slowly around. The sun, bright and gleaming as it skirted the perimeter of the structure, refused to enter beyond more than a few feet. Inside, the building was oppressively dark. The steel girders stood like dusky sentries with secrets, mocking her with their silence.

There was only the sound of her breathing.

A fragment flashed through her mind. She'd been breathing hard, her lungs almost bursting as she ran, afraid to look back. Knowing what was behind her. Praying that it would somehow vanish.

She felt as if the structure were going to close in on her. As if it would collapse, sealing her in. She had to get out.

Rebecca dug her nails into Angus's arm.

She felt his hand close over hers.

"This is the place, isn't it?" he said.

For a second, she could only nod. And then, she regained her voice. "I need to get out of here." She turned her eyes toward him. "Please."

Chapter 6

Rebecca paled right before his eyes. For one terrible second, Angus thought that she was going to faint. Moving quickly, he slipped his arm around her, just in case.

She felt frailer than she looked, he thought. Protectiveness welled up within him.

"All right," he agreed as he slowly turned her toward the entrance again. "I'll tell you what. Why don't you just sit in the car while I look around?"

The edges of her vision had grown black, closing in on all sides like the screen of a dying television set. Employing every bit of concentration she could scrounge up, Rebecca struggled to hold the world around her in focus. She was *not* going to play the melodramatic heroine and pass out, she insisted fiercely to herself.

With effort, she forced herself to listen to what Angus was saying. Something about needing to look around.

"For what?" The words sounded almost breathless to her own ear. As if she'd been running a great distance.

If he knew the answer to that, maybe he'd already be on his way to discovering who she was, Angus thought dryly.

"That's half the challenge of this job. Most of the time, you don't know what you're looking for. You just know it when you see it." A whimsical smile played on his lips as he reflected on his words. "It's a little, I guess, like love. You might have some preconceived notions of what you want in the person you want to marry, but nothing really concrete. Until you see the one person who knocks you back on your butt and she's not a damn thing like what you expected."

He'd succeeded in rousing a smile from her. Rebecca looked at him, humor bringing the color back to her cheeks. "Very romantic."

He felt his smile widen and lifted his shoulder in a half shrug. "Hey, I have my moments." His smile softened as he took her elbow. "C'mon, I'll walk you back to the car and—"

Rebecca shook her head, easing her elbow away. She'd had enough time to pull herself together. And more than enough to become both embarrassed and annoyed at her lapse.

"No. The least I can do is stay and try to help. I was behaving like an idiot. I'm sorry." She had no patience with herself for giving in to the feeling that threatened to overwhelm her. "I can't run from some nebulous 'something,'" she told him, searching for the right words. "I'm over it now." She exhaled, as if that was all it took to blow the fear away from her. "It was just a temporary lapse."

She was trying too hard, he thought, unconvinced. There was still a small bead of perspiration on her forehead. Fear's imprint. She'd been frightened when she'd looked around. Was still frightened—and ashamed to admit it. People who didn't admit to being afraid were only fooling themselves, or worse, they were fools.

She didn't strike him as a fool. Only someone whistling in the dark to keep herself brave. He wondered what she would think if she knew that he had the urge to hold her until she stopped being afraid.

Probably that he was trying to take advantage of her. All things considered, he couldn't say that he'd have blamed her.

"The biggest guy I ever knew," he told her, "was afraid of spiders. He was six-four and over three hundred pounds. The sight of a wolf spider would send him running." His eyes touched her face gently. "Everyone's got fears, Becky. Everyone's afraid of something."

An odd expression crossed her face as she looked at him. The lady should never be allowed to get in a poker game, he mused. Every emotion she felt was there, on her face, in her eyes.

"What?"

"I don't think anyone's ever called me Becky before." Even before the words were out, she laughed at herself in disbelief. "Isn't that ridiculous? I have no idea who I am, where I came from, yet I can stand here, being almost positive that I never heard anyone calling me by a nickname."

"Not so ridiculous," Angus countered. "There's no size-places, no alphabetical order or priorities for a mind to follow. It's all just random. Things pop into your head normally without warning. And that's when your head's filled to capacity. When there's very little available to hang on to, it all seems random and odd." He peered into her eyes, looking for a glimpse of the woman she'd been forty-eight hours ago. Would she be so very different from the one standing before him right now? He was beginning to hope not. "Do you mind being called Becky?"

She didn't mind, she rather liked it. Maybe it was silly, too silly to admit to Angus, but it made her feel closer to him, as if she actually belonged somewhere.

"No, I don't mind," she replied softly. "You can call me Becky if you like."

Holding a shiver in check as she looked around the gray girdered structure, she dug in, refusing to be cowed by fears. It didn't matter that Angus gave her excuses—she didn't excuse herself. Whatever was out there, she was going to face it. She had to.

Rebecca drew a deep breath. "Okay, let's look around."

The word *gutsy* floated through his mind. Angus took the lead.

They combed the area slowly, going from space to space. Rebecca remained by his side every step of the way.

For all the good it did, she thought ruefully. There was nothing to trigger any further bursts of memory. Though she tried very hard to summon back her initial reaction when she'd entered the structure, nothing materialized.

Instead, there was just a vague disquiet that stood in the shadows, mocking her. Feeding her feelings of frustration. Making her feel that someone was watching.

But there was no one here but Angus. Not even a single car had pulled in since they'd arrived.

She was surprised at how methodical Angus was. Had it been up to her, she would have elected a simple drive through the area, and would have thought that was enough. Obviously, he didn't agree. He examined every wall, every girder they passed, looking for that elusive, hidden-in-plain-sight clue he'd talked about.

She still didn't know what he hoped to find. Certainly nothing tangible. If her purse had been lost here, she was certain that someone would already have picked it up and taken whatever there was inside that was valuable.

She didn't know if she'd been carrying anything valuable. For that matter, she didn't think she would have been able to identify her purse, or any of its contents even if they did come across it.

Frustrated, she struggled against the shackles of uselessness. Damn it, there had to be something here, something that would make her remember at least a single fact.

But there was nothing. Nothing to tell her why she'd been here, nothing to tell her who she'd been before yesterday afternoon.

Nothing. The word ate away at her.

She wanted so badly to know.

Was she an active person, or a passive one? Did she allow life to roll right over her, or did she fight back with every fiber of her being? Who *was* this person she'd woken up inside of?

A piece of a newspaper flew across her path, chasing itself as the wind blew it end over end. It occurred to Rebecca that she didn't even know what day of the week it was.

"Becky, over here."

Startled, Rebecca looked around and realized that Angus had turned a corner without her. She'd been lost in thought—or what passed for thought, she amended ruefully.

Hurrying to catch up, she found him on the other side of the wall, standing by a dilapidated car. From its condition and the heavy layer of dust on it, it had been parked here for a while—obviously abandoned.

Like her?

She squeezed the thought out. It wasn't like her to feel sorry for herself.

Was it? a small voice whispered uncertainly.

She shut that out, too. Faced with a clean slate, she was determined to do some of the writing on it herself.

Apparently pleased with his find, Angus indicated a very small hole right below the car's rear window. Surprised, she raised her eyes to his and he nodded in response.

"It's a bullet hole." Angus confirmed her silent observation. "Judging from the angle, unless he was shooting from the hip, whoever was chasing you was shorter than average." He looked at her. "Or driving a car."

She had remembered being pursued by a car. She stared at the hole, fascinated. A bullet hole. Meant for her. It didn't seem real. "How do you know it's fresh?"

Angus produced the handkerchief he'd used to inspect the point of entry and showed it to her. "The hole itself is clean. No dust like the rest of the car."

Shoving the handkerchief back into his pocket, Angus tried the door. It amazed him that even though the car was abandoned, it was locked. He wondered if the owner had meant to return and hadn't—or if this was just the final disgruntled act of an unhappy driver. Either way, the car had to be opened.

He felt Rebecca watching him as he took a tool out of his pocket and began working the lock. "What are you doing?" she asked.

He cocked his head slightly, listening for just the right sound. "Something I learned in my misspent youth." That had been the Colonel's term for it—a term that had

gotten even more judgmental as Angus grew older and
began exercising his own will.

"Breaking into cars?" she asked.

Amusement curved his mouth as he spared her a glance
over his shoulder. "Unlocking cars for ladies who had
accidentally locked their keys inside," he corrected.

She couldn't tell if he was being serious or not, but she
had her suspicions. She wondered just how grateful these
"ladies" had been for his services.

"There." He pulled open the door, pocketing his tools.
Pocketing, too, a small sense of accomplishment. "Contrary to what the Colonel believed, I did pick up a few
things that turned out to be useful in my later life."

Rebecca stood back as Angus got in and searched the
back of the car. Questions multiplied in her mind as she
watched him go over every inch of the back seat. Questions that had nothing to do with her.

"Was he really that hard on you?"

Angus thought of the strap his father favored over conversations and lectures. But that was all tucked away in
the past. There was no point in talking about it. He
shrugged carelessly as he went on looking.

"He thought he was doing me some good. That somehow, it would make me tough, make a man out of me."
At least, those were the reasons that the Colonel gave
when he *did* bother talking to him.

Angus had other ideas about the methods the Colonel
used.

She noticed that he didn't really answer her question.
Maybe in not answering, Angus had done just the opposite, she thought. The Colonel had been hard on him and
Angus didn't want to talk about it. "Well then, I guess
he succeeded beyond his wildest dreams, didn't he?"

This time Angus did turn around. "How so?"

The smile on her lips was heartfelt. "You're a knight in shining armor, aren't you?"

The fact that she'd put it that way amused him. The image of a knight dovetailed with his weakness for damsels in distress.

"Tarnished armor," he amended.

Shifting, he went over another section of the back seat. It was dark within the car and the upholstery was a dirty, stained burgundy. He wished he had thought to bring a flashlight.

The next moment, his fingers came in contact with a deep impression in the material.

"Bingo." Using the same tool he'd used on the lock, Angus dug something out of the back of the rear seat.

"Did you find something?" Rebecca asked, eagerly, peering over his shoulder.

"Another piece of the puzzle." Not one that fit readily into anything right now, he thought, but it might eventually.

As he got out, he tucked the tool back into his pocket. His other hand was tightly closed around the handkerchief he used to house what he'd found. He opened it for her benefit.

There was a bullet laying on the white cloth.

Rebecca stared at it. A bullet. "It still doesn't seem real to me. Doesn't look very big, does it?"

"Doesn't have to be big, just accurate." Very carefully, he refolded the handkerchief, trapping the prize inside. He tucked it into his breast pocket. Biordi was going to see this. The bullet looked to be a 9 mm. If a weapon had been fired, that made Rebecca's case something more complicated than just a missing person and an unexplained case of amnesia.

Angus glanced at Rebecca. Did she realize that she

might very well still be a walking target? He noticed for the first time that she'd taken off her bandage. If the bullet had been a fraction of an inch closer, the two of them wouldn't be standing here together, looking for clues.

His scrutiny made her feel nervous. It was the fluttery kind of nervous, rather than the panicky kind. She pressed her lips together. "Why are you looking at me like that?"

"I was just thinking that you were one lucky lady."

Her eyes held his for a minute, her nervousness increasing.

"So was I."

She tried to shake the feeling from her, the one she told herself was due only to an overwhelming wave of gratitude. But the feeling wouldn't leave, wouldn't allow itself to be reasoned away. She was attracted to Angus. There was no denying it. No denying the fact that, in unguarded moments when their eyes met, she felt something. A pull.

A very strong pull.

But she had no business feeling anything until she knew who she was. And who, if anyone, was in her life.

Stepping back from Angus, but not from the feeling, she gasped as she stumbled. One of her heels had gotten stuck in the grating that ran parallel to the wall.

"Hold it." Angus caught her before she fell ignobly at his feet.

"Thanks," she murmured. She was acutely aware of him, of the scent of his aftershave. Of the scent of his body permeating the musty air in the structure. It all surrounded her like a futuristic force field, keeping everything else out. Keeping her in.

After a second, she thought to step back. But she still couldn't move. The grating was holding her heel captive. Embarrassed, she slipped out of her shoe and began to reach for it.

"Wait a second." Angus stopped her, bending down himself. Gripping the heel, he slowly rocked the shoe back and forth until he managed to work it free. The grating, intended to offer a semblance of drainage for the structure—which was built on a downward slope—was hopelessly clogged. No one had bothered to service it for some time.

Angus wondered if it would be worth his while to pull a few lengths of it off and see if anything had gotten trapped there.

Rather than hand her the shoe, Angus cupped her heel and slipped her foot into it.

Lightning raced up her leg. Her eyes widened slightly as she felt her pulse accelerate.

His smile as he looked up at her was soft, easy. Sensuous. "Cinderella, I presume?" Rising, he dusted off his hands. "I seem to keep giving you shoes."

Her mouth felt completely dry. "Like I said, a knight in shining armor."

"Or a frustrated shoe vendor." Angus looked around, pretending to himself that he hadn't become completely distracted. "That's probably how you lost your shoe yesterday," he speculated, trying to remember that a detective was the only thing either one of them needed him to be. Not a man drawn to a very attractive woman. "The heel got caught while you were running."

Looking down at the grating, he wondered just how far it extended. "I'm going to check out the rest of the grating. Are you tired? Do you want to go back to the car?"

She had no intention of retreating now. "In for a penny, in for a pound." Rebecca blinked. That sounded hopelessly quaint to her. "I wonder how many other trite sayings I've got stored up within me."

Rebecca felt the sensual moment disappearing.

Angus laughed. "I can't wait to find out."

They found her other shoe stuck in the grating at the rear of the structure. Squatting, Angus pulled it free. The heel was not only stuck, it was broken. As he stood, Angus absently looked out beyond the perimeter of the exit.

Across the way was a Dumpster, so full that its lid was not quite closed. It was located at the rear of a Vietnamese restaurant.

The alley Rebecca thought she found herself in, Angus realized.

"Look familiar?" he asked her. The small, sharp intake of breath told him it did.

The next moment, she was leading the way. Minutes later, her heart hammering, Rebecca walked from one side of the Dumpster to the other. It wasn't quite flush against the wall. There was some space there. A small space, big enough for a child. Or a small woman.

The strong aroma of curry assailed her as the wind shifted in their direction. It aroused another fragment of a memory.

So did the smell of smoke that suddenly seemed so prevalent.

She had been here, she thought excitedly, a tiny part of the fog lifting from her brain. She'd woken up here, roused by the rain and the smell.

"It was here," she told him, adrenaline pumping through her veins. "I came to…here."

The excitement at the revelation diminished slightly. Though she remembered waking up behind the Dumpster, she had no memory of how she'd gotten there.

"Maybe you ran across from the parking structure and hid back here, then blacked out because of your wound," Angus offered.

It sounded plausible. She looked back over her shoulder at the parking structure. The view was plain enough from the right place. If she could just remember.

"But why didn't whoever was chasing me look here?" It seemed so obvious to her. "All the person had to do was look."

"Maybe he was going to," Angus suggested. "But someone scared him off." The Dumpster was only a few feet from the rear door. "Someone from the restaurant could have come out just then—to empty the trash or take a cigarette break. Who knows?"

What he *did* know was that he was grateful that she'd managed to escape.

He took her hand and began to walk toward the edge of the restaurant.

Beside him, still holding onto her shoe, Rebecca walked quickly, so as not to slow his pace. "Where are we going?"

We. It had the sound of a partnership, he thought. Well, why not? It was her life they were dealing with—or at least trying to reconstruct.

"To see if anyone in the restaurant noticed anything suspicious yesterday." It was too much to hope for, he knew, but every once in a while, you got lucky.

He wondered if she felt lucky.

As they circled the building, the smell of smoke became more acute. "Look." Rebecca pointed to the building three doors down. The front was completely charred.

"Now we know where the smell's coming from. Must have been within the last couple of days."

Angus remembered she'd smelled slightly of smoke when she came to his office. So…she'd been here, during the fire. Maybe there'd been too much going on for her assailant to get a clear shot at her, he thought.

The front of the restaurant had an ornate canopy to offer protection from the sun. Angus tried the door, but it was locked.

Rebecca placed her hand on his shoulder, calling his attention to a sign in the lower corner of the window. Further view into the restaurant was blocked by a beige curtain.

The sign was written in two languages, the second of which was English. "It says they don't open until eleven-thirty."

"They're not opened to do business yet," he corrected, knocking again louder.

There was still no answer.

"Maybe nobody's in," she suggested.

Angus glanced at his watch, though it was a redundant gesture—he'd always had an innate sense of time. "It's after eleven. There must be someone there," he assured her. "They have to get ready before they open."

He continued knocking until someone finally came to the window, pulling back the curtain.

The small, wizened woman looked at him through the glass with tired, dark eyes that were older than time. She shook her head and pointed to the sign. Her expression was a testament to incredulity that he should be knocking when the sign clearly indicated the establishment's hours.

Rather than retreat, Angus dug into his pocket and took out a ten-dollar bill. He held it up. The curtain dropped back into place.

A moment later, the woman cautiously opened the door a crack. She looked solemnly from his face to the money in his hand.

Angus placed his hand on the door, preventing her from shutting it again. "I'd like to come in and ask a few questions, if you don't mind."

The woman stared at him in silence, as if she were trying to process his words in her mind. "No ask. Eat," she finally told him.

If that's what it took, he thought philosophically, they'd eat. "All right, we'll order something," he agreed.

But she still didn't admit them. "Closed," the woman insisted. "Come later."

Before the limited, halting conversation could continue, the old woman was joined by a much taller, much younger man. He looked as robust as she was frail. The smile on his face when he looked at Angus was polite, but dismissive.

"I'm sorry. My grandmother doesn't speak English very well. We're not opened yet." He moved to close the door on them.

Angus's hand remained on the door. "We're not here to eat," he informed the younger man. "We'd just like to ask a few questions."

A trace of suspicion entered the dark eyes. They shifted from one face to the other. "About what?" he asked guardedly. "If it's about the fire, we already talked to the inspector. We didn't see anything."

Angus would have preferred to come in and discuss the matter under friendlier circumstances, but he'd conducted inquiries under less favorable conditions than these.

"We're not here about the fire. Did any of your employees see anything strange taking place yesterday around noon?"

There was no indication that the man knew what Angus was talking about.

"Specifically, did you see anyone hanging around back? Maybe running from the parking structure across the way?"

The young man shook his head. "Nobody said anything

to me about it and I was here all day." His gaze shifted from Angus to Rebecca again. His brow furrowed in concentration. When he saw the shoe she was holding, it came to him. "You're the woman with one shoe. Yeah, I saw you yesterday." His expression grew more affable. "Sorry, you all tend to look alike to me." He grinned at his own witticism, growing friendlier. "Is that what you're asking about?"

Angus exchanged looks with Rebecca. She appeared to be hanging on the man's every word. Maybe they were finally getting somewhere. "Partially. Was there anyone chasing her?"

The question didn't seem to surprise the man. The neighborhood obviously wasn't the best. "No, I just saw her crossing the street in front of the restaurant when I looked out the window. She almost got hit by a car, but the guy just shouted at her and drove off. If there had been anyone chasing her, I would have gone out."

The man did look as if he knew how to take care of himself.

"Do you remember what time that was?"

He answered without bothering to think. "Yeah, two-thirty. The lunch crowd had just cleared away. We were starting to get ready for dinner."

Angus had a feeling that he'd gotten about as much information as he was going to get. He took out his card and handed it to the man.

"If you think of anything else…anything at all…we'd appreciate it if you called this number."

As the man pocketed the card, Angus saw that the old woman was still eyeing the ten-dollar bill he hadn't bothered putting away. With a polite, formal bow of his head, Angus offered it to her.

Embarrassed, the woman's grandson waved the money away. "That's okay."

Angus knew by the look in the old eyes that it was definitely *not* okay to withdraw the money. The woman might not understand the language all that well, but she understood the currency. He pressed it into the wrinkled hand.

"Consider it a down payment on a tip," Angus told her grandson.

Nodding, he thanked Angus, said something to his grandmother and closed the door.

Rebecca blew out the breath she'd been holding. Turning, she began to retrace her steps with Angus. Her head was aching. She wondered if it was the tension or the wound. Probably a little of both.

"So, now what?" she asked him.

"Now we know where it happened and the time frame when you came to, and we have a bullet," he enumerated, patting his pocket. "We can get the make and model of the gun that fired it."

None of that gave her a last name, she thought. "Is that helpful?"

"It might be," he allowed, "in the long run. Can't hurt at any rate." He looked at her. "Are you hungry? We could find a restaurant—"

"How about a grocery store?" She was thinking of the one near his apartment complex.

"Sure, we could go to a grocery store." He knew of a couple that had a deli section and were set up to accommodate a few people who chose to eat their purchases on the premises. But he had a hunch that wasn't what she had in mind. "Why?"

"Because I want to cook something for lunch. I feel

like doing something, and I'm definitely no help here."
She looked at him. "Call it therapy."

Part of surviving was knowing when to give in. Angus
gave in. "Therapy it is."

Chapter 7

Detective Al Biordi rocked back in his chair, thinking. The resulting creak of protest the chair made was swallowed up by the constant low hum of activity within the squad room. He looked at the single spent bullet Angus had brought to him. Now antiseptically encased in a clear plastic bag, it was lying on his desk, right next to a half-empty mug of what could, quite possibly, be the world's worst-tasting coffee.

He didn't hold out much hope.

"Looks like a pretty unremarkable 9 mm. My guess is that it's from a Beretta. I'll run it by ballistics for you, Angus, but I'm not making any promises. I don't know when they're going to be able to get to it." He gestured vaguely to the folders haphazardly scattered over his desk, effectively covering every square inch. The desk was a carbon copy of every other desk in the squad room.

"Caseloads are pretty heavy around here right now. Must be the weather," he mused more to himself than to his friend, then raised his eyes. "And remember, there's no urgency. It's not like there's a crime being reported in connection with it."

Angus leaned a hip against the desk. One of the files fell off, landing at his feet. He bent over to pick it up and tossed it on the desk. Every time he came by, the stacks got a little higher, a little messier. The hallmark of a growing city, he thought with a twinge of regret.

"Bullets found in the upholstery of abandoned cars pretty commonplace these days?"

Biordi took no offense at the light sarcasm. Very carefully, he enumerated the reasons on his fingers. "One, no body. Two, no injured party—"

Angus didn't quite see it that way. "Rebecca." She had been injured, physically and certainly emotionally.

Biordi stuck by his opinion. "She's not bringing up charges."

A glimmer of temper flashed in Angus's eyes before fading. "Charges? Hell, Al, she can't even remember what happened."

Like a smug lawyer resting his case, Biordi spread his hands. "My point exactly."

Angus shook his head, not really clear on what his friend's point was. "Maybe whoever shot at her is out there, still looking to finish the job." He didn't like thinking of her as a walking target, even if she was with him. He could only do so much for her—had only so many resources at his disposal. Biordi had the entire police force if he needed it.

Biordi steepled his fingers together, thoughtfully. "Maybe," he allowed. "And maybe it was just a run-of-the-mill mugging that got out of hand. My brother, he picked up a saying while he was in medical school: if you hear hoofbeats, it's probably just a horse, not a zebra."

Sitting up, he leaned forward, narrowly avoiding hitting the mug. Looking slightly annoyed at the near mishap, he set it off to the side. "In other words, Angus, it's probably just something routine, nothing exotic. No hit man," he added for good measure. Seemingly satisfied he'd made his point, he reverted back to being Angus's friend. "Want my advice?"

Angus laughed shortly. He had a feeling he wasn't going to like what he heard. "No, but that's never stopped you before."

Biordi continued as if Angus hadn't said anything.

"Take it easy, do what you're best at," Biordi counseled with a broad wink. "See if you can find out who she is, since that's what she wants to know. And in the meantime, enjoy the lady while she's around."

Biordi was his friend and there was no reason to take offense, Angus told himself. And yet, part of him did. For Rebecca's sake. "What's that supposed to mean?"

If the slight shift in Angus's tone registered, Biordi didn't show it. He glanced at the framed photograph on his desk. Surrounded with files, it was partially buried—out of sight. There were times, like right after an argument, when he liked it that way.

"That means—off the record—if I weren't married to a very special lady with a hell of a right hook, I might be putting in a lot of time on this thing myself. This Rebecca's a looker. Even beneath those big shoes you stuck her in, and that dirty raincoat."

He almost looked as if he were waiting for a few intimate details, except that Angus knew better. Biordi wasn't the type to indulge in vicarious experiences.

The smile on Biordi's lips took the years away from his face, making him look like a boy rather than a police veteran. "I bet she cleans up real nice."

"She does." He moved his wife Emily's photograph forward. The frame fell, face first, into a pile of folders. "My advice to you is, go home to your wife, Al."

Picking up the photograph, Biordi righted it on the opposite side of his desk. A devilish gleam entered his eyes. "Yeah, I think I just might at that."

As Angus got up to leave, he nodded at the bullet still on Biordi's desk. "You'll let me know if you come up with something?"

Biordi rose to his feet. "You'll be the first to hear."

Angus was backing away slowly. He'd settle for being in the top five. "And if a missing person report comes in on her—?"

Biordi rolled down his second shirtsleeve, then reached for his jacket. "First button I hit on the speed dial," he promised.

Maybe not the first, but pretty close, Angus was willing to bet. "You're a prince."

Biordi stopped, one arm about to slide into his jacket. He grinned. "Captain doesn't seem to think so, but thanks."

He slammed down the telephone, shattering the still air around him. Struggling for composure, he crossed out another hospital on the list he'd printed out.

She wasn't there. Hadn't been there.

He was tired of repeating the same question. Tired of getting the same answer.

She hadn't gone home, he knew that for a fact. Hadn't gone home, hadn't crawled off to die. Hadn't gone to any of the hospitals or walk-in clinics he'd called.

People didn't just vanish.

He was going to make her pay for this when he found her. And he was *going* to find her.

It was just a matter of time.

Composed again, he tapped out the next number on his list.

Angus had put one foot inside the apartment when the aroma greeted him like a warm, seductive woman, seeping into his senses before he even realized it. The delicious smell evaporated any words that were on his tongue.

Surprised that smells so good could be coming from his apartment, Angus paused, trying to place the aroma. All he knew was that his reaction to it was instantaneous—hunger, deep and overwhelming, taking large chunks out of him.

A different kind of hunger had eaten away at him this morning when he'd seen Rebecca standing there in his jersey. But it had been just as instantaneous, just as intense.

Seeing her that way had made him remember, completely without his consent, that it had been a while between women. A long while. And far longer since he'd cared about a woman in any other than the most cursory manner.

Over seven years, to be precise. Jane had been the only one to whom he'd ever opened up his heart. And hadn't that turned out just dandy? he mocked himself.

But they'd had their moments, their time together before it had gone sour. It wasn't that Jane hadn't loved him—she had. He knew that. She'd just loved her freedom more. And he had wanted her so badly, he hadn't understood. Hadn't realized that if you loved someone, freedom was the greatest gift you could give them.

All he'd felt at the time was betrayed.

Now, in a way, he understood. But it was a lesson he figured he was never going to get a chance to put to use.

Because he wasn't ever going to paint himself into that kind of corner again.

That the thought, the memory, should turn up now, skimming across his consciousness, made him wonder a little. Then he shrugged it away.

The aroma grew more tempting as he came closer.

Just the way Rebecca did.

His reaction to her was something he was going to have to shrug away, too, he told himself. There was absolutely no use in setting himself up for another fall. Once was plenty for any man—and more than enough for him.

With all this firmly in place in his mind, Angus indulged himself a moment. Leaning against the wall of the tiny entranceway, he watched Rebecca in the kitchen, moving around the small space like a whirlwind.

Vikki was trying to keep up. That tickled him most of all. If he didn't know any better, he'd have thought he'd wandered in on a scene right out of some family program on TV.

TV was all he could liken it to. There hadn't been any scenes like this in his own life.

He pushed away the longing that suddenly rose up.

"Lucy, I'm home," he announced, grinning, just as two sets of eyes looked his way.

Angus saw the pleased smile on Rebecca's face and felt himself reacting to it. She was getting to him, he realized. He should have left Biordi's office, Angus thought, before the man thought to tender his "advice."

Vikki wrinkled her nose as she rubbed an itch away with the back of her wrist. "Who's Lucy?"

"Someone on a classic sitcom," he told her. He laid a hand on her shoulder by way of a greeting. "It just seemed appropriate at the time." He looked at Rebecca. She took this cooking thing seriously, didn't she? "What are you two up to?'' And what was Vikki doing here, now that he thought of it? He'd left her at Jenny's when Rebecca and he had gone out. Angus looked from his daughter to his houseguest. ''Everyone all right?''

Rebecca had more than an hour embroiled in preparing a meal that she felt far more confident about when she began, than when she finally slid the pan into the oven. Looking at Angus now, she caught her bottom lip between her teeth. ''That all depends.''

Angus had the strongest desire to nibble on her lip for her. It took a lot of willpower to drag his eyes away. ''On what?''

''On whether you like Italian food.'' She tried to sound nonchalant. It was silly to feel this way. But there was very little in her world right now—and every correct turn, every minor success, was important. That included cooking a meal for someone who had been good to her.

''Love it,'' Angus swore. He thought of the place near his office he liked to frequent. ''There's a little rest—''

''*Homemade* Italian food,'' Rebecca interjected before he could start reciting the virtues of yet another restaurant. She was beginning to suspect that as far as Angus was concerned, the stove was just a fixture that came with the apartment—like electrical outlets.

''Whose home?'' he asked guardedly, turning his eyes toward Vikki.

Dimples winked around the child's mouth as she announced proudly, ''Ours.''

Cupping her chin in his hand, Angus rubbed a dab of what looked like whipped cream away with his thumb. Obviously, she had been sampling whatever it was that they were making. The image of Rebecca and Vikki, their heads together, creating something—however inedible it finally turned out to be—warmed him.

"I didn't think anything could be cooked in our apartment. You mean the microwave still works?"

"Not the microwave. Rebecca used the oven," Vikki informed him importantly. "Rebecca even let me turn the dials."

"We have an *oven?*" He pretended to look around. "Where?"

"Here, silly." Holding onto one arm, Vikki dragged him over to it. "See?"

He could just barely make out the shape of a pan behind the stove's tinted glass. "And here I thought it was only for storing dirty plates in."

Rebecca had taken care of those, washing and then stacking them in the cupboard. "Speaking of which," she asked, one hand on her hip, "how does a man who never cooks manage to accumulate so many dirty dishes?"

He was the soul of innocence. "Talent."

"Well, plant your other talents on the chair." Rebecca nodded toward the table. "Dinner is about to be served."

So saying, she took a quick peek into the refrigerator. A plate piled high with the dessert over which she and Vikki had labored, was on the top shelf, chilling. Rolled pieces of pastry, stuffed to the brim with white, foamy filling dotted with bits of dark chocolate, lay like tiny promises of ecstasy, waiting for consumption. Closing the door again, she announced, "Everything's ready."

He was just standing there, looking at her as if he had no idea what was going on. "You're not sitting," she accused.

"I'm sitting, I'm sitting," he obliged, moving toward the table.

A table—he noticed for the first time—that was actually set. He couldn't remember the last time he hadn't begun a meal by grabbing utensils on his way to the table. There were three settings. Three. There had never been more than a deuce before. Ever. First his father had sat across from him. Then Jane. Then Vikki.

Three had a nice feel to it, he mused. Too bad it was only temporary.

Angus nodded at his plate as Rebecca took the hot pan out of the oven. "When did this miracle start taking place?"

"Just after you left." She hoped she hadn't left anything out of the recipe. The next moment, the thought struck her as almost ludicrous. Recipes rose up, whole and intact in her mind, and yet she still didn't have a clue as to something so simple as her last name.

Rebecca transferred the contents of the pan to a large plate and brought it over to the table. Very carefully, she slid two wide-mouthed shells filled to capacity with meat, sauce and cheese onto his plate.

"By the way, you owe Jenny a can of tomato paste."

"She said she wanted to have some of the mana— manni—" Vikki stopped, apparently frustrated that she couldn't wrap her tongue around the word.

"Manicotti," Rebecca supplied.

"Yeah, that—if it came out all right," Vikki concluded.

Angus could feel the vibration of Vikki's feet as she swung them back and forth, hungrily eyeing the food being placed on her plate. It certainly looked good, he mused. And smelled good.

Almost as good as Rebecca did, he thought. He caught a whiff of something enticingly sensual as Rebecca bent over Vikki's plate.

The next moment, his mouth felt like cotton—cotton left out in the sun for a week. His caught just the merest hint of the swell of her breasts peeking out over the top of her blouse. He had trouble concentrating on what he was saying. "Then invite her over."

Vikki looked reluctant to leave her plate.

"Why don't you taste it first," Rebecca suggested, "and see if you should be inviting guests?"

Was she uncertain about her efforts? he wondered. "Now you're beginning to sound mysterious."

She shrugged. "Just cautious."

And maybe, just maybe, she added silently, a little proprietary. She wanted Angus to taste this first effort of hers without distracting neighbors around, no matter how likable they were. She had no idea why it meant so much to her not to share this moment with anyone else—but it did.

"Okay, Jenny can wait," he told Vikki.

Bracing himself, Angus took a bite, knowing he was going to have to be polite about it, no matter what it tasted like. He was the first one to admit that things didn't always live up to their promise.

But the promise was not only lived up to, it was exceeded. The manicotti all but dissolved on his tongue, leaving behind an intense desire for more.

Angus looked up at Rebecca, pleasure and wonder in his eyes. "Hey, this is good."

She discreetly let go of the breath she'd been holding. Now she could afford to brazen it out. "You say that as if you're surprised."

The smile on his face was nothing if not endearing. It was the kind that could have coaxed forgiveness out of the hardest of hearts. And hers was far from that.

That much she could sense.

"Well, you *did* lose your memory."

She certainly couldn't argue with that. But apparently

some fundamentals hadn't been erased. "Selectively, it seems. I still remember how to walk and talk—and cook."

Vikki already seemed to have sunk into ecstasy, wolfing down her portion. She grinned happily at her father, eyeing the large plate and obviously hoping for more. "This is even better than takeout, Angus."

He winked at Rebecca, unaware of the flutter that created in her stomach. "I think you've just been given the ultimate compliment." Angus watched as Rebecca slid another two shells onto Vikki's plate. Her own was still empty. "Aren't you going to have any?"

"I'm not all that hungry." For form's sake, she took a single shell and placed it on her plate before retiring the spatula. "I nibbled a lot while I was making this," she explained when he looked at her quizzically, hoping that he wouldn't guess at her real reason.

The knot in her stomach was just now loosening. If Angus seemed surprised that she could cook well, he wasn't the only one. When she'd gone to the supermarket with him to purchase the ingredients she needed, she'd only had a vague feeling that she knew what she was doing. Halfway back to his apartment, she had silently experienced a panic attack, afraid that she'd taken on more than she could handle.

The panic had receded as she had gotten immersed in a ritual that slowly began to feel familiar to her. She did things by instinct, not by memory. Vikki became her assistant and unofficial cheering section. She'd gone to Jenny's to pick the little girl up after Angus had left her, because she'd needed someone to talk to. Someone to keep the void from returning for her.

And, she reasoned, Vikki needed to feel included just as much as she did. After a few suspicious minutes had passed, it became evident that Rebecca's reasoning was right on the money. Vikki liked being consulted, liked helping. And *really* liked sampling.

Rebecca smiled as she watched the two of them eat with relish. "So, I guess we can take the hospital emergency phone number off the speed dial?"

Angus nodded, washing down the last of his meal with a swig of soda. "Unless we have to go there because we've all eaten too much." Not standing on ceremony, he helped himself to more. "How did you learn to—" He stopped abruptly, his eyes shifting to her face. It was a stupid, thoughtless blunder. "Sorry, wasn't thinking."

"It's all right," she said, unfazed. "You've done enough thinking for one day."

"Can she stay, Angus?" Vikki suddenly asked, her mouth full.

Angus raised an eyebrow. "What?" He had heard her, but couldn't believe he'd heard correctly.

Vikki swallowed, then took a deep breath before continuing. "Rebecca. Can she stay here with us?"

What was she getting at? "She *is* staying here with us."

But Vikki shook her head. The look she shot Rebecca was entirely different from the one she'd aimed at her less than half a day earlier. Obviously, some sort of treaty had been formed in his absence. "I mean, forever."

For a second, Vikki had left him speechless. Recovering, he tried tactfully to ease his way out of the situation without insulting Rebecca or hurting Vikki. "I don't think that'll work out. Rebecca has another life she has to get back to."

Vikki didn't quite understand. "What life?"

Angus noticed that Rebecca was leaving this all up to him. He felt like someone struggling to stay afloat in progressively stormier waters. "The one she had before she came to me."

"But she doesn't remember that one. Maybe it was bad. You don't want her to go back to a bad life, do you? Can't she stay?" she repeated. Her eyes shifted hopefully to Rebecca.

Vikki sounded as if she thought she had it all worked out. "It's not that simple, Vik."

"Sure it is," Vikki insisted. She looked at her new friend. "Right, Rebecca?"

Touched, Rebecca ran her hand along the back of her neck. She wasn't quite sure how to handle the question. She met Angus's quizzical look over the little girl's head.

"We bonded while you were out. Frying ground beef together will do that to you." Taking a deep breath, she plunged into what she hoped was a good answer. "You and your father are a family. I can't just come and move in on you."

"But you already did," Vikki reminded her.

"Not permanently," Rebecca stressed. She saw distress in the girl's eyes. Rebecca didn't want to ruin the evening. "I tell you what, let's just take this one step at a time and we'll see what happens, okay?"

Since there weren't any other deals up for consideration at the moment, Vikki agreed. "Okay."

Rebecca saw admiration on Angus's face. She also saw him beginning to take a third helping. "Leave room for the cannoli," she cautioned.

The spatula halted in midslide. "You made cannoli?"

"*We,*" Rebecca corrected him. "We made cannoli."

Vikki sat up a little straighter, evidently pleased with the recognition.

Yes, he could see that they'd bonded. In less than two days, Rebecca had made more headway with his daughter than he had in six months. He mentally took his hat off to her.

He placed the shell he'd begun transferring onto his plate. "Don't worry, I've always got room for dessert."

It was other things that he didn't have room for. Other things like feelings for a woman who wasn't meant to be in his life, who wouldn't be in his life once she had a direction. And it was his job, he reminded himself, to find that direction for her.

Talk about a catch-22 situation, he mused, watching as she cleared away her own plate and Vikki's.

Angus waited until later that evening—after Vikki had obligingly fallen asleep, and he was getting ready to bed down on the sofa—before he said what had been on his mind for most of the afternoon.

"She's taken to you a hell of a lot faster than she did to me."

Rebecca paused, wondering if that bothered him. He didn't strike her as the type given to petty jealousy. She was going with instincts again, she thought, rather than any knowledge she could draw on.

She didn't *have* any knowledge she could draw on, she reminded herself. But some things, you just knew.

Rebecca relieved him of the bedding. She shook out the top blanket before draping it over the sofa. Curious, she asked, "Do I remind her of her mother?"

Angus shook his head. "You're not a thing alike. Jane was a go-to-hell type of woman from the minute she was born." He took one end of the blanket and helped her spread it out over the cushions. "The poster child for independence. She didn't have a vulnerable bone in her body."

Rebecca tucked the ends of the blanket around the perimeter of the cushions, working quickly, competently, her mind on what he was saying. And not saying. "And I do?"

"Just enough to make you appealing." He tossed a pillow on one end of the sofa. "I didn't mean that in a bad way."

Without thinking, she picked the pillow up and fluffed it before returning it to its place. "I didn't take it in a bad way."

"Good."

The conversation was halting. Because he wasn't thinking about what he was saying. He was only thinking of her. Of what it might be like if he *did* follow Al's advice.

Of what it might be like to taste those lips that lifted so beguilingly in a half smile.

Before he could stop himself, Angus gave in to impulse. Ever so lightly, he feathered his fingers over her hair, his hand coming to rest against her cheek.

She could feel her pulse quickening as she turned her face up to his. "Does vulnerability turn you on?"

"No," he answered truthfully. "Not usually."

She cocked her head just a little, her eyes searching his face. She hadn't a clue what she was looking for. Acceptance? Affection? Something else? Something more?

"Then?" The single word came out in a soft, breathy whisper.

It would have been so very easy to give in, to bend his head just slightly and satisfy this unreasonable craving that had been dancing through him all day. Very easy. And very unprofessional. He struggled and won. And lost a little as well.

"But you do. Turn me on," he added needlessly. Taking a deep breath, he stepped back from her. But not from the desire that insisted on tempting him. "I thought you should know."

Was he being gallant again? For a moment—a wonderful moment—she had thought he was going to kiss her. She knew she was supposed to feel guilty about that, but she couldn't. All she felt was disappointment that he hadn't. If there was someone she was guilty of betraying because of these feelings, she felt no sense of shame. She didn't know of anyone else. She knew only Angus.

She was rationalizing, she thought ruefully. And he was being a gentleman, telling her his feelings instead of acting on them.

"You're telling me so I can prop a chair under the doorknob in my room?"

He liked her sense of humor. "I'm not going to pull a Stanley Kowalski on you." He realized that she had no way of knowing what he was talking about. "That's from—"

"*A Streetcar Named Desire.*" Her surprise mirrored his, as the title of the play popped out. "Right?"

"Right." He knew he should be retreating, putting space between them. But since she had his room, there was nowhere for him to go. "Like I said, a box of surprises." He smiled at her.

She made no effort to leave. God help him, he didn't want her to. And that was a mistake.

"Is there anything you need?" he asked her. "I mean, for tonight?"

"Yes." She hesitated. "Could you hold me? Just for a minute?" She didn't want him to misunderstand. This wasn't a come-on, just one human being needing another. "I mean, I know how that must sound, but right now, I suddenly feel very afraid."

She was, he realized. Had he inadvertently said something? "Of what?"

There was no one else to share her feelings with, and

she needed to share. Needed to talk and pretend that her words mattered to someone.

"That I won't get it back. That this is as far as my memory will go. Just enough to have me functioning, not enough to let me remember."

He knew she could be right. There were cases where people didn't regain their memory, even when they were surrounded with everything that was familiar to them. And Rebecca didn't even have that.

So he did as she asked. He took her into his arms and held her. And was only remotely aware that by doing so, he had taken the first step in a direction he'd vowed never to go in again.

Chapter 8

It wasn't that Angus didn't want to kiss her. He did. Very much. At that one moment in time, he couldn't think of anything he wanted more than to kiss Rebecca.

What he didn't want was for that kiss to be the start of something.

Angus had a sinking feeling that it might already be too late for that. Something had already begun—begun before he ever touched his lips to hers. How far it went depended on him.

Or so he wanted to believe, because that still left a semblance of control in his possession.

More than anything, he would have hated to think that he had no say in the matter.

Even if he really didn't.

So he held her and pretended that every fiber of his body wasn't wanting her at this moment. He didn't convince himself. He'd never been very good when it came to pretending.

When he felt her cheek move along his chest, felt her breath as it softly skimmed his shirt until it seeped through the cloth and penetrated his skin, saw the look in her eyes as she turned her face up to his, Angus knew that the pretense he had hoped to nurture had died before it was ever born.

There was no course open to him but the one he followed.

It seemed as natural to him as breathing.

Looking into her eyes, he was filled with her, with the scent and the desire of her. He couldn't resist any more than he could stop his heart from pounding.

Nor did he want to resist.

But if his heart was hammering, hers had stopped. As if she were watching something happen outside of herself, Rebecca held her breath, waiting, hoping.

Wanting.

Gently skimming her throat with his fingertips, Angus framed her face with his hands, then lowered his mouth to hers. And kissed her.

Kissed her to kiss away her fears, her gut-wrenching loneliness. She had no way of knowing that in that same moment, he also kissed away his own peace of mind.

All she knew was that he'd kissed her. It was a gentle kiss, a soft kiss. She clung to it, responded as it unearthed so much more within her than she'd thought was there. The breath she'd held had been snatched away from her, leaving her entirely without air. She didn't care. All she knew was that she wanted him to go on kissing her forever.

He tasted her need as it mingled with his, forming a unit that overwhelmed him. Her lips parted in an unspoken invitation.

It didn't go unanswered.

His hands dropped from her face and he enfolded her in his arms. His hands lightly grazed her back, as if to assure himself that he wasn't, after all, merely imagining this.

His imagination had never been that good. Not about things like this. He was always the last to understand his own feelings, the last to even acknowledge their existence. He had no choice this time. They slammed through him, demanding his attention. Demanding release.

But that wasn't possible.

What he had left of his control, he used, tightening the rein on his desire.

Tightening his arms around her.

Rebecca felt the moan of raw pleasure as it rumbled along her throat. His kiss had gone beneath the layers of the civilized, lost woman she thought herself to be, to something far deeper, far more basic that existed underneath. It reached down and touched her at her very core.

Rebecca felt the outline of his hard body against hers. Whether it was because he held her so tightly, or because she'd pressed herself to him, she didn't know. Point of origin didn't matter. What mattered was the excitement it generated. Excitement that exploded within her, going off like a battery of photographers' flashbulbs at a state wedding the moment the bride and groom exited the church.

She had no idea she was harboring feelings like this. There'd been no hint that her emotions went this far, this deep. Or were this strong. Stunned, she could only hold on and go along for the ride.

He felt her heart pounding against him. Or was that *his* heart trying to break free of the confines he'd been so certain he'd imposed on it? He realized he'd forgotten what it was like to really want a woman. To burn in frustrated unfulfillment because he couldn't have her.

Just the way he couldn't have Rebecca.

No matter how he looked at it, how much he wanted it, making love with her wasn't right.

Very slowly, Angus drew his head back. He wanted to hold her just a little longer, but he knew if he did, he might not have the strength to let her go again. He dropped his arms to his sides. "I'd make that two chairs if I were you."

Feeling even more dazed than when she'd first come to, and stumbled away from the Dumpster yesterday, Rebecca could only stare at him. Her mind wasn't processing his words.

"What?"

"Against your doorknob." He repeated his previous warning. There was a great deal more conviction behind it now. "I'd make it two chairs instead of one tonight, just in case my common sense decides to evaporate."

"Oh." The fog that had enshrouded her brain began to lift. "Right."

Shaken, struggling for some sort of composure, Rebecca dragged a hand through her hair. He was right, of course. She couldn't say she was very happy about it at the moment, but she was grateful to him for not pressing his advantage. She had no idea what had come over her. She didn't behave this way—did she?

She blew out a breath. That was just it—she had no idea how she behaved. She didn't know if this was normal for her, or a wanton departure brought on by need, by the chemistry between them and by a desire so strong she was powerless to resist it on her own.

Instinct told her it was the latter. Instinct also told her that sleeping with Angus would only further complicate a situation that was already far too complicated.

The thought that she was behaving sensibly failed to cheer her.

Rebecca took a step back, testing the integrity of her bone structure. Contrary to what she'd thought, her legs hadn't been transformed into Silly Putty. She could still walk away. At least physically.

She tried to tell herself that what she felt, what she *thought* she felt for Angus, was a result of her being so alone in this world. His was one of the first faces she'd seen, certainly the first she'd focused on. He was Adam to her Eve. Once she got past that, she might feel different about him.

Maybe. Maybe not.

"I'll see you in the morning," she murmured. He looked relieved that she was retreating, she thought. It stung a little.

He only nodded in response, not sure just how long he could remain this noble. It had been a long time since he'd felt a pull as powerful as the one holding him in its grip right now.

He needed a cold shower, he thought as he watched her disappear into his room, closing the door behind her. He tried not to think about her putting on that same jersey—his jersey—and then getting into bed. His bed.

She was in his bed in his jersey.

Without him.

But the only shower in the apartment was accessible only through his bedroom. He knew if he entered the room right now, he might never make it to the stall.

Might? There was no question about it.

Resigned to spending a restless night alone, Angus lay down on the sofa. There was comfort in knowing that ultimately, he was doing the right thing. But not much.

* * *

"Would you mind if I came along today?"

Angus stopped riffling through the papers scattered on the coffee table and looked up at Rebecca. Somewhere amid this mess made up of the Sunday paper and miscellaneous other things was an address he needed.

Her question had caught him completely off guard. Sunday had been spent cautiously regaining ground that had been sacrificed in the aftermath of the few unguarded moments they'd shared before they'd each retreated to their separate corners—their separate worlds—the night before. By the time Sunday was over, they were back to where they'd been, somewhere between P.I. and client and two people on the cusp of what could be a budding friendship.

With the advent of Monday, things promised to return to the regular routine—with one notable exception. Vikki was going to school and he was going to work. He'd figured that Rebecca, the new, temporary ingredient in this mixture, would just remain here.

"Where?" he asked cautiously.

Her shoulders rose, then fell. She had no specific answer. "Wherever you're going."

She probably thought he was going to continue looking for clues to her identity. Much as, for her sake, he would have liked to devote himself to that exclusively, there were other things that demanded his attention.

"I've got other cases pending, Becky. I need to devote some time to them." He didn't want her thinking he was abandoning her. "That doesn't mean I'm not going to try to find out who you are, but—"

She placed her fingertips on his lips. The contact, their first since Saturday night, momentarily shifted her focus.

Realizing the effect it was having—on her if not him—
Rebecca dropped her hand again.

"You don't have to apologize," she said quickly. "Especially since I can't pay you yet. You've got a living to
make, I understand that. I'm grateful for everything
you've done so far." She searched for the right words,
her brain still a little addled. Touching him had just underscored the unanswered desire that hummed within her.
"I just thought that maybe I could help in some way, you
know, in lieu of paying you right now."

Not being beholden to him seemed to be important to
her. Was she independent to a fault, too, the way Jane
had been? "And what way would that be?"

Again, specifics eluded her. "I don't know." She
thought for a second. "Maybe you need your office
straightened out." From what she remembered seeing of
it, even in her disoriented condition, the place had been
in semichaos.

"It's an organized mess," he qualified. And he liked it
that way. "Besides, I'm not going to the office until later
this afternoon. After I check in with Al, I'll be tied up
doing surveillance work."

The thought intrigued her. "What kind of surveillance?"

Still rummaging, Angus finally found what he was
looking for—the address he was going to, after stopping
at the station. Folding the paper, he put it into his pocket.

"Mrs. Angela Clarence Madison wants to get the goods
on her gigolo of a husband so she doesn't get stuck with
paying him a hefty alimony. She was born to the money,
he married it," he explained.

As he saw it, the woman who came from third-
generation money had purchased herself a handsome man
and then done everything in her power to make him regret

selling himself to her. In Angus's estimation, they deserved each other. But his job was not to make a moral judgment, just to take photographs and provide his client with the proof she needed to make her point in court.

He looked at Rebecca. She'd be much better off spending the day here, though he had to admit that the thought of her company was tempting.

He had to watch that word *tempting*, he thought. If he slipped and gave in to it, it could foul him up royally in the long run.

"That means I get to spend a lot of time in my car, parked in some unobtrusive place with great visibility, biding my time until I can take the photographs that make Angela Madison's case for her."

He made it sound so tedious. "Sounds like an exercise in boredom."

That summed it up neatly, he thought. He shrugged. "Part of the job."

And he took pride in doing his job well, in giving his clients their money's worth, she guessed. "Would you like company?"

He would, but there was an inherent problem with that. "You'll distract me."

The last thing she wanted was to get in his way. But the idea of staying here alone wasn't appealing. There were no thoughts to sustain her, and she had already cleaned up his apartment yesterday. Even now, she was making neat piles out of the scattered newspaper. That was the last of it. There was nothing to do. The restlessness weaving through her would drive her crazy if she remained by herself.

"I'll be quiet," she promised.

He smiled. Whether she was quiet or not made no difference. "You'll still distract me."

She thought of the other night and knew that he was thinking of it, too. A warm sensation curled through her, like hot coffee on a cold morning. She really wanted to go with him. When she was with Angus, she didn't feel so lost. He made her feel safe; without saying a word or making promises he couldn't keep, he made her feel as if everything would turn out all right.

"Two sets of eyes are better than one?" She looked at him hopefully.

There was that, he supposed. But more important, maybe if she was with him, if they went on talking as they sat, watching the rest of the world go about its business, something would occur to her.

He was rationalizing, but it was still worth a try.

"Okay," he agreed, "you can come with me. But just remember, this isn't going to be anything like *Magnum.*"

"Magnum?" she repeated blankly.

The name obviously meant nothing to her. Vikki and Jenny were glued to the set every day at seven, watching reruns of the show on a cable channel. "It was a TV show about a private investigator."

"Never saw it," she told him. At least, as far as she knew she never had.

"Then we start out even." He had never caught it, either, when it was on originally. And now, he heard rather than saw it whenever he came home at that time.

"Vikki," he called to her, "you've got ten minutes before school starts."

Several beats passed before Vikki came out of her room, dragging her feet. She looked like a portrait of the petulant child. "Can't it start without me?"

"It can, but it won't." He took out his wallet, looking for two dollar bills to give her. But the smallest he had was a five. Angus handed it to her. "Here, lunch money. I expect change."

Eyes that were just a shade too innocent looked up at him. "How much change?"

"Do the math," he told her. Grabbing her backpack—a hot purple knapsack that had spent all weekend on the stool near the front door where she had dropped it—he ushered Vikki out the door.

"Are you going to school with me?" she asked Rebecca as she climbed into the back seat.

"No, she's coming to work with me," Angus answered. He got in behind the wheel.

Vikki slid the metal tongue into the slot on her seat belt. Angus listened for the telltale *click*.

"Can I get her tomorrow?" Vikki asked.

"Vik, Rebecca isn't a toy to be passed back and forth, she's a person with feelings." Looking over his shoulder, he backed out of the spot.

"I know that." Vikki looked miffed at the suggestion that she didn't. "I just want to bring her in for show-and-tell. They never saw anybody with 'nesia before."

He slanted a look at Rebecca. She seemed to be taking it well, but he still apologized for Vikki. "Sorry about that."

"Don't be. At least I'm useful for something." Turning, she looked at the little girl. "You clear it with your teacher, Vikki, and I'll come."

He laughed, glancing on both sides of the car before pulling out of the complex. "I think I call that valor above and beyond the call of duty."

A smile that he was tempted to sample firsthand curved her mouth. "I think I'd call it fun."

Fun. He could only shake his head. "To each his own, Becky, to each his own."

* * *

They dropped Vikki off at school and went directly to the police station. Biordi was out on call, but he had left a message for Angus with the desk sergeant. There was no change in status. No one matching Rebecca's description had been reported missing.

It didn't make sense to Angus. If she'd been his, he would have reported her missing fifteen minutes after she was late.

He wasn't being objective about this, he thought, driving down the street noted on the paper in his pocket. Hell, he'd stopped being objective when he had decided not to drop her off at the shelter.

The entrance of the building that Angela Madison owned—where Ryan Madison supposedly worked whenever he felt like showing up—was located in the middle of a long, busy block in the heart of Bedford's newly completed industrial area.

Angus considered himself lucky when he found a parking place almost directly opposite the building. Ryan— Mrs. Madison had called to inform Angus—had taken great pains to tell her that he was going in on Monday to take care of a few details. Mrs. Madison figured the details were all located in strategic places on the body of the newest woman in his life.

"It must be awful," Rebecca said with a sigh when Angus explained this to her.

"What is?" He wasn't sure which part of his explanation she was referring to.

"To know that the man you love is cheating on you."

"I don't know about love, but there's little doubt about the cheating part."

An eyebrow arched in surprise. "You don't think Mrs. Madison loves her husband?"

Angus laughed softly at the innocence of her question.

He wondered if the woman she really *was* was this innocent. "I think Mrs. Madison wanted to wear her husband like a prized piece of jewelry. I doubt that love ever entered into either side of it, unless you're talking about love of the good life or love of money."

It sounded like a sad commentary on two lives. "You really think rich people are that cold?"

"Not rich people, just *these* rich people," he corrected. "I did some checking and asking around. It was a match made in a bank vault. She had it, he wanted it."

"What did he have that she wanted?"

Amused, Angus looked at her pointedly.

"Oh."

Angus grinned. "Charm and looks gets 'em every time."

"If that's true, why isn't there anyone in your life?"

She wasn't being coy, he realized, but serious. Which left him at a loss for an answer.

He was spared fielding the question. A dark limousine with plates matching the ones Angela Madison had given him drew up to the entrance of the Clarence Building. Madison had arrived.

"Show time," he said under his breath.

Rebecca leaned over Angus, trying to get a better view, curious to see what Angela Madison's money had bought and paid for. A well-groomed, strikingly handsome man emerged from the back of the vehicle.

He looked awfully young from where Rebecca was sitting. She turned to Angus. "How old is he?"

She was too close, he thought. Maybe bringing her along *had* been a mistake. "Not nearly as old as Angela Madison."

Madison said something to his driver, then stepped back on the curb as if to walk into the building. But the moment the limousine drove off, Madison was back at the curb, signaling for a cab. One arrived almost instantly.

He'd obviously called ahead, Angus thought.

"Looks like he's taking his business on the road," Angus told her. Making a U-turn on the island in the middle of the street, Angus followed the cab.

It was a bonafide chase scene, even if it was in slow motion. Rebecca got into the spirit of it, sitting as close to the edge of her seat as her seat belt allowed. "I thought you said this wasn't going to be interesting."

"I didn't think we'd be going anywhere this soon. The man doesn't even have enough brains to go in and let a few people in the office see him before he takes off."

His comment intrigued her. "Is that how you'd do it if you were cheating on your wife?"

"I wouldn't cheat on my wife," he informed her. "There's no point in being married if you're going to cheat."

She liked his philosophy. The woman who got Angus was going to be a very happy, very lucky woman, she thought. A touch of wistfulness whispered through her. She couldn't help wondering if she had a husband and if he felt that way about her.

With each day that passed, the possibility that she was married seemed more and more remote. The thought didn't bother her.

"What are you going to do when he stops?" she asked, watching the cab intently.

"Depends on where he stops." The light was turning yellow. Angus sped up and just made it through in time. Though two cars separated them, the cab was still in sight. "Hopefully, it'll be at a hotel. Once I get the photographs, it'll be over."

She read into his tone. "You don't like doing surveillance?"

It wasn't the work he minded, it was what it was tied to. "Not this kind."

She didn't understand. "Then why do you do it?"

"It pays the bills. In this case, it pays pretty well. Mrs. Madison is very anxious to get her hands on some incriminating photographs of her wandering spouse."

She couldn't see him being a private investigator if he didn't like it. "Do you work other kinds of cases?"

He nodded. "I do a lot of background checks for places that require security clearance on their employees. And I used to try to locate runaways." Those cases had been some of his most challenging ones—until Rebecca had walked into his office. "But I don't handle runaways anymore. I had to give them up."

"Why?" Was he subtly telling her that he hadn't been good at that sort of thing?

He sometimes missed the travel, the challenge of piecing clues together. But he'd had no choice. "Taking those kinds of cases would have taken me away from home too much. I figure Vikki has had enough upheaval in her life. What she needs right now are roots and a father who comes home to her every night."

The next moment, they slowed down as the cab pulled into a parking lot of a hotel.

"He's stopping." She didn't bother disguising the excitement in her voice.

"Looks that way." Her reaction amused him. To him this was all routine, but he supposed there was nothing right now that was routine to Rebecca.

Madison got out at the entrance of the Excelsior Hotel as soon as the cab stopped. In his hurry, he left the car door ajar.

The driver called after him to shut it, then got out, grumbling obscenities about cheap fares. When he slammed the door, the sound echoed through the street. Madison was oblivious to the anatomical instructions hurled his way as he took the red-carpeted hotel steps two at a time.

Fascinated, Rebecca kept her eyes on the man while Angus parked the car. "He must be in a hurry."

So should he be if he didn't want to lose Madison, Angus thought. He leaned over the back of his seat to retrieve his camera case.

"I don't know how long I'll be," he warned as he got out.

But she was already closing the passenger door behind her. "I'm coming, too." It wasn't a request until she saw the look of surprise on his face. "Maybe I can help."

He had no idea what she thought she could do, but he didn't have time to talk her out of it now. Madison had already disappeared into the hotel. Besides, as long as she was with him, he could keep her out of danger.

"All right, let's go."

Slanting a look at her as they hurried across to the entrance, he couldn't help thinking she looked like a kid at Christmas. At least this was taking her mind off her own situation, he thought. Maybe that was all she needed—to relax—and then she'd start remembering. Things had a way of linking up in the mind. Maybe he'd get lucky on two counts.

They made it into the lobby in time to see Madison heading away from the front desk and toward the bank of elevators. Rebecca, energized, took the lead, quickening her step.

"C'mon, you don't want to lose him."

Wanting to keep a low profile, he'd intended to find

out what floor Madison was going to by distracting the front desk clerk long enough to take a look at the computer screen. Riding up with his quarry wasn't his first choice, but Rebecca seemed to have other ideas.

They took the same elevator as Madison getting on just as the doors were closing. Rebecca stole a triumphant glance in Angus's direction. Angus was beginning to get the feeling that whoever Rebecca was in her other life, the word *reticent* didn't apply to her.

When Madison got off on the eleventh floor, Rebecca followed in his wake, her hand locked tightly around Angus's wrist.

Pulling back just a little to give Madison time to get ahead, Angus whispered, "Whose case *is* this, anyway?"

"Yours," she answered automatically, her eyes trained on Madison.

The man was handsome, she thought, in a plastic sort of way. On an absolute scale, he was better looking than Angus. But there was an electricity about Angus, an instant draw that seemed to be missing from Madison—at least at this distance.

Maybe her knowledge of what he was up to was coloring her perception, she thought. But she doubted it. Angus was miles ahead of the man in front of her on any scale.

Following a few feet behind, they stopped when Madison did. His hand on the doorknob, the man looked in their direction, mild suspicion crossing his picture-perfect features.

Rebecca turned on Angus, her hands on her hips. "Don't tell me you forgot the card again." She raised her voice in annoyance. "'Don't take your purse,' you said. 'You won't need it,'" she added in a mocking, singsong voice meant to mimic him. "Now what are we going to do?"

Recovering quickly, Angus picked up his cue. "Go down to the lobby and have them let us in. No big deal."

"No big deal?" She tossed her hair over her shoulder. "They're going to have to change the access code for us. Again. They're not going to be happy about it, Howard."

Bored, Madison lost interest in the exchange. If he wanted to listen to harping, he would have spent his evenings at home. A shapely brunette, clad in something that appeared vaguely translucent, was in the doorway the moment he opened the door. She purred a greeting and drew him into the room.

Angus looked at Rebecca, new respect in his eyes. It was coupled with amazement. "That was very good." He made a note of the number on Madison's door. "Who's Howard?"

She had no idea. "Just a name that popped up in my head."

Howard. Was he just a friend, or her husband? Lover, perhaps? Angus did his best to lock away the feelings that went along with the question. "Anything else popping up in there?"

She shook her head. She wasn't even thinking about that. She was getting wrapped up in what Angus was doing. "Only that this is exciting."

That was the word for *her*, he thought, looking at her profile. Exciting.

Chapter 9

"So now what do we do?"

He could feel the enthusiasm radiating from her. Somewhere along the line, between his apartment and the eleventh floor of the Excelsior Hotel, Rebecca had dealt herself in.

The idea of being his not-so-silent partner seemed to please her. He supposed there was no harm in it. If anything, seeing his work through her eyes gave him a fresh outlook. Angus figured that could only help.

If she brought this sort of excitement to a routine assignment, he found himself thinking, what could she do with lovemaking?

That was something he wasn't about to find out and there was absolutely no point in torturing himself by wondering.

The thought refused to go away, though, hovering instead within the distant recesses of his mind. Curiosity, he'd long ago discovered, could be a damn annoying thing.

Angus led the way back to the elevators. He only hoped that his luck, as far as the Madison case went, was holding.

"Now we go down and get a room around the corner from Ryan Madison and the current light of his life. And we hope that being on the eleventh floor mutes his sense of discretion enough to make him forget to draw the curtains while he grabs a little afternoon delight."

He pressed for the elevator. The doors seemed to open instantly, as if eager to please.

She walked ahead of him into the empty car. "It's only nine-thirty," she pointed out.

Leaning in front of her, Angus pressed the button for the lobby. "Poetic license. By the time they're through, it might be afternoon."

Their car was an express, skipping the next ten floors and arriving at its destination in a matter of seconds. It took several more before Rebecca's stomach caught up.

She swallowed, and her ears popped. "They should book this elevator as a ride in an amusement park," she murmured, linking her arm with his.

She was doing things like that more and more, he noticed. Touching, making contact, using her hands as an extension of her voice and the personality he saw unfolding before him. It all came naturally to her, without any thought.

Was the true Rebecca emerging? Or was this a part of herself she'd kept hidden when she was her usual persona? Would what he saw now—what attracted him so strongly to her—fade away and die once she remembered who she was?

It didn't matter, he thought. He wouldn't be around to

see or be affected one way or the other. By then, his job would be done and he'd have signed off.

And as far as jobs, Angus reminded himself, he had one to see to now.

The twenty-story Excelsior Hotel was shaped like an ornate horseshoe, its inner perimeter closing ranks around a huge circular swimming pool and recreation area built exclusively for the use of the hotel guests. Familiar with the hotel's interior from past experience, Angus knew that there were a handful of rooms on each floor that faced one another. Privacy was maintained by virtue of the distance between the two sections of the building.

But privacy didn't reckon on a powerful telephoto lens like the one in his camera case.

With Rebecca beside him, Angus asked the desk clerk for room 1125. It was situated so that he'd have a clear view of Madison's room, provided Madison hadn't become shy. Or cautious.

The clerk's small, sharp eyes narrowed over the bridge of his hawklike nose. Most guests didn't specify a room by its number.

"It's my lucky number," Angus supplied amiably in response to the clerk's quizzical look.

"Eleven-twenty-five?" It hardly sounded like a run-of-the-mill choice.

"It's my birthday," Rebecca put in. "November twenty-fifth," she added when the clerk continued to stare uncomprehendingly.

"Oh. I see," he murmured. The answer seemed to satisfy him. "Well, I see that your luck seems to be holding. The room is unoccupied at the moment."

The clerk took down the necessary information, then took Angus's charge card and fed the numbers into his

computer. Waiting for confirmation, he eyed the camera
case hanging from Angus's shoulder. It was the only piece
of luggage between the couple.

"Traveling light, sir?"

Angus never missed a beat. "We're only in town for
the day."

The hotel frowned on being the site of assignations,
which was what this appeared to the desk clerk to be. But
there was little that could be done. Angus's charge card
had gone through, authorizing payment.

With a holier-than-thou sniff, the man handed them the
card that would get them into the room.

"We hope you have a pleasant stay with us."

Angus had heard more sincere recorded messages from
government switchboards. "I'm sure it will be," he replied, ushering Rebecca away.

Laughter, light and musical, broke free as soon as they
turned toward the elevators. She looked up at Angus. "I
think the clerk thinks that *you're* the one in the market
for a little afternoon delight."

He wasn't in the market for it, but it certainly kept
popping up in his shopping cart. At least the thought of
it did. Keeping his mind on business was becoming almost
a Herculean feat. Who knew how long they were going
to have to remain in the room before the opportunity for
a good photo presented itself? Meanwhile, another opportunity—a far more tempting one—was already present.
If he examined it logically, the timing was perfect. And
as a bonus, he wouldn't have to worry about Vikki coming up on them unexpectedly.

But something else was coming up on him unexpectedly: his sense of honor, of fair play. Maybe Rebecca
belonged to another man, and maybe she didn't. But without definite proof one way or another, it was the *maybe*

that was the stumbling block. If she did, and they made love, she would feel as if she'd betrayed someone. And if something should come of their being together, if Angus began to care for her and she went back to that someone, then *he* would feel betrayed. Just the way he'd felt when Jane left.

The only way he could win at this game was if he didn't play at all.

It sounded good in theory. Execution was another matter.

A smile curved his mouth. If he couldn't allow himself to have her, he could at least enjoy her in other ways. There was no harm, he told himself, in looking. From what he could see, a lot of other men were indulging already.

"The clerk probably took one look at you and wished himself in my place."

The smile she tendered in response to his words began in her eyes and quickly spread to all parts of her, like the rays of the early morning sun on the land. "Thanks, I needed that."

He couldn't see why, if she'd taken even so much as a cursory glance at herself as she passed a mirror. She couldn't be oblivious to the way she looked, no matter how overwhelmed she was by her amnesia. When they'd walked through the lobby, men's heads had turned, their glances simultaneously admiring and envious.

A beautiful woman who wasn't aware of it. The hoofbeats he was hearing really did belong to a zebra, he thought, ushering her into the elevator. Maybe even a unicorn.

Madison had obligingly left the curtains open, allowing the bright Southern California sun, and Angus, access to what was going on inside the room.

From the looks of it, what was going on was exactly what Angela Madison had suspected.

"Looks like you don't have to wait," Rebecca commented as they walked into their room.

From where she stood, all she could see were the shadowy figures of two unclothed people apparently wrapped around each other. Their identities, if she hadn't known, would have been anyone's guess.

"I love a cooperative subject." This made his work easy for him.

Angus put the camera case on the bed and snapped open the dual locks. He took out a miniature tripod. When he released the three locks along the legs, three lengths of metal came shooting out, tripling the tripod's height.

Tuning out the passionate nude couple across the way, Rebecca watched, fascinated, as Angus began to set up his equipment by the window. "Do you think you can get a clear shot?"

Angus unscrewed the lens from his camera, then carefully took out a second one from his case. The latter looked like a small telescope.

"I think so," he said mildly. When he raised his eyes to hers, she saw the amusement.

Moving away from the window, she crossed to the bed.

"That looks as if it would give you a clear shot of two people making love on Mars."

He laughed as he attached the lens to his camera. The equipment represented a sizable investment, but it was necessary for the kinds of cases coming his way. He had enough of the latest technology to be a state-of-the-art Peeping Tom, he thought wryly.

"Maybe not Mars," he said, "but I could certainly get

a clear shot of the fly on the wall that's watching our two friends in room 1109."

She watched as he mounted the camera. She had her doubts about it remaining steady. "Do you need any help holding it up?"

A grin teased his mouth and he bit his tongue so as not to quip. "I'm fine. The tripod can support it."

Angus propped up the center of the lens with something that looked like another, more sophisticated tripod. Set, he peered through the viewfinder. Perfect. Angela Madison was going to be one very satisfied client, he mused.

Positioning himself, Angus took careful aim. For the next twenty minutes, the only sound within the room was the soft click the camera made as Angus shot photograph after incriminating photograph. He used up two rolls of film, just to play it safe.

Though she couldn't see clearly without the benefit of Angus's lens, Rebecca felt like a witness to a desecration of something precious. An odd feeling slithered through her.

Moving away from the window, she crossed her arms in front of her to ward off the chill she felt. How would she have reacted, finding the man she loved in bed with someone else?

And then she knew the answer. She would have reacted with hurt and anger and an enormous sense of betrayal if her man had so wantonly violated something that meant so much to her.

"I hope she rakes him over the coals."

Angus could imagine the subjects of his photographs rolling straight into the fireplace in their passion—but he assumed that wasn't what Rebecca meant.

"Who?"

"Mrs. Madison." Unable to stop herself, she glanced

back at the couple. They were back on the bed again. She felt indignation for a woman she'd never met. "He deserves everything he's getting."

Angus laughed. "Right now, I think he'd tend to agree with you."

She flushed. "I didn't mean—"

He nodded, getting her off the hook. "I know what you meant."

Angus removed the camera from its support. He had two complete rolls, thirty-six shots each. There were bound to be enough clear photographs there to put the nails into Madison's coffin.

Sitting down on the bed with the camera next to him, he glanced Rebecca's way. She looked uncomfortable, he thought. Angus gestured toward the television set. "They get several of the movie channels. Why don't you put one on?"

She was being silly, she thought. But there was this cloak draped over her. This sudden, oppressive feeling mocking her when she looked at Madison flagrantly breaking his marriage vows.

Still cold, Rebecca ran her hands along her bare arms. "I'm sorry, it's just that, watching him, I—"

Angus stopped disassembling the camera. "What? Are you remembering something?"

"Something," she agreed. It was such a nebulous word, used to describe such a nebulous feeling. "But I don't know what." She couldn't pin down the feeling, much less the memory it generated. Stymied, Rebecca shrugged. "Maybe it was just a program I saw on TV."

But maybe it was more than that, Angus thought. Setting the camera aside, he got up and crossed to her. Maybe she wasn't married, but divorced. Maybe she had caught her own husband cheating on her just the way Madison was cheating on his wife. It would explain why her reaction was so vehement.

Now he knew for sure that he wouldn't be partaking of any "afternoon delight" with Rebecca. It was for the best in the long run, he told himself. No complications.

Like hell there were no complications, he thought, looking down at her face.

Gently, he placed his hands on her shoulders. The anguish in her eyes had returned. He couldn't stand for her to look like that—especially when he couldn't do anything about it.

"I've got enough on film," he told her. "Why don't we get out of here?"

Rebecca took a deep cleansing breath. If she couldn't remember, then she didn't want to dwell on a half memory. Especially one that felt so unpleasant.

"I'd like that."

Angus offered to take her home before he went to his office, but she turned him down.

"I'm all right, really," she assured him again.

Rebecca was already feeling foolish about the way she'd acted in the hotel. There was no reason to become upset over what a stranger was doing. And if it echoed of something else, something in her lost life—well, until she could put a name to it, there was no reason to behave this way. Or to disturb Angus with it. The last thing she wanted was to be a millstone around his neck.

Where were these sayings coming from? she wondered again. She wasn't even sure she knew what a millstone was.

"I'm sorry about before," she apologized as they walked up the stairs to his second-floor office. "It was just that I got such a strange, strong feeling of *déjà vu* when I was watching him. Or imagining what he was doing," she amended, feeling a slight tinge of color creeping up to her face. "But I don't even know if I was feeling bad for his wife, or reliving something."

Hiking the camera strap farther up his shoulder, Angus put his key in the lock. His guess was that it was probably the latter. Sympathy entered his eyes as he looked at Rebecca. This had to be hell for her. "It would be nice if you could just snap your fingers and have it all come back."

Would it be nice? she wondered. When she'd come to his office the first time, she would have said *yes* immediately. But now, she didn't know. Did that life hold something better for her than what was happening here? Or something worse?

"Maybe," she allowed slowly.

He thought she would have adamantly agreed with him. Angus held open the door for her. "Maybe?"

She walked inside. "As long as everything that was happening now didn't go away. I'd hate to forget these last few days."

Maybe that sounded pushy, she realized. But she couldn't be anything but honest, especially after watching that exercise in dishonesty at the hotel.

He flipped on the lights, telling himself not to read too much into her words. "Maybe it would be an even trade."

She looked at him. There were feelings rippling through her that she didn't quite understand yet. Feelings that were related to him. "I don't think so."

Suddenly awkward, Rebecca looked away from him and at the office. She hadn't been here since that first afternoon.

Angus watched as she looked around. Was she looking for something? "Trying to remember?"

She wasn't sure what she was doing right now. She felt like a time traveler trapped between two worlds—one she didn't know and one she wanted to know.

She moved toward the window and leaned against the sill. She felt the dust beneath her fingertips. It made her smile. In his own way, the man was in desperate need of help himself.

"I'm thinking something might hit me that hasn't before," she explained. She turned around to face him, mechanically wiping one hand against the other to get rid of the grit. "You know, like *déjà vu* that widens like the rings in a pool?"

He took out his handkerchief and offered it to her, nodding at her hands. A hint of a smile slipped over her lips as she accepted it. "I'm not sure," he said, "but I think you just mixed your metaphors."

"I also didn't come up with anything." Rebecca handed the handkerchief back to him. "Thanks." This time, when she looked around, she saw the office as it was. A small fifteen-by-eighteen room that stood like a wobbly survivor in the aftermath of a hurricane. "How do you function in a place like this?"

He took no offense. He knew he was far from neat. "Well enough to pay the rent on the office and the apartment and eat every other Tuesday." He saw the way she was eyeing his desk. Like Biordi's desk at the precinct, there wasn't a single inch on it that was uncovered. "An empty desk is the sign of an empty mind."

She raised an amused eyebrow. "Does that saying extrapolate to a messy desk?"

He saw where she was heading with this. "It only goes as far as I want it to."

For a moment, humor receded as she looked up at him.

"Does that go for you, too? Do you only go as far as you want to go?"

Was he that in control, that in charge of himself? Or was he like her—the way she found herself to be right now? Not quite in control of what she felt unfolding inside of her.

"Sometimes." The air within the office suddenly seemed in short supply, he thought. And he was once more fighting off urges that were steadily wearing him down. "Maybe you could straighten up a few things."

The moment, with its tension and promise, was gone. Her grin flashed. "I thought you'd never ask." As she turned her attention to the blizzard of papers on his desk, he started to leave. "What are you going to be doing?"

"Developing photographs," he said. He held up the rolls of film.

"You're leaving?" she asked, surprised.

"Only to the next room. The closet, actually." He nodded toward a recessed door in the rear. It was next to the bathroom. "Otherwise known as my darkroom."

The man had a multitude of talents. "You develop your own photographs?"

She said it as if he'd just told her he enjoyed strolling across the ocean to Catalina every afternoon at three.

"I took an extension course at the university taught by that photojournalist who got all those awards. Callaghan, I think his name was. Anyway, developing my own film is a lot faster than taking to the corner pharmacy. This way, if I want to enlarge something I find in one of the photographs, I don't have to waste time going back and forth and waiting for some lab to process it."

She had another suggestion for him. "You could do that with a good software package. If you had a digital camera, you wouldn't even have to bother with any chemicals.''

He turned to look at her, the rolls of film and what was on them temporarily forgotten. He gauged by her expression that she was just as amazed as he was to hear the advice she was giving.

''How do you know about digital cameras and software packages?''

She had an eerie feeling, as if someone was channeling through her.

''I don't know, I just do.'' She concentrated, exploring this new avenue that had opened up. The words came without any conscious effort on her part. ''I know that they've made great strides in utilizing computers when it comes to touching up photographs and basically making anything you want appear on the page. You can make composites, create scenes by merging images.''

Excitement began to undulate through her. She was remembering.

For the first time, she noticed the computer that was standing off to the side on a rickety card table, like an uninvited guest who had crashed a party. ''You've got one there.''

Crossing to it, she ran her fingers along the keyboard. Despite the layer of dust on this, too, she felt a sense of homecoming.

Angus deposited the rolls of film into his front pocket, more interested in tapping further into her mind. ''One of my clients gave me that in lieu of payment. I figured I'd eventually take it home for Vikki.''

She pressed the ''on'' button, but there was no response from the machine.

''It's not plugged in,'' he told her.

Rebecca looked at him incredulously. "You don't use it?"

He had no burning desire to join the swelling ranks of the computer world. "Other than as a giant paperweight, no."

Spying an outlet, she plugged the computer in. "You could input all your files on it."

The thought had no appeal for him. "I like the feel of paper."

That was no excuse. "Get a printer."

He laughed, playing this out, seeing just how much she could recall without his pressing the issue directly. She did better when she was relaxed.

"Why should I go through all that trouble when all I need is just a piece of paper to begin with? And maybe a file folder," he added, although he had to admit that a lot of his papers hadn't found their way into folders yet. But he had a system. Not an orthodox one, but it worked for him.

"Storage, for one," she answered his question. "You could definitely do with the extra space that getting rid of all this would afford you." She saw the resistance in his face. "You don't like progress, do you?"

He saw the way she looked when she touched the keyboard. That was definitely progress, he thought. Computers obviously figured into her life and not in a small way.

"Depends on the kind you mean. If it's with a small *p*, then yes, I do."

He'd lost her. "Small *p?*"

Angus elaborated. "Progress in a case. Progress in understanding something. Progress with Vikki, with a relationship." He stopped before he went too far, said something that was better left unsaid. "As for 'progress' as in the advance of technology—no, I can't say I'm crazy about it."

She curbed the desire to play around with the computer, see what sort of programs were on it. His desk was what needed her attention first.

"Why? The computer's a wonderful tool." She picked up a handful of paper from the top. It started a minilandslide as several dozen sheets cascaded to the floor.

They both stooped down to pick up the papers. "It's a depersonalizing tool." He shoved the papers back on the desk, only to have them rain down again on him. "It separates people from people."

She stifled a laugh and regathered the strewn pages. "Chat rooms," she countered. Making a neat pile, she decided to set it aside on the floor for the time being.

He sat back on his heels, watching her. "If I'm going to 'chat' with somebody, I want to see them. I want to be able to look into their eyes and see what they're thinking."

The corners of her mouth rose. "You don't use the phone?"

He hadn't meant that. "Okay, at the very least, I want to hear their voice."

Still on her knees, she stretched to reach for several sheets of paper that had fallen under his desk. "They have accessories that do that."

He knew he should be the one crawling under the desk instead of watching her and enjoying the view. But a man had to allow himself some small pleasures.

"I'd rather have flesh and blood." As she snaked back out, he covered her head with his palm to keep her from hitting it on the desk above. "My senses can handle it from there." His senses, he thought, were doing a lot of handling lately.

"Just where is all this knowledge coming from?" he prodded.

She was no closer to knowing that now than she'd been when she started down this road. "Beats me. It's just something I know."

Rising, he offered her his hand. "Like cooking."

She curled her fingers around his, then got to her feet. "Like cooking," she agreed. "Speaking of which, what are you in the mood for?"

Humor glinted in his eyes. "After watching Madison and his lady, you don't want to know."

She felt color streak up her neck as an image flashed through her mind. Angus, his body hard and lean, holding her in his arms, making love with her. Slowly, she exhaled a long, slightly shaky breath.

He looked at her quizzically.

But it was a lot safer if she didn't respond to that look. "I meant for dinner tonight."

It was all one and the same to him. "Surprise me. I'm easy."

"I wouldn't say that."

At this rate, he was never going to make it into the closet. But she intrigued him far more than any photographs he'd taken, sizable retainer notwithstanding. "Oh? And what *would* you say?"

Here, too, she could only be honest. "That you're a very kind, very decent, very complex man."

"Complex?" Angus echoed. He'd never thought of himself as particularly complicated.

She gave up pretending that she was paying attention to what she was doing.

"I see things in your eyes, Angus. Hear things in your voice." She took a breath. "There's some kind of struggle going on inside you."

Not bad, he thought. "I once saw a cartoon. I snuck out to Jimmy Noonan's house to watch—the Colonel didn't approve of cartoons," he explained when she raised an eyebrow at his digression. "There was this character and he had a devil on one shoulder and an angel on the other. They fought constantly." His eyes held hers. "That's kind of how I feel."

Rebecca wasn't aware of the breath she was holding. "About?"

He wasn't free to talk about that, to let her peer any further into that part of his world. It was a very fragile place, and he hated to feel that there was anything about him that was fragile.

Angus fished the film out of his pocket. "I'd better get this developed."

He'd almost reached the closet when she asked, "That cartoon you mentioned."

He looked over his shoulder at her. "What about it?"

"Which side won?"

He shook his head, as if mourning the fact. "The angel. Every time."

A quirky smile played over her mouth just before she went back to sifting through papers. "Too bad."

"Yeah," he said, under his breath, "I know."

Chapter 10

Something warm and formless spread through Angus. When he'd come out of the bedroom, preoccupied with the phone call he'd just taken, the sight of his daughter and Rebecca had caught him by surprise. Like an extra gift at Christmas, hidden behind the branches and discovered much later, the scene appeared before him, unexpected and pleasing.

He stopped just short of the kitchen and silently stood watching them. The two, sitting at the table that had just recently been cleared of the dinner dishes, had their heads together over Vikki's schoolbooks.

And Vikki was actually paying attention, Angus marveled.

Getting Vikki to do her homework each evening was a test of patience and ingenuity. She hated anything associated with school. He remembered how she'd resisted mightily when he had enrolled her in the elementary school that was located less than a mile away. Vikki was not about to give up the fight any time soon.

In a way, he understood. School represented another new thing she had to endure, another new hurdle she didn't want to jump. Vikki had never attended school before. Jane had been lax when it came to Vikki's formal education, though, to her credit, Angus thought, she had made sure that their daughter knew her numbers and how to read.

According to Vikki, the lessons, such as they were, had been taught in the back rooms of the casinos where she had roamed around free, being virtually everyone's pet. She'd been doted on, made to feel special. Here she felt like just another student behind a desk. That, plus being confined in a place for a regulated number of hours each day, just didn't sit well with Vikki.

In the latter, Angus couldn't help thinking, she'd taken after him. He'd certainly had his fill of structure and regulations. His childhood and teen years had been full of both. As had the time he'd spent in the navy. The very thought of reverting back to that, of being just another cog in the system, left him cold.

But though he fully empathized with Vikki, there was no way she was going to get out of attending school, at least not for the next ten years. He might be a nonconformist in some respects, but he damn well knew the value of an education—and Vikki was going to get one.

Vikki's angry, tearful retort to his efforts had been that Jane had treated her better. When he first enrolled her, she'd retreated into herself for a week. Ever so slowly, he had managed to coax her into giving up the silent treatment, but the sailing so far had been far from smooth.

Acutely aware of her unhappiness and of his new responsibility, Angus had made it a point to do Vikki's homework with her whenever he was home. It wasn't exactly something either one of them looked forward to, but it had to be done.

Tonight, the phone had rung just as the books had come out. Rebecca had answered and returned to tell him that Angela Madison was on the line, wanting to speak to him. Since he had given the woman the photographs and received his check from her secretary, he assumed that their association was terminated. Her call was unexpected.

It was also long.

Angus was certain that by the time he came out of his bedroom—a room that now retained the haunting scent and feel of Rebecca everywhere he turned—Vikki would be firmly engrossed in a video game, or over at Jenny's apartment glued to the big-screen TV while one of Jenny's action videos flickered.

The very last thing he'd expected to find was Vikki where he had left her, frowning over her math book, her head propped up on her hand.

As he drew closer, he realized she wasn't frowning over the opened math book. She was frowning at the cards on the table next to the math book.

What was she doing, playing cards when she had homework to do?

Rebecca could feel his eyes on her. She savored the sensation for a second before relinquishing it. Even though her attention was on the cards in front of her, she'd been aware of his presence the moment he'd approached the kitchen.

He didn't look happy. Had it been bad news? she wondered.

She set the deck down. "I didn't know how long you'd be," Rebecca explained, "and Vikki was having trouble with her math."

"So you set it aside and opted to play cards?" he asked. Apparently Rebecca had as much trouble saying *no* to Vikki as he did. He didn't fault her. Vikki could be damn persuasive when she wanted to be. Persuasive or not, Vikki couldn't be allowed to get away with it.

"We're not playing cards," Rebecca corrected him. "We're *using* cards."

He didn't follow. It certainly looked as if they were playing cards. "Using them how?"

"She's a better teacher than you are, Angus." There was enthusiasm in Vikki's voice as she gave Rebecca the seal of approval.

Embarrassed and afraid that she'd usurped him or, worse, that he might be hurt by Vikki's comment, Rebecca tempered the declaration. "I just put it in terms she'd understand."

He came around to their side of the table and looked down. The card arrangement was classic. "By playing blackjack?"

"By making her add up the numbers and comparing that to the problems she has to tackle in her math book. I told her to think of it as one great big hand of blackjack, without any upper limits." She gathered the cards together and returned them to Vikki, who'd brought them out of her room. "She seemed to catch on better after that." The legs of the chair scraped along the vinyl flooring as Rebecca moved back. "Here, sit down. I've kept your place warm for you."

That wasn't the only thing she was making warm for him, Angus thought.

But he declined to take her place. "Why don't you just keep on teaching?" he urged. "From the sound of it, you're doing a great job. I've never heard Vikki do anything but moan whenever I've mentioned the word *math*."

He'd never looked forward to this part of the day, anyway. It was a relief to hand over the reins to someone else, even temporarily. And the bottom line, after all, was Vikki. If she learned better with Rebecca's help than his, that was fine with him. "I've got some things to catch up on."

Rebecca looked at him hesitantly. Was he just saying that to cover up wounded pride? "You're sure?"

The very last thing she wanted was to repay his kindness by coming between Angus and his daughter. Not as a bone of contention and certainly not as someone who drew Vikki's budding affection away from Angus.

"I'm sure."

Angus crossed to the sofa and sat down, dropping a file folder on the coffee table. But as he made himself comfortable, his attention kept veering back toward the kitchen.

This wasn't good, he thought, though he wasn't quite able to muster the conviction necessary to reinforce his feelings. The problem was that he was getting used to this, used to seeing Rebecca here day in, day out. Two weeks had passed. Hardly any time passed in the grand scheme of things, and yet, in a way, it seemed as if this was the way it was always meant to be.

What's more, Vikki was getting used to having Rebecca around, as well. Vikki might even have felt it before he did. She'd been the one that first day to ask if Rebecca could stay. He realized now that it wasn't just because Rebecca was another female. It went deeper than that. She was kind, helpful and caring with the little girl. Not many women would have allowed themselves to be dragged off to school and used for show-and-tell. But Rebecca had, and she had been a rousing success, according to a pleased

Vikki. It was the first time Vikki had actually *wanted* to go to school.

Having Rebecca here was obviously helping Vikki with the transition she was making from being the daughter of a nomadic card dealer to someone with roots in a place that had none of the glitter to which she'd become accustomed.

Would all the progress that was being made crumble once Rebecca was gone? Would everything revert back to square one? It was something to think about, even though he didn't want to. And he wasn't worried only about losing ground with Vikki. The thought of Rebecca leaving brought a feeling with it that he didn't want to think about or explore.

The sound of Rebecca's voice and Vikki's occasional laughter hummed in the background, creating a soothing atmosphere. Nevertheless, Angus found himself staring at the same paragraph he'd been reading and rereading for the last ten minutes. His mind just was not on his work. Slowly, he closed the folder to listen to the two in the other room.

After all, he rationalized, Rebecca wasn't going to be here that much longer. He might as well enjoy her teaching Vikki while he could.

A pang drifted through him. He tried to shut it out. This was ridiculous. He had to face the fact that this was just a temporary situation, albeit a pleasant one, and at bottom, he knew he wanted it that way. He wanted it to remain temporary, without strings or entanglements.

And yet....

Maybe it wouldn't change, he thought suddenly. Maybe her memory had gone as far as it could go. There hadn't been any further breakthroughs on any front in the last week. Biordi still had nothing on her, no missing person report that even vaguely fit her description. Maybe it was time to face the idea that for Rebecca, there was no going back—only forward.

Would it be such a terrible thing for her if her memory never returned? he wondered. She certainly seemed to be adjusting. More and more, he saw her opening up, not just absorbing things around her, but enjoying herself.

And if feeling useful was her thing, she was certainly seeing to that. She'd accompanied him to the office on a regular basis. True to her promise—or veiled threat, depending on how much trouble he had finding something—she'd cleaned it up and then turned her hand to inputting all his files on the computer.

Finished in what seemed to him an incredibly short amount of time, she'd set her sights on teaching him the system. As a result, he could no longer brag about being computer illiterate and the last holdout in a technological world.

She took delight in every detail she recalled, and no longer seemed disturbed by the fact that the details were all impersonal. Beyond her own abilities, no memories returned. No faces from her past, no fragments of things she'd done. In the last couple of days, she'd even stopped asking if Biordi had called.

It was almost as if she were settling in. Angus smiled to himself. A lot of men would have envied the position in which he found himself. A beautiful, vibrant young woman with no preconceived notions, no history to drag her down or get in the way, had dropped out of the sky practically on his doorstep and was living in his bedroom. For all intents and purposes, she was a clean slate for him to write on. To leave his mark on if he so chose.

The way she was apparently leaving her mark on Vikki, he thought, watching them.

And on him.

Closing the book, Rebecca raised her eyes toward Angus. His expression left her wondering what he was thinking about. "We're finished with the math. Do you want to help her with her reading?"

He shook his head. She was probably better at that, too. He might have his talents, but teaching didn't number among them. "You're doing fine without me."

Yes, they were. Did that bother him? she wondered again. His expression gave her no indication that it did. A man didn't smile like that if something was bothering him.

How would you know? a voice whispered through her mind. *How would you know anything?*

It was true. There was nothing to base any of her speculations on, and yet she *felt* she knew things. Except when it came to herself. There were so many questions. Had she been experienced? Had there been many men in her life before now? Or none?

Since she couldn't remember, she supposed that no matter what had happened before, Angus would be her first. Her pulse quickened even as the thought drifted through her mind, teasing her. Making her wistful.

Vikki was shoving a red covered book into her hands, indicating the page she'd marked with her index finger. "We're supposed to read from page 76 to 87." She was frowning distastefully.

Rebecca collected herself, forcing her mind away from Angus. "Is that all? Piece of cake. You'll have it done in no time." She laid the book open between them, turning it so that it was directly in front of Vikki. "Okay, read to me."

In the face of such faith, Vikki lost her desire to denigrate the assignment. Instead, with a proud little shake of her head, she launched into a halting rendition of a toiling little crimson chicken and her lazy circle of friends.

Each time Vikki stumbled, Rebecca gently coaxed her into sounding out the word that needed to be conquered. Minitriumphs punctuated the eleven pages.

Angus listened. Though he tried not to think about it, he knew the scene he was watching represented something he'd wanted all his life: A sense of family.

Too bad they weren't one, he mused, watching Vikki.

Was it so wrong, he thought, his not wanting Rebecca's memory to return? Not wanting to give this up?

Yes, it was. He was being selfish and he knew it.

Knew too, that even under the best of circumstances, it would have been difficult for him to open up his heart to accept any woman. He'd been wary of being hurt before he had met Jane, wary of letting anyone into his life. After she left, his wariness had returned in such increased proportions that it had completely hardened his heart.

Oh, he could still easily be friends with a woman, but to trust her emotionally, well, that was something of which he didn't think he was capable anymore. It wouldn't be fair to Rebecca, after what she had been through, to have to deal with that. She deserved far more than emotional limbo.

Angus knew all this, knew all the reasons against forming any sort of relationship with Rebecca. So why the hell did he still continue wanting her?

He had no answer. He could only hope that the question would never be asked aloud. If he kept her at arm's length, it never would be.

"I want to talk to you."

The words stopped him in his tracks the moment he came out of Vikki's room.

For once, Vikki had allowed him to read something other than her beloved *Whose Shoes are Those?*. Instead, he'd read about a family of rabbits. It was a book, he was informed as he tucked Vikki in, that Rebecca had picked out earlier, saying Vikki might enjoy it.

The woman was a miracle worker, he thought, silently blessing her as he read the new tale.

The miracle worker apparently had something on her mind. A strange, uneasy feeling came over him. Like the gatekeeper admitting the Trojan horse into the city, he had no idea what was coming. He didn't like not knowing.

She'd already made up the sofa, he noticed. Though he'd told her time and again she didn't have to, she seemed determined to take on a myriad of little details that went into making life more pleasant. Making a home. A man could get used to this, he thought. He knew he'd already gotten used to her homecooked meals.

As he approached Rebecca, he took her hand in his. It felt icy, he realized as he sat down with her.

"And I'd like to talk to you," he said. "I don't think I've thanked you enough."

She blinked, thrown off. "Thanked *me?*"

He was the one who had taken her in, put no limitations on his generosity, made her feel useful. Rebecca felt that she would forever be indebted to him for that. There was no way she could ever pay him back, but at least she could cease being a burden.

Angus was surprised at her reaction. Was she really that oblivious to the effect she had on those around her? To the contributions she had given so freely? It was hard for him to believe anyone could be that unassuming.

"You cook like an angel, have the patience of a saint with Vikki. You know how to program the computer so that it practically runs the office." He grinned. "Not to mention being very easy on the eye. I'm beginning to think I made you up.''

The small laugh that escaped her lips almost sounded disparaging. She'd been so wrapped up in thinking about what course she should take, that she'd gone almost a whole day without thinking about about the life that had been lost to her for two weeks now. "Considering that nobody's filed a report on me, maybe you did.''

"My imagination would never be this good.''

It was happening again, Angus thought. He felt that strong, demanding pull that gave him no peace.

He sifted a lock of her hair through his fingers. The silkiness ate through a layer of his resistance. Something flickered in her eyes before she drew back. Desire? He didn't know if it was worse to hope it was—or pray that it wasn't.

"What did you want to talk to me about?'' he asked.

It wasn't easy, but then nothing had been since she had woken up in that alley. Nothing, except being here with Angus and Vikki. But she didn't really belong here, no matter how much she wanted to.

She rose, suddenly restless, and began to pace around the sofa. "I can't stay here indefinitely.''

Was that her pride talking? Or something more? In either case, Angus knew she didn't have the resources to go anywhere. Watching her circle around like a sleek cat in a cage, he kept the concern out of his voice.

"A week is not indefinite.''

"Closer to two,'' she corrected. She couldn't continue taking advantage of him like this. It wasn't fair. And she would become too accustomed to being here. Too accustomed to seeing him each morning. The longer she stayed, the harder it would be to go.

It was hard already.

"Okay, closer to two," he accepted. "Still not indefinite."

Torn between what she felt was right and what she wanted, Rebecca turned and looked at him. "And what comes after two weeks?"

"Fifteen days?" he hazarded.

A smile twitched her lips, defusing the moment. "Don't make me laugh." But she already was. "I'm being serious."

Shifting, he perched on the arm of the sofa. She'd stopped pacing and he caught her hand in his. He ignored the warning signs that went up within him—the warning signs that told him he'd missed his chance to keep things from becoming even more complicated than they were.

Maybe a little complication was good for the soul. And besides, he was still in control of things. Nothing to worry about.

"I like it when you laugh. And you're hardly *The Man Who Came to Dinner,* Becky." An appreciative smile curved his mouth as he let his eyes drift over her. It didn't matter if she was wearing jeans and a T-shirt from a discount store. Clothes loved her. "For one thing, you're the wrong gender. For another, I just enumerated a few of the ways you've found to 'repay' me. You've even managed to do the impossible and organize my office and my home. Hell, you've got me eating vegetables, and Vikki doing math. That alone should buy you a month."

He saw the look that entered her eyes. No matter that her memory was in limbo, she wasn't a woman who accepted a free ride. Though it got in the way right now, he couldn't help but admire that.

"I understand that this situation is making you edgy, but you don't have a choice," he said softly. "There's nothing you can do but wait it out. Why not do it in surroundings that have become familiar?''

He was making sense, she thought. Sense for her, but not for himself and his daughter. There was no way around the fact that she was putting them out. ''And what? You'll go on sleeping on a sofa while I'm taking up your bed?'' It just wasn't right.

He shrugged casually. Amusement entered his eyes. ''Unless you have another arrangement in mind.''

And then he approached her protest seriously. ''If the sleeping arrangements make you uncomfortable, we could take turns. You can have the sofa once in a while. I'll even throw in a hair shirt for you to sleep in.''

He was trying to make her feel better about it. Her resolve softened a little. Her heart already had. ''Maybe we can skip the hair shirt.''

Good, she was coming around. For a moment, she had him going. Angus paused, trying to come up with something that would soothe her chafing conscience.

''Would it make you feel better if I called you my secretary and had you officially working at the office?'' It was the only solution that occurred to him on such short notice.

''Secretary?'' she repeated.

She said it as if it were a foreign word. ''You know, answer the phone. Update any files that might have fallen in the cracks and eluded your sweeping purge.''

It had taken her three days to clear away the folders and type them onto the hard drive. He'd been amazed at how fast her fingers flew over the keyboard. Concert pianists had nothing on her dexterity. And she'd been right—the office did look larger without files strewn all over it.

But it also seemed smaller for having her in it. He was just going to have to find a way to deal with that.

"How about office manager?" she suggested. "That has a nicer ring to it."

So, she was ambitious. Angus added ambition to the list of personality traits he was mentally tallying. A very savvy lady was being pieced together, though the title she'd chosen seemed a little out of line. "The only thing you'd have to manage is the files—and me."

The way he said that, the way he was looking at her, generated an aura of intimacy. More than anything, she wanted him to hold her, to kiss her again. But the moves—whatever they were going to be—had to be up to him.

She smiled. "You could be a handful, given the right situation."

If he didn't know better, he would have said that she was... He cocked his head, studying her. "Why, Becky, are you flirting with me?"

Nervousness, warm and delicious, skittered through her, a long-legged spider on a slippery floor. "I don't know, am I?"

There was a sweet vein of innocence amid the sensuality. He might have been able to resist one, but not both. He was being reeled in, Angus realized, as helpless as a fish being yanked out of the water. It didn't immediately occur to him to resist.

"Yeah," he told her, "you are. And I'm a sucker for a brazen woman." He looked down into her eyes, wanting nothing more than to take her into his arms and kiss her. But if he did that, there would definitely be more.

So he kept himself in check.

His voice softened. "So, is it all settled? No more talk

about wrapping up your belongings in a scarf, putting it on a stick and striking out on the open road?''

She didn't want to run away, not from the only things she knew. It was just him she was thinking of. "If you're sure I'm not in the way."

He couldn't resist saying, "Well, you are that, but only in the nicest possible way."

She had that to keep her warm, she thought. Rebecca turned down the covers on the sofa. "I'll take the sofa tonight."

He knew she was going to say that. There was no point in trying to talk her out of it. "And I'll prop two chairs against the doorknob."

"To keep me out?" she asked in surprise.

He'd already crossed to the bedroom, putting distance between them. When you weren't sure how to contain the fire, it was best not to strike a match. "No, to keep me in."

As he closed his door behind him, Angus had a clear understanding of the way the early Christian martyrs must have felt. Sacrifices—even for all the right reasons—were hell.

Chapter 11

Angus felt good.

There was nothing like the satisfaction of wrapping up a case, of knowing that there was money in the checking account and that, for a while at least, there would be no wolf at the door. Not only had he taken care of Angela Madison's problem to the lady's overwhelming satisfaction, but he had also managed—on the heels of that case—to bring two other investigations to a timely end.

At the moment, the only outstanding case he had concerned Rebecca, and if he wasn't in a complete hurry to see that wrapped up—well, Angus felt he couldn't be entirely faulted.

He really liked having her around.

She had, as of this morning, turned her attention to the state of his accounts, or lack thereof. He was the first to admit that his system was not the garden-variety type that kept accountants happy and sane, but it worked for him. When he remembered to make entries.

After writing his final notes to himself on the surveillance he'd completed for a data corporation, Angus closed the folder and rocked back in his chair, content just to watch Rebecca for a while.

He would have done better by her, he lectured himself, if he spent less time gazing at her and more time looking into leads that might yield some information about her identity.

That was just the trouble. There weren't any leads. At least, none that he could come up with, and he *had* tried. It was as if she'd been born, fully grown, barely two weeks ago. No one had seen her previous to the time she had stumbled out of the alley. No one had heard gunfire. Of course, given the area and the fact that there had been a fire going on at the time, that wasn't surprising.

He'd even tracked down the number of the fire company that had been out there that evening, hoping someone might have noticed something—a man hanging back in the shadow of the parking structure, perhaps. It was a thousand-to-one shot and it hadn't paid off. Everyone had been too busy with the fire and with keeping civilians back to notice.

Biordi had suggested running her picture in the local paper. Angus had vetoed that immediately. There was always a chance that whoever had been shooting at her might see it, too. If it hadn't been a random mugging— if it was someone who had wanted her dead—Angus didn't want to risk making her a target again.

So here she sat, with her life on hold, organizing his accounting system as if doing so was really important to her. Try as he might, he couldn't detect a trace of bitterness in her. No self-pity and no hopelessness. She bore up and went on.

Rebecca whatever-her-last-name-was was one hell of a rare woman.

It was a thought that had occurred to him a lot in the last fourteen days.

The desire to be close to her brought him to his feet. He crossed to her, giving in to an impulse he had been weighing all morning. "Would you like to get away for a while?"

She'd been concentrating so hard, she hadn't heard him. Rebecca glanced up, a bemused expression on her face.

"I *am* away," she reminded him. "Away from everything I supposedly know." Frowning, she held up an entry he'd made when he obviously had other things on his mind. "Is that a three or an eight?"

It took him a minute to decipher his own writing. "It's a zero." Or at least he thought it was.

But he had more important things on his mind. Taking the ledger from her, he closed it and set it aside. Her protests fell on deaf ears. "And I mean getting away the traditional way. For the weekend," he explained.

All morning—ever since last night's phone call actually—he'd been mentally listing the pros and cons that went along with his question. The con column was longer. The pro one carried more weight. And he knew what, deep down, he wanted. What wasn't good for him, or her.

So he went with his gut instinct. "The phone call I took last night was from Mrs. Madison."

The sympathy was instant and full-blown, coming from a region she had yet to uncover. "Was she very upset about the photographs?"

Angus shook his head, amazed that Rebecca could feel so much for a woman she didn't know. Was there something there, in her past, that caused her to unconsciously empathize with the Madison woman's situation, or was it just that she had a heart as great as Yosemite?

He would have felt better if he knew for certain that it was the latter.

"No, she was upset about her husband, but that was when she'd first discovered he was being unfaithful."

Angela Madison was not a woman who took being crossed lightly, either in business or in love. Especially not in love. The fact that she was rich due to a late husband's nest egg and her own business acumen, and looked twenty years younger than her age, just made her that much more formidable. Her young stud of a husband should have realized that before he ever agreed to rendezvous with the tasty little tart with whom he'd been immortalized, Angus thought.

"Mrs. Madison was thrilled about the photographs. So thrilled," he elaborated, "that she wants us to have a free weekend away at the casino she owns in Tahoe."

"Us?" As far as Rebecca knew, Mrs. Madison didn't know she existed.

Angus grinned. He'd taken a liberty, but he figured he was entitled. "Well, me, really," he admitted. "But she said accommodations were for two." And there was no one else other than Rebecca that he wanted to complete that number.

As much as she wanted to say yes, there was someone else to consider. Someone else who wouldn't take kindly to being left behind. "Don't you think you should take Vikki instead of me?"

Her thoughtfulness struck an appreciative chord within him, but Vikki was the last person he wanted to bring with him to the casino resort.

"I'm trying to wean Vikki away from that kind of life. Taking her to a resort built around a casino might dredge up too many memories she might not be up to dealing with yet.'' His smile was intimate. ''While taking you to one might just stir some up.''

She could feel a host of little nerves executing a series of jumping jacks up and down her body. ''How do you figure that?''

He actually did have a sound basis for inviting her to the resort, but it just hadn't been the first thing that had prompted him to extend the invitation. It had come in a distant second.

''If you're relaxed,'' he said, toying with a strand of her hair, ''who knows? Things might suddenly come back to you. Just like cooking and working on the computer did.'' Angus glanced around his office. ''And being compulsively neat.''

Taking exception to his evaluation, and feeling a bit unnerved by his touch, she extracted her hair from his fingers. ''I am *not* compulsive.''

He could argue that, he thought genially, but he let it go, simply saying, ''To me, anyone who hangs up his clothes is compulsive. I don't even recognize my bedroom anymore.'' The bed was made each morning. There were no clothes on the floor or draped over every available surface in the bathroom. And toilet paper was even on the roll instead of sitting on the floor.

''You don't recognize your bedroom because you haven't been in it for two weeks,'' she pointed out, ''except for last night. And even then, you spent only a few minutes there before going back to the sofa.''

There seemed to be no end to his chivalry. Even after agreeing to take the bed, he'd come out to tell her that he'd gotten used to sleeping on the sofa and that he'd wanted to switch back.

It was a lie, of course, but such a sweet one. Even the

man's lies were endearing. With each day that passed, Rebecca was more and more afraid that whatever life she'd left behind couldn't be as good as the one she was now enjoying.

A part of her, she realized, no longer wanted to find that lost identity. She liked being Becky far too much.

Angus was still waiting for her answer. Or maybe just for the right answer—the one he wanted to hear. "So, how about it?" His eyes coaxed her to say *yes*. "Will you come to Lake Tahoe with me?"

It wasn't in her to say *no*. Not because she wanted to remember the past, but because she wanted to remember the present. A present she was sharing with him.

Very slowly, a shy smile took possession of her lips. Just as he wanted to take possession of them, he thought, watching the smile progress until every part of her seemed to be caught up in it.

"All right," she finally agreed. "Like you said, who knows what kind of memories might be stirred up?"

Yeah, who knows? Angus knew that he was already stirred up, and they hadn't even gone anywhere yet.

It was a step he hadn't wanted to take, a step that left him vulnerable.

But no more vulnerable, he reminded himself, banking down his rage, than it made him having her alive.

There were no options left, no avenues open. If she was dead and no one had discovered her body, it made no difference.

If she was alive, he needed to know. Needed to find her.

And to do that, he needed help.

Before the others discovered the error and made the

trail end with him.

He picked up the receiver and dialed.

Angela Madison, they discovered when they arrived at the lavish Paradise resort, was a generous woman when she was happy. And from all appearances, she was very happy. She'd left instructions for the second-best suite in the resort to be set aside for Angus and his guest. The first was always reserved for any reigning celebrity or politician who might be visiting.

It didn't matter. Second best was far better than anything Angus had expected. Seeing the light in Rebecca's eyes as she surveyed their quarters was worth every minute of the three-hour trip over winding roads that it had taken to get here.

"This is second best?" Rebecca turned a full three hundred sixty degrees in the huge room. The suite, complete with a sitting room, looked to be the size of Angus's apartment. "First must be a palace."

"Very nearly," the bellhop told her. After setting down their suitcases, he moved to the bay window and opened it to give them a spectacular view of the lake. "You can see the Sierras from here."

Paradise was a good name for the resort, Rebecca thought, crossing to the window. The view, unobstructed by any signs of civilization, made her feel as if she were standing on the edge of eternity.

Angus dug into his pocket as the bellhop passed him on his way to the door. The latter shook his head, refusing the bill Angus produced.

"Oh, no, sir. Mrs. Madison would have my head."

Angus had a feeling that his declaration wasn't that far from the truth.

"She specifically called to say that everything is on the house, including the service." He'd reached the door before he remembered to add, "Oh, there are chips set aside in your name at the casino. We hope you enjoy your stay with us." With that, he closed the door.

"Enjoy it? I'm beginning to hope she adopts me," Angus murmured.

But he was only kidding. This was the kind of life that had attracted Jane—the excitement of enormous amounts of wealth passing from person to person, and perhaps, by proximity, to her. Money, other than for necessities, had never had much of an allure for him.

This weekend would have translated to a hefty bill if they had been paying. Rebecca turned to look at Angus. "She *really* liked those photographs."

"Yes, she did," he agreed. "Because of them, there'll be no extenuating circumstances concerning the divorce." Which meant that Angela Madison would continue keeping company with her money, and that Ryan Madison was out on his ear with little to show for the time he had put in as her husband except for a small assortment of personal effects.

But Angus hadn't come here to think about either one of the Madisons. His agenda was to pay exclusive attention to the woman who had softly crept into his life and turned it on its proverbial ear.

Angus turned to take in the surroundings that had awed Rebecca. It really was like being in another world here, he thought. The bed, a major focal point of the room, was raised on a platform that was accessible by five steps, which spread out like the fan of a coquettish *señorita* from Old California.

It looked like something out of a movie set, he thought. As did she.

Both Rebecca and the bed were looking more and more

tempting by the moment. He desperately needed some air, he thought. Or a cold shower. Maybe both.

"What would you like to do first?" he asked her, trying to distract himself from his thoughts.

Make love with you, she thought. *Now wouldn't that shake you up?*

"I don't know," Rebecca admitted aloud. She turned to him, her face shining with innocence. "Why don't I just put myself in your hands—and you can take it from there?"

He wondered if there was a special place in heaven for detectives who resisted temptation when it came in such pretty wrappings.

Ever so lightly, he brushed a wayward hair behind her ear, his fingertips caressing her face. It was all he would allow himself. "Oh, Becky, you've got to stop saying things like that. A man can be noble for only so long."

She could hear her own heart beating in her breast. Beating so hard, it sounded like the drum of a marching band. "And then?"

For one moment, he entertained the idea of spending the entire weekend in this room, making love with her on every flat surface they tumbled onto. But then, he had a hunch—looking at the tempting line she called a mouth—he would be hopelessly and irrevocably hooked. Better not to start what in all probability wouldn't finish to his liking.

Moving back from her upturned face, and from temptation, Angus picked up his suitcase and took it to the sofa in the sitting room. "Why don't we go down to the lake before I'm tempted to show you?" he suggested.

After much deliberation, and because there would be a full evening ahead of them, they finally settled on a peaceful activity. They went canoeing.

Time with Rebecca, Angus realized soon into it, would be peaceful only if he was dead. There was nothing peaceful about paddling on a crystal clear lake with no one else around and Rebecca only inches from him. She filled his senses with her fragrance, filled his soul with yearning.

Lucky for him, he had a paddle in his hands, he mused, so he wouldn't give in and do something stupid. He'd told her they were here to help her relax. How relaxed was she going to be if he pounced on her like some sex-starved college freshman?

Rebecca craned her neck to look at him behind her. He had a pensive look on his face. What was he thinking? Was he thinking about her? She was too self-centered, she thought, but that was only because she had no clue about what existed at her center.

She could only hope.

"You've been paddling much too long," she told him. "I'll take a turn and you can lie back and relax."

Not unless someone shot him with a tranquilizer dart, he thought. But he kept that to himself.

When she reached for the paddle, he asked, "Do you know how to paddle a canoe?"

She took it from him. "You stick it in, stroke it and take it out. How difficult can it be?" Her eyes narrowed as he broke up and nearly doubled over. "What are you laughing at?"

He was laughing so hard, he thought he was going to capsize the canoe. Angus made an effort to draw in air to steady himself. It took him a minute before he could talk.

"I'm not sure, but I think you just gave a young boy's description of sex." He struggled not to laugh again, this time at the bewildered expression on her face and the streak of crimson on her cheeks.

"And," he continued softly, "like sex, there's a great deal more to it than just that." He nodded at the paddle. "There's a rhythm you have to hit, a feel you're going for. Otherwise, you won't do it right. Here." He scooted flush against his corner of the canoe. "Get directly in front of me and I'll show you."

Rebecca did as he asked, sitting between his legs, her back flush with his chest. She was about to hand him back the paddle, but he told her to hold it as if she were going to paddle. Then he placed his hand over hers and guided her through the movements.

The paddle dipped into the water, softly, lyrically parting the waters. "Like that—gently, firmly. Remember, do it like a lover, not an adversary. This is for pleasure. You're romancing the water, not assaulting it."

It wasn't only the water that he was romancing, she thought.

They worked together as one, slipping the edge of the paddle into the water, pushing it back, then raising it to begin the process all over again. And, as promised, pleasure filled her. But then, it had begun as soon as she felt his chest against her back, his hands on hers.

She didn't know anything about canoeing, but this had to be a new approach to it. "Did you learn this from your father?"

"Hardly." She felt the dry laugh as it rumbled in his chest and along her back. She didn't have to turn around to know that there was no smile on his face. She felt its absence. "The Colonel thought that everything was accomplished by issuing orders. If you knew what was good for you, you obeyed. He never took the time to study the psychology behind things, never tried to understand how people worked. With him it was all black and white. Cause and effect.''

''I'm sorry.''

Her comment caught him unprepared. Sorrow didn't enter into what he'd just been telling her. ''About what?''

''That you didn't get along with your father.'' She had a feeling that it was something he regretted deeply. And something, she knew with a rock-solid certainty, that the Colonel had no idea he had missed.

Angus dismissed her words and the feeling they generated. ''I got over that a long time ago.''

He was lying to her, she thought. And maybe to himself. ''I'm still sorry that you didn't have the kind of childhood a boy should.''

She could feel him shrug. It rippled against her, making her smile. Making her dream. ''I grew up all right.''

Rebecca turned then. Her hair, teased by the breeze, brushed along his chin and his throat as she looked up at him. He felt the muscles in his stomach tightening so hard that a solid punch wouldn't even have registered.

''Yes,'' she agreed softly, ''you did.''

He would have to have been made out of stone not to kiss her then. And even stone cracked sometimes.

Cupping her chin with his hand, Angus tilted her head back just a little more and then brushed his lips softly over hers. When she sighed her contentment, all the demanding, delicious sensations he'd experienced earlier returned full grown. Just as he'd left them. Detonating within him.

Urging him on.

He skimmed his hands over her shoulders, just barely touching her.

Burning to touch her.

Unable to resist, Angus gently slid his palms over her

breasts. The moan that echoed in his brain in response ignited desire within him, a torch to him. All he could think of was having her.

He couldn't do it in the middle of the lake. By the time they returned to the shore, he could only pray that common sense and control would, too.

With effort, he managed to resist the urge to kiss her again. "I think we should get back."

A sense of loss sliced through her like the point of a rapier. He was being noble again. She wondered if the rescued princesses in medieval times had run into this sort of thing, and if any of them had felt as frustrated as she did right now. "So soon?"

He smiled. Not soon enough to spare him the sharp jabs that came from frustration. "I don't want to give the fish anything to talk about."

Reluctantly, he picked up the paddle. "I'll take it from here," he told her. "I need to work off some steam."

She felt like Cinderella.

The fact that she actually recalled the fairy tale went a long way in pleasing her. It made her feel less like a walking vacuum, more like a person. A person better equipped to sustain Angus's interest.

The Cinderella feeling had originated when her protest that she had nothing to wear to the casino had been answered with a trip to the shops that comprised the resort's small but exclusive mall.

Now, as she modeled the glamorous evening wear the saleswoman had brought her, she felt even more of a princess.

Angus stood, admiration in his eyes, watching as she came out of the dressing room in gown after gown, wondering just how much temptation one man could endure before meeting his breaking point. He began to realize that his theory that clothes loved her was a vast understatement. She brought a grace and style, which she didn't seem to know she possessed, to everything she wore.

His knowledge of fabrics ended with being able to identify corduroy. But he knew what he liked, and he liked what he saw on her. Each new gown made that itch he was feeling just a little more pronounced.

When she mentioned how generous Mrs. Madison was being to let her buy a new outfit, it didn't register at first. He was too distracted by the way the silver gown dipped almost all the way to her waist, making him acutely aware of her firm breasts. "This one's on me," he finally said.

She turned from the mirror, a myriad of silver flashes winking at him as her skintight gown caught and reflected every glimmer of light in the room.

Her expression turned serious. The line had to be drawn somewhere. She couldn't just keep taking from him. "But I can't—"

"Yes, you can," he cut her off. Then, to assuage her conscience, he added, "Consider it on the tab if it makes you feel better."

She caught her lower lip between her teeth, debating. So far, everything she owned came from him. "If this keeps up, the only way I'll be able to pay you back is by giving you my firstborn."

He laughed, "Thanks, but one surprise kid on my doorstep is definitely enough for me." Looking at her, he let his mind wander for just a fraction of a second. "At least for the time being," he added more softly.

She could feel the way his eyes touched her. Warmed her. "Do you want more children?"

"Eventually," he allowed guardedly. "The thought of having one or two more is not unpleasant." He'd always hated being an only child. "I'd like to be there when they say their first word, and *not* have it be the kind nuns liked to tackle with a bar of soap."

The store clerk approached Rebecca with two more gowns, but Rebecca held up her hand, wanting to hear what he was saying first. "Is that what Vikki was like the first time you met her?"

It was easier to talk about, now that it was six months in the past. And he couldn't fault the child—she had been afraid. "Pretty much. She wasn't happy about being shipped out to a father she'd never seen."

"That wasn't your fault," Rebecca said defensively. "You didn't even know about her existence. And the important thing is, you're getting along now."

Even so, it had been a long, hard road from there to here. And it still had a somewhat tentative feel to it. Not one he wanted to talk about. Vikki had been entitled to her anger. Life had dealt her a hard hand. He was going to make it up to her if he could.

Leaving all that unsaid, he merely shrugged. "Things have a way of working themselves out."

She knew there was much more involved here than whimsical fate. There was patience and kindness and a man struggling with a situation with which he had no prior experience. All the same qualities that he was demonstrating with her.

The clerk was still standing off to the side with the new gowns. Her arms, Angus noted, were beginning to droop under the weight. "So, have you made your mind up yet?" Angus asked Rebecca.

She had, but not about the gown. That was a minor, negligible detail. "Since you're laying out the money, why don't *you* choose?" It was Angus she wanted to please with the gown, anyway.

Crossing to the clerk, he selected one of the gowns she was holding. The one with the least amount of material. It was a cream-colored gown that looked as if it had been spun out of moonbeams—loosely joined moonbeams, and not too many at that.

He held it up for her perusal. "How about this one?" She reached for it. "I'll try it on."

He placed his hand on hers. "No, surprise me."

She liked the sound of that.

He'd never had much thought about visions, never really believed that people had them. Certainly not ordinary people like him.

He didn't believe in them, until he saw Rebecca that evening.

They had taken turns in the shower. He went first, then dressed and left her to get ready in peace. He thought of going to get a drink at the bar but wound up going for a walk along the resort's grounds instead, trying to figure out what the hell he thought he was doing. He hadn't brought Rebecca here to help her remember. If he was being honest with himself, he had to admit that he'd brought her here to be alone with her. No matter what he tried to pretend to the contrary, he wanted this time alone with her in a make-believe place where people came believing in mythical things like luck and dame fortune, and hoping to be touched by magic.

Maybe he wanted a little of that magic himself, if only for the space of a weekend.

When he returned to their suite, Rebecca was standing by the window. Moonlight draped itself along her skin, turning it golden.

It was then that his opinion about visions changed. *She* was a vision.

Rebecca couldn't read his expression. A flutter of nerves threatened to take possession. Rebecca looked down at the gown, trying to see it through his eyes. "You don't like it?"

How could she possibly think that? "If I liked it any more, it'd probably be considered illegal in at least eight states."

The gown clung to her body like a shimmering waterfall. Every breath she took only reinforced that image, arousing a desperate thirst within him. But sampling the waters wouldn't begin to quench it. Sampling, he knew, would only intensify his thirst.

Rebecca glanced, undecided, at the wrap she'd left on the bed. "Do you think it might be chilly?"

"Not once you walk in," he promised. Picking it up, he slipped the wrap around her shoulders. With a formal bow, Angus presented his arm to her. "I've always wanted to make a roomful of men jealous."

She slipped her arm through his, his compliment warming her. "That doesn't sound like you."

She said it with such conviction that it made him smile. Angus closed the door behind them, escorting her down the hall to the elevator. "There's a great deal about me you don't know."

She never hesitated. "Then I'd like to learn."

The problem was, he wanted to teach her. And she wasn't his to teach.

But for now…for this evening…he could pretend that she was. He could pretend that there was no world for her to return to once she remembered. Pretend, too, that trusting someone with a piece of himself wasn't impossible.

After all, they were in a place where magical things happened. Once in a while, someone did manage to win against the house.

Chapter 12

The wall of noise from the casino followed them, finally fading as they got on the elevator.

His hand lightly pressed to the small of her bare back, guiding her into the car, Angus was oblivious to everything but Rebecca.

Who was this woman that fate had so whimsically dropped into his life? Where had she come from? How many men had wanted to possess her—but hadn't?

And how many had wanted to—and had?

She couldn't answer any of those questions for him and in the long run, it was better that way. Maybe he really didn't want to have them answered—at least, not the last question. He would rather pretend that there had been no one else in her life. She couldn't tell him different.

But if there had been a legion of men or none at all, it wouldn't have made a difference—not the way he felt about her tonight.

It wouldn't have altered the fact that he wanted her so much it hurt to breathe.

There were five other people in the elevator car with them, but they were a blur in the background to her, just as the casino noise had been. All Rebecca noticed, all she sensed—as she had all evening—was Angus. The way he had looked at her when he first saw her standing by the window, wearing the gown he'd picked for her. The way he had touched her, lightly, naturally, yet somehow intimately, in a crowd of people. The way he had held her as they danced in the small club after dinner. The way his breath had teased her skin when he blew on her dice for luck.

Was this what it was like to want someone? To love someone?

She had nothing to fall back on, no experiences, vicarious or otherwise, to map out the way for her, to tell her she wasn't just letting her imagination run away with her. In her small scope of life, there was absolutely nothing that could validate what she thought she was feeling.

But somehow, she knew. Knew in a special, deep-down-to-the-core kind of way that what she was feeling wasn't just born of the moment. She loved him.

The feeling that told her she was right was different from that which had brought all the other pieces of herself back to her—like cooking and knowing her way around a computer. This emotion she knew by pure instinct. There was no vague, formless feeling that she was attempting to reach for something, to bring it into the light so she could see it more clearly.

This just *was*.

The elevator doors slid open. Instantly, anticipation began to hum through her body. This was their floor.

She felt each one of his fingers against her back as he

gently escorted her out. Hopes and fears collided against one another like two misrouted commuter trains coming from opposite directions.

What if he just left her in her room, like all the other nights, and went to sleep on the sofa?

What if he *didn't?*

Stopping before their suite, Rebecca stared down at her bulging purse. It was stuffed to the bursting point with chips they hadn't bothered to take to the cashier to exchange for currency, as if doing that would somehow bring an end to the dream they were both having.

"Do you think Mrs. Madison will let us keep it?" Was that her voice that sounded so reedy? She cleared her throat. "The money we won?"

Angus unlocked their door. "The chips were ours, and *we* didn't win anything." He followed her in, then closed the door. "You did."

The sound of the door closing echoed in her brain. Vibrated in her breast. She forced herself to calm down. This was still Angus, still her. Nothing had changed.

But it might. Sweet heaven, it might.

"But there wouldn't have been anything to win with if Mrs. Madison hadn't left the chips in your name," Rebecca insisted.

With a shake of his head, he laughed softly, then bracketed her shoulders with his hands. His eyes delved into hers, as if he were examining her, looking for clues. "You have undoubtedly got to be the most honorable woman I know."

"Since you probably know a great many, that's a pretty big compliment." Hesitating, Rebecca fidgeted with the ends of her wrap. It wasn't any of her business. She told herself not to ask, but couldn't resist. "How many women *do* you know?"

He dropped his hands and moved away. It had been a long day, Rebecca had to be tired. "Billions," he said flippantly. Then something in her eyes stopped him—she was serious. "None."

After Jane, there had been none that he had bothered to get to know, none he'd wanted to get to know. Until Rebecca had appeared, dripping, lost and semibarefoot in his office.

She shouldn't have pressed. The smile on her lips was self-mocking. "I guess the answer's somewhere in the middle."

The lone lamp that had been left on in the suite was just behind her. Its light mingled with the fabric of her gown, rendering it almost nonexistent. It illuminated her body so clearly that he could see every soft, tempting inch of her outline.

His mouth went dry. "Closer to none than billions."

If he continued looking at her like that, she thought, as if she were a hot fudge sundae and he had a congenital weakness for ice cream, she wasn't sure how much longer she could keep from throwing herself at him.

With an effort to try to maintain her composure, she held out her purse to him.

"All right, if the chips are ours, then I want to give you my half." She saw his eyebrow rise. "As a down payment on my debt." She wished she didn't feel as if she were babbling.

He made no move to cross to her or to take the purse. Did she really think he'd take money from her? he wondered. That all there was between them was business?

His voice was low, too low for her to hear anything but the words. "You don't have a debt."

She didn't understand. He was trying to find out her identity, what had happened to bring her to that parking structure, running for her life. She'd taken up his time as well as his space. "But you're working for me."

The smile that curved his mouth touched her soul. "I'd rather think I'm working *with* you."

From across the room, his voice seem to whisper along her body, making it quicken. Making her feel warm, so unbearably warm. Her eyes never leaving his, she slowly shed her wrap, letting it slip from her shoulders and gently drift to the floor.

He would have given anything for a drink right now, something hard and potent to numb his body. To anesthetize it so that he wouldn't feel all the sensations that were racing through him at urgent, breakneck speed.

He had to leave, now, before his self-control gave out completely. "I guess we'd better call it a night."

But he remained where he was.

Slowly, she moved toward him, a dream drifting on the sultry summer wind. "I guess so."

Mesmerized, held tightly in the grip of something to which he couldn't put a name, he could only watch her.

"I'll take the sofa."

Standing before him now, Rebecca took his hand, weaving her delicate fingers through his. They felt powerful. Gentle. She had no idea where her courage was coming from, but she prayed it wouldn't desert her.

"The bed's big enough for the entire cast of the revue we saw tonight. It would almost be like sleeping in separate rooms."

He shook his head, unable to drag his eyes away from her face. His head was filled with her fragrance. The scent drove out the last of his common sense. "Too small. I'd find you."

She was a hair's breadth away from him now, her face turned up to his. Her body enticing his.

"I wouldn't hide," she said softly.

He could feel her breath on his skin. It sent tremors through his body. Huge tremors that spelled a complete, total collapse of every shred of resistance he had.

There were a thousand reasons this shouldn't be happening. She was his client, he had professional ethics; there might be a man waiting for her, a husband, a lover, someone who had a right to her affections.

There was only one reason it *should* be happening. Because he wanted her.

"That's just the trouble," he told her, doing his best to warn her away even while everything within him pleaded with her to stay. "You *should* hide."

She wasn't going anywhere. Any lingering crumbs of conflict she might have felt had been laid to rest by the light in his eyes.

"Tell me why." No matter what he said, she knew she wouldn't listen.

He couldn't think clearly, not when needs were slamming through him like pre-game football players in a locker room, threatening to overpower him. "For so many reasons," he said.

There was no space between them, not even for a prayer, if he could have remembered any. His mind was as empty of all other thoughts as hers had been when she'd first come to him.

All there was, was her.

Letting her instincts lead her across this fresh, new ground on which she was treading, Rebecca raised herself on her toes. Her heart pounding, she skimmed her lips along his throat. Electricity flowed through her veins as she felt his reaction to her.

Her voice was soft, seductive as she coaxed, "Name one."

Angus didn't want to. He should have, but heaven help him, he didn't want to. What he wanted now, what he realized he had wanted from the very first moment he'd laid eyes on her, was Rebecca.

Her hands feathered along his chest, toying with the buttons on his shirt. Toying with his heart.

Unable to take any more, he caught up her hands in his, and held them. He searched her eyes, looking for answers to questions that tormented him.

"I don't want you to regret this, Rebecca. I don't ever want you to regret this."

He said it like a plea, not a warning, and if she'd had even the tiniest inclination to stop, to withdraw, it disintegrated in the face of his words.

"I won't," she promised.

He framed her face between his hands, his eyes intense. He'd know if she was lying. "No matter what."

"No matter what," she echoed. How could she ever regret what she wanted now with every ounce of her being?

The last of his resistance snapped. His mouth came down on hers, taking what she offered so selflessly. The urgency rushing through him, stunned him. He'd always been a gentle lover, a considerate lover, able to give while holding just a little of himself back, able to watch with detached pleasure as he placed someone else's needs above his own.

While the desire to pleasure her existed now, there was something else possessing him, something he'd never dealt with before. A ravaging, all-consuming desire that he felt unable to contain.

He wanted to take her here, now, while his blood pumped hot and his body pulsed and throbbed from wanting her. Angus felt like a man obsessed.

Over and over again, his mouth took hers, humbled by what she offered, greedy for more. Insatiable. His hands roamed her body, seizing possession of every curve, every dip, urgently seeking to burn away the touch of any man who had been there before him.

Her animal-like whimper stopped him cold.

What was he doing, taking her like some bull in heat? With almost superhuman effort, Angus drew his head away from her.

Dazed, she could only look at him. Had she done something wrong? "What is it?"

He dropped his hands. "I don't want to hurt you." He'd never forgive himself if he did. She was a beautiful, delicate woman in a very vulnerable state, and *he* was behaving like a damned rutting stag.

"You won't." Very deliberately, she covered his hands with hers and moved them back to where they had been on her hips. "But I'll be forced to hurt *you* if you back away now."

The savage tension of the moment receded as he laughed, pulling her even closer. "You and whose army?"

She raised her chin, equal to his challenge. "Haven't you heard? The pure of heart are their own army." Her eyes softened, blurred with desire, with wanting him. She could sense what he was thinking. "You'll be my first, Angus. I don't remember anyone else, so there wasn't anyone. Only you." It was as simple as that.

He wanted to be the first. Heaven help him but he wanted to be her first. And her last. And even as that evoked fear within him, it was burned away in the heat of his desire.

"And you won't remember anyone else," he promised, for even if her memory returned, he meant to obliterate that part of it. He wanted her to remember no other lover but him.

The moment he brought his mouth to hers, the fire ignited all over again, exploding around them. Consuming them.

As if to reassure himself that she was real, he swept his hands all along her body, claiming her. Branding her. His hands gripping her buttocks, he molded her to him.

His kiss deepened, widened, drawing her in. Submerging him.

Feeling himself shaking inside, he slid the thin straps of her dress down her shoulders until the material was trapped between their bodies.

Angus stepped back just enough to allow her gown to pool to her waist. It rested there as it waited for him to urge it down completely.

To take what was already his.

For a moment, he could only look at her. Angus groaned as a new volley of desire delivered a powerful salvo to his midsection and regions beyond. With skin as white as virgin snow, she was so beautiful she robbed him of his last snatches of breath.

Like a reverent penitent, he worshipped her with his hands, with his lips, caressing her bare skin as he tugged her gown away from her hips.

Underneath she was nude. "No underwear?"

His hot breath vibrated against her belly. "No need," she whispered hoarsely, her eyes fluttering shut as she absorbed sensation after delicious sensation.

A thrill passed through him as Rebecca ran her hands through his hair, pressed his head to her breast.

Her breath was ragged as she tried to drag it back into her lungs, vainly struggling to hang on to her mind before it went reeling away.

She didn't want to be passive, didn't want to merely receive, but to give. She might not remember any men before Angus, but there was nothing wrong with *his* memory. Other women resided there, other women he had loved, had slept with. Rebecca wanted at least to hold her own against them, if not completely eradicate those other women from his mind.

One by one, she undid the rest of the buttons on his shirt. Though she wanted to rush, she forced herself to move as slowly as she could. What she lacked in experience, she meant to make up for by tantalizing him.

The fire in his eyes told her she was succeeding.

Dressed only in heels and his desire, she tugged his shirt from his arms, tossing it to the floor. The breath whooshed out of Angus as she surprised him, pushing him back onto the bed.

Pinning his shoulders to the mattress, she loomed over him, a goddess no sculptor had ever had the honor of immortalizing.

With her palms splayed across his chest, Rebecca held him prisoner as she inclined her head, bringing her mouth down on him.

Angus watched, desire tightening his gut, as, using just the tip of her tongue, Rebecca anointed skin that was already moist with anticipation. Skimming along it, working her way ever lower, she dipped her tongue around his navel, outlining it.

Her eyes were wicked as she raised them to look at him. A sense of power filled her as she felt his taut belly quiver in response. She sat back on her heels, her body teasing him, enticing him. With slow, deliberate movements, she began to unbuckle his belt.

Completely at her mercy, Angus covered her hands with his own and helped her pull his trousers from his hips. They were discarded, as were his briefs. He couldn't contain himself anymore.

The next moment, cupping the back of her head, he brought her face up to his, sealing his mouth to hers. The time for playing, for teasing, was over.

Hungry, their bodies tangled, nearly fusing from the heat. Over and over again, their lips met and remet. Lost in the throes of passion, to everything but what they were feeling, they came perilously close to falling off the edge of the world. And nearly did fall off the bed.

Angus felt her laughter vibrating within his mouth and raised his head, one eyebrow arched in silent inquiry.

"You were right," she explained breathlessly. "The bed isn't big enough."

"I'm always right," he told her, catching both of her hands in his. She looked at him in surprise. "You tortured me—it's my turn to return the favor."

And return it, he did. Pushing her up higher on the bed, he used his tongue, his teeth and his lips to weave a soft, moist web that generated throbbing pulse points all along her body. He feasted and teased, aroused and withdrew, until she ached beneath him, with such a crying need for him to fill her emptiness that she thought she was going to explode.

Satisfied that he had given as good as he'd received, Angus dragged his body up along hers, pleasuring himself in the feel of skin rubbed against skin, until he could look into her eyes again. Humbled by what he saw there, he kissed Rebecca with all the passion she inspired within him.

Her eyes fluttered shut, only to fly open again in surprise as she felt his fingers lightly probe the very center of her desire, outlining it. Then he began to rub, ever so gently, until he brought her up and over the first climax.

Overwhelmed, Rebecca grabbed the covers beneath her, her body trembling as she absorbed the sensation.

Then she looked at him in breathless, dazed wonder, only to have him begin all over again. And again.

Exhausted, she summoned strength from some distant reserve as he began to caress her yet again. "Not without you," she declared weakly.

Grabbing onto his shoulders, she arched her body toward him, parting her legs farther. The silent invitation was impossible to resist. Moreover, he'd reached the end of his tether. Angus couldn't have held back any longer if the fate of the world had depended on it.

With his eyes on hers, he slowly slid into her, taking possession. Taken prisoner.

Hearts racing, they let themselves be swept away by the rhythm that beat within them. They danced the dance of lovers, the music growing steadily more frenzied until it suddenly peaked, then faded away.

Spent, weary, they collapsed against each other, too tired to move. Too content to care.

Ever so slowly, after what seemed like eternity, the world began to come back into focus. Little by little, Rebecca again became aware of everything. Of the imprint of his body as it pressed down on hers, of the way his breath was tickling her shoulder. Of the way the breeze was stirring the curtains at the window just beyond his head. Rebecca cataloged every last detail and pressed them between the pages of her mind.

Angus raised himself up on his hands, afraid his weight was too much for her. A smile played on his lips as he looked at her. She had been everything he had thought she'd be. And more. He only hoped that she could bring herself to forgive him for succumbing to his own desire so ruthlessly.

"So, now what do you want to do?" he teased.

"Do?" she repeated innocently, as if she were giving it serious consideration. And then her eyes glinted. "I want to do it again."

"Again?" He rolled off her. Tucking one arm beneath her, he drew Rebecca to him and pressed a soft kiss to her temple. "Lady, you've got the wrong man for that. I'm dead. You managed to completely sap all my strength."

"Dead, you say?" She turned her body into his.

He could feel her heating him. Could feel himself growing enticed again. It amazed him. "Completely."

With skillful strokes that surprised her as much as it did him, Rebecca dipped her hand low and began to move her fingers lightly over him.

"Are you sure?"

"I *was*." He could feel desire rebuilding itself at a prodigious rate. He wouldn't have thought it was humanly possible to be so ready again so quickly.

But then, he'd never made love with Rebecca before.

Pushing him back into the mattress, she rose, straddling him. "Think again."

"*You* think," he told her, a wicked grin taking hold. "I'm going to be busy."

"Damn straight, you are." Fitting herself against him, she took him in and began to move her hips ever so slowly, in a tempo far less frantic, far less urgent than before. She knew what was waiting, and half the fun, half the joy, was the journey.

This time, he was the one who arched and swayed, covering her breasts with his hands, teasing her nipples with his palms until they hardened like two perfect ripened berries.

The tempo increased.

Rebecca moved her hips faster, driving him further along the upwardly spiraling road. Hoarsely, Angus murmured endearments until, unable to hold himself back any longer, he pulled her down to him.

His mouth found hers as they took the last leg of the journey together. And became eternally one.

Chapter 13

The jarring sound sliced through his sleep like the whirling blades of an incoming helicopter. Before it woke him, it ruthlessly broke apart the dream he was having. Angus resisted opening his eyes, resisted giving up the last tiny remnants of the contentment that swaddled him.

When he felt her stirring beside him, the realization that it hadn't been a dream came to him, preserving the euphoric feeling.

It was real.

Last night had been real. It had just *felt* like a dream.

Like a blanket slowly being tugged away from her, sleep drifted away from Rebecca. Turning, curving her body into his warmth, Rebecca reached for Angus before she even opened her eyes. There was something infinitely comforting about lying there, her arm extended over his chest, her face nestled against his shoulder. She could have stayed like this forever.

The telephone rang a third time.

Rebecca sighed, opening her eyes. "Are you going to let that go on ringing?"

Angus smiled at her. With her hair tousled and falling into her eyes, the scent of last night's lovemaking still fresh on her body, she was even more beautiful than she'd been when he'd taken her down to the casino. Because then he'd only dreamed about having her. Now, she was his.

"I'm thinking about it."

He crooked his finger beneath her chin, tilting her head and bringing her lips to his. The kiss was whisper-soft and carried with it the promise of the day. He felt his body yearning.

Incredible. First thing in the morning and all he could think of was having her again. He toyed with abandoning the agenda they'd planned and just making love with her until check-out time, or until both were dead from exhaustion—whatever came first.

Curiosity got the better of Rebecca before the magic of Angus's hands drove the ability to think completely away. "It might be important," she pressed.

"Like what?" He couldn't think of a single thing worth the effort of making contact with the outside world. It was probably the resort, calling to see if everything was satisfactory. He nibbled on her shoulder, feeling her move against him. He could definitely say, without any reservations, that everything was *more* than satisfactory.

Rebecca's mind was already clouding, the phone notwithstanding. It took effort to stay focused. "Like Vikki."

He paused, his mouth inches away from the soft white column of her throat. "If it was Vikki, my cell phone would be ringing." He'd given his daughter the number so she could reach him any place, any time. So far, she'd never used it.

But because the telephone went on ringing, determined to shatter the blissful euphoria that surrounded them, Angus gave in. With a muttered oath, he reached for the receiver. It was the exact moment Rebecca chose to burrow under the covers to investigate just how sleepy he still was.

"Hello?" The greeting was almost choked out as he sucked his breath in sharply.

Cradling the receiver against his neck and shoulder, he reached for Rebecca, dragging her back against him. There was no way he could listen to whoever was calling while she was doing *that*. Her eyes were laughing at him. He promised himself to pay her back as soon as he got rid of the caller.

"About time you answered." Biordi's voice filled the receiver. "I was beginning to think they connected me to the wrong room. Where the hell were you?"

"Bed." Angus ground the word out. Biordi had picked a hell of a time for a call. He was tempted to let the receiver drop back into the cradle. Trapped against his side, Rebecca was now doing wicked things to him with her mouth. His very flesh was quickening. The last thing he wanted to be doing was talking into the phone.

"Bed?" Biordi's voice was incredulous. "Do you know what time it is?"

As if that mattered. Angus was in a place where time had no meaning. "Haven't got the foggiest." He caught Rebecca by the wrist as she began to cup him. Man oh man, but she was an endless source of surprises. Who would ever have thought—looking at that classic, heart-shaped face—that a tigress existed just inches below the surface? "Look, Al, can this wait until I get back?"

"No, it can't."

There was something in his friend's tone that warned

Angus to take notice. He shook his head at Rebecca, silently telling her to wait.

"I've got news, Angus. I tracked you down because I know you've been waiting for this." He paused, letting the words sink in. "Someone filed a missing person report on your mystery lady. Turns out her name's Rebecca Conway."

Angus stiffened, instinctively bracing himself. There was no reason to fear what Biordi was about to tell him. This was what he'd wanted all along—to help Rebecca discover her identity and, with any luck, her memory.

So why did he feel like the hull of the Titanic a moment before the iceberg ripped through it?

As he sat up, he felt Rebecca staring at him, but all his attention was centered on the voice on the other end of the line.

"Someone," he repeated slowly, as if merely saying the word left a bitter taste in his mouth. "A male someone?"

"As a matter fact, yes." Angus felt his stomach sinking as Biordi continued. "Her fiancé. He said Rebecca was supposed to be in Japan on business. When she didn't call him, he didn't think anything of it at first. Seems he has a 'full schedule.'" Biordi's tone sounded mocking. "According to him, she has a tendency to get caught up in her work and forget about everything else. When he finally tried to get in touch with her, there was some kind of mix-up with her hotel reservations. He had a hard time finding someone who could give him a straight answer. Nobody seemed to know where she was."

I do, Angus thought, his gut wrenching. *She's right here.* But she was slipping farther away from him with every word Biordi said.

The playfulness drained from Rebecca. There was

something in Angus's eyes that made her uneasy. A nameless fear began working itself up from her toes, laying a shroud over her entire body.

Biordi's voice continued buzzing in his ear as Angus struggled to make sense of the words and fit them into his life.

"When the guy finally got frustrated and called the airline, they told him she was never on the flight. That's when he came to the police. Better late than never, I guess, right?"

No, never would have been better, Angus thought. He felt cheated, robbed and explosively angry, with no target to lash out at.

"Angus, did you hear me?" Biordi asked. "Are you there?"

Angus looked at Rebecca. Everything inside him was crashing. "Yeah, I'm here. Look, we'll be there as soon as we can."

"Good, I'll fill you in on the rest of it then. You know where to find me." Biordi hung up.

The dial tone was buzzing in his ear. Feeling like a man trapped in a nightmare, Angus let the receiver drop back into the cradle. He felt like hurling the telephone across the room. It took his last ounce of strength to pull himself together.

Rebecca was sitting up. She'd drawn her half of the sheet tightly around her, but it didn't ward off the chill she felt. For a moment, while he had listened to someone on the other end of the line, Angus's face had been an impassive, unreadable mask. She didn't even recognize him.

But it was his eyes that made her afraid. The light had gone out of them.

She lay her hand on his arm. Whatever it was, she could

help him face it. There wasn't anything that they couldn't face together.

"What's the matter, Angus?" she asked softly. "Who was that?"

The touch of her hand underscored the helplessness he felt. Unable to deal with it, he lifted her hand from his arm and placed it on the bed.

When he looked at her, his eyes seemed to bore into hers, as if he were searching for something. "Does the name Conway mean anything to you?"

She tried to shut the hurt out, telling herself he meant nothing by it. She tried instead to concentrate on the name he said. Rebecca thought a moment, then shook her head. "No, nothing. Why?"

He wanted to reach for her, to hold her and make love with her again. But it wasn't right. Not anymore, not when he knew that there was someone else waiting for her. "It should," he told her quietly. "It's yours. That was Biordi on the phone."

Biordi. The police detective. What else had he found out? Why was Angus looking at her like that?

Very carefully, she said the name out loud, "Rebecca Conway," and waited for the sound of it to become familiar, like a photograph slowly developing in a darkroom.

It didn't happen. The last name meant nothing to her. She shrugged. "It doesn't feel like it's mine."

That was just the amnesia talking, Angus thought. He had no foundation to build his hopes on. "According to the man who filed the report, it's yours."

She froze. "What man?"

"Your fiancé." Angus tried hard to keep the bitterness out of his voice. It remained an invisible marauder, hacking away at him.

The ground suddenly opened up beneath Rebecca's feet, sending her plummeting. There was no bottom to the ravine. "I have a fiancé?" she whispered.

The planes of his face had hardened, locking him away from her. It mirrored what was going on inside. He couldn't have dealt any other way with the pain that threatened to consume him. "That's what the man told Al."

She wanted to deny it, to shout at the top of her lungs that it was a lie. But the truth was, she didn't know. She didn't know if Conway was her real name or if Rebecca Conway did or didn't have a fiancé. What she did know was that she didn't *want* there to be a fiancé. She didn't want any other man in her life besides Angus.

Anguish turned to anger. Rebecca rebelled against what he was telling her. There had to be some mistake. Someone, for reasons she didn't understand, was lying about her.

"Where was this so-called 'fiancé' all this time?" she demanded. "Why didn't he come forward as soon as I— as soon as this Rebecca Conway—was missing?"

Angus was torn between doing what he wanted to do, and what he knew was right. What was right was making this easier for her. He didn't want to make it easier. He didn't want to make it happen at all.

He repeated what Biordi had told him. "He said you were supposed to be in Japan. He's been trying to track you down."

"Japan?" she echoed. None of it made any sense to her. None of it struck even a remote chord in her mind. It *had* to be a lie. "What was I doing in Japan?"

"I don't know! Some kind of business!" The sharp flash of temper took him by surprise. Blowing out a breath, he fought off the urge to drag her toward him, to lose himself in her, to deny that the phone had ever rung and shattered his world. Under control again, he apologized. "I'm sorry. Al said he'd fill us in on the details when we got to the station."

And he was just going along with this? Didn't last night mean anything to him? Rebecca felt beside herself, as if freshly constructed walls were collapsing in on her. "I don't want to be filled in. I don't want to go anywhere."

He hated seeing her like this. It was his fault. He was the one who should have maintained the boundaries of their relationship instead of succumbing to the desires that had clawed at him.

He reached to touch her shoulder. "You don't mean that."

She shrugged him off. "Don't tell me what I mean. You have no idea what I mean, what I feel." She was being redefined again, in terms she didn't know, didn't understand.

"Yes." His voice was so quiet, she had to strain to hear. "I do."

The fire went out of her. Hot tears threatened to spill down her cheeks.

"Hold me," she implored. "Just hold me." Everything would be all right if he just held her.

He wanted to, heaven help him. He wanted to hold her—and hold the rest of the world at bay. But it wasn't right. *He* had no right.

"Rebecca, I really don't think that's such a good idea." Every word felt like a shard of glass in his mouth. "This changes everything."

Panic scampered through her on tiny, nimble feet with sharp claws. He was pulling away from her, deserting her. "It doesn't have to. We're still the same people we were last night, the same two people who made love. If you never picked up the telephone...if it never rang...we wouldn't know about the report.''

It was ripping him apart, but for her sake he had to be strong. She'd made a commitment to someone before him. To someone she loved. It wasn't fair to take that away from her, to take advantage just because she couldn't remember.

"But it did ring," he told her firmly. "And I did answer it. And we do know."

He reached for the pants that had been discarded last night in the heat of passion, tugged them on, then rose from the bed.

He couldn't remember ever feeling this tired, this defeated. "I'll shower first, give you a chance to pull yourself together."

She watched him leave the room. She didn't think pulling herself together was possible.

"Will you go with me?"

At first, he thought he'd imagined it. Imagined her asking him for a favor. She hadn't said a word to him since he'd gotten out of the shower. Not then, not when they checked out of the resort. Not even during the last two hundred miles as they drove back. He'd thought it was because she'd had a chance to think things over and now, because she was finally being reunited with her life, she was embarrassed about last night.

As for him, all he could think of was that it was happening again. He had allowed himself to feel something for someone, allowed himself to begin to dream just a little, and the door had been abruptly slammed in his face.

It wasn't fair.

His lips twisted in a cynical smile. Since when was life supposed to be fair?

He looked at her now. "Did you say something?"

She wanted to scream at him, to beat at him with doubled-up fists and demand to know what he thought he was doing, driving her to another man. Driving her away from him. But at the same time, she could feel herself being drained. The fight was going out of her and a numbness was setting in.

"I said, will you go with me?" she repeated flatly.

"Where?"

Rebecca pressed her lips together. She wasn't going to cry. He had already pushed her away and she wasn't going to let him see that she hurt. Wasn't going to beg. "To the police station."

How could she ask? "Do you think I'd let you go alone?"

"I don't know." She struggled to keep the anger from taking hold again. "I don't know what to think anymore."

He had been so cold to her since the telephone call, as if he'd just as soon forget what had happened the night before. Who knew—maybe he was even relieved to be rid of her. He certainly didn't behave as if he wanted her to stay. Would he be taking her so quickly, so calmly to the arms of a stranger if he cared?

She hated the answer that was staring her in the face.

"I'll come with you," he said quietly.

He didn't want her to go. Suddenly, with every fiber of his being, he wanted to turn the car around and just head for parts unknown. Some place where this fiancé who had crawled out of the woodwork would never find them.

"Rebecca?"

Her eyes were shining with angry, unshed tears. "What?"

He opened his mouth to tell her—to say that they were going away—but he couldn't do it. Couldn't give in to impulse. There was Vikki to think of. And a life waiting for Rebecca that had no place for him. "Never mind."

Very slowly, she let out a ragged breath. Shifting, she continued staring straight ahead of her as the miles and the scenery all melded together.

The words on the missing person report swam in front of her:

Rebecca Conway, twenty-nine. Female, white Caucasian. Blonde, five foot four, 115 pounds, violet eyes, senior computer programmer, DATA International.

Details, just sterile details that neatly summed up a life. A life she didn't remember having.

The emptiness, far worse than what she had experienced when she first walked into Angus's office, refused to go away.

"None of this sounds familiar." She handed the report back to Biordi.

A sergeant walked by with a rectangular box that, according to the outside log, had once held size ten loafers. He was taking up a collection for the captain's wife, who had just had twins. "Anything you think you can spare." The policeman thrust the box toward Biordi.

Biordi dropped the report on his desk and dug out his wallet, parting with a five-dollar bill.

His face was kind as he looked at Rebecca. "I don't know much about amnesia, Ms. Conway, but maybe once you're back home, things will start coming back to you."

"Rebecca, please," she corrected. That was who she was. Rebecca, just Rebecca. Not even Becky anymore. "Maybe," she murmured.

But what if she didn't want things to come back? What if she didn't want any of the things written down on that piece of paper to come back to her? What if she wanted her new life instead, the one she had just begun forming?

It didn't matter, she thought dully. Her new life didn't want her. Angus didn't want her. If he did, he wouldn't have suddenly grown so distant. He would have at least said something, hinted that he wanted her to stay.

But he hadn't, and his silence gave her the answer. An answer she didn't want, but had to learn to live with.

"What about her getting shot at?" Angus wanted to know. That aspect of the case seemed to have gotten lost in the shuffle. What if there was still someone out there after her?

Biordi's thin shoulders rose and fell. "We investigated, but nothing turned up. As far as the police are concerned, it was just another random, senseless mugging."

"And that's it?" Angus demanded, raising his voice. He knew he sounded unreasonable, but right now he wasn't feeling very reasonable.

Several heads turned in their direction.

"Hey, you find something, I'll run with it," said Biordi.

Angus dragged his hand through his hair, feeling like an idiot. Losing his temper and yelling at Al wasn't going to accomplish anything.

"Okay, sorry." He slanted a look at Rebecca, wishing the wall he was trying to put between them would hurry up and block her out. She had come to him as a client and he had to keep that uppermost in his mind. The rest of it shouldn't have happened. "Now what?"

Biordi sat down behind his desk and pulled the telephone closer. "Now we call Howard Dunn and tell him we found his fiancée." Out of consideration for Angus, he'd held off calling the man.

Howard. The name that had popped out of Rebecca's mouth at the hotel when he was tracking Madison. It was all coming together now. And he wished to God it wasn't.

"Howard Dunn?" Rebecca repeated.

The note of recognition in her voice pierced Angus, killing the last iota of hope. "Familiar?"

"No." She didn't want it to be, but there was something. Something. "Yes."

His eyes narrowed, pinning her. "Well, which is it, yes or no?"

"Vaguely familiar," she snapped out. "It's vaguely familiar—are you happy now?" She felt as if her voice were going to break.

"Very," he said, his tone the antithesis of what he was saying.

Biordi felt as if he'd stumbled into a combat zone. He'd never seen Angus like this, and they went back a long way, through some pretty hairy situations. Angus had always been levelheaded, cool. In control. But there had never been a woman involved before.

Biordi opened the file. "It says here that he's her boss as well as her fiancé. Maybe that might account for the ambiguity on some level." He raised his eyes and looked from Angus to Rebecca. "All right if I call him now?"

Angus shrugged, but the decision wasn't his to make. Biordi waited. Rebecca took a deep breath and then nodded. Biordi looked at the number written on the inside cover, and dialed.

She didn't know him, didn't know the man who was hugging her with such abandoned relief. His touch brought back no memories, no feelings.

All she could remember was the way she felt in Angus's arms.

The scent of the man's cologne nudged at her consciousness, but that could have come from anywhere. If he was her boss, she could have caught a whiff of the scent in the office at any time. It didn't mean Howard Dunn was who he said he was. It didn't mean he was her fiancé.

Wouldn't she remember if she loved him?

Why would he lie?

Why didn't she *feel* something?

Stepping back, overcome with emotion, the tall, darkly handsome man looked as if he could hardly believe she was here.

"Rebecca, I've been out of my mind with worry. Thank God you're safe. I feel like someone just handed me a brand-new life." He ran his hands up and down her arms, oblivious to the way she stiffened at his touch. "Are you all right? Were you hurt? Where have you been?"

He seemed obviously concerned and relieved to see her. Rebecca tried to muster a smile but couldn't. She felt too hollow. "I really don't want to talk about it right now."

And that was that, Angus thought. Their whole time together summed up in one sentence: She didn't want to talk about it.

He couldn't blame her, even though a part of him might have felt better if he could. She had acted as if she were free and now she'd found out that she wasn't. There had to be guilt attached to that.

This was exactly what he'd tried to avoid. Her guilt, his pain.

Obviously without success, he thought cynically.

Slipping one arm around her shoulders in a possessive gesture that set Angus's teeth on edge, Dunn looked at him. "Were you the one who found her?"

As if she were some lost puppy he'd come across. "Actually, she found me."

Dunn appeared to hardly hear. "Well, whatever the circumstances, I owe you a huge debt." Withdrawing his arm hesitantly, as if he were afraid that he would lose her again, Dunn reached into his pocket and took out his checkbook. "Name your price."

It took everything Angus had not to take a swing at Dunn. The thought of drawing blood from that perfect, aquiline nose vastly appealed to him.

"Put it away." It was a quietly issued order, but there was no mistaking the steel reinforcing it. "You don't owe me anything."

Chapter 14

Dunn's expression told Angus that the man was annoyed by the rebuff. But he was also intimidated. Apparently more than willing to placate Rebecca's protector, Dunn put his wallet away, fumbling slightly as he slid it into his pocket.

"All right, have it your way," he told Angus. "No money. But I'm still in debt to you for taking care of Rebecca."

Dunn turned to her, obviously eager to be on his way. "Are you ready to come home?"

No, not with you! her mind cried in distress. But if Angus didn't want her coming with him, where did she have to go? She was still a woman without any choices.

Her back stiffened. She wasn't just going to let herself be swept along. There had to be another choice. If there wasn't, she'd create one.

"Do we—" She took a breath, forcing the question out. "Do we live together?"

Angus noted that the fact that she didn't know didn't seem to trouble Dunn. If anything, it appeared to amuse him, as if her amnesia were some sort of game.

"No, we don't. You like maintaining your independence. It's one of the things I love about you."

"If you're her fiancé," Angus began, measuring each word out slowly, "why isn't she wearing an engagement ring?"

"Rebecca doesn't believe in archaic symbols. She doesn't want to wear a wedding ring, either." There was a trace of annoyance in Dunn's eyes, then he dismissed Angus. Dunn took Rebecca's hand again, his eyes searching hers. His manner seemed to be a shade more at ease now than when he had first entered the squad room. "You really don't remember anything?"

When Angus saw her shake her head in response, he wanted to pull her away from Dunn. The man had no business holding her hand like that if she thought of him as a stranger, no business crowding her into mental corners.

And what business did Angus have, crowding her? Didn't the same set of rules apply to him? Wasn't he still almost as much of a stranger to her as her fiancé was?

"Nothing about us?" Dunn pressed gently. "Nothing at all?"

"She said *no*," Angus pointed out tersely. "She has amnesia—it's not going to disappear just because you showed up." He ignored the look Biordi gave him. Maybe he was behaving like an ass, but right now he couldn't seem to help himself.

"And *you're* a doctor?" There was a snide, mocking edge to Dunn's voice.

"I took her to one," Angus retorted coldly.

Dunn withdrew, his manner once more congenial.

"Yes, of course." He flashed an apologetic grin. "I'm sorry. This has all been very emotionally trying for me. I was afraid I'd lost Rebecca for good. Finding her only to discover that she doesn't know me, well, I'm not sure how to react." His eyes shifted toward her. "We've been so close for so long...." He let his voice trail off.

Angus shoved his hands deep into his pockets, forming fists.

Just then, Biordi jumped in as referee. "I think you should take her to her place, Mr. Dunn. The sooner she gets into familiar surroundings, the better." He glanced toward Angus. "Right, Angus?"

"Right," Angus bit off.

"Will you excuse us for a minute?" Biordi took Angus aside not bothering to wait for the man to nod.

"What's the matter with you?" Biordi demanded in a low voice once they were away from the others.

Angus wasn't sure how to put what was bothering him into words that didn't make him sound like some kind of raving idiot.

"Something's not right, Al. I can feel it. Dunn's not what he seems, I'd bet money on it." Right now, all he had was a gut reaction. His eyes narrowed to cold slits as he looked back at Dunn. The man had his head in close to Rebecca's, sharing some kind of confidence with her, rubbing her hand between his as if that would somehow bring her memory around. "I don't like him."

"You can't think a guy's suspicious just because you don't like him." Biordi's voice softened with understanding. "Just because he's her fiancé."

Angus really hadn't expected any support from Al.

The detective was far too levelheaded to understand an irrational hunch. "*You* can't," Angus corrected. "I can."

With that, he walked back to Rebecca and Dunn. The

man looked up, and Angus could have sworn that the relief he saw in Dunn's eyes was almost smug. The back of his neck prickled again. Something didn't fit.

"We'll be going now, Detective." Dunn addressed Biordi, looking right through Angus. "Taking your advice, I want to get her into familiar surroundings as soon as possible."

Angus made up his mind. "I'm coming with you."

Dunn looked startled. He missed the ray of hope that leaped into Rebecca's eyes. "I find that highly inappropriate."

From the look of it, the man's suit could have paid the rent on his place for a month. That still didn't make him anyone important in Angus's book. "You can find it anything you want, Dunn. But Becky's been thrown into enough unknown situations for a while. The bottom line is, she doesn't remember you—and she *does* remember me. So whether you find it 'appropriate' or not, I'm going along to help her make the transition."

Dunn shot a look at Biordi to see where the detective stood on this barely veiled threat. Biordi merely raised and lowered his eyebrow, as if he thought that, just possibly, the annoying bastard who'd wedged himself into Rebecca's good graces was making sense.

Outnumbered, Dunn relented. "Very well, I can see where it might be a temporary comfort for her to have you around."

Rebecca's head snapped up. That did it. She'd had enough. She was tired of being discussed as if she weren't even in the room, and there was no way she'd stand around accepting crumbs of charity from Angus. He could just take those crumbs and shove them. Amnesia or not, she could look after herself. All she needed was to collect her things and have someone point her to her house, or apartment, or wherever it was she was supposed to have set up living quarters.

"Wait a minute, don't I get a say in any of this?" she demanded, her eyes spitting fire.

Surprised by the sudden outburst, Dunn was quick to placate. "Of course you do, dear."

His tone only rankled her. She found it hard to believe that, despite his looks, she could have been attracted to Dunn, much less engaged to him. The man was a snob.

"Don't patronize me," she warned. "I have a case of amnesia—not stupidity. First, I want you to show me where I live." Her eyes swept toward Angus. "And then I want to go to your apartment and collect my things." Things he'd bought her. The memory stung. Just being around him like this felt as if someone were twisting a knife in her heart. But that would be over with soon enough, she promised herself.

And then the real pain would begin.

"I'll pay you back for everything you spent," she informed Angus frostily. The question of her finances came to her suddenly. She looked at Dunn. "Do I have a checking account?"

"Yes, of course," he assured her. What was she getting at? "Your salary's in the six-figure range."

"Good." She nodded, her eyes blazing as she looked in Angus's direction. "I'll write you a check before you leave."

"Fine," Angus bit off.

"Fine," she snapped back.

Not so fine, Biordi thought, watching them leave the squad room. He wondered if he should give the guys working domestic violence today a call and alert them of a possible problem. From all appearances, Angus and Rebecca reminded him of two red-hot kettles, about to blow.

Dunn would probably get caught in the cross fire. He supposed, to Angus's way of thinking, that would make it all worthwhile.

"But I don't understand. Don't you like it here anymore?" Vikki demanded, her petulance giving way to distress as she followed Rebecca around the room. She was doing her very best not to act like a baby and throw her arms around Rebecca, begging her to stay. That didn't help, anyway. Mommy hadn't stayed when Vikki had begged her to.

Tossing her other pair of jeans into the suitcase that she hadn't bothered to unpack, Rebecca looked over toward Angus. He was standing in the doorway, one shoulder against the jamb, silently watching her. For once, Jenny, who'd been baby-sitting Vikki when they returned, faded into the background and kept her peace.

Angus left the ball in Rebecca's court, refusing to come to her rescue.

Rebecca damned his soul to hell as she squatted down to Vikki's level. "I don't belong here, Vikki. I have my own place."

Vikki stared at her, doing her best to understand what was happening. "Your 'nesia's gone?"

No, she thought in frustration, that still hung down before her like an asbestos curtain, separating her from her past, refusing to part.

Looking at Vikki, she shook her head. "No, but someone who knows me came to the police station to tell them where I lived. That's where I'm going now." She couldn't stand the shattered look on the small face. At least *someone* wanted her to stay—and it hurt like hell to tell her that she couldn't. "Here, let me write the address down for you. This way, you'll know where I am." Reaching for the magazine Vikki had left on her bed, she flipped it over and wrote the address along the margin.

Dunn had taken them to the small town house right after they had left the station. As soon as he unlocked the door, he had received a page from his office. Though he'd looked perturbed about it, he said he had to get back to smooth over what was turning into a transcontinental crisis. Rebecca's failure to arrive in Japan and meet with the prospective buyers had triggered it, he had explained.

Leaving them in the town house, Dunn drove off, promising to call and return the next morning.

Though Rebecca had been quick to leave, there had been a vague, familiar feel to the place, as there was now, writing the address down for Vikki. But it was a distant feeling, as if she'd experienced it a long time ago, or maybe even felt it vicariously while watching a movie.

She just didn't know anymore what was real and what wasn't.

"Here." She handed the magazine to Vikki. "Now you can always find me if you need me."

Vikki hugged the magazine to her. "But why do you have to go?" she demanded again.

"Leave her alone, Vik," Angus ordered sternly. "Rebecca has to be going."

The sooner the break was made, the better it was for Vikki, he thought. He was annoyed with himself for not suggesting that he just bring Rebecca's things to her later. But he supposed that Vikki needed closure, needed to say goodbye.

He sure as hell didn't know what *he* needed.

He couldn't wait to be rid of her, Rebecca thought, biting back angry words. She wasn't going to yell at him in front of his daughter, no matter how much he deserved it. She wouldn't do that to Vikki.

Feeling a sudden rush of emotion, Rebecca kissed Vikki's cheek. In response, Vikki dropped the magazine and threw her arms around Rebecca's neck. Rebecca absorbed the bittersweet sensation, holding the child to her for a long moment.

She felt as if her heart were breaking.

But then it was time to go. Very gently, she pried the small arms away, and then rose.

"I'll call you soon," she promised Vikki. Without a word to Angus, Rebecca picked up her suitcase and walked past him. When he reached to take the bag from her to carry outside, she jerked it out of his reach. "I can handle it."

He raised his hand in retreat. "Suit yourself."

She felt as if the broken pieces of her heart had been shoved into a deep freeze. "I will." She turned to Jenny and said her goodbyes.

Jenny surprised Rebecca by giving her a quick hug. "Take care of yourself, kid."

Not trusting her voice, Rebecca merely nodded, then walked out the door on legs that didn't quite feel as if they belonged to her.

It didn't help her to hear Vikki's whimper of anguish in the background.

The trip seemed longer because of the silence, but it took only twenty minutes to drive to Rebecca's town house. Finding a spot not too far from the front door, Angus parked the car and got out.

Rebecca was already out. She yanked the cloth suitcase out of the back seat, determined to get away quickly.

"You don't have to bother coming in." Her tone dismissed him.

She wanted him to be on his way before she broke

down in front of him. She wasn't sure how she'd managed to hold back her tears this long.

"Yeah, I do." He wanted to look around her house, make sure everything was all right. The phrase mocked him. Everything would probably never be "all right" again.

With deliberate effort, Angus blocked out emotions that were gathering within him. The ones that would make him say things to her he knew he couldn't...shouldn't...say.

"That's right," she realized. "I haven't written out your check yet."

She walked ahead of him, afraid he would read things in her eyes that she refused to let him see. Her eyes blurry, Rebecca jabbed the key Dunn had given her into the lock—and missed. When she tried a second time, she dropped it.

Angus stooped down and picked the key up before she made the effort.

"I don't want your damn check," he growled, unlocking the door for her.

She lifted her chin. "You don't want mine, you won't take Howard's. Keep that up and you'll wind up starving to death."

With a toss of her head, she walked into the house, wishing she could slam the door in his face. But he was too close.

"Consider it on the house," he said bitterly, following her inside.

Angus glanced around. The town house looked just the way it had earlier. Incredibly neat, incredibly organized, just like Rebecca. Not a thing was out of place. Nothing to give him a clue what had happened that last day, just before her world had become a blank.

He stopped before clusters of photographs that lined

both walls of the tiny hallway leading to the back of the house. "Do any of these look familiar to you?" he called to her.

Curious despite herself, Rebecca came into the hall. The photographs—a compilation of professional and candid, black-and-white and color, portrait and group activity shots—came in various sizes and frames. For now, the faces captured there were strangers to her. Even her own face among them felt to her like that of a stranger.

She shook her head, not daring to look at him.

Sympathy tugged at him despite his mind-set. "Maybe later."

"Maybe." But she was beginning to disbelieve that. She was going to be trapped here, in a life she didn't remember, with a man she didn't want. The thought appalled her.

Angus went into her bedroom. The soft, gentle fragrance that also lingered in his room at home was here to greet him. He tried not to let it distract him. Looking around, he found the same neatness here as everywhere else in the house. A place for everything and everything in its place.

He checked the closet. Her clothes were arranged by color and hanging in one direction. There were no empty hangers, no spaces.

Wouldn't there have been spaces, he wondered, if she had packed for a trip?

Probably not. Knowing her, she would have reapportioned the spacing. Forgetting about the question, Angus closed the sliding door.

He had to go—now, while his strength was there and he still could.

Turning, he found her watching him.

Angus crossed to her. He knew he had to say something, he just couldn't leave without a word.

"Listen," he began, then stopped, at a loss. What could he say that wouldn't sound like begging? That wouldn't let her know that he wanted her to go with him—not stay with someone else who could offer her, in all probability, so much more.

Except for love. No one could offer her more love than he could.

But it wasn't fair to her to tell her that.

"If you say it's been fun," she warned, her throat constricting, "you're not going to live to make it out that door."

Her expression was stony, but the look in her eyes got to him. It was the same vulnerable look he'd seen that first day.

Being very careful not to touch her, Angus said the only safe thing he could think of. "If you ever need me...if you ever need anything, day or night, just call."

Yes, I need you. I need you to hold me. I need you to love me, the way I love you. But she said none of that. What was the point? He was just talking to her in his professional capacity. Maybe he even felt a little guilty about what happened—who knew?

"Thanks," she muttered. "I still have your card."

He nodded. "Yeah, that's right." There was nothing left to do but go.

Angus never saw the tears that came to her eyes as he shut the door. He wouldn't have been able to leave if he had.

"What did you do to her? What did you say to make Rebecca leave?" Vikki's questions assaulted him as soon as he walked through the door.

He exchanged glances with Jenny. The older woman, her expression sober, slipped past him and murmured good-night as she shut the door.

"What did you say?" Vikki demanded again, her voice hitching.

"Nothing, Vik." God, but he was tired. Tired enough to drop in his tracks. "I already told you, she found out where she lived." He flipped the lock on the front door, closing up for the night. "She gave you the address, remember?"

She didn't care about another address. She wanted Rebecca back at their address. "She liked us. She would have stayed. You said something to make her go," she accused. "Unsay it, Angus. Unsay it and make her come back. I promise I won't ever ask you for anything else—not even a dog. Just get Rebecca to come back."

He didn't want to take the emotions he was feeling out on Vikki. She didn't deserve it. But he had never felt this kind of frustration before, this kind of helplessness. And rage was a new feeling entirely.

"I can't, Vik. Now go to bed, it's late and I'm not writing another note for you for school tomorrow."

Vikki stood in the kitchen, a tiny bantam rooster spoiling for a fight. She opened her mouth to defy him, then shut it abruptly.

To his surprise, Vikki walked out of the kitchen without another word, clutching her magazine to her. She went to her room, obviously intent on giving him the silent treatment.

He didn't need the silent treatment, he was in hell already.

Stripping off his shirt, he walked into his room. The moment he entered, Rebecca's fragrance came to him—soft, seductive. It was all around him. On the pillows, on the comforter, in the closet when he opened the doors. Like an invisible conspiracy, it encircled him.

Silently reminding him of what he had lost.

He grabbed a worn T-shirt and stalked out of the room. He'd sleep on the sofa again tonight, he told himself. There was no way he would be able to get any sleep in that bed.

Sitting down on the sofa, not bothering with any pillow or sheets, he glanced at his watch. With a start, he realized he'd sent Vikki to bed before seven-thirty. What's more, she had actually gone.

He didn't blame her. He wouldn't have wanted to be around him, either.

Restless, Angus got up and prowled around the apartment, unable to find a place for himself. Unable to get at what was nagging at him, daring him to find it. Something was bothering him—something beyond the emptiness in his apartment, in his life—now that she was gone.

He supposed that in some way this had to be what Rebecca had felt like: unable to remember, unable to catch hold of something elusive that teased her with its formless shape.

What *was* it? What was it that he was missing? Was Al right? Were all his suspicions magnified just because he didn't like Dunn, because he resented the man's presence in Rebecca's life?

Or was there something else? Something in plain sight that he saw, but wasn't, seeing?

First thing tomorrow morning, he was going to investigate the man from top to bottom.

But what would he do with the endless night that was facing him?

Frustrated, he yanked open the refrigerator door and looked in. He wasn't hungry, though he hadn't eaten all

day. Rummaging through the refrigerator was an automatic response. There was just a sliver left of the quiche
lorraine that Rebecca had made for them before he'd
taken her up to Tahoe. He left it for Vikki.

"Guess it's back to takeout," he muttered under his
breath.

He didn't realize that he had slammed the refrigerator
door until it made contact. The glass Vikki had left on the
edge of the counter fell off, jarred by the vibration. It
smashed on the kitchen floor. One loud noise came on the
heels of the other. It sounded as if he were having his
own riot.

Great, he thought, throwing the pieces away, Vikki
would think he was losing his mind. Just what he needed.

He had to get hold of himself—for her if not for him.
Vikki needed a father. A *sane* father. It was time he
started acting like one again.

The first thing he had to do was reassure her. He knew
Vikki was going to miss Rebecca. But some things just
didn't turn out the way you wanted them to, he thought.
You had to move on.

He had to move on.

Calmer now, he began to piece together what he wanted
to say to Vikki to make her understand that this was no
one's fault, that he hadn't driven Rebecca away. Their
paths had just gone in different directions.

Philosophical garbage, but maybe it would work on
Vikki. At least, it was worth a try.

"Vik, you up? I'm sorry if the noise scared you," he
said as he knocked. When she didn't answer, he opened
the door to her room.

Her bed was empty. Vikki was nowhere to be seen.

Chapter 15

The small scrap of paper with childish writing across it stared up at him from the center of the rumpled bed.

I went to Rebeka to fix things.

Swearing, Angus shoved the note into his back pocket. Why couldn't that kid stay put?

With hope that had little foundation, he leaned out the window, scanning the area in both directions. Maybe she'd just left and hadn't gotten very far.

He saw a couple necking in the shadows, and a man walking a dog. There was no one else out.

Now what? He shut the window so hard that it rattled. Vikki could be anywhere. She had no idea where Rebecca lived.

And then he remembered the magazine she was clutching when she went into her room—the magazine with Rebecca's address in the margin.

Her place was twenty minutes away by car—how long

would it take to reach on foot? On two very small feet? And how many wrong turns could those two small feet take? He didn't even want to think about it.

Angus swore again as he picked up his car keys and left the apartment.

It struck him as ironic that until Vikki had come into his life, part of the money he made came from tracking down runaways. Now he was tracking his own runaway. Mentally, he apologized to any parent he might have un-intentionally seemed insensitive to while conducting those investigations. Now he understood the anguish.

Angus was backing out of his parking place even before the gears had time to properly shift.

This was his fault. He should have stayed with Vikki tonight, explained things to her more carefully. He shouldn't have sent her off to her room while he licked his wounds like some damn wounded bear.

Hell, he should never have brought Rebecca to his apartment in the first place. Then none of this would have happened. Vikki wouldn't have gotten to care so much about Rebecca and he—he wouldn't have fallen in love with her.

The car ahead of him was moving too slowly. Glancing to the side, he changed lanes, then sped up. He should have seen it from the start. They didn't belong together, he and Rebecca. She and Dunn did. They were the very picture of a perfect couple.

Picture.

And then it hit him, opening in his brain like a quick blooming flower. He knew what had been nagging at him since he'd gotten home.

Angus pressed down on the accelerator, his gut instincts telling him to hurry before it was too late.

* * *

If this was her house—and from all the photographs she saw of herself, it was—Rebecca found no peace in it tonight. It made her feel caged in, restless. Like an animal waiting to be executed.

She couldn't focus, couldn't think. A myriad of diametrically opposed emotions swirled around her in endless confusion.

Wandering around the town house, opening closets, investigating drawers, touching knickknacks, she waited for a sign, a feeling to tell her that she'd come home. If it existed, it was blocked out by her agitation.

She was relieved that Howard wasn't coming back tonight. She didn't want to have to deal with him on a one-to-one basis yet. More than anything, she just wanted to be left alone.

No, that wasn't true, she thought ruefully. She put down the book she was paging through. More than anything, she wanted Angus.

Which just showed her how very mixed-up she was. Thinking about Angus, wanting him, was useless. Worse than useless. Angus was history. Past history in what was still a very brief life. If she was going to get on with it, and somehow piece it all together, she was going to have to put him out of her mind. Permanently.

Easier said than done.

She found herself in the kitchen. Without thinking, she opened the refrigerator and looked in. The lone occupant of one shelf—a little box of baking soda—looked as if its sides were caving in. Moisture had weakened it. There were fruits tucked in one drawer and three kinds of vegetables in the other. A carton half filled with milk was inside the door, just beneath a tub of barely-used fat-free margarine.

If she was such a terrific organizer, why had she left a half-stocked refrigerator when she was supposed to be going on an extended business trip to Japan?

It didn't make any sense. But she couldn't make sense out of anything—not when she was feeling like this. Not when she was feeling as if everything had been drained out of her, leaving an empty shell.

Rebecca let the door close.

Frustrated, she went into the living room and switched on the television set, hoping for some sort of distraction. She burrowed into the oversize beige sofa, tucking her legs in under her and clutching the remote.

A used car salesman was riding a dolphin to the edge of the tank. He never made it. She pressed the channel button before he could begin his pitch. Staring ahead, glassy-eyed, Rebecca flipped from one station to another. Old movies and episodes from series long laid to rest chased one another from the screen.

This was ridiculous, she thought. She wasn't going to find anything to occupy her mind if she just kept flipping around like this. Rebecca stopped on the next channel she came to, and put the remote down. She was going to watch and pay attention no matter what was on.

An old black-and-white movie that had somehow escaped being colorized flickered unevenly on the screen. Judging by the scenery, it was set in the thirties or forties. Rebecca forced herself to concentrate.

Someone was running down an alley, fleeing from an oncoming old roadster. The driver, his machine gun butted up against the outside of the car door, was spraying the fleeing man with a shower of bullets. Through the inventive genius of Hollywood, every single bullet miraculously missed its target. Sirens screeched in the background as police cars materialized from nowhere.

The noise blended and swirled, throbbing in her head.

Rebecca leaned forward on the sofa, riveted, afraid to take a breath.

Lights began to wink madly in her head, making her dizzy. Rebecca struggled against the light-headedness that threatened to black out everything.

The sound from the television melded with the bright lights flashing through her brain.

Lights.

Headlights.

Headlights were coming after her. She was running from them. Her breath hitched, backing up in her lungs as she looked over her shoulder to see the car getting closer. She darted between two steel pillars, tripping as one of her shoes was yanked off her foot. Terrified, she left the shoe behind.

She had to get away. Get away before he killed her.

She heard a loud noise, felt something strike her. Was she imagining it?

No, something sticky was sliding down her temple. Blinking, she sought to keep it out of her eyes. Half-blinded now with fear, she kept running toward the noise. Toward people, people would keep her safe.

She hit something. A wall, a metal wall.

There was a space behind the wall. She dropped to her knees and crawled behind it, praying that *he* hadn't seen her.

She made herself into a tight little ball as everything grew smaller around her. Soon, there was nothing there at all.

Gasping for breath, feeling as if her brain were about to explode, Rebecca remembered. Remembered running, remembered trying to escape.

But from what? From whom? Who had been after her and why?

Her hands shook as she pulled Angus's card from her pocket. She'd kept it there all the while like a talisman— a piece of him to make her feel safe. Maybe he could somehow help her remember the rest of it.

Maybe he could just hold her and help her stop trembling.

Her heart was hammering as she went to the telephone in the kitchen.

The knock on the door nearly made her jump out of her skin. The receiver slipped out of her hand, banging against the wall as it came to the end of its cord.

Rebecca dragged air into her lungs. This was ridiculous, she had to calm down. There had to be some sort of a sane explanation for all this. If she went to pieces, she'd never find that explanation.

Trying to contain the nervousness that was pulsing through her, making her knees weak, she went to the door. "Who is it?"

"It's Vikki. Please let me in."

Vikki? What was she doing here? Was Angus with her? Oh, God, she hoped so.

Rebecca didn't even pause to look through the peephole. Yanking the door open, she found Vikki and a thin, reedy man standing on her front step. Her heart dropped.

The man smelled faintly of peppermint and had a face that looked like a road map that had been refolded too many times.

"Is she yours?" he demanded.

Rebecca looked from his face to Vikki's. "What's going on?"

Vikki wrapped her hands around Rebecca's arm in mute supplication. Her words came out in a rush.

"I had to come see you, Rebecca. I saw a number on the bus bench for a cab and I called it. I used the money I had from Momma to pay. But he said he wanted to see for sure that I knew where I was going. That it was okay. Tell him. Tell him I'm yours."

Nothing would have made her happier than if the words were true. Rebecca placed her hand protectively on Vikki's shoulder, drawing the little girl to her. She looked at the cabdriver. Thank God he was concerned enough to watch out for Vikki. She didn't even want to think about what could have happened to a little girl alone at night.

"She's mine. Thank you for bringing her to me." It seemed like such a feeble phrase to express her gratitude. "Do I owe you anything?"

"I got paid," he grumbled. His mouth didn't look capable of forming a smile. "But you could do yourself and the kid a favor by keeping better tabs on her." With that, he shuffled off, muttering something about parents these days.

Rebecca didn't know whether to hug Vikki or to shake her. When she saw the expression on the child's face, Rebecca gave in and hugged her.

Drawing back, she scanned the small face. Had something happened to Angus? Was that why she had come? "What are you doing here?"

Vikki shifted uneasily. "I had to see you. Whatever Angus said, he didn't mean it. He's real upset you're gone. Please come back."

If Angus was upset, she doubted very much it had to

do with her. Still, she was touched by the plea. Rebecca ran her hand over Vikki's head. "Oh honey, it's not that simple."

Vikki planted small hands on her hips. "I want you. Angus wants you." Her mouth drooped at the corners as she entertained the next thought. "Don't you want us?"

Rebecca hugged Vikki to her again. The last thing she wanted was for Vikki to think she was being rejected. "Oh, so very much."

Vikki's voice was muffled against her shoulder, creating a warm spot close to Rebecca's heart. "Then it's simple."

"No, I—" Rebecca's head jerked up as she heard the key being inserted in the lock. Some inner instinct had her instantly gaining her feet, warning her not to remain where she was.

Grabbing Vikki's hand, Rebecca pulled the little girl after her, down the hall and into her bedroom.

"What's the matter?" Vikki demanded, confused. "Why are you running?"

Rebecca couldn't explain, didn't even know why she was running but something urgent within her told her they weren't safe. "I have to get you out of here."

Vikki didn't understand. Shaking, she fought against tears. Rebecca was scaring her. "Why?"

Rebecca heard nothing but the pounding of her heart.

There was someone else inside her house. She knew it, sensed it. Someone was coming after her. To kill her.

"Don't ask questions, just climb out the window." Moving quickly, Rebecca slid the sash to the side as quietly as she could. "As soon as you're out, call your father."

Vikki seemed almost paralyzed with fear.

"But—"

"I mean it, Vikki. Call your father. Tell him to come quick." The window screen refused to budge when she tried it. Afraid of wasting any more time, Rebecca shoved her hand against it hard, pushing it out. The screen fell into the bushes outside. "Go, go," she urged.

Coming to life, Vikki jumped on the sill and started to climb out.

Suddenly someone reached from behind Rebecca and grabbed Vikki's leg, jerking her back inside. Stifling a scream, Rebecca caught the child before she hit the floor. But even as she swung around, she felt Vikki being yanked from her arms.

Her breath froze in her throat as Rebecca looked up into the eyes of Howard Dunn.

The handsome face was contorted with a mocking malevolence. "You *remember,* don't you?"

He had been afraid of that, afraid that he'd finally pushed his luck too far. As soon as he saw Rebecca at the window trying to get the brat out, he knew. He didn't need her answer.

"Let go of her," Rebecca ordered, reaching for Vikki.

He pulled the child aside, out of Rebecca's reach, as if Vikki were nothing more than a pawn to be bargained for. "No, I don't think so. As long as I have her, you'll do anything I want."

His eyes were cold, merciless. Rebecca struggled to think, knowing Vikki's safety depended on what she did in the next few seconds.

"I'll do what you want," she said evenly, managing to eradicate the fear from her voice, "if you let her go. She doesn't know anything. She can't hurt you."

But Vikki *could.* "She can put me here, with you." He

couldn't risk the police finding that out. His eyes narrowed to small, steely slits, slicing through her. "And that would be a very bad thing. Later."

Her blood ran cold. He was going to kill her. Just as he tried to before.

Dunn was the one who had shot at her. It all came back.

"Rebecca? Rebecca, open up the damn door. Let me in."

The loud pounding, coupled with Angus's voice, momentarily distracted Dunn. On reflex, he turned his head toward the sound.

It was all Rebecca needed. She lunged for him, grabbing the hand with the gun. With the element of surprise in her favor, she managed to jerk his hand upward. The gun discharged, lodging a bullet in her ceiling.

"Run, Vikki, run!" she cried.

Instead of going out the window, Vikki darted from the room into the hall.

"Daddy, Daddy, save her," she screamed as she ran to the door. Her fingers were slippery with sweat when she yanked it open.

She never called him *Daddy*. Angus grabbed her, his heart pounding with an unnamed fear. Vikki's face was a mask of terror and tears.

"She's in the bedroom, fighting with a bad man. Rebecca!" Angus was already running, two-thirds of the way there. "He's got a gun," she called after him.

"Stay put!" he ordered, praying she'd listen for once. Praying he was in time.

His gun was in his hands by the time he ran into the room. The scene registered in a single glance. Rebecca, blood trickling from her mouth where Dunn had hit her with the gun, was grappling with him for possession of the weapon.

"Drop the gun!" Angus ordered.

Swinging around, Dunn whipped one hand around Rebecca's clavicle, using her as a human shield. The other hand held the gun to her temple.

Hatred blazed in Dunn's eyes as he looked at Angus. "My thoughts, precisely. Drop yours—or she dies right here in front of you."

Angus couldn't get off a clear shot. With little margin for error, he had no choice. One hand raised, he slowly used the other to begin to set his gun down on the floor.

"Let her go, Dunn. You can't get out of here. I've already called the police." It was a lie, but Dunn didn't know that.

"Then they'll be just in time to find three dead bodies," Dunn declared.

He was going to kill them, thought Rebecca. Her, Vikki, Angus. They were going to die. All because of her. She had one chance. Desperate, Rebecca brought her heel down on Dunn's foot, grinding the three-inch spike in as she simultaneously jerked her head down and sank her teeth into his hand. She bit him as hard as she could.

Dunn howled and the shot he fired went wild.

Taking aim quickly, Angus fired and hit Dunn in the shoulder. Obviously stunned, Dunn jerked his gun into position, but Angus fired again. The second bullet hit his knee.

Screaming obscenities, Dunn went down at Rebecca's feet.

"Daddy, Daddy, are you all right?" Vikki came running into the room.

Angus caught her by one arm, keeping her back. "I thought I told you to stay put."

"I was scared you were hurt," Vikki protested. She had a death grip on his arm.

His face softened, but he kept his arm around her and his eyes still trained on Dunn, just in case. But the man seemed to be out cold.

"You never called me *Daddy* before."

Flustered, she began to apologize. "I'm sorry, I didn't—"

"It's okay," he said softly. "I like it."

Vikki turned her face up to him. Her voice was small as she told him, "Me, too."

His attention shifted to Rebecca. "Are you all right?" he demanded, concern and raw fear putting an edge on his voice.

Numb, she could only nod. "Thanks to you."

He put his other arm around her, allowing himself one quick hug to reassure himself that she was unhurt. "I've got to call Biordi."

"And an ambulance," Rebecca added. She looked at Dunn. He was still breathing. "He's just unconscious."

The fact didn't impress him. "I'll take my time with the ambulance." Taking her hand, he placed his gun in it. "Can you use this?"

She nodded. "If I have to."

"Good. If he makes a move, don't hesitate. Shoot him."

Biordi sighed, surveying the scene. "You keep bringing me business like this and we're going to have to put you on the payroll."

He had arrived soon after getting Angus's call. Having

been quickly filled in, Biordi told them he'd hold off calling for backup until he completed assessing the situation.

Right now, it was just him and two paramedics crowding into Rebecca's town house. Biordi had asked the paramedics to step into the other room with Vikki while he remained with the three key players.

The color was just now beginning to return to Rebecca's face. She'd been whiter than Sierra snow when he'd first arrived.

"Look, you can tell me all about it tomorrow." He smiled at her. "I type slow, anyway."

Rebecca shook her head. "No, I want to get it all out now." It was important to her to tell him everything, before any of the details were lost again. "None of this would have happened if I'd told the police my suspicions in the first place."

Biordi exchanged looks with Angus. Neither had any idea what she was talking about. "Go ahead, then." Biordi took out his notepad and waited.

With Angus's arm around her for support, Rebecca took a deep breath and began.

"Last month, I overheard part of a conversation that made me think Dunn was involved in selling security-sensitive software to an international conglomerate that had its eye on a hostile takeover of our company."

"The people in Japan?" Angus guessed.

"Their headquarters were domiciled there, yes."

"What was your part in this?" Angus asked.

But she shook her head. "I didn't have any. I was never supposed to go to Japan. That was just what he told you." It was hard to sort the lies from the truth, but she tried. "That's why I had your card in my pocket. I didn't want to make accusations I wasn't sure about. After all, Dunn is one of the key people in a very lucrative, cutting-edge software company. The government is one of its clients. If I accused him without proof, it would be my neck on the chopping block, not his." She took another cleansing breath. "I asked around about a private investigator and someone told me about you. She said you were very good at conducting discreet investigations. I was going to ask you to investigate Dunn for me." She bit her lip, looking over toward the man laying on the gurney.

Dunn had come to as the paramedics had worked over him. His hostility was ripe. "I'm going to bleed to death here, listening to her lies. Get me to the hospital," he ordered.

Angus moved over to glare down at him. "You're in no position to give any orders." Then, to Rebecca, he said, "Go ahead, Becky."

"I was working late one evening, trying to get the bugs out of a new program. When I went to my car in the company garage, it wouldn't start."

"He tampered with it," Angus accused.

"Probably. Dunn came by just as I got out of the car, asked me if I was having any trouble. When I said it wouldn't start, he offered to give me a lift. I didn't think that was a good idea and I turned him down, but he insisted. He said this seemed to be fate because he'd been meaning to talk to me about my future with the company. I didn't think he knew that I'd overheard him and I didn't want to arouse his suspicions by saying no, so I got in." She let out a ragged breath.

"Take your time," Biordi advised.

"He seemed agitated," she recalled. It was all so clear now. "He took me some place I'd never been to before." She looked at Angus. "That parking structure we found.

I began to get very uneasy. When I told Dunn that I was going to get out and call a cab, he reached into the glove compartment. As soon as I saw the gun, I pushed the door open and jumped out of the car. It was still moving.''

She pressed her lips together. It was coming back almost too fast now, rushing at her like an oncoming train.

''He chased me with the car, but I managed to get away. Then I heard this loud *pop* and felt something—the bullet grazing me.

''I remember seeing the Dumpster. There were fire engines all over. The store near the restaurant was burning. I thought I could lose him in the confusion. I ran toward the Dumpster in back of the restaurant and hid there, hoping he'd give up. That's all I remember. I must have passed out.''

Angus guessed at the rest. ''And he couldn't do anything because of the firemen. By the time he came back looking for you, you were gone. Right, Dunn?''

The man glared at him in stony silence.

Rebecca had a question of her own. ''How did you know where to find me?'' she asked Dunn.

Clutching his bandaged arm, he growled, ''I'm not saying anything without my lawyer.''

Angus squatted beside the gurney. Removing the revolver from his waistband, he pressed the muzzle against Dunn's cheek, hard enough to hit the bone. ''The lady just asked you a question. I'd answer it if I were you.''

Rage and fear mingled in the look Dunn shot Biordi. ''Are you going to just stand there and let him do that to me?''

Biordi appeared to think the question over, then smiled mildly. ''Yeah. I am.''

When Angus cocked the trigger, Dunn began to shake.

"All right, all right, I'll tell you. I didn't know where she was. I called all the hospitals and someone matching her description had been brought in to one—but the name was all wrong. I knew I had to find her. I figured a missing person report was the fastest way." His eyes gleamed with hatred as he looked at Rebecca. "I couldn't take a chance on you talking to someone." He answered her question before she asked. "I saw you eavesdropping and knew I had to get rid of you."

"But when you found me, I had amnesia," Rebecca protested. Why had he come after her?

"You could always get your memory back." A smile, like dark, crude oil seeping out of the ground, spread over his face. "You two idiots realize that none of this is admissible in court?" he jeered at them. "You got it out of me at gunpoint, without my lawyer present. They'll throw it all out."

"Not all. We've got you on attempted murder—" Angus countered, mimicking Dunn's smile. "—Rebecca's. We don't need your confession."

"You son of a bitch!" Dunn tried to get up, only to fall back in pain.

"You guys can come on back in now," Biordi called to the paramedics. "It's time to take the garbage out before it completely stinks up the lady's house." As the two men came in, bringing Vikki back with them, Biordi turned to Rebecca. He tucked his notepad back in his pocket. "I think I've got enough down to keep me typing all morning. Come in tomorrow afternoon and I'll have it ready for you to sign."

She nodded, relieved beyond words to finally have this all behind her. "I'll be there." She looked at Angus. If he hadn't shown up when he did...

"What made you come here?" she asked him.

"He was looking for me," Vikki piped up.

Angus grinned as he felt Vikki tighten her arms around his waist. It felt as if they were hermetically sealed together. Which was fine by him.

"That," he agreed, "and I realized that your so-called fiancé wasn't on your wall."

He'd lost her. "What?"

"The photographs." He nodded toward the hallway. "You didn't have any of him. That didn't seem very loving. Or very plausible, given all the other photographs you had. I knew he had to be lying. If he was lying about that, maybe there were more things he was lying about."

One arm around Vikki's shoulders, he slipped the other around Rebecca and drew her to him. "C'mon, let's get out of here. I'm going to take you home."

She liked the sound of that.

Angus sat with Rebecca on the sofa, his arm tucked around her shoulders. She rested her head against his. Between them, they had finally managed to settle Vikki down and gotten her to bed, but only after Angus had promised that tomorrow they were finally going shopping for a dog. Rebecca had read to Vikki until she'd drifted off to sleep. Reading had soothed them both.

"Well, I guess you're down one fiancé," Angus observed.

She felt too exhausted to raise her head or take exception to the term. They both knew Dunn had never really been her fiancé. That was a lie he'd concocted to make himself seem more sympathetic and to allow him easier access to information about her.

"Yes, I guess I am."

Very slowly, he ran his fingers along her arm, stroking her. "Want another?"

Her heart thudded against her chest as she looked at him. Was he asking her to marry him? "That all depends," she said slowly.

With the tip of his finger, he outlined her lips. "On what?"

Her mouth tingled. As did the rest of her. "No, on who."

"Me." He held his breath, waiting. Hoping.

Her smile went from ear to ear. "That's the first right answer. Want to try for the second?"

"A second?" Angus studied her face. He wasn't sure he knew what she was getting at. "All right, what?"

"Why?" she countered.

The smile was quick, bright, warming her in its light. "Because I love you."

It was all she wanted to hear. To know that he loved her. "And the man gets the prize."

"Yes." His arms tightened around her as he drew her onto his lap. "I sure do."

She touched his face, her heart bursting. "I love you, too," she whispered softly. "So, when do you want to get married?"

"As soon as possible. I can't wait to start doing my husbandly duties."

There was laughter in her eyes as she brought her mouth to his. "Never too early to start practicing."

"That's why I love you, Becky, you're so much smarter than I am." His lips covering hers, he gave up resisting altogether. There was no more reason to.

* * * * *

SILHOUETTE·INTIMATE·MOMENTS®
commemorates its

15th Anniversary

15 years of rugged, irresistible heroes!

15 years of warm, wonderful heroines!

15 years of exciting, emotion-filled romance!

In May, June and July 1998 join the celebration as Intimate Moments brings you new stories from some of your favorite authors—authors like:

Marie Ferrarella
Maggie Shayne
Sharon Sala
Beverly Barton
Rachel Lee
Merline Lovelace
and many more!

Don't miss this special event! Look for our distinctive anniversary covers during all three celebration months. Only from Silhouette Intimate Moments, committed to bringing you the best in romance fiction, today, tomorrow—always.

Available at your favorite retail outlet.

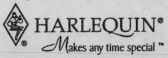

PAULA DETMER RIGGS

**Continues the
twelve-book series—
36 Hours—in May 1998
with Book Eleven**

THE PARENT PLAN

Cassidy and Karen Sloane's marriage was on the rocks—and
had been since their little girl spent one lonely, stormy night
trapped in a cave. And it would take their daughter's wisdom
and love to convince the stubborn rancher and the proud
doctor that they had better things to do than clash over their
careers, because their most important job was being Mom and
Dad—and husband and wife.

For Cassidy and Karen and *all* the residents of Grand Springs,
Colorado, the storm-induced blackout was just the beginning
of 36 Hours that changed *everything!* You won't want to miss a
single book.

Available at your favorite retail outlet.

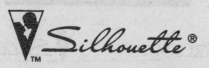

FIVE STARS
MEAN SUCCESS

If you see the "5 Star Club" flash on a book, it means we're introducing you to one of our most STELLAR authors!

Every one of our Harlequin and Silhouette authors who has sold over 5 MILLION BOOKS has been selected for our "5 Star Club."

We've created the club so you won't miss any of our bestsellers. So, each month we'll be highlighting every original book within Harlequin and Silhouette written by our bestselling authors.

NOW THERE'S NO WAY ON EARTH OUR STARS WON'T BE SEEN!

OVER
5 MILLION
BOOKS SOLD
SPECIAL OFFER INSIDE

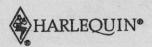 

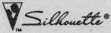